FIGURE 1: David Jones in his room at Calvary Nursing Home, Harrow, 1973. Film still from the interview transcribed in chapter four (David Jones Society).

DAVID JONES ON RELIGION, POLITICS, AND CULTURE

UNPUBLISHED PROSE

Modernist Archives Series

Series Editors: *Matthew Feldman (Teesside University, UK) and Erik Tonning (University of Bergen, Norway)*

From letters, journals, and notebooks to unpublished or out of print works, unfamiliar but important writings in translation and forgotten articles, Bloomsbury's *Modernist Archives* series makes available to researchers at all levels historical archival material that can reconfigure received views of Modernist literature and culture.

Annotated throughout and supported by extensive contextual essays by leading scholars, the *Modernist Archives* series is an essential resource for anyone with a serious interest in twentieth-century literature and culture.

Published titles

Ezra Pound and Globe Magazine: The Complete Correspondence
Edited by Michael T. Davis and Cameron McWhirter

Forthcoming titles

W. B. Yeats's Robartes-Aherne Writings
Wayne K. Chapman

The Correspondence of Ezra Pound and the Frobenius Institute, 1930–1959
Edited by Ronald Bush and Erik Tonning

Global Modernists on Modernism
Edited by Alys Moody and Stephen J. Ross

DAVID JONES ON RELIGION, POLITICS, AND CULTURE

UNPUBLISHED PROSE

Edited by Thomas Berenato, Anne Price-Owen, and Kathleen Henderson Staudt

BLOOMSBURY ACADEMIC
LONDON • NEW YORK • OXFORD • NEW DELHI • SYDNEY

BLOOMSBURY ACADEMIC
Bloomsbury Publishing Plc
50 Bedford Square, London, WC1B 3DP, UK

BLOOMSBURY, BLOOMSBURY ACADEMIC and the Diana logo are trademarks of Bloomsbury Publishing Plc

First published in Great Britain 2018

Cover design: Daniel Benneworth-Gray
Cover image © Mark Gerson / National Portrait Gallery, London

A catalogue record for this book is available from the British Library.

A catalog record for this book is available from the Library of Congress.

ISBN: HB: 978-1-4742-7413-5
ePDF: 978-1-4742-7415-9
eBook: 978-1-4742-7414-2

Series: Modernist Archives

Typeset by RefineCatch Limited, Bungay, Suffolk

To find out more about our authors and books visit www.bloomsbury.com and sign up for our newsletters.

Parentibus nostris

CONTENTS

EDITORIAL PREFACE TO MODERNIST ARCHIVES

Archival excavation and detailed contextualization is becoming increasingly central to scholarship on literary modernism. In recent years, the increased accessibility and dissemination of previously unpublished or little-known documents and texts has led to paradigm-shifting scholarly interventions on a range of canonical authors (Beckett, Eliot, Joyce, Pound, and Woolf, among others), neglected topics (the occult, 'primitivism', fascism, eugenics, book history, the writing process), and critical methodologies (genetic criticism, intertextuality, and historical contexts). This trend will surely only increase as large-scale digitization of archival materials gathers pace and existing copyright restrictions gradually lapse. *Modernist Archives* is a book series that aims to channel, extend, and interrogate these shifts by publishing hitherto unavailable or neglected primary materials for a wider readership. Each volume also provides supporting, contextualizing work by scholars, alongside a critical apparatus of notes and references.

The impetus for *Modernist Archives* emerges from the editors' well-established series, *Historicizing Modernism*. While *Historicizing Modernism*'s focus is analytical, *Modernist Archives* will make accessible edited and annotated versions of little-known sources and avant-texts. The monographs and edited collections in *Historicizing Modernism* have revealed the extent to which contemporary scholars are increasingly turning toward archival and/or unpublished material in order to reconfigure understandings of modernism, in its broader historical rootedness as well as in its compositional methodologies. The present series extends this empirical and genetic focus.

Understanding and defining such primary sources as a broad category extending to letters, diaries, notes, drafts, and marginalia, the *Modernist Archives* series produces volumes that not only unearth significant unpublished material and provide original scholarship on this material, but which also develop cutting-edge editorial presentation techniques that preserve as much information as possible in an economical and accessible way. Also of note is the potential for the series to explore collections pertaining to the relations between literary modernism and other media (radio, television), or important cultural moments. The series thus aims to be an enabling force within modernist scholarship.

It is becoming ever more difficult to read this extraordinary period of literary experimentation in isolation from contextualizing archival material, sometimes dubbed the 'grey canon' of modernist writing. The difficulty, we suggest, is something like a loss of innocence: once obviously relevant materials are actually accessible, they cannot be ignored. They may challenge received ideas about the limits or definition of modernism; they may upend theoretical frameworks, or encourage fresh theoretical reflection; they may require new methodologies, or revise the very notion of 'authorship'; likewise, they may require types of knowledge that we never knew we needed – but *there they are*.

However, while we are champions of historical, archival research, *Modernist Archives* in no way seeks to influence the results or approaches that scholars in this area will utilize in the exciting times ahead. By commissioning a wide range of innovative and challenging editions, this series aims to once more 'make strange' and 'make new' our fundamental ideas about modernism.

Matthew Feldman
Erik Tonning

ACKNOWLEDGEMENTS

The authors wish to thank Mark Aeron-Thomas, Leo Aylen, Peter Barry, Cate Berenato, Stephanie Bernhard, Roger Billcliffe, Francesca Brooks, Sharon Burger, Jamie Callison, Paul Cantor, Colette Dabney, Nia Mai Daniel, Thomas Dilworth, Lorraine Douglas, Johanna Drucker, Lucas Elkin, Nicholas Elkin, Katherine Fox, Andrew Gent, Thomas Goldpaugh, Warner Granade, Brad Haas, Kevin Hart, Sandra Hicks, Paul Hills, Jo Hornsby, Stanley Honeyman, Andrew Isidoro, Ted Jackson, Matthew Jarvis, Benjamin Kohlmann, the Kularatne family, Michael Levenson, Ceridwen Lloyd-Morgan, Patricia McCarthy, Jerome McGann, Darragh O'Donoghue, Alex Patterson, Fr John David Ramsey, Sarah Rhys, Paul Robichaud, Chris Ruotolo, Nicholas Scheetz, Rebecca Somerset, Andrew Stauffer, Michael Suarez, Anna Svendsen, Scott Taylor, Luke Thurston, Erik Tonning, Herbert Tucker, David Vander Meulen, Nigel Wattis, Jessica Williams, Sarah Williams, and Tom Woods.

This project would not have been possible without the cooperation of the Booth Family Center for Special Collections at the Lauinger Library of Georgetown University Libraries, the John J. Burns Library at Boston College, the curators of the David Jones Papers at the National Library of Wales, Aberystwyth, and the generosity of the Buckner W. Clay Endowment for the Humanities, the David Jones Society, the University of Virginia Institute of the Humanities and Global Cultures, the Modernist Studies Association, Rare Book School, the South West Film and Television Archive, and the Trustees of the Estate of David Jones.

EDITORS AND CONTRIBUTORS

Thomas Berenato is a PhD candidate in the English department at the University of Virginia.

Oliver Bevington is an Assistant Professor of English Literature at Yeni Yüzyil University in Istanbul. He completed his PhD at Aberystwyth University on the political writings of David Jones. He has published articles in the *Modern Language Review*, the *New Welsh Review*, and the *Times Literary Supplement* and is currently the Reviews Editor for the *International Journal of Welsh Writing in English*.

Jasmine Hunter Evans recently completed her interdisciplinary PhD in English Literature and Classics at the University of Exeter. Her research contextualizes Jones's reception of ancient Rome in the wide-ranging discourses of civilizational decline in the twentieth century. Since publishing, in 2014, a transcript of a rediscovered 1965 BBC interview with Jones, she has co-led, with Anne Price-Owen, the David Jones Society's project to digitize 16-mm film interviews and programmes on Jones.

Anne Price-Owen is Research and Postgraduate Tutor at the University of Wales Trinity Saint David, Swansea Campus, UK. She is co-editor, with Belinda Humfrey, of *David Jones: Diversity in Unity* (University of Wales Press, 2000). She re-launched the David Jones Society in 1996.

Kathleen Henderson Staudt teaches at Virginia Theological Seminary and the Henry Luce III Center for the Arts and Religion at Wesley Theological Seminary in Washington, DC. Her poetry, essays, and reviews have appeared in *Contemporary Literature*, *Modern Language Studies*, *Spiritus*, *Christianity & Literature*, *Cross Currents*, *Sewanee Theological Review*, the *Anglican Theological Review*, and the *David Jones Journal*, among others. She is the author of *At the Turn of a Civilization: David Jones and Modern Poetics* (University of Michigan Press, 1994) and three volumes of poetry, most recently *Good Places* (Finishing Line Press, 2017).

Tom Villis is Professor of History at Regent's University London. He studied at the universities of Edinburgh and Grenoble and completed his PhD at St John's College, University of Cambridge. His research interests lie in early twentieth-century cultural politics and religion. Villis is the author of *British Catholics and Fascism: Religious Identity and Political Extremism Between the Wars* (Palgrave Macmillan, 2013) and *Reaction and the Avant-Garde: The Revolt Against Liberal Democracy in Early Twentieth-Century Britain* (I.B. Tauris, 2005).

Rowan Williams is Master of Magdalene College, University of Cambridge. Archbishop of Canterbury from 2002 to 2012, Williams is a scholar, poet, and translator of poetry with a long-standing interest in David Jones. He serves as the current honorary president of the David Jones Society.

LIST OF ILLUSTRATIONS

Note: Figures 1–5 appear courtesy of the David Jones Society, Swansea. Manuscript images in chapters one, two, and three are reproduced with the permission of the Trustees of the Estate of David Jones and the John J. Burns Library, Boston College, Chestnut Hill, MA, and the Booth Family Center for Special Collections, Lauinger Library, Georgetown University Libraries, Washington, DC.

FOREWORD

ROWAN WILLIAMS

Scholarly and critical interest in David Jones continues to grow – now further assisted by the publication of Thomas Dilworth's comprehensive biography.[1] That Jones is one of the most serious modernist artists of twentieth-century Britain is hardly in dispute, and recent exhibitions of his visual work have been enthusiastically received. Recent commemorations of the First World War have prompted some revisiting and reworking of *In Parenthesis*, notably Iain Bell's operatic version of 2016. Practically no one would now read this extraordinary work as a 'romanticizing' of the experience of the trenches, as some were doing forty or fifty years ago. Discussion of Jones's religious and aesthetic ideas has not been lacking by any means, but – especially in the last ten to fifteen years – the study of the fluid frontier between modernist aesthetics and some currents of Catholic thought in the early twentieth century has developed considerably, with Stephen Schloesser's 2005 monograph opening up a rich seam of investigation.[2] And this has an enormous amount to offer to new readings of Jones. On this side of the Channel, not only the abiding debt to Maurice de la Taille and Jacques Maritain, but the long friendship with Christopher Dawson will bear a good deal more research.

But this does indeed, as the contributors to this book acknowledge freely, raise issues about the intersection of Jones's aesthetics with his ideas about politics and society. It is important to confront and examine the uncomfortable elements in this intellectual world and Jones's own response to them. One of the ironies of the early twentieth century is that aesthetic modernism could live in surprising proximity to ideologies of the far right as well as the far left (think of Pound and Wyndham Lewis), and that courageously innovative artists wrestling with the burden of cultural fragmentation and what they saw as the commercial debasement of art and culture could sometimes be capable of translating this into fiercely anti-democratic opinions. Add to this the very deliberate and self-conscious concern of many in Jones's circle to look away from British or English insularity towards a more lively set of debates about theology and civilization in continental Europe, and it is not difficult to see how a particular kind of 'radical' Catholicism could be associated with some sort of fascist agenda by unsympathetic observers – and sometimes by the radical Catholics themselves. (Bernard Bergonzi's 1981 novel *The Roman Persuasion* dramatizes some of these debates as they evolved in the early 1930s.)

The Concordat between Mussolini and the Vatican and Franco's militant defence of Spanish Catholic identity fostered the idea that fascist polities might serve a renascent and rejuvenated Catholic social ideal which could replace capitalist, individualist systems with something more attuned to grace and communion. And Hitler – whose theory and practice hardly suggested that he would be sympathetic to that sort of rapprochement – was at least,

[1] Thomas Dilworth, *David Jones: Engraver, Soldier, Painter, Poet* (London: Jonathan Cape, 2017).

[2] Stephen Schloesser, *Jazz Age Catholicism: Mystic Modernism in Postwar Paris, 1919–1933* (Toronto: University of Toronto Press, 2005).

in the eyes of some British observers, an enemy of atheistic state socialism and unbridled capitalism alike. It would take time for the implications of his racial convictions and his absolute disdain for legality to become clear to such observers; Jones's letter to Chamberlain in 1938 is still poignantly myopic about the nature and scale of Hitler's threat.

Of course, by 1939 most illusions about Hitler as a potential guardian of traditional European civilization had become completely unsustainable. (Interestingly, Christopher Dawson had been pretty consistently unimpressed by fascism and had a lot less to recant in 1939 than some did.) Jones, to his great credit, *does* acknowledge that the philosophy of race and blood in Hitler's autobiography must ultimately vitiate his political vision; and he readily admits his failure to read the runes accurately in the 1930s. But the full text of his proposed reflections on all this, now available here for the first time, allows us to follow the complex turnings of his mind and imagination on these matters. There remains from the First War the obstinate conviction that the 'ordinary' German soldier was not the real enemy. (Jones never forgot that Hitler fought in the engagement at Mametz Wood.) There is the feverish impatience with international financial regimes and with a romantic and sanitized version of British imperial history which allows open hypocrisies about justice and aggression to flourish unchecked. There is the paradoxical linkage of the belief that war is invariably hideous and dehumanizing and to be avoided at practically all costs with the sense that Hitler's appeal to a kind of cathartic violence is no less morally defensible than the concern of Hitler's enemies to safeguard the market. Jones's piece is anything but lucid, and the anguished rambling (if that isn't too contradictory a description) shows the depth of his bafflement and unease. As with his comments on *Mein Kampf* to Harman Grisewood, these pages illustrate both his honesty and the limits of his perspective. But they also pose a challenge to his admirers at least to see why his questions were serious – why a sensitive, compassionate Christian with no time for classical Catholic anti-Semitism might briefly believe, or toy with believing, that Hitler was not self-evidently the worst threat to the civilized world, even that Hitler was on the frontier of mystical insight – one of Jones's more startling moments.

Hence, as the contributors to this book emphasize, his focus on 'the Question' – the 'Question Not Asked' which appears in the Grail romances. Failure to ask the question delays the healing of the wounded Fisher King, and thus the rescue of the land from devastation and sterility. That Question is sometimes represented as the question of what the King suffers and why, and so of why the land is laid waste. But the earliest version renders the Question as 'Whom does the Grail serve?' Paraphrasing this, it is the question of where the symbolic systems of human culture point or tend; what is culture *for*? Jones's appropriation of the idea of the 'Break' in cultural history on whose far side we now stand is closely related to this.

What has not always been brought out clearly in discussions of Jones's achievement is how he sees the cultural climate of industrial and functional modernity as eroding something fundamental about human language itself. Art in general, the reading and composing of poetry in particular, are a form of archaeology – not simply excavating antique objects, but excavating connections. The artist uncovers 'root systems' in human imagination and communication and displays the virtual infinity of ways in which one thing is what it is because of countless others and one word is anchored in entire systems of myth and perception. Every thing and every word is thus *for* a whole ecology of meaning, in whose completeness (a completeness that of course resists possession or definitive expression) the unequivocal gift of God is mediated, the gift of both being and bliss. The acts of redemption in the life, death, and resurrection of Christ are not episodes in a plain historical sequence, but uniquely concentrated manifestations of the interconnectedness of culture and speech: this is what *The Anathemata* sets out to show us. And if the root systems are ignored or denied, every thing and every word shrinks into itself alone, reduces to its immediate function within our pragmatic management of the environment. When this happens, we are deprived of our metaphorical repertoire; and this is not just the loss of a useful dressing-up chest, but a blow to the nature of distinctively human speech. In a world where the Question is not asked, the Grail becomes a convenient receptacle for whatever we choose to put into it. And the result is that healing is indefinitely postponed, because the resources of meaning at every level are blocked up. (It is tempting to cast a sideways glance at a theme that emerges in a number of Jones's visual exercises as well as in his letters: 'freeing the waters'.)

So what he has to say about Gerard Manley Hopkins in the prolonged but pregnant essay included here is an affirmation of Hopkins's importance for grasping the scale of the Question. Hopkins's metaphorical exuberance, but also his deliberate playing with the stress on the wildly oscillating surface of his lines; Hopkins's appropriation of Scotus, and his vision of the one Christ 'playing' in the immeasurable diversity of distinct created lives – all this shows what poetry needs to be if it is alive to the Question, and it explains why Hopkins is not just a late Victorian but a precursor of aspects of modernism: that modernism which both threatens ultimate dissolutions of meaning and allows dangerous and unlooked-for recoveries of connection and mutuality. Hopkins is a paradigmatically modern poet as well as a paradigmatically Catholic one, and, as we should expect, Jones helps us see that these characteristics can belong together in the most fruitful tension. Awareness of the Question means that Hopkins restores to language the 'pregnancy' that belongs to it; so far from being exotic or eccentric, this register of speaking exhibits the central 'humanness' of language – as of course does the writing of Joyce, another modernist with (somewhat convoluted) Catholic elements. Uncovering the root systems will always risk the odd and even the apparently anarchic, but the alternative is a speech that does not restore wastelands and so is ultimately empty.

What we have in the texts and discussions in this book is a deeply welcome tranche of material for the fuller understanding of what Jones believed he had to witness to and conserve in 'the dialect of the tribe' – to quote another uncomfortable dweller on the modernist–Catholic frontier. Jones, quintessentially a private person, is unsurprisingly confused and disturbed when he tries to make sense of public events; but it would be a mistake to say that this is no more than the ill-informed rumination of an unworldly artist. At least he does not advance the confident and alarming political theses of a Yeats. But beneath the very uneasy surface and the jejune thoughts about the international scene, Jones is pushing forward his focal and vital question: how do we enact our distinctive human destiny as sign makers, witnesses to the connection of all things in the eternal Word, in a culture that systematically disconnects? Global political schemes, whether liberal or totalitarian, fail to answer; art itself answers in broken, difficult ways ('*A, a, a, Domine Deus* . . .'); but its confidence in answering, even in fragments, depends on a metaphysical passion and insight that constantly have to be renewed and recovered. And so Jones raises his *anathemata*, even his *vexilla*, to invite us to join the excavations.

Introduction

The Unpublished Prose of a Practical Saint

THOMAS BERENATO

'I cannot read *The Anathemata*', admits the Dominican Dantist Kenelm Foster, opening his review of *Epoch and Artist* for *Blackfriars* in 1959 with a candid disclaimer. But, Foster adds, 'I am ready to spring to attention as soon as Mr Jones starts discoursing in prose'.[1] This volume culls from Jones archives in the United Kingdom and the United States four pieces of Jones's prose either previously unpublished or previously published only in abridgment. The interest of such a collection to Jones's admirers is not in question. Anyone acquainted with the visual art, poems, essays, and correspondence already available hungers for more from the heap of material whose patient presentation to the public will be the heavy but happy task of a generation of editors. The appetite for Jonesiana feeds on a leading feature of the artefacts themselves, their insatiability for the meaningfulness that comes of connection. A survey of the work maps a mind astride an eddy arising from the confluence of memory and desire: the desire and pursuit of the whole – what Jones, describing Ezra Pound's *Cantos*, calls 'a *unique integrity*'.[2] This mind rides, sometimes foundering in, the crosscurrent formed by the centrifugal force of its evident delight in allusion and its centripetal impulse to gather all things in.[3] Jones wants an artwork not only to 'gather recession from the past' but also to 'project itself forward so that other works of art and nature, perhaps trivial, perhaps of only remote association, are in our minds, conditioned by it'.[4] The beholder of a page or canvas by Jones turns away exhausted and exhilarated in equal measure by exposure to the rhythm of recession and projection that puts its elements everywhere at odds with themselves and to the common rhythms of everyday life.

The intent of the editors for this book is to expose its readers to 'the sudden violences and the long stillnesses, the sharp contours and unformed voids' of a few underexposed

---

[1] Kenelm Foster, OP, 'David Jones on Art and Religion', *Blackfriars* 4, no. 475 (October 1959): 421.

[2] See Jones's letter of 29 December 1952 to the engraver Desmond Chute in David Jones, *Inner Necessities: The Letters of David Jones to Desmond Chute*, ed. Thomas Dilworth (Toronto: Anson-Cartwright Editions, 1984), 24.

[3] See David Jones, 'The Myth of Arthur', in Harman Grisewood (ed.), *Epoch and Artist* (London: Faber & Faber, 1959), 243: '"All must be safely gathered in", as Mr. Stanley Spencer said to me, with reference to the making of a picture (a more apt expression of the artist's business I never heard).'

[4] Jones, 'The Myth of Arthur', *Epoch and Artist*, 250.

specimens of Jones's prose.[5] Of Jones's prose Kenelm Foster writes in his review, with a nod to Robert Herrick, 'its rambling "sweet disorder", its frolicsome imagery, has a heart-lightening quality; for the images do not merely frolic, they really aid intelligence'.[6] Foster had not seen the items gathered here. One of them is the uncomposed prose of transcribed speech, likely the last interview for which Jones sat. Two of them, a letter and an essay written in the wake of 'Munich', may discompose the reader disinclined to agree with the painter Julian Bell that 'Jones's opinions were a matter of the utmost political inconsequence'.[7] In the other item, an abandoned attempt, circa 1968, to assess the influence on a belated epoch of Gerard Manley Hopkins, decomposition is both theme and ruinous form.[8] No single topic is common to these four generically disparate pieces. If anything unites them it is what Bell aptly characterizes as Jones's 'concessionary, democratic reasonableness of address'.[9] They are of timbre all compact. Jones was hypersensitive to the sound of the human voice, experiencing it on occasion 'as if it were a *physical touch* – a healing thing'.[10] The formal, almost oratorical, address of the open letter on Hitler and the private letter to Chamberlain does not disguise the foundational presumption of anterior intimacy between himself and his readers on which Jones premises all of his prose. This knack for buttonholing his audience while playing the Wedding Guest shapes even the terrible halting cadence of the drafts on Hopkins and the lost, late interview. Both mesmerize on the strength of their very tentativeness, their irresistible blend of wild civility and fine distraction.

Jones's prose strikes the same pose with respect to the rest of his work as Jones depicts, in the painted inscription he places at the head of *Epoch and Artist*, 'the bards of the world' assuming before 'the men of valour'.[11] The prose-pieces, like the poets, execute an assessment without passing judgement. Their virtue is 'practive': to strengthen the base from which art might issue.[12] The place of Jones's prose along the sweep of his oeuvre cries out for greater specification than scholars have yet accorded it. Such is the aim of the rest of this introduction.

* * *

[5] David Jones, *In Parenthesis* (London: Faber & Faber, 1937), x.

[6] Foster, 'David Jones on Art and Religion', 424.

[7] See Julian Bell, 'Moon Behind Clouds: The Wounded Vision of David Jones', *Times Literary Supplement*, 5 April 1996, 10. On the question of Jones's 'sympathies for Fascism', see also the exchange of letters between Thomas Dilworth and the painter Timothy Hyman in the *Times Literary Supplement*'s correspondence pages, issues of 22 and 29 January 2016, respectively, 6.

[8] See Harman Grisewood's introduction to the first posthumous collection of Jones's prose in David Jones, *The Dying Gaul and Other Writings*, ed. Harman Grisewood (London: Faber & Faber, 1978), 10: 'Like G. M. Hopkins in the 1930s, David Jones needs to be "re-discovered" by those who are at some distance from the time in which he wrote.' Grisewood discusses the unexpected incursion of Hopkins's poems into his and Jones's 1930s milieu in his memoir *One Thing at a Time: An Autobiography* (London: Hutchinson, 1968), 86.

[9] Bell, 'Moon Behind Clouds', 10.

[10] See Jones's letter of 11 July 1958 to Harman Grisewood in David Jones, *Dai Greatcoat: A Self-portrait of David Jones in his Letters*, ed. René Hague (London: Faber & Faber, 1980), 175. It is the female voice of a certain quality to which Jones is particularly susceptible: '*Voices are extraordinary*, I *think*, they have almost limitless power to deject, repel, bore, or elevate, enchant, console, attract and all the rest.'

[11] Jones takes the text of this inscription, which faces the title page of *Epoch and Artist*, from the Welsh poem Y *Gododdin* and the Vulgate's Book of Ecclesiasticus. For details, see Nicolete Gray, *The Painted Inscriptions of David Jones* (London: Gordon Fraser, 1981), 37.

[12] See Jones's 1958 'Preface by the Author', *Epoch and Artist*, 12. For a host of practical reasons, Jones would not have authorized the present edition of his prose.

'I feel that my stuff, such as it is, is much more "prosaic" than they imagine.'[13] So writes Jones to Harman Grisewood in a letter of 22 May 1962. 'They' are 'chaps who, for one reason or another, think "academically" or, on the other hand, "imaginatively" – in the Yeats tradition'.[14] The 'stuff' in question is Jones's poems published so far: *In Parenthesis* (1937) and *The Anathemata* (1952). Jones is careful not to call his poetry prose. But he acknowledges – he insists upon – something unpoetical about it. It eludes exclusive claims to comprehension by visionaries and pedants alike. 'Academic' is a dirty word for Jones – down there with 'rhetorical' – and his 'stuff' answers indifferently to professors and prophets, aspires to the condition of neither commentary nor revelation.[15] 'Ars' is rather 'an infantryman's job'.[16] The valley of its making is a trench where 'staff-wallahs' have no business.[17] His 'stuff', Jones explains to Grisewood, has an 'altogether different point of departure' to that of '"poetry" or "prose" as conceived by "writers", whether good or bad'.[18] The 'writers' on Jones's mind at this moment are Rupert Brooke, Wilfred Owen, Siegfried Sassoon, Robert Graves, and '*even*' T. S. Eliot.[19]

On what grounds does Jones except himself from this select club? He begins by refusing to recognize its rules. The opposition of prose to poetry is not in fact one to which this poet-painter pays homage. Jones likes to quote James Joyce: 'practical life or "art" . . . comprehends all our activities from boat-building to poetry'.[20] The inverted commas around 'art' suggest that Joyce means to bring the idea of art down a notch – onto the plane of 'practical life', which is reciprocally dignified by the offhand equation coordinated by the conjunction 'or'. Jones likewise plays the leveller when, later, he considers an artwork 'as a making, as *poiesis*'.[21] This apposition simply literalizes the Greek term of art, but the effect is to siphon off the aura it has accumulated over millennia of feverish theorizing. Jones wishes to isolate the 'prosaic' kernel of *poiesis*.

In an essay of 1921 T. S. Eliot identifies the need for a fourth term to complete the analogy between poetry and prose: 'we have the term "verse" and the term "poetry", and only the one term "prose" to express their opposites'.[22] Jones has one to hand, plucked from Aristotle's *Nicomachean Ethics*: *praxis*.[23] The paradox at the heart of Jones's artistic practice is that for him *poiesis* is most gratuitous – which is to say, for Jones, nearest its true self, 'intransitivity and gratuitousness' being for him the soul of art – when it is most practical.[24] Practicality is synonymous on this account not with 'utility', in its narrow denotation of 'the merely utilitarian' or the 'simply functional',[25] but with *prudentia*,

[13] Jones, *Dai Greatcoat*, 189.
[14] Jones, *Dai Greatcoat*, 189.
[15] Jones, *Dai Greatcoat*, 89.
[16] See David Jones, 'The Utile', *Epoch and Artist*, 183.
[17] Jones, *Epoch and Artist*, 183.
[18] Jones, *Dai Greatcoat*, 188.
[19] Jones, *Dai Greatcoat*, 188.
[20] David Jones, 'The Preface to *The Anathemata*', *Epoch and Artist*, 108. Jones gives the quotation again in his essay 'Art and Sacrament', *Epoch and Artist*, 172. Jones cites Oliver St. John Gogarty's record of Joyce's remark in *As I Was Going Down Sackville Street* (London: Rich & Cowan, 1937), 287.
[21] Jones, 'Art and Sacrament', *Epoch and Artist*, 172.
[22] T. S. Eliot, 'Prose and Verse' (1921), in T. S. Eliot, *The Complete Prose of T. S. Eliot: The Critical Edition: The Perfect Critic, 1919–1926*, ed. Anthony Cuda and Ronald Schuchard (Baltimore, MD, and London: Johns Hopkins University Press and Faber & Faber, 2014), 324.
[23] Jones, 'Art and Sacrament', *Epoch and Artist*, 172.
[24] Jones, 'Art and Sacrament', *Epoch and Artist*, 149.
[25] Jones, 'Art and Sacrament', *Epoch and Artist*, 176.

which Jones understands to be a contraction of *providentia*: 'So we use Prudentia for convenience to denote, as it were, the tutelary genius who presides over the whole realm of faith, moral, religion, ethic; she is thought of as Holy Wisdom.'[26] Since Jones understands absolutely everyone – from the saints of legend to the 'party-leaders' of the present – to fall under the jurisdiction of 'a *Prudentia*', the only distinction that matters to him is that between what he calls the 'the validity of a word' and its invalidity, which is a function of the '"situational problems"' of a particular 'civilizational phase'.[27]

At issue is the efficacy of signs: whether what Jones calls an 'efficacious formula' has been uttered.[28] As Jones puts it in *The Anathemata*, 'It all hangs on the fiat. If her fiat was the Great Fiat, nevertheless, seeing the solidarity, we participate in the fiat – or can indeed, by our fiats – it stands to reason.'[29] The participation of 'our fiats' in 'her fiat' offers a vivid image of the relationship between prose and poetry in Jones's work. Prose is the 'matrix' of all verse-forms.[30] The prosaic is the general mother of the poetic, its womb.[31] And the parturition of the poetic proceeds by 'fiat'. Jones exploits the active-passive ambivalence of the word. The first 'fiat' is God's *fiat lux* of Gen. 1.3, but it is the *fiat mihi* of the Theotokos that Jones invokes in *The Anathemata*.[32] This prosaic act of receptive perception primes the mother of God for the inception of the poem with which she follows it up: the Magnificat or Canticle of Mary.[33]

With the same sly spirit that he brings to bear upon the transvaluation of 'anathemata', Jones redefines poetry as 'propaganda'.[34] His impertinent equation draws attention to 'the "dangerous" element' in art. 'Poetry is to be diagnosed as "dangerous" because it evokes and recalls, is a kind of *anamnesis* of, i.e. is an effective recalling of, something loved. In that sense it is inevitably "propaganda", in that any real formal expression propagands the reality which caused those forms and their content to be."[35] The '"danger"' lies in the degree of that 'reality' with which the poet's fiat confronts the fiats of a society's 'rulers'.[36] The poet's reality carries the dangerous potential of overruling the rulers' reality insofar

---

[26] Jones, 'Art and Sacrament', *Epoch and Artist*, 145.

[27] Jones, 'The Preface to *The Anathemata*', *Epoch and Artist*, 118–19.

[28] Jones, *In Parenthesis*, xii. See also *In Parenthesis*, 53, for 'the efficacious word'.

[29] David Jones, *The Anathemata* (London: Faber & Faber, 1952), 214.

[30] See Walter Benjamin's essay of October 1936, 'The Storyteller', trans. Harry Zohn, in Walter Benjamin, *Walter Benjamin: Selected Writings, Volume 3: 1935–1938*, ed. Howard Eiland and Michael W. Jennings (Cambridge, MA, and London: The Belknap Press of Harvard University Press, 2002), 154: 'great prose is the creative matrix of the various metrical forms'. Compare Jones in his poem of 1960, 'The Tutelar of the Place', in *The Sleeping Lord and Other Fragments* (London: Faber & Faber, 1974), 62, where one of the tutelar's titles is 'mediatrix of all the deposits'.

[31] See the last line of 'The Tutelar of the Place', in *The Sleeping Lord*, 64, where the tutelar is identified as the 'Womb of the Lamb'.

[32] For Mary's *fiat mihi* see Lk. 1.38 in the Vulgate. Compare Jones, *The Anathemata*, 189, and the poem 'from *The Book of Balaam's Ass*', in *The Sleeping Lord*, 108, where the dying soldiers of Passchendaele call 'On Mary because of her secret piercing, and because, but for her pliant *Fiat mihi*, no womb-burden to joust with the fiend in the lists of Hierosolyma, in his fragile habergeon: HUMANA NATURA'.

[33] See Jones's 1964 essay 'An Introduction to *The Rime of the Ancient Mariner*', in *The Dying Gaul and Other Writings*, 225, where he justifies the presence of a swinging censer in 'the last of the eight full-page illustrations', published in 1929, that he had made for Coleridge's poem: 'It is at Vespers that the altar is censed during the singing of the Magnificat, her song who is called the Star of the Sea.' (A 'little vesper bell' calls the Mariner to prayer near the end of the last part of *The Rime*.) See also Allen Grossman, *The Sighted Singer: Two Works on Poetry for Readers and Writers* (Baltimore, MD: Johns Hopkins University Press, 1992), 237: 'The biblical type of the poem is the *Magnificat* (Luke 1:46–55).'

[34] Jones, 'The Preface to *The Anathemata*', *Epoch and Artist*, 118.

[35] Jones, 'The Preface to *The Anathemata*', *Epoch and Artist*, 118.

[36] Jones, 'The Preface to *The Anathemata*', *Epoch and Artist*, 118.

as it offers a stronger link to the past. The poet is 'by profession the custodian, rememberer, embodier and voice of the mythus', Jones writes.[37] The poet's reality exerts an 'influence' on the ruler's reality by means of what Jones calls a 'most adverse magic'.[38] This 'influence' is the burden of the past, which, 'lifted up' by the poet in the 'magical' act of *anamnesis*, serves to put a damper on the politician's 'progress'.[39]

The poet stands askance of history. With respect to the past the poet's role, as Jones conceives it, is 'legatine', vicarious rather than prophetic.[40] In section xv of the introduction to the first volume of *The Decline of the West*, Oswald Spengler demands that men born in 'the early winter of full civilization' embrace their historical burden head-on and without illusion: 'Everything depends on our seeing our own position, our *destiny*, clearly, on our realizing that though we may lie to ourselves about it we cannot evade it. He who does not acknowledge this in his heart, ceases to be counted among the men of his generation, and remains either a simpleton, a charlatan, or a pedant.'[41] At this point in the margin of his copy of the book, Jones objects: 'He might be simply an intelligent person who knows he is living in a kind of hell.'[42]

The Jonesian poet cuts a figure less poetical, and more practical, than that of a Spenglerian hero of fate. He confronts what Jones calls 'the present culture-situation' squarely, but he refuses to deduce from what he sees a diagnosis of its unidirectional declension. A vector quantity that might be called culture's Junonian crosscurrent runs counter.[43] Jones deems Spengler to be swimming in 'a male thought-world entirely', from which source directly flows his fatalism.[44] Jones complements Spengler's deterministic *Weltanschauung* with what he christens 'the "optimism" of the Saints'.[45] The sign of such optimism is, to use a word Jones borrows from Blake, 'trembling'.[46] Artists tremble in the fearful act of affirming delight, which is the goal of painting, according to a maxim that Jones, approving, attributes to Poussin.[47] Any artwork worthy of the name registers the seismic shocks of belief – of a poetic faith in the constitutive human capacity for significant making.[48] The tutelar of this

---

[37] Jones, 'The Preface to *The Anathemata*', *Epoch and Artist*, 117.

[38] Jones, 'The Preface to *The Anathemata*', *Epoch and Artist*, 118.

[39] Jones, 'The Preface to *The Anathemata*', *Epoch and Artist*, 125.

[40] Jones, 'The Preface to *The Anathemata*', *Epoch and Artist*, 130.

[41] Oswald Spengler, *The Decline of the West*, trans. Charles Francis Atkinson (London: George Allen & Unwin, 1926), I, 44. A copy of this edition (two volumes in one), dated 19 August 1941, is in Jones's personal library, preserved at the National Library of Wales, Aberystwyth.

[42] Cited by Kathleen Henderson Staudt in her essay 'The Decline of the West and the Optimism of the Saints: David Jones' Reading of Oswald Spengler', in John Matthias (ed.), *David Jones: Man and Poet* (Orono, ME: National Poetry Foundation, University of Maine, 1989), 458.

[43] See Jones's letter to Harman Grisewood of 26 February 1942, in Jones, *Dai Greatcoat*, 115, where he observes that Spengler 'has liquidated *Juno*'.

[44] Jones, *Dai Greatcoat*, 115.

[45] Jones, 'Art in Relation to War', *The Dying Gaul*, 159. This long essay, first published, posthumously, in 1978, is dated on p. 166 as '1942–3, 1946'. In a letter of early August 1943, T. S. Eliot recommended that Jones expand it into a book. See Thomas Dilworth, *David Jones: Engraver, Soldier, Painter, Poet* (London: Jonathan Cape, 2017), 228 and 259.

[46] Jones, 'Art in Relation to War', *The Dying Gaul*, 129, n. 1.

[47] Jones, 'Art in Relation to War', *The Dying Gaul*, 129: '"The goal of painting is delight," said Poussin. No one ever said truer word.'

[48] See Jones's remark in a letter of 4 July 1963 to Thomas Gilby, OP, reproduced in Aidan Nichols, OP, *Dominican Gallery: Portrait of a Culture* (Leominster: Gracewing, 1997), 421: 'Poor old Galileo's *Eppur si muove!* is what we cry in the presence of any decent art-work.' Thomas Dilworth reports that Jones shared with his friend (since spring 1924) the collector and curator Jim Ede a 'belief in the importance of a sense of movement' in an artwork. See Dilworth, *David Jones: Engraver, Soldier, Painter, Poet*, 89 and 107.

faith is the order of value that in the culture of the West goes by the name 'feminine'.[49] A favourite phrase of Jones's is an epithet for the God-man that he adapts from the Gradual for the Feast of the Maternity of the Blessed Virgin Mary: 'That which the whole world cannot contain, is contained.'[50] The container in question of course is the Virgin Womb.

In the long essay 'Art in Relation to War', his major prose-work of the 1940s, Jones identifies the gauntlet thrown down by this sacred text as the 'cause' of Blake's 'fear and trembling'.[51] The challenge to contain the uncontainable 'drums in the head of the artist'.[52] To meet it takes something Jones finds in short supply: 'intellectual courage'.[53] Courage is one of the four cardinal virtues, alongside prudence, justice, and temperance. 'Intellectual' courage – as distinct from 'moral' or 'physical' courage, which Jones finds 'readily supplied' – is the moral virtue of prose.[54] Its hallmark is a kind of political realism. 'World history' tests the mettle of anyone who aspires to intellectual courage in contemplation of its 'rake's progress'.[55] Anyone who flinches from recognizing the course of history as up and down 'a criminal dissipation of noble things' must be called an intellectual coward.[56] Anyone who avoids this terrible acknowledgement is guilty of the unsaintliest false '"optimism"'.[57] 'We must call deaths, deaths, and admit a real loss', Jones writes.[58] Such an admission is the precondition of artistic vision, which is courageous comprehension *par excellence* – comprehensive of '*real* loss and *real* gain' alike.[59] It is the vision of Eliot's blind Tiresias, who, as Jones often reminds his readers, 'foresuffered all'.[60] Tiresias's all-encompassing glance is the look of art: 'What Tiresias *sees*, in fact, is the substance of the poem', Eliot indicates in an endnote.[61] It takes in what Jones calls the '"swing and roundabout" situation' that obtains at 'every big turn in human history'.[62]

For Jones, history is a 'tangled brake' that the poet, hunting forms, cannot escape.[63] Viewed from without, the poet seems to lack direction, looks lost in a 'muddle'.[64] But as his 'meander' gains momentum it sets in motion a logic of 'inner necessities' that discovers form.[65] Suddenly the tangled brake assumes the shape of a sacred wood. The end of man is 'happiness', Jones believes.[66] Happiness – the optimism of the saints – is also the end of

---

[49] On this motif, see Kathleen Henderson Staudt, *At the Turn of a Civilization: David Jones and Modern Poetics* (Ann Arbor: University of Michigan Press, 1994), 86–7.
[50] Jones, 'Art in Relation to War', *The Dying Gaul*, 142.
[51] Jones, 'Art in Relation to War', *The Dying Gaul*, 142.
[52] Jones, 'Art in Relation to War', *The Dying Gaul*, 142.
[53] Jones, 'Art in Relation to War', *The Dying Gaul*, 147.
[54] Jones, 'Art in Relation to War', *The Dying Gaul*, 147.
[55] Jones, 'Art in Relation to War', *The Dying Gaul*, 154.
[56] Jones, 'Art in Relation to War', *The Dying Gaul*, 154.
[57] Jones, 'Art in Relation to War', *The Dying Gaul*, 153.
[58] Jones, 'Art in Relation to War', *The Dying Gaul*, 153.
[59] Jones, 'Art in Relation to War', *The Dying Gaul*, 152.
[60] See *The Waste Land* (1922), l. 243, in T. S. Eliot, *The Poems of T. S. Eliot: Volume 1: Collected and Uncollected Poems*, ed. Christopher Ricks and Jim McCue (Baltimore, MD, and London: Johns Hopkins University Press and Faber & Faber, 2015), 64. Jones quotes this line in 'The Preface to *The Anathemata*', *Epoch and Artist*, 122, and elsewhere in his prose.
[61] See Eliot's endnote to *The Waste Land*, l. 218, in *The Poems of T. S. Eliot*, 74.
[62] Jones, 'Art in Relation to War', *The Dying Gaul*, 153.
[63] For two of many instances of Jones's use of this phrase, see *Epoch and Artist*, 116, and *In Parenthesis*, 52.
[64] See Jones's letter of 9 October 1961 to Harman Grisewood, in Jones, *Dai Greatcoat*, 185.
[65] For one mention among many of 'the meander', see the last lines of Jones's poem *The Kensington Mass*, in *The Roman Quarry and Other Sequences*, ed. Harman Grisewood and René Hague (New York: Sheep Meadow Press, 1981), 92. For 'inner necessities', see Jones's letter of 29 December 1952 to Desmond Chute in Jones, *Inner Necessities*, 24.
[66] Jones, 'Art in Relation to War', *The Dying Gaul*, 135.

art, which ends on earth not in 'fulfilment' (the prerogative of heaven) but in 'struggle'.[67] Writing of painting in some notes he made for his psychiatrist on 8 October 1947, Jones gives a succinct definition of poetic happiness: 'Painting odd in that one is led partly by what evolves as the painting evolves, this form suggesting that form – happiness comes when the forms assume significance with regard to this juxtaposition to each other – even though the original "idea" was somewhat different. The consequent extreme difficulty of "talking about" or explaining a painting. The happiest ones seem to make themselves.'[68] To strive for 'the felicity of forms', which is what Jones declares here that he is 'really after', takes the fortitude and gives the happiness of the saints.[69] Once the poet acknowledges it as 'the chief occasion of fear', *poiesis* can serve as 'the chief release from tension'.[70]

Jones identifies as one of the 'efficient causes' of poetry the employment of a particular language 'at an especially heightened tension'.[71] This formulation recalls Gerard Manley Hopkins's dictum that the 'poetical language of an age shd. be the current language heightened', next to the citation of which in his copy of *A Hopkins Reader* Jones made a mark in the margin.[72] A footnote to 'Art in Relation to War' includes the parenthetical remark that 'painting is poetry'.[73] But what Jones elsewhere designates as 'written poetry' does not include 'prose', except when the latter takes its place as an element (another being 'verse') in a *prosimetrum*, as it does in *In Parenthesis*, *The Anathemata*, and the sequence of shorter poems that compose *The Sleeping Lord*.[74] For Jones the difference between prose and verse rests solely on the look of the page of text as the printer has set it up in accordance with the poet's instructions in manuscript, where Jones marks the ends of lines of verse with a red-pencil solidus.[75] Lines of prose lack this mark and so run on to the right margin and down the page at the printer's convenience. The work of 'poetry' is performed by the juxtaposition on the page of prose and verse (and image, when Jones inserts reproductions of his drawings or painted inscriptions into his books of poetry).

This work is the fruit of play: 'My "method"', Jones writes in a letter of 29 December 1952, 'is merely to arse around with such words as are available to me until the passage in question takes on something of the shape I think it requires & evokes the image I want. I find, or think I find, the process almost identical to what one tries to do in paintin' or

[67] Jones, 'Art in Relation to War', *The Dying Gaul*, 135.
[68] Jones, *Dai Greatcoat*, 137.
[69] Jones, *Dai Greatcoat*, 138.
[70] Jones, *Dai Greatcoat*, 139.
[71] Jones, 'The Preface to *The Anathemata*', *Epoch and Artist*, 117.
[72] See p. xxiii of Jones's copy, in the National Library of Wales, Aberystwyth, of John Pick (ed.), *A Hopkins Reader* (London: Oxford University Press, 1953). For a brief discussion of Jones's interest in Hopkins's remark, see Jonathan Miles, *Backgrounds to David Jones: A Study in Sources and Drafts* (Cardiff: University of Wales Press, 1990), 76.
[73] Jones, 'Art in Relation to War', *The Dying Gaul*, 137.
[74] See the Hopkins essay manuscript, pp. 161, 171, 249 below.
[75] See for instance file LR7/1 of the David Jones Papers at the National Library of Wales, Aberystwyth, Jones's manuscript for *The Book of Balaam's Ass*. In his letter to Vernon Watkins of 11 October 1957, in David Jones, *Letters to Vernon Watkins*, edited with notes by Ruth Pryor (Cardiff: University of Wales Press, 1976), 41, Jones shows in a series of red-pencilled diagrams how he '*indicates to the printer which are the "prose" bits and which the so-called "poetry" bits*' of 'The Wall', whose first British publication Watkins was editing for a Christmas poetry supplement. See Vernon Watkins (ed.), *Landmarks and Voyages* (London: Poetry Book Society, 1957). 'The Wall' had been published in *Poetry* 87, no. 2 (November 1955), 68–74, and Jones wished to take this opportunity to adjust the layout and make other corrections.

drawin'.'[76] In a letter of 11 April 1939 Jones describes his poetic method (or, as he puts it, 'method') in terms of 'a sort of Balaam business': 'how if you start saying in a kind of way how *bloody* everything is you end up in a kind of *praise – inevitably*'.[77] 'Arsing around' is the artistic activity – of 'Gathering all things in' – prelusive to that 'acid twist' by which form is found in the scatter of *materia poetica*.[78] In *The Book of Balaam's Ass*, his half-abandoned post-*In Parenthesis* project, Jones figures as a feminine power the 'sweet influence' by which 'all the disorder and deadness' of 'the hard steel world' 'takes shape and life'.[79]

What Jones once refers to as 'this contingent "real" world, so called' is what Hegel in his lectures on aesthetics of the 1820s called, without caveat, 'the prose of the world': 'a world of finitude and mutability, of entanglement in the relative, of the pressure of necessity from which the individual is in no position to withdraw'.[80] Jones's sacramental vision illumines for him the poetic side of the prose of life. In his view, the poetic is the soft underbelly of the prosaic that it is the poet's task to protect and nurture – but, crucially, without rejecting the prosaic 'fact-world' out of hand.[81] Instead the poet must suffer the prosaic to 'turn a corner' into the poetic.[82] The poetic – in an analogy with the line of verse – is an inflection of the prosaic.[83] By the end of *Balaam's Ass* the poet has demanded of 'the perfected steel: Bend your beauty to my desire.'[84] But Jones knows that this fiat is unenforceable. The poet must render himself susceptible to influence, accepting that 'her fiat is our fortune'.[85] The poetical potential of the prosaic answers not to an imperative but an interrogative. The poet must put questions to, not place demands upon, the prosaic if he wishes to winkle out its formal beauty. And he must make the interrogation a phase of self-interrogation: 'for space itself, they say, leans, is kindly, with ourselves, who make wide deviations to meet ourselves'.[86] Poetry arises from the poet's willingness to be wounded by the world's perfected steel. The poet draws strength to bear the blow from the belief – in a truth at once natural and supernatural – that man is by nature *homo faber*.[87]

But this belief is not consolatory: 'Indeed, it is that conviction which strips off all defensive armour, so that the sharp contradictions and heavy incongruities may at least be

---

[76] Jones, *Inner Necessities*, 24. On Jones's notion of '"man as artist" at play', see the discussion of 'Art in Relation to War' in Dilworth, *David Jones: Engraver, Soldier, Painter, Poet*, 228.

[77] Jones, *Dai Greatcoat*, 91.

[78] See 'The Tutelar of the Place', in Jones, *The Sleeping Lord*, 61, and 'Art in Relation to War', *The Dying Gaul*, 140.

[79] See *The Book of Balaam's Ass* in Jones, *The Roman Quarry*, 209, and Jones's letter of 11 April 1939 to Jim and Helen Ede, in Jones, *Dai Greatcoat*, 91.

[80] Jones, *Dai Greatcoat*, 91; G.W. F. Hegel, *Aesthetics: Lectures on Fine Art: Volume 1*, trans. T. M. Knox (Oxford: Clarendon Press, 1975), 150.

[81] See Jones's poem 'The Agent', *The Roman Quarry*, 145.

[82] See Jones's 1941 essay 'Religion and the Muses', *Epoch and Artist*, 102: 'The springing to life of an art-form is subject to no constraint and no good-will can call it into being. It would seem to rise from breakdowns and fusions to produce a new and unexpected life. (Something of this sort seems sometimes to take place also when individual artists turn a corner, or suddenly achieve something worth looking at.)'

[83] See Jones's preface to *In Parenthesis*, xi: 'A new line, which the typography would not otherwise demand, is used to indicate some change, inflexion, or emphasis.'

[84] Jones, *The Book of Balaam's Ass*, *The Roman Quarry*, 211.

[85] Jones, *The Anathemata*, 128.

[86] Jones, *The Book of Balaam's Ass*, *The Roman Quarry*, 188.

[87] See Jones, 'Art in Relation to War', *The Dying Gaul*, 141, n. 14. Art's '"fidelity to nature" consists in its being fidele to "super-nature" in some way'. And see Jones, 'Art and Sacrament', *Epoch and Artist*, 178: 'in spite of any appearances, man remains, by definition, man-the-artist'.

felt.'[88] To 'make a shape in words' is to turn the other cheek.[89] The poet is neither a hero nor a saint, and a 'writing' is not a martyrdom, but a poem does give a picture of the world under the aspect of its vulnerability to the prosaic. The object of Jones's prose is to make the world safe for his poetry, which is to say all that is vulnerable in the world. In the midst of the 'world-storm', devotion to delicacy at this extreme makes sense only in the light of the tutelary title: 'Womb of the Lamb the spoiler of the Ram'.[90] A poem is at once wound and bow, calm and storm, peace and war, lamb and lion.[91] Poetry, the issue of prose, leans on prose and ends up embracing it: 'rite follows matriarchate'.[92] Of prose the poet never stops asking, 'Are you my mother?' As long as he asks, the reply remains always in the affirmative.

In this collection of poet's prose we watch Jones ask this question of, in turn, '"the Austrian ex-house painter"' Adolf Hitler, the Launcelot-like prime minister Neville Chamberlain, the time-travelling *makar* Gerard Manley Hopkins, and, finally, of himself, at the hands of a pair of interviewers just over a year before his death.[93] All of these pieces of prose – including the dictated prose of Jones's transcribed speech – are poetic insofar that they wallow in the depth of their own devising. They meander, as does all of Jones's writing, but forgivably, for within the ambit of the 'crooked labyrinth' they explore, 'the extraneous is inconceivable'.[94]

What Jones says of the 'arts' applies as well to the overgrown letters, unfinished essays, and long conversations gathered here: they 'abhor any loppings off of meanings or emptying out, any lessening of the totality of connotation, any loss of recession and thickness through'.[95] The archive of Jones's unpublished prose is thick. A vertiginous, if not absolutely infinite, recession of overlapping arguments awaits unpacking and unpicking.[96] Their annotation will be an editorial anabasis. This necessarily narrow selection of Jones's comments on religion, politics, and culture seeks to gauge the rake angle at which his incisive artist's mind cuts across its epoch, struggling and sometimes succeeding in an unabashed attempt to integrate its disparate data into a single tolerable shape.

---

[88] Jones, 'Art and Sacrament', *Epoch and Artist*, 178.

[89] Jones, *In Parenthesis*, x.

[90] See the last line of Jones's poem 'The Tutelar of the Place', *The Sleeping Lord*, 64.

[91] See Jones, 'Art in Relation to War', *The Dying Gaul*, 141. Great painting, Jones says there, '*is* both peace *and* war; it must make the lion lie by the lamb *without anyone noticing*, it must hint at December snow, when summer's heat is in the text. In painting a persistent "desire and pursuit of the whole" is needed.'

[92] See Jones, 'from *The Book of Balaam's Ass*', *The Sleeping Lord*, 110.

[93] On Hitler as painter, see p. 73 below.

[94] Jones, *The Kensington Mass*, in *The Roman Quarry*, 92; 'Art and Sacrament', *Epoch and Artist*, 169.

[95] Jones, 'The Preface to *The Anathemata*', *Epoch and Artist*, 120.

[96] See René Hague's estimation, in his preface to *Dai Greatcoat*, 13, of the number of words from which he culled his selection of Jones's correspondence for that volume.

CHAPTER ONE

David Jones, Letter to Neville Chamberlain, 18 December 1938

OLIVER BEVINGTON

INTRODUCTION

'Lo ye all Englishmen'

— *Le Morte d'Arthur* and David Jones's Response to the Appeasement of Adolf Hitler in 1938

On 18 December 1938, David Jones wrote a letter to Neville Chamberlain in which he told the then Prime Minister of Great Britain that he wished to express his gratitude 'for all you have done and are continuing to do to mend things in Europe and to save us from the worst'.[1] Jones's letter was written in support of Chamberlain's policy of appeasement in the face of German territorial expansion into Czechoslovakia prior to the start of the Second World War and, more specifically, in response to Chamberlain's apparent success at the Munich Conference of September 1938, an achievement that had temporarily forestalled all-out war between Britain and Nazi Germany. Although 'appeasement' has since become what Larry William Fuchser has called 'a metaphor for weakness and the cowardly abdication of power in the face of the malevolent',[2] Dan Stone has more recently established that a significant section of the British population during the late 1930s supported Chamberlain's policy. Moreover, such support did not necessarily come from those who unambiguously advocated fascist ideologies, but, in fact, often derived from people who held a wide range of political perspectives: 'Whether they made their decisions for fear of the Soviet Union, in defence of the empire and British trade, or out of a desire for peace and a blind trust in Hitler's similar desire, there is a parabola of appeasement here ranging from naive pacifist to pro-Nazi, with many gradations in between.'[3] Jones's own stance towards this provocative issue falls somewhere on this 'parabola of

[1] All references to Jones's letter to Chamberlain in this chapter are to the facing-page facsimile reproduction of its pages and the transcription of them in this edition below.
[2] See Larry William Fuchser, *Neville Chamberlain and Appeasement* (New York: Norton, 1982), 2.
[3] Dan Stone, *Responses to Nazism in Britain, 1933–1939* (London: Palgrave Macmillan, 2003), 9.

appeasement', and his letter to Chamberlain of 1938 represents a key articulation of his views on this subject.[4]

Jones's letter includes a set of important allusions to Sir Thomas Malory's fifteenth-century work *Le Morte d'Arthur*.[5] Through these allusions Jones creates an intertextual link between the letter and his first significant literary text *In Parenthesis*, a work that also features numerous allusions to *Le Morte d'Arthur* and which Jones also sent to Chamberlain as a gift on 18 December 1938.[6] Such allusions in *In Parenthesis* – which is a quasi-autobiographical account of Jones's experiences of the First World War – have provoked significant debate among critics of Jones's writing. Paul Fussell accuses Jones of naively attempting to situate the mechanized warfare of the First World War into a tradition of honourable and heroic conflict, claiming that the intent of 'the poem, for all its horrors, is to rationalize and even to validate the war by implying that it somehow recovers many of the motifs and values of medieval chivalric romance'.[7] Others, such as Paul Robichaud, disagree, claiming that *In Parenthesis* 'uses the Middle Ages to gain an ironic purchase on the experience of modern warfare'.[8] Extending such critical concerns to Jones's use of Malorian allusions in his letter, we might also view them as attempts to 'rationalize and even to validate' the policy of appeasement by situating it within a subjectively defined tradition that may indicate, to some critics, a quasi-reactionary perspective. Others might wonder if the attempt to gain 'ironic purchase' on Chamberlain's appeasement of Hitler through Malorian allusions is nuanced enough to adequately reveal Jones's views on the matter.

Nearly all the existing critical engagements with Jones's use of allusions in *In Parenthesis* appear to assume that the book is, primarily, a retrospective appraisal of the First World War. Jones himself supports this opinion in his introduction to the work when he writes that within the book he 'attempted to appreciate some things, which, at the time of suffering, the flesh was too weak to appraise'.[9] By considering the text in this way, and by noting that its earliest compositional phases fell between 1928 and 1932, we might easily situate *In Parenthesis* within the 'war-books boom' of the late 1920s and early 1930s.[10] However, although chronologically the dates of its initial composition suggest such an affiliation, the fact that Jones revised sections of the book before its publication in 1937

[4] The Chamberlain letter has not previously been reproduced in full or considered at length, although it has been mentioned by other critics. For example, Thomas Dilworth mentions Jones's letter to Chamberlain in 'David Jones and Fascism', in John Matthias (ed.), *David Jones: Man and Poet* (Orono, ME: National Poetry Foundation, University of Maine, 1989), 146. Neil Corcoran also refers to it in his essay 'Spilled Bitterness: *In Parenthesis* in History', in *David Jones: Man and Poet*, 215, n. 4. Neither critic reproduces the letter in full, although Dilworth quotes from it, and neither of them discusses the link between its two Malorian allusions and *In Parenthesis*.

[5] Thomas Malory, *Le Morte d'Arthur*, ed. Ernest Rhys (London: Dent, 1933). I cite from this edition of Malory's text because Jones owned a copy of it; he may have consulted it during the late stages of *In Parenthesis*'s preparation. It is now held in Jones's archive at the National Library of Wales, Aberystwyth, as item 393 in the catalogue of his personal library. See Huw Ceiriog Jones, *The Library of David Jones (1895–1974): A Catalogue* (Aberystwyth: National Library of Wales, 1995), 189. Jones's underlining in this copy often corresponds with passages of the *Morte* that figure in *In Parenthesis*.

[6] David Jones, *In Parenthesis* (London: Faber & Faber, 1937).

[7] Paul Fussell, *The Great War and Modern Memory* (Oxford: Oxford University Press, 1975), 147.

[8] Paul Robichaud, *Making the Past Present: David Jones, the Middle Ages, and Modernism* (Washington, DC: Catholic University of America Press, 2007), 2.

[9] Jones, *In Parenthesis*, x.

[10] Andrew Frayn, *Writing Disenchantment: British First World War Prose, 1914–30* (Manchester: Manchester University Press, 2014), 201.

problematizes such a grouping and suggests that it may be equally as valid to consider *In Parenthesis* in relation to a later context. Neil Corcoran has suggested that, partly due to such revisions, *In Parenthesis* can be seen to be a text that

> offers itself or insinuates itself as an element of intervention, even of propaganda, in the political life of Britain in the thirties. It becomes thereby a contemporary poem, a poem of the moment of its own publication – 1937 – rather than a poem definable by the period (1915–16) which it describes.[11]

This perspective is particularly apposite when considering Jones's partial dedication of *In Parenthesis* to 'the enemy front-fighters who shared our pains against whom we found ourselves by misadventure'.[12] The manuscript drafts of *In Parenthesis* suggest that this sentiment was added to the original dedication at some point in 1937,[13] a revision that becomes politically significant when it is considered in relation to Jones's desire to 'pal up to Germany proper and let the other buggers do what they choose' in the wake of Hitler's remilitarization of the Rhineland in March 1936.[14] Moreover, Jones's gift of *In Parenthesis* to Chamberlain as a response to the Munich Conference further confirms Corcoran's opinion, as expressed above, regarding *In Parenthesis*'s level of intervention in the political life of the 1930s.

Taking these issues into account, I propose first to situate the letter to Chamberlain within the critical debate surrounding Jones's allusions to chivalric and romantic materials in *In Parenthesis*; second, I shall examine the intertextual relationship between *In Parenthesis* and the letter, as facilitated through their shared use of Malorian allusions, exploring how this relationship may offer us both a new interpretation of one strand of allusions within Jones's first major work, and a more comprehensive understanding of Jones's responses to both appeasement and National Socialism during the late 1930s. Ultimately, I propose that Jones's support for Chamberlain's policy of appeasement was partly influenced by his strong sense of soldierly solidarity with the German 'enemy front-fighters' against whom he found himself by 'misadventure'.[15] However, by 1938 Jones's view had calcified into an inflexible and entrenched anti-war stance towards Hitler's Germany. Consequently, he refused to adequately acknowledge any of the troubling elements of that country's altered political landscape.

Critical debate

The critical debate surrounding Jones's use of allusions to chivalric and romantic literature[16] in *In Parenthesis* falls into two camps: those who criticize Jones for glorifying the First World War by situating it within a tradition of noble combat, and those who perceive a level of irony in his use of such allusions. John H. Johnston, whose work Jones

---

[11] Corcoran, in Matthias, *David Jones: Man and Poet*, 213–14.

[12] Jones, *In Parenthesis*, xvi.

[13] For the final manuscript version of the dedication, see David Jones, folder LP 2/1 of the David Jones Papers at the National Library of Wales, Aberystwyth. The revised text of the dedication, which includes the reference to 'the enemy front-fighters', appears as a handwritten annotation to a typescript version of the original dedication that was produced in 1937 and that can be found in folder LP 3/2 of the same collection.

[14] David Jones, letter to René Hague, Easter 1936, in folder CD 1/15 of the David Jones Papers at the National Library of Wales, Aberystwyth.

[15] Jones, *In Parenthesis*, xvi.

[16] With the phrase 'romantic literature' I refer to the type of medieval prose and verse romances that continued to be popular into the early modern period. Malory's *Le Morte d'Arthur* is a well-known example of such a work.

himself considered to be 'the only decent analysis of I. P. that's ever appeared',[17] discerns an essential difference between Jones's poem, which was published nineteen years after the armistice, and the work of those poets, such as Wilfred Owen and Siegfried Sassoon, who wrote during the war.[18] Johnston believes that Jones's use of allusions to heroic texts – such as *Le Morte d'Arthur* – allows his poem to transcend the purely personal, and narrowly emotive, focus of the earlier lyric First World War poetry of Owen and Sassoon. Moreover, he goes on to point out that within *In Parenthesis*, whenever we discern an analogy 'between the heroic past and the heroic present, we are impressed by the fundamental unity of human experience',[19] and yet when such allusions seem incompatible 'we are conscious of ironic discrepancies which emphasize the unprecedented violence and suffering imposed by the conditions of modern technological warfare'.[20] Johnston's point of view proposes several problems, not least of which is the idea of a 'fundamental unity of human experience'. Can we really view the horrors of mechanized trench warfare as being comparable to the chivalric conflict depicted in Malory's work? Furthermore, if such is Jones's intent, would this not represent a rationalization of the horrors of the First World War, rather than a criticism of them?

Other critics have not been so sympathetic with regard to their stance on Jones's use of such allusions. For example, many of the questions that are provoked by Johnston's reading have been asked in Fussell's *The Great War and Modern Memory*. Fussell describes Jones as a 'turgid allusionist',[21] and goes on to suggest that his evocation of images of martial glory from both literary and historical sources within the book attempts to assimilate the warfare of the First World War into a tradition of noble conflict, a view that is not, ostensibly at least, disparate from Johnston's.[22] But Fussell believes that 'by placing the suffering of ordinary modern soldiers in such contexts as these, Jones produces a document which is curiously ambiguous and indecisive'. Ultimately, Fussell sees propaganda where Johnston sees irony:

> The poem is a deeply conservative work which uses the past not, as it often pretends to do, to shame the present, but really to ennoble it. The effect of the poem, for all its horrors, is to rationalize and even to validate the war by implying that it somehow recovers many of the motifs and values of medieval chivalric romance.[23]

Fussell concludes that Jones's book is an 'honourable miscarriage' that ultimately fails to ground the soldierly experience of the First World War with previous historical examples of conflict.[24] Even to attempt to do so, for Fussell, is to romanticize twentieth-century warfare and to fail to discern a fundamental change in the nature of human conflict. In this way, Fussell sees Jones as condoning the struggle in which he participated.[25]

---

[17] David Jones, letter to Harman Grisewood, 22 May 1962, in David Jones, *Dai Greatcoat: A Self-portrait of David Jones in his Letters*, ed. René Hague (London: Faber & Faber, 1980), 188.

[18] John H. Johnston, *English Poetry of the First World War: A Study in the Evolution of Lyric and Narrative Form* (Princeton, NJ: Princeton University Press, 1964).

[19] Johnston, *English Poetry of the First World War*, 304.

[20] Johnston, *English Poetry of the First World War*, 304.

[21] Fussell, *The Great War and Modern Memory*, 144.

[22] Fussell, *The Great War and Modern Memory*, 144.

[23] Fussell, *The Great War and Modern Memory*, 146–7.

[24] Fussell, *The Great War and Modern Memory*, 147.

[25] Fussell, *The Great War and Modern Memory*, 144.

This view has been denied stringently by Vincent Sherry, who claims that Fussell's reading of Jones's work 'compulsively associates heroic literature and false glorification'.[26] '[L]ooking closely at the heroic allusions,' Sherry surmises, 'we can see Jones making a recondite and precise judgment on the unheroic nature of technological war, and conveying this judgment in controlled, imaginative artistry.'[27] Moreover, Sherry again points to Jones's ironic use of heroic allusion, and provides an example in the form of an allusion to the ancient war god Mars's original function:

> Mars the war god originated as a fertility god, Jones knew from reading James Frazer and Jessie Weston. The primitive saw connections between fertility and war, between natural and martial vigour; spring was the fighting season. But how does the modern author respond to this ancient heroic concept? Mars's original role as a life-giving god, seen against the technological weapons which effect massive destruction, becomes profoundly ironic. Witness the first shell-burst of *In Parenthesis*, where Jones contrasts the motifs of fertilizing energy and destructive effect with great irony.[28]

Within his description of this 'first shell-burst', Jones refers to it as a 'Pernitric begetting'.[29] Sherry points out that 'Pernitric' is 'the chemical term for compounds containing nitrogen, and nitrogen's two uses – in fertilizer and explosives, in "begetting" and "unmaking" – match the double role of Mars'.[30] Therefore, the term oscillates between the duality of both the chemical agent and the pagan deity, creating – in Sherry's view at least – a type of sardonic, and yet poignant, commentary on both the interrelatedness of war and culture and the willingness of man to exploit the natural world for his own brutal ends.

In a similar vein, Jonathan Miles has claimed that 'Fussell misunderstands Jones's attempt to comprehend an experience which both shared similarities with what had gone before and yet was quite unlike anything that had gone before because of the more insidious nature of the technical role and the resultant magnitude of the suffering.'[31] He goes on to say that 'Fussell does not appear to understand that the heroic allusions in *In Parenthesis* are not celebratory of the war but work in a complex manner; indeed they sometimes celebrate aspects of experience but more often than not they function as ironic critiques.'[32] Here Miles seems to echo Johnston's reference to 'ironic discrepancies'. He suggests that Jones's allusions are partially, and deliberately, inappropriate and that through that inappropriateness they convey a sense of the uniqueness of the current conflict.

At the heart of this debate seems to be the idea that Jones's allusions to *In Parenthesis* contain two distinct, and at times opposed, points of view: one that sees the First World War as an entirely unique, and exceptionally horrific, phenomenon, and another that seeks to situate its terrors in relation to earlier forms of conflict. For Johnston, Sherry, Miles, and Robichaud, the way in which these perspectives are embodied and interact within a given allusion demonstrates Jones's sincere attempt to reconcile the strangeness of his experience with what he could only conceive of as its uncanny familiarity.

---

[26] Vincent B. Sherry, 'David Jones's *In Parenthesis*: New Measure', *Twentieth-Century Literature* 28, no. 4 (Winter 1982): 375.
[27] Sherry, 'David Jones's *In Parenthesis*', 376.
[28] Sherry, 'David Jones's *In Parenthesis*', 376.
[29] Jones, *In Parenthesis*, 24.
[30] Sherry, 'David Jones's *In Parenthesis*', 377.
[31] Jonathan Miles, *Backgrounds to David Jones: A Study in Sources and Drafts* (Cardiff: University of Wales Press, 1980), 82.
[32] Miles, *Backgrounds to David Jones*, 82–3.

However, for Fussell this same duality seems to imply a sort of moral relativism and creates a 'curiously ambiguous and indecisive text'.[33] The charges of moral ambiguity that Fussell levels at Jones regarding the use of this technique as a response to the First World War become ever more difficult to contend with when such allusions are considered in relation to, or used as a response to, the highly charged political climate of the late 1930s.

In his 2007 article, 'War Trauma and Religious Cityscape in David Jones's *In Parenthesis*', Charles Andrews offers us an alternative way of understanding Jones's use of heroic allusions.[34] Refuting Fussell, Andrews offers a fresh explanation of Jones's choice of the 'literary' over the 'literal'. He maintains that '[i]n Jones's representations of military life, the allusions and mythic parallels become a means of coping with trauma'.[35] Andrews sees Jones's use of heroic allusions as a means of dealing with his own trauma by facing the traumatic event through the refracting lens of literary allusion. Ultimately, he concludes that '[t]he overall form of *In Parenthesis* displays an excess that functions as the traumatic kernel rupturing the narrative from inside'.[36] Here, then, the potential moral ambiguity implied by Jones's allusions is symptomatic of his own personal confusion regarding his participation in the First World War. They reveal a mind traumatized by a unspeakable event attempting to come to terms with it through literary images that are at once evocative of and disassociated from that event.

Luke Thurston has also argued that Fussell misreads Jones's use of heroic allusion in *In Parenthesis*,[37] suggesting that Jones's allusive technique is 'bound up with an apprehension of how the event of the war – both for Jones as an individual and for the culture at large – had marked a decisive shift in the very meaning of history, corresponding in effect to the breakdown of its essentially modern European, post-Enlightenment conception as progressive, teleological narrative'.[38] Thurston proposes that the war was traumatic on both a personal level for those who participated in it and on a cultural level for European society as a whole. He believes that Jones's allusions to Malory in the poem are especially apt because both Malory and Jones shared the fate of writing 'at a point of cultural breakdown where experience as such becomes an enigma: both a monstrous, illegible aberration and a source of unparalleled poetic creation'.[39] The setting of Malory's *Le Morte d'Arthur* – the disintegration of the chivalric world of Arthur's Round Table – is a literary depiction of a similar cultural circumstance.

Through his allusions to Malory's work, Jones draws upon these other instances of 'cultural breakdown' in order to display his own sense of moral uncertainty regarding the First World War. This becomes apparent in Colin Wilcockson's 1995 essay 'Presentation and Self-Presentation in *In Parenthesis*', which analyses the various forms of authorial 'self-presentation' in Jones's book. The opening pages of the essay discuss Jones's 'authorial association with particular characters in the narrative'– such as Privates John

---

[33] Fussell, *The Great War and Modern Memory*, 146.

[34] Charles Andrews, 'War Trauma and Religious Cityscapes in David Jones's *In Parenthesis*', *Journal of the Midwest Modern Language Association* 40, no. 1 (Spring 2007): 87–96.

[35] Andrews, 'War Trauma and Religious Cityscapes', 88.

[36] Andrews, 'War Trauma and Religious Cityscapes', 94.

[37] Luke Thurston, 'David Jones' Disaster: *In Parenthesis*', *Almanac: Yearbook of Welsh Writing in English: Critical Essays* 16 (2012): 151–72.

[38] Thurston, 'David Jones' Disaster: *In Parenthesis*', 158.

[39] Thurston, 'David Jones' Disaster: *In Parenthesis*', 163.

Ball and Walter Map – through his use of first- and third-person pronouns.[40] Subsequently, Wilcockson moves on to analyse how the allusions to Malory in the text allow 'Jones to present himself via the subtext of Malorian association', a topic that takes up the rest of his essay and which is of particular relevance to our current discussion.[41] Wilcockson writes:

> Within *Le Morte d'Arthur*, the character who pre-eminently represents moral confusion is Lancelot. Not only the reader, but also the characters within the fiction, cannot decide whether he is a hero or villain. Even Arthur himself, wronged by Lancelot's affair with his queen, is confused and prefers to turn a blind eye. When the king is compelled to sanction Lancelot's exposure, it is only because the degenerate Agravaine and Mordred force him to do so, against the wishes of the other knights. Finally, Mordred kills Arthur, his uncle-father, before Lancelot can return from exile to save the king.[42]

Wilcockson believes that Jones especially empathizes with the figure of Lancelot, claiming that 'even when the Malorian references are not specifically to Lancelot, they are almost always to characters whose lives are closely involved with his'.[43] This close association between Jones and Lancelot will be of central importance to this chapter as one of the Malorian quotations that Jones incorporates in his letter to Neville Chamberlain also concerns Lancelot.

In summary, we can begin to see that Jones's use of Malorian allusions – specifically those pertaining to the ambiguous figure of Lancelot – reveal Jones's attempt to understand his own participation in the First World War, which has been conceived of as both a personal trauma (Andrews) and a point at which traditional European cultural and intellectual norms and received forms of artistic communication become inadequate (Thurston). Here, then, the potential moral ambiguity and indecision that Fussell finds at the heart of Jones's heroic allusions are symptomatic of the poet's own personal confusion regarding his involvement in the First World War. Jones's ambivalent perception of the First World War is also indicative of his stance towards the political events of the late 1930s.

Jones's romantic response to the First World War

In Jones's use of Malorian allusions as a response to the First World War we can discern a convergence of his lived experience and an interest in romantic literature that goes back to the pre-war period. Robichaud has suggested that 'Jones's interest in the medieval past and legends of King Arthur goes back to his late Victorian childhood,'[44] a childhood that Thomas Dilworth believes imbued in Jones 'idealistic, patriotic, imperialist values'.[45] Dilworth has offered a comprehensive discussion of Jones's formative reading habits, and, in reference to the *Books for the Bairns* series of monthly literary volumes to which his parents subscribed during his childhood, Dilworth says, 'David wanted read to him

[40] Colin Wilcockson, 'Presentation and Self-Presentation in *In Parenthesis*', in Howard Erskine-Hill and Richard A. McCabe (eds), *Presenting Poetry: Composition, Publication, Reception* (Cambridge: Cambridge University Press, 1995), 237.

[41] Wilcockson, 'Presentation and Self-Presentation in *In Parenthesis*', 240.

[42] Wilcockson, 'Presentation and Self-Presentation in *In Parenthesis*', 244–6.

[43] Wilcockson, 'Presentation and Self-Presentation in *In Parenthesis*', 246.

[44] Robichaud, *Making the Past Present*, 17.

[45] Thomas Dilworth, *David Jones in the Great War* (London: Enitharmon, 2012), 19.

"always Arthurian things", and his favourite in the series was *King Arthur and the Knights of the Round Table* (1899), an adaptation of stories from *The Mabinogion* and Sir Thomas Malory.'[46] For Dilworth, this early interest in romantic literature was one of several strands of reading that allowed Jones to delve deeply 'into the national romance of imperial Britain'.[47] Ultimately, Dilworth goes on to explain that '[b]efore enlisting in the army [Jones's] sensibility was historical and literary and his imagination thoroughly romantic'.[48] The implication here is that Jones's conception of the First World War, and his own participation in it, may have been partially informed and shaped by his 'thoroughly romantic' imagination, as imparted by his early engagement with 'the national romance of imperial Britain' through the romantic texts described above.

Several documents seem to support this idea, and two in particular – which are reproduced in Dilworth's *David Jones in the Great War* – reveal just how thoroughly romantic Jones's early view of the First World War was. The first of these is an essay entitled 'A French Vision', which Jones wrote while on leave in 1916.[49] It is the earliest surviving specimen of Jones's writing, and Dilworth tells us that it is 'the only contemporary written record of his thoughts and feelings about his early combat experience'.[50] In this essay, Jones rhetorically questions the validity of the war and its value. The line 'IS IT WORTH IT?' is repeated throughout, but Jones also seems to condemn any thought of 'giving up' as 'un-British', and, in so doing, he effectively undermines his own questioning attitude towards the war. He notes the dissenting voices of 'a young lieutenant' and a 'Varsity man', but he finally contradicts their opposition by making a sustained allusion to the Battle of Agincourt. The narrator slips into a sort of reverie and has the eponymous 'vision' of a medieval battlefield that is steeped in Jones's romantic notions regarding chivalric conflict:

> If one had lived in the old days, war was so different then! And one mentally pictures a sunlit valley, massed squadrons of emblazoned chivalry with lances couched; and behind, bowmen armed 'cap-a-pie' with short sword and buckler. Suddenly the bowmen, with a fierce and mighty cry, charge madly to the valley, and the arrows fly thick and fast! The imagination carries one away, it is so fine. How grand to have lived then, to have heard the stirring fanfare of the heralds' trumpets, to have seen the pennons dancing in the sunlight![51]

In the next section, the vision changes:

> And now the vision passes. Night falls, and another, and far different scene presents itself. The same valley lit by the pale moon; the groans of the wounded and dying break the silence. 'Was it worthwhile for these men', five centuries, maybe, ago. By their fierce conflict, and their outpoured blood, they freed the land from the tyrant's yoke! Worthwhile? Perchance Europe in thralldom still would be, but for that battle on that sunlit day.[52]

---

46 Dilworth, *David Jones in the Great War*, 19.
47 Dilworth, *David Jones in the Great War*, 19–22.
48 Dilworth, *David Jones in the Great War*, 26.
49 For 'A French Vision', see Dilworth, *David Jones in the Great War*, 127–9.
50 Dilworth, *David Jones in the Great War*, 126.
51 'A French Vision', in Dilworth, *David Jones in the Great War*, 127–9.
52 'A French Vision', in Dilworth, *David Jones in the Great War*, 128–9.

Here, the darker side of the conflict is revealed. However, it is the ideological and propagandist implications of this allusion, rather than 'the groans of the wounded and dying', which are most troubling. Though we might view the Hundred Years War as a dynastic conflict fought between the medieval houses of Plantagenet and Valois, the Battle of Agincourt is often seen as a defining moment and a foundational myth of English nationhood, a belief that seems to be implied by Jones when he refers to the battle as having freed Europe from both the 'tyrant's yoke' and 'thralldom'. Moreover, Jones draws a direct comparison between this ideologically loaded image of the Battle of Agincourt and the First World War itself:

> And but for the holding of that trench – but for the blood spilt – the ruined homes – the stricken hearts of thousands – but that one stood in the muddy trench in cold and misery – but that the young lieutenant, 'so bored', had left the vision in the drawing-room to cry her eyes out, perhaps – but that the 'Varsity man had left his books – Europe to-day might lie prostrate 'neath the iron heel of the Teuton terror.[53]

In this way, Jones utilizes a highly propagandist medieval battle – one that Jones describes in both effusive and romantic terms – in order to justify his own participation in the First World War by suggesting that the two conflicts are morally analogous and honourable. The result for both a modern reader and, as we shall see, the mature Jones, is both naive and, ultimately, propagandist.

The second document that reveals Jones's engagement with 'the national romance of imperial Britain' through romantic medieval imagery is a three-page string-bound pamphlet entitled *The Quest*.[54] This pamphlet is comprised of both a cover illustration and what Dilworth refers to as 'a short pseudo-medieval allegory in the style of William Morris's late prose romances'.[55] It was completed in 1917 while Jones was in the trenches, and in the same year he sent it home to his parents so that his father could have it printed as a New Year's card.[56] The story begins as a Knight, a Lady, a Minstrel and a Man of Letters set out to discover the 'Castle called Heart's Desire'. On discovering the castle, the group find that it is a utopian society in which '[h]e who was lord, and kept the place, was a mighty lord withal; yet held he neither slave, serf, nor unwilling vassal'. Finding themselves unable to enter, each is entreated by the castle's Lord to return home to work honestly at his or her respective discipline. Only in this way might they gain access to the 'Castle called Heart's Desire'. Dilworth insists that the allegory 'reflects irritation at the inequalities of military rank and the class system, and reveals an affinity with Morris-like Socialism'.[57] This link between Jones and Morris has also been noted by Robichaud, who suggests that Jones's 'markedly Pre-Raphaelite enthusiasm for medieval authors, particularly Sir Thomas Malory, 'was an important catalyst in the development of his unique Modernist style'.[58] Little of this style is evident in *The Quest*, and indeed it was many years after the war that Jones was finally able to develop it in the form of *In Parenthesis*. For this reason, this allegorical piece of writing should not be seen as a genuinely mature example of Jones's *oeuvre*. Robichaud writes that within *The Quest*

---

[53] 'A French Vision', in Dilworth, *David Jones in the Great War*, 128–9.

[54] For a reproduction of *The Quest*, see Dilworth, *David Jones in the Great War*, 180–3.

[55] *The Quest*, in Dilworth, *David Jones in the Great War*, 179.

[56] For a reproduction of this illustration, see Dilworth, *David Jones in the Great War*, 180.

[57] Dilworth, *David Jones in the Great War*, 183.

[58] Robichaud, *Making the Past Present*, 5.

'[m]edieval chivalry is held up as an ideal to be emulated by the modern soldier, an ideal promulgated by the popular literature of the late Victorian period'.[59] Moreover, the invocation for the Knight to 'strike not but to make men free' implies, for Dilworth, 'an altruistic belief in the Allied cause'.[60] Such a reading of the text is certainly similar to the seemingly propagandist use of chivalric imagery in 'A French Vision'. The illustration that is on the cover of Jones's pamphlet, depicting the four questing characters within the story, is also highly reminiscent of a certain type of allegorical and propagandist drawing that Jones made while in the trenches. Such illustrations as 'Is there Peace?' (New Year's 1917), 'Germany and Peace' (20 January 1917), and 'Captive Civilization and the Black Knight of Prussia' (13 July 1918) were published in *The Graphic* magazine while Jones was still in the trenches and depict Germany and Britain as two knights battling for the hand of the maidens 'Peace' and 'Civilization'.[61] Such work would seem to align with what Jonathan Miles and Derek Shiel have described as Jones's intention at that time to 'dedicate his precocious drawing talents to historical illustration'.[62] *The Quest* would seem to be a literary extension of this intent.

These works clearly demonstrate Jones's early use of chivalric imagery as a response to the First World War. They imply a simplistic comprehension of the moral causes of that conflict on Jones's part. However, there is evidence that shows that this conception of the First World War was not one that Jones held after its cessation. In his essay on Hitler of 1939, Jones declares:

> Those of us who fought in the last war are by this time very conscious that our heads were filled with a good deal of nonsense as to the nature and need of that struggle. That war may have been politically 'unavoidable' – that makes the exploitation of our youthful innocence even more a matter for anger.[63]

Here Jones evokes the sort of propaganda that was disseminated by Britain – and, as we have seen, also by himself – during the First World War, supporting the notion that the fight against Germany was both necessary and morally unambiguous. However, from these lines, written on the eve of the Second World War, we can also perceive Jones's sense of disillusionment with the sort of naive and romantic stance he himself had previously taken at the start of the First World War.

Miles has pointed out that Jones's negative stance on his own idealization of the war also features in an excluded section of 'Part 1' of *In Parenthesis*. This deletion details the enlistment of the 'slacker' Bobby Saunders and 'chronicles the nurturing of the blindly patriotic mood which swept through England at the outset of the Great War'.[64] In this section, which Miles claims 'reveals the kind of pressures that patriotism exerted on the youth of England in 1914',[65] we are told that the mind of Bobby Saunders – a former Peace Scout and boy soldier – was 'moulded and informed' by a visit to his school by Commander Shackleton, who 'spoke with emotion of the Bull-dog breed, of the Union Flag in very hot, and very cold places, / of how the sea was free',[66] and by heroic images of 'Kitchener',

[59] Robichaud, *Making the Past Present*, 2.
[60] Dilworth, *David Jones in the Great War*, 183.
[61] For reproductions of these pictures, see Dilworth, *David Jones in the Great War*, 144–5 and 189.
[62] Jonathan Miles and Derek Shiel, *David Jones: The Maker Unmade* (Bridgend: Seren, 1995), 214.
[63] See Tom Villis's edition of this essay, p. 59 below.
[64] Miles, *Backgrounds to David Jones*, 89–91.
[65] Miles, *Backgrounds to David Jones*, 89.
[66] Miles, *Backgrounds to David Jones*, 89–90.

'Florence Nightingale' and 'Nelson, who existed uncreated and who stood / as he were Zeus, behind the Gods'.[67] Fed on an ideological diet that explicitly preached British moral superiority, Saunders comes to the paradoxical conclusion that the 'war to end war seemed the very thing for a / Peace Scout'. Though the referenced influences here are not primarily romantic or chivalric in origin, we can see that the negative attitude displayed by Jones within this omitted section towards 'the exploitation of . . . youthful innocence' is as applicable to Jones's own wartime experience and romantic conception of the war as it is to the fictional character of Saunders. Moreover, of this omitted section Miles writes that:

> its inclusion might have clarified aspects of the relation of Jones's use of literary scraps from a heroic past to the deployment of heroic sentiments by the jingoists, for it catalogues the pressures of imperial propaganda that were active prior to and in the early years of the war.[68]

For Miles, and in keeping with his view regarding the function of heroic allusions in *In Parenthesis*, this suggests that with the inclusion of the Bobby Saunders section Jones would have more clearly indicated that his 'use of literary scraps from a heroic past'[69] was essentially ironic, and yet Jones's deliberate omission of the section complicates such a reading. Nevertheless, the Bobby Saunders section clearly demonstrates a critical attitude towards the ideological justifications of the First World War that, Jones believed, had been impressed upon its participants.

Corcoran offers another textual example of Jones recanting his previously naive and romantic conception of the war when he refers to a section from Jones's poem 'from *The Book of Balaam's Ass*', which was published in *The Sleeping Lord and Other Fragments* sequence of 1974 but composed between 1934 and 1937. This section refers to the telling of old war stories. It reads:

> Tilly-vally Mr Pistol that's a petty tale of y'r Gallia wars. Gauffer it well and troupe it fine, pad it out to impressive proportions, grace it from the ancients. Gee! I do like a bloody lie turned gallantly romantical, fantastical, glossed by the old gang from the foundations of the world. Press every allusion into Ambrosian racket, ransack the sacred canon and have by heart the sweet Tudor magician, gather your sanctions and weave your allegories, roseate your lenses, serve up the bitter dregs in silver-gilt, bless it before and behind and swamp it with baptismal and continual dew.
>
> No, Lavinia, won't wash, and that you know well enough. To adopt the initial formula, 'Ladies and gentlemen, I will remove the hat.' You will observe the golden lily-flowers powdered to drape a million and a half disembowelled yeanlings.
>
> There's a sight for you that is in our genuine European tradition.
>
> Lime-wash over the tar brush?
>
> No, but rather, cistern the waters of Camelot to lave your lousy linen. The salient is Broceliande, these twain indeed are one.[70]

Corcoran takes Jones's reference to 'Gallia wars' to mean the First and Second World Wars and Jones's description of 'a bloody lie turned gallantly romantical' and the 'golden

---

[67] Miles, *Backgrounds to David Jones*, 90.
[68] Miles, *Backgrounds to David Jones*, 93.
[69] Miles, *Backgrounds to David Jones*, 93.
[70] David Jones, 'from *The Book of Balaam's Ass*', in *The Sleeping Lord and Other Fragments* (London: Faber & Faber, 1974), 99–100.

lily-flowers powdered to drape a million and a half disembowelled yeanlings' to constitute criticism of those conflicts. Moreover, the Arthurian allusion that reads 'cistern the waters of Camelot to lave your lousy linen' seems to condemn the use of romantic imagery as a response to the First World War as a form of propagandist sanitization. Ultimately, such indicators lead Corcoran to conclude that, due to the period in which it was composed being contemporaneous with Jones's final edits to *In Parenthesis*, this section represents 'a savagely hostile criticism of the procedures of *In Parenthesis* composed by the author himself prior to the work's completion'.[71] Corcoran detects within this passage a criticism of the type of glorification of the First World War that may be directed at *In Parenthesis*. If the omitted Bobby Saunders section of *In Parenthesis* represents a self-critical appraisal of Jones's own romantic image of the First World War, as evidenced by the juvenilia that he produced during that conflict, then this section of 'from *The Book of Balaam's Ass*', for Corcoran, represents a critical reappraisal of Jones's response to the war that is to be found within *In Parenthesis* itself. This reading suggests that, even before its publication, Jones believed that his attempt to describe his wartime experiences accurately had been compromised in some essential way. We can gain some insight into this attitude from a letter to Jim and Helen Ede of 11 April 1939 in which Jones describes the subject of *The Book of Balaam's Ass*: 'I think it is really about how if you start saying in a kind of way how bloody everything is you end up in a kind of *praise* – *inevitably* – I mean a sort of Balaam business.'[72] This might also be read as a description of Jones's own feelings toward *In Parenthesis* at this point in time. Balaam – who against his own desires and inclinations becomes the reluctant mouthpiece of God – is a suitable analogue for Jones because both are forced to acknowledge the self-defeating nature of their own intentions. Balaam may not speak his mind, and Jones may not describe the horrific events and actions he witnessed during the First World War without also resorting to the complex framework of literary and cultural associations that shaped how he originally experienced them.

Thus *In Parenthesis* seems caught between two opposed conceptual impulses: a naive form of oversimplified propaganda, as demonstrated by two pieces of juvenilia, and a self-critical appraisal of the cultural origins of that same naive response, as suggested by the omitted section of *In Parenthesis* and *The Book of Balaam's Ass* section. The fact that the omitted Bobby Saunders section's self-critical appraisal makes no significant reference to either romantic or chivalric imagery reveals Jones's commitment to the continued validity of such material as a response to the First World War during the early compositional stages of *In Parenthesis*. And yet, the seemingly bitter and sarcastic tone of the allusion to 'the waters of Camelot' in *The Book of Balaam's Ass* section would appear to represent Jones unambiguously critiquing the use – perhaps his own use – of such material to describe twentieth-century conflict. We might choose to view the allusions to Malory in *In Parenthesis* as a missing link between Jones's youthful and naive use of romantic allusion and the eventual critique of such a technique to be found in *The Book of Balaam's Ass*. Although Jones's use of such romantic material continued through the 1930s and beyond, his conception of that material, and the poetic uses to which he believed it could be put, became ever more complex. Hence the survival of his belief in its usefulness for the task of formulating an artistic response to both the First World War and, eventually, the increasingly aggressive actions of Hitler's Germany in 1938.

[71] Corcoran, 'Spilled Bitterness', 210.

[72] David Jones, letter to Jim and Helen Ede, 11 April 1939, in Jones, *Dai Greatcoat*, 90–2.

Allusions to Le Morte d'Arthur *in* In Parenthesis

There are numerous allusions to *Le Morte d'Arthur* in Jones's first book, but two types are of particular importance to note here. The first set refer to Lancelot, and the second to fratricidal conflict brought about through inadvertent or malicious actions – what Jones might refer to as 'misadventure'.

Lancelot

In 'Part 3' of *In Parenthesis*, Jones describes a night-time march of his unit to a forward position on the front line:

> Past the little gate,
> into the field of upturned defences,
> into the burial yard –
> the grinning and the gnashing and the sore dreading – nor
> saw he any light in that place.[73]

In his note for this section, Jones claims that it was inspired by 'book vi, ch. 15' of Malory's text.[74] In the preceding chapter, Lancelot has been led to an 'old manor' by a hunting hound he encounters in a forest. From this manor, a weeping lady comes and tells Lancelot of her dead husband 'Sir Gilbert the Bastard' who, she tells him, has been slain by another knight who had himself been wounded in the fight. The lady enigmatically claims that, although she is not aware of the name of her husband's antagonist, 'he that did the deed is sore wounded, and he is never likely to recover, that shall I ensure him'. Lancelot then departs and in the forest encounters another 'damosel' who tells him that it was her brother, Sir Meliot de Lorges, 'a fellow of the Table Round', who fought and killed Sir Gilbert, and that Sir Gilbert's wife, who is revealed to be a sorceress, has laid a curse upon her brother so that his wounds will never heal until his body is 'searched' with a sword and bloody cloth that may only be found in the 'Chapel Perilous'.[75]

Accordingly, Lancelot rides to the Chapel Perilous and ties his horse to a 'little gate', a phrase that is repeated in Jones's allusion and which signals its commencement. He enters the graveyard and sees 'on the front of the chapel many fair rich shields turned up so down', several of which he recognizes. Then he is confronted by 'thirty great knights'.[76] In his allusion to chapter fifteen, Jones uses the words 'grinning' and 'gnashing', which in the original text are used to refer to the manner in which the thirty knights react to Lancelot's approach. At this sight, Lancelot himself is said to have 'dread him sore', a line that Jones evokes through his own 'sore dreading'. Finally, after the knights scatter before Lancelot's approach, he enters the chapel itself in which he sees 'no light, but a dim light burning', a description that Jones partially echoes in the concluding lines of his version: 'nor / saw he any light in that place'.[77] Of his use of allusions, Jones has said:

> One of my rules is that when one uses some quotation or even a name that evokes some past author or event or some past literary association one must have an

[73] Jones, *In Parenthesis*, 31.
[74] Jones, *In Parenthesis*, 194.
[75] Malory, *Le Morte d'Arthur*, 173.
[76] Malory, *Le Morte d'Arthur*, 174.
[77] Malory, *Le Morte d'Arthur*, 174–5.

> experiential, concrete, contactual matter in the narrative that corresponds in some way or other with the quoted situation or name.[78]

In this instance, the shared words in the original text and Jones's allusion suggest such an 'experiential' correspondence between the two works. Lancelot must pass through a gate under cover of darkness, and he is then confronted by a seemingly insurmountable group of foes, who have, if we infer from the upside-down shields on the chapel wall, already vanquished many of his fellow knights. His fear is related to the anxiety of being about to engage in combat with an all too present enemy, but it is also the terror of the unknown. Such sentiments would seem to be a broadly adequate analogue for the inner feelings of a First World War soldier moving towards the front line at night, passing abandoned defences and the discarded arms of their lost comrades, and all the while being painfully aware of the enemy's increasing nearness. This way of forming an 'experiential' correspondence between Malory's text and Jones's own lived experience of the First World War offers us a rather simple interpretation of Jones's use of such allusions, which in this particular instance does not seem to allow for the sort of ironic commentary on the continuity of experience between modern warfare and the heroic past that some of Jones's critics have discerned within his use of heroic allusions.

If we consider both the origin of Lancelot's mission to the Chapel Perilous and its conclusion, then we may perceive that this allusion contains more sinister implications. Inside the chapel, Lancelot discovers the body of Sir Gilbert the Bastard, whose sorceress wife he had encountered in the previous chapter. He takes a piece of the bloody cloth covering the knight's body and a 'fair sword' that appears before him. Lancelot departs from the chapel and is once again confronted by the thirty knights who now insist that he leave the sword behind. Lancelot refuses, and passes through them unharmed once again. Beyond the chapel yard, he encounters a 'fair damosel' who warns him that if he does not leave the sword behind, he will die, and she then threatens that he will never see 'Queen Guinevere' again if he refuses.[79] Undeterred, Lancelot declines to leave the sword, so instead the 'damosel' asks him to kiss her. Lancelot again refuses, and the 'damosel' reveals herself to be both 'Hellawes the sorceress'[80] and, it is strongly implied, the wife of Sir Gilbert, whom Lancelot had previously encountered. She explains that the whole adventure to the Chapel Perilous had been nothing more than a subterfuge orchestrated by herself. The thirty knights were just a seemingly phantasmagoric ploy to mask the real danger of his situation. She tells him that if he had left the sword, or had he kissed her, then he would have died. Disgusted by the sorceress's trick, Lancelot returns to Sir Meliot and his sister in order to heal the wounded knight with the sword and bloody cloth.

The first point to note about this extended context for Jones's allusion is the role of the sword. Normally a symbol of conflict, in this quest the sword is both a weapon and a restorative agent with the capacity to heal the injured Sir Meliot. Moreover, to leave it behind in the chapel would mean Lancelot's death, and in this way, in an allegorical sense, the taking up of arms becomes an ambiguous act. Perhaps more important than this image within the quest is that all of the conflict has been brought about by duplicitous means. The thirty knights in the graveyard, Lancelot's most visible foes for the majority of the

[78] David Jones as quoted in Colin Hughes, 'David Jones: The Man Who Was on the Field: *In Parenthesis* as Straight Reporting', in Matthias, *David Jones: Man and Poet*, 179.

[79] Jones in Hughes, 'David Jones: The Man Who Was on the Field', 174.

[80] Jones in Hughes, 'David Jones: The Man Who Was on the Field', 175.

tale, are shown to be nothing more than a ruse. When deployed in reference to the First World War, such imagery suggests a critical stance towards that conflict that seems consonant with Miles's reading of the omitted Bobby Saunders section of *In Parenthesis*.

The fourth part of *In Parenthesis* opens with another allusion to Lancelot: 'So thus he sorrowed till it was day and heard the foules sing, then somewhat he was comforted,'[81] which Jones states is an allusion to 'book xiii, ch. 19' of *Le Morte d'Arthur*.[82] This chapter forms part of the story of Lancelot's quest for the Holy Grail, and it describes how Lancelot discovered his unworthiness to obtain it. In the previous chapter, while asleep outside a chapel to which he has been unable to gain entrance, Lancelot hears the approach of a wounded knight. Unable to wake, but still aware of everything that transpires around him, Lancelot witnesses the healing of this other knight by the Holy Grail, which comes forth from the chapel. Upon being healed, the formerly wounded knight wonders about the slumbering Lancelot. His squire conjectures that Lancelot's inability to wake is due to the fact 'that he dwelleth in some deadly sin whereof he was never confessed' and is therefore unworthy of the Grail.[83] Subsequently, in the chapter to which Jones's allusion refers, Lancelot, knowing that the sin that prevents his acquisition of the Grail is his adulterous love for Queen Guinevere, spends the night lamenting the fact that he is unable to complete his quest: 'So thus he sorrowed till it was day and heard the foules sing, then somewhat he was comforted.'[84] 'Part 4' describes a typical day on the front, and so it is probable that Jones used this line at the start of this part of the book because of the reference to Lancelot waking to the sound of a cockerel, which would indicate dawn.[85] However, when considered within its Malorian context, the fact that Jones chose to describe the waking of his comrades in the same manner to that of Lancelot implies that the sleep from which they have just awoken has been filled with impotent restlessness and deeply troubled moral self-recriminations. Jones's allusion to Lancelot's own existential epiphany suggests that they have also begun to question the ethical validity of their participation in the war. As with Lancelot, the cock's crow is comforting for the soldiers because it signals an escape from the unresolvable moral qualms, doubts, and fears that have troubled their sleep.

Later in 'Part 4', in a section in which Private John Ball looks out at Mametz Wood – the place where the climactic battle of the book will take place in 'Part 7' – Jones declares, 'Or come in gathering nuts and may; / or run want-wit in a shirt for the queen's unreason'.[86] In his note to this allusion, Jones states that it refers to 'the madness of Launcelot because of Guenever's stupidity when he lay the second time with Elaine unwittingly, and by enchantment'.[87] Jones also cites the lines, 'He lept out at a bay window and there with thorns he was all scratched of his visage and body; and so he ran forth he wist not whither, and was wild wood as ever was man; and so he ran two years, and man might have grace

---

[81] Jones, *In Parenthesis*, 59.

[82] Malory, *Le Morte d'Arthur*, 189–90.

[83] Malory, *Le Morte d'Arthur*, 188.

[84] Malory, *Le Morte d'Arthur*, 189.

[85] There is also an allusion here to Peter's denial of Christ at cockcrow. See Mt. 26.74–5.

[86] Jones, *In Parenthesis*, 66.

[87] Jones, *In Parenthesis*, 203. In *In Parenthesis*, Jones usually spells the names of Malory's characters as they appear in the edition by Ernest Rhys of *Le Morte d'Arthur* that he owned, as is the case with 'Launcelot' and 'Guenever'. Throughout this chapter, I have retained Jones's original spelling of these names within the quotations that I have drawn from his writings. Otherwise I employ modern spellings of such names, e.g. 'Lancelot' and 'Guinevere'. In his letter to Chamberlain, Jones transcribes the title of Malory's book as 'the Morte D'Arthur'. I retain Jones's version of this title when citing him but otherwise give it as *Le Morte d'Arthur*.

to know him.'[88] Lancelot's hysterical departure from Camelot is provoked by Guinevere's discovery that he has slept with the lady Elaine, the future mother of his son Sir Galahad, for a second time. However, in Malory's book, Lancelot's two encounters with Elaine are brought about against his will – the first time by enchantment, and the second by deceit – a narrative device that is similar to the one deployed in the Chapel Perilous quest discussed above. In all three allusions to Lancelot discussed so far we can see Jones focusing on the knight's vulnerabilities and weaknesses. In the first, he is blind to the manipulations of Hellawes and is only saved by his innocence and love for Guinevere. In the second, he is revealed to be both spiritually unworthy and impotent in the presence of the Grail. And here, in this third allusion to Lancelot, he is once again easily manipulated and, in the face of disaster, is shown to be a hysteric. Such depictions reveal him as falling very short of the paragon of manly, chivalric virtue we might expect him to uphold. In this way, Jones alludes to the vulnerabilities of himself and his comrades, and focuses not upon their martial valour or bravery but on the sort of psychological pressures that must be exerted upon soldiers while in combat. In addition, the theme of the wild man of the wood configures the wood as a place of madness, a negative liminal space outside of normative society. Just a few lines before his reference to 'the queen's unreason' Jones writes, 'To the woods of all the world is this potency – to move the bowels of us. / To groves always men come both to their joys and their undoing.'[89] In a sense, Lancelot's mad rush into the woods prefigures the chaos that will ensue within 'Part 7' of *In Parenthesis* when the soldiers attack the enemy in Mametz Wood, the place where many of them will find 'their undoing'. Therefore, the allusion may also be read as suggesting that such conflict, like Lancelot's madness, may be the result of manipulation and deceit.

Misadventure

A second set of Malorian allusions refer to fratricidal conflict brought about through inadvertent or malicious actions.

In the section of *In Parenthesis* known as 'Dai's Boast' (79–84), the eponymous Dai cites his ancestral pedigree and situates himself in a tradition of foot soldiers who have participated in innumerable conflicts since time immemorial. In his footnote to this section, Jones twice makes explicit reference to Malory's work. Subsection F of footnote 37 refers to these lines, which Jones cites as originating in 'Malory, book xxi, ch. 4':

> I the adder in the little bush
> whose hibernation-end
> undid,
> unmade victorious toil:[90]

These lines refer to the climactic battle of Malory's book between the forces of Arthur and Mordred. As the two antagonists parley with one another before both armies, an adder comes and bites one of the attendant knights. In response, the knight draws his sword to kill the adder. Viewing the drawing of the sword as an act of betrayal, both sides attack, and the battle that will end in the death of Mordred and the mortal wounding of Arthur commences.

[88] Jones, *In Parenthesis*, 203. Jones mistakenly cites 'book xi, ch. 3' of the *Morte* as the source of these words when in fact they are found in book xi, ch. 8. See *Le Morte d'Arthur*, 134–5.
[89] Jones, *In Parenthesis*, 66.
[90] Jones, *In Parenthesis*, 80.

The allusion suggests that the conflict and, therefore, the breakdown of Arthur's idealized societal order are brought about by an inadvertent action and seemingly against the wishes of the constituent parties. The second reference to Malory within Dai's boast reads:

> O Brân confound the counsel of the councillors, O blessed
> head, hold striplings from the narrow sea.
> In the baized chamber confuse his tongue:
> that Agravaine.
> He urges with repulsive lips, he counsels: he nets us into expeditionary war.
> O blessed head hold the striplings from the narrow sea.[91]

Jones explains the connection of this section of the poem to Malory in a note that maintains that the section alludes to '[t]he part played by Agravaine toward the climax of the *Morte d'Arthur*'.[92] Here Jones references Sir Agravaine's attempts to reveal the illicit affair between Lancelot and Guinevere, which will lead to fratricidal war and, ultimately, the breakdown of Arthurian society. Where the former reference to the adder suggests calamity brought about by misfortune, this allusion refers to calamity brought about by manipulation and subterfuge. Corcoran has offered an allegorical reading of this section of *In Parenthesis* that responds to both the political climate immediately prior to the start of the Second World War and to Jones's own anti-war stance in that same period. In Corcoran's view, 'the baized chamber is the House of Commons; Agravaine is the representative of those who urged a stronger line against Hitler (Churchill himself?); the expeditionary war is the envisaged war in Europe'.[93] In this way, Jones's plea to the tutelary head of 'Brân' to 'hold striplings from the narrow sea' refers to the young men who may be asked to sacrifice their lives should war commence. Moreover, it recalls the 'million and a half disembowelled yeanlings' who died in the First World War that Jones references in 'from *The Book of Balaam's Ass*'.[94] Once again, Jones focuses on both the innocence and the vulnerability of those who, like Lancelot, are brought into conflict against one another by 'misadventure' and manipulation.

This idea occurs again in 'Part 6':

> He said that
> there was a hell of a stink at Division – so he had heard from
> the Liaison Officer's groom – as to the ruling of this battle –
> and the G.S.O.2 who used to be with the 180th that long bloke
> and a man of great worship was in an awful pee – this groom's
> brother Charlie what was a proper crawler and had some posh
> job back there reckoned he heard this torf he forgot his name
> came out of ther Gen'ral's and say as how it was going to be a
> first clarst bollocks and murthering of Christen men and reckoned
> how he'd throw in his mit an' be no party to this so-
> called frontal-attack never for no threat or entreaty, for
> now, he says, blubbin' they reckon, is this fellowship
> wholly mischiefed.[95]

---

[91] Jones, *In Parenthesis*, 83.
[92] Jones, *In Parenthesis*, 209.
[93] Corcoran, 'Spilled Bitterness', 216.
[94] Jones, 'from *The Book of Balaam's Ass*', *The Sleeping Lord*, 100.
[95] Jones, *In Parenthesis*, 138.

In his citation to this passage, Jones remarks that 'Various passages of Malory have influence here. Particularly book xx, ch. 1.' As with the second Malorian allusion to be found in Dai's boast of 'Part 4', this allusion refers to the attempt by Mordred and Agravaine to convince Gawain, Gaheris, and Gareth to tell Arthur of Lancelot's betrayal. Gawain, Gaheris, and Gareth refuse to tell Arthur the truth, but they do not prevent Mordred and Agravaine from doing so despite the fact that Gawain is only too aware of the civil war that will ensue from this action. In the quoted section, Jones compares this moment in Malory's book to the dissent among Jones's superior officers regarding a planned 'frontal-attack'. The line 'is this fellowship wholly mischiefed' is adapted from Malory's statement, 'Alas, said Sir Gawaine and Sir Gareth, now is this realm wholly mischiefed, and the noble fellowship of the Round Table shall be disparply [dispersed]: so they departed.'[96] Here we are once again made to understand that it is the hidden, malicious motivations of Mordred and Agravaine and not Lancelot's adulterous passion for the queen that leads to the destruction of the brotherhood of the Round Table. Moreover, the allusion seems to question both the motivation and unity of opinion between those, such as the commanders at 'Division', who are directing the army's actions – actions configured as an ill-conceived, mysterious affair carried out in the face of apocalyptic cultural breakdown.

'Part 6' also opens with a section of writing that is a pastiche of three quotations that are taken from *Le Morte d'Arthur*. It reads:

> And bade him be ready and stuff him and garnish him . . . and laid a mighty siege about . . . and threw many great engines . . . and shot great guns . . . and great purveyance was made on both parties.[97]

The first quotation is taken from 'book i, ch. 1'. This chapter describes how King Uther Pendragon prepares to wage war on the Duke of Tintagil so that he may seduce the Duke's wife, Igraine. In full, the quotation reads, 'Then the king was wonderly wroth. And then the king sent him plain word again, *and bade him be ready and stuff him and garnish him*, for within forty days he would fetch him out of the biggest castle that he hath'.[98] In the quoted section, Uther warns the Duke to prepare himself for a siege, as he intends to attack within 'forty days'. The second quotation is taken from 'book xxi, ch. 1', though Jones inaccurately cites it as being from chapter 2 in which Sir Mordred has usurped Arthur's throne and seeks to marry Queen Guinevere in order to secure his position. Hence, he lays siege to the Tower of London, which is where Guinevere is hiding. The section from which Jones takes his lines reads:

> Then when Sir Mordred wist and understood how he was beguiled, he was passing wroth out of measure. And a short tale for to make, he went *and laid a mighty siege about* the Tower of London, and made many great assaults thereat, *and threw many great engines* unto them, *and shot great guns*.[99]

The final quotation comes from 'book xx, ch. 12'. In full, it reads:

---

[96] *Le Morte d'Arthur*, book xx, ch. 1, 339–40.
[97] Jones, *In Parenthesis*, 135.
[98] *Le Morte d'Arthur*, book i, ch. 1, 5–6. Italics added to indicate text omitted by Jones.
[99] *Le Morte d'Arthur*, book xxi, ch. 1, 379–81. Italics indicate text used by Jones.

> And so they departed either from other; and then either party made them ready on the morn to do battle, *and great purveyance was made on both parties*; and Sir Gawain let purvey many knights for to wait upon Sir Launcelot, for to overset him and slay him.[100]

This section refers to the siege of Lancelot's castle, Jouyous Gard, by the forces of King Arthur and Sir Gawain. Eventually this siege comes to an end in a pitched battle when Lancelot's forces sally forth. For Jones, the medieval slow war of attrition, with its deprivations and enforced inaction, must have seemed an adequate 'experiential' correspondence to the trench warfare in which he himself participated. However, the moral elements of these allusions are also worthy of note. Observe how the motivations of the besieging forces (Uther and Mordred) in the first two allusions are morally reprehensible, and the siege in the final allusion, which pits Arthur against Lancelot, is caused not by Lancelot's infidelity but by the manipulations of Mordred and Agravaine. If we follow the thread of the allusions, we see that the warfare they allude to is seen as morally reprehensible and, in the last case, fratricidal.

In summary, Jones's use of romantic imagery within *In Parenthesis* is significantly more complicated than has been discerned in the two pieces of juvenilia that he produced during the First World War. Jones's Malorian allusions often speak of morally ambiguous conflict and of men being forced to fight against one another through either manipulation or 'misadventure', a view that also informs the scathing indictment of imperial propaganda to be seen in the omitted Bobby Saunders section discussed above. In this way, such allusions suggest regret, disillusionment, and, when viewed in relation to the political climate of the late 1930s, an entrenched desire to avoid either active or passive participation in such acts again. Ultimately, this desire can be seen to have preconditioned Jones's positive response to Nazi Germany regarding Hitler's territorial ambitions in relation to Czechoslovakia in 1938. However, whether these allusions can be said to function ironically, or are, conversely, part of an attempt to situate the First World War in a tradition of honourable conflict, is difficult to say. Jones's desire for a direct 'experiential' correspondence between his lived experience and the work to which he alludes incorporates both the physical similarities of the described experience – as with the analogue between contemporary trench and medieval siege warfare – and the ethical implications that such experiences provoke, as with the allusion to Lancelot's moral epiphany over his inability to obtain the Grail. Considered in this way, we can see that it is often the ethical insinuations of such allusions that seem to be of central importance to Jones, and such implications rarely seem to reveal an ironic stance. Nevertheless, we can see that by drawing his allusions to Lancelot from chapters and specific quests in which the character's vulnerability and moral weaknesses are most openly displayed, Jones seems to deny the sort of heroic imagery we might normally associate with him. In this way, Jones would appear to pre-emptively challenge, at least in regard to his allusions to Lancelot, Fussell's belief that Jones attempts to glorify the First World War.

Lancelot is, in fact, shown to have a fair range of complex psychological emotions, in some of which Jones must have perceived a direct 'experiential' correspondence with his own experience. If Wilcockson is right that in *In Parenthesis* Jones especially empathizes with the figure of Lancelot, we can see that through Lancelot's terror, confusion, moral self-recriminations, and hysteria we are able to gain an insight into the sort of personal tensions that beset Jones and his comrades during the war. Perhaps this is not a perfect comparison,

[100] *Le Morte d'Arthur*, book xx, ch. 12, 359. Italics indicate text used by Jones.

and so, even despite the credibility of such a response for Jones, it is understandable that for some critics such a literary technique occludes, and therefore fails to truthfully represent, an experience that would be more authentic for them if it were communicated in a more literal manner. However, Robert Graves, who was also a member of the Welch Fusiliers during the First World War, once wrote that 'the memoirs of a man who went through some of the worst experiences of trench warfare are not truthful if they do not contain a high proportion of falsities'.[101] Graves's opinion speaks to both the lack of desire on the part of the individual to recall or recount certain traumatic experiences and the inability of language to fully convey them. In this way, Graves's point is in keeping with Andrews' belief that '[i]n Jones's representations of military life, the allusions and mythic parallels become a means of coping with trauma' and that although trauma may lie beyond language, its expression is, nevertheless, dependent upon it. In this way, we can see that Jones's use of Malorian allusions is a means by which he communicated the uncommunicable through the imperfect medium upon which that communication depended. In addition, we might also question whether this is the reason behind the condemnation of the use of romantic imagery as a response to the First World War to be found in 'from *The Book of Balaam's Ass*'.

Nevertheless, what we can see is that at least two strands of Malorian allusions within *In Parenthesis* suggest a highly critical stance towards the causes that lay behind the First World War. Furthermore, Jones draws attention to such allusions in *In Parenthesis* by his accompanying letter when he sends Chamberlain a copy of *In Parenthesis* in 1938. Jones's sending of *In Parenthesis* to Chamberlain may be interpreted as a form of affirmational anti-war propaganda. However, we will see that in his letter to Chamberlain, the generalized anti-war stance that can be discerned through the allusions to *Le Morte d'Arthur* within *In Parenthesis* becomes compromised by Jones's feelings towards Nazi Germany during the late 1930s.

Jones's response to Chamberlain's policy of appeasement

In 1938, *In Parenthesis* was awarded the prestigious Hawthornden Prize. In the same year, Hitler was insisting that the President of the Czechoslovakia, Edvard Beneš, give the German minority within the country autonomy within the Sudetenland. Throughout the year, tensions between the two countries escalated, and German troop levels on their shared border grew. With Hitler having annexed Austria earlier in the year, Chamberlain feared that if a similar fate befell Czechoslovakia the member states of the League of Nations would be obliged to intervene, an action that could lead to all-out war in Europe. Accordingly, throughout September 1938 Chamberlain conducted several personal meetings with Hitler in an attempt to resolve the situation peacefully. The first of these meetings took place in Berchtesgaden in Germany on 15 September. Frank McDonough has described what took place at that first meeting:

> Chamberlain was informed in no uncertain terms by the Nazi leader that he intended to 'stop the suffering' of the Sudeten Germans by force. After this prolonged harangue, Chamberlain asked Hitler what was required for a peaceful solution. Hitler demanded the transfer of all districts in Czechoslovakia with a fifty percent or more German speaking population.[102]

---

[101] Robert Graves, *But It Still Goes On* (New York: Jonathan Cape and H. Smith, 1931), 33.

[102] Frank McDonough, *Neville Chamberlain, Appeasement, and the British Road to War* (Manchester: Manchester University Press, 1998), 63–4.

In response, Chamberlain said that 'he had nothing against the idea in principle', but that he would have to overcome several practical issues if such demands were to be accepted by the other member states of the League of Nations. Subsequently, on his return to England, Chamberlain held talks with the French Prime Minister, Édouard Daladier, which resulted in an Anglo-French agreement to 'placate German demands', an agreement that the Czech government was forced to accept for fear of having to face the military might of Germany without the aid of Britain or France.[103] During his second trip to Germany, on 22 September, Chamberlain told the German leader of his success, but Hitler then went on to make a set of further demands:

> He wanted the immediate occupation of Sudeten areas and non-German-speakers who wished to leave would be allowed to take only a single suitcase of belongings with them. He also added certain areas with less than fifty percent German speakers and raised Polish and Hungarian grievances in other areas of Czechoslovakia.[104]

Though shocked by these requests, Chamberlain returned home, and over the next few days he attempted to convince the British cabinet to agree to meet Hitler's demands. In response to this situation, on 24 September Jones wrote to Grisewood to say, '*what* a business – have we come to it at last – all these years something of this sort has haunted me . . . only I always vaguely hoped it might be averted'. He went on to say:

> Yes, I heard Chamberlain's grand little speech on his first return. I did like it more than I can say. He is simply the real goods, there is no doubt about that – the only bright spot – But Lord, what a weight the poor man has to carry, and hardly any bugger to give him proper support. (The *Times* have been all right, I think. Thought leading article for yesterday, 23rd, masterly and unanswerable.) You already know what I think about the Left – League [of Nations] and Co. – the 'idealisms' that have terrified one with their unrealities for years – and Chamberlain, I felt, from the beginning of his taking office, saw real issues and has struggled valiantly to do something – but I fear now, too late, perhaps – I feel I don't know for certain about that – but I do know that on 'our' side the follies and dangerous untrue ideas have been contributing to a disaster. The infernal thing is that once there is a show-down no ideas matter much and one can't see any light at all as to what might happen. If one could, one might not feel so wretched. Lord, how different all this is from 1914 – but I suppose I personally must take into account that now I'm a buggered-up neurotic and then I was an innocent uninformed boy . . . *bugger bugger bugger* I do wish everything was nicer. We are an unfortunate generation.[105]

In these last few lines, we can discern how Jones himself perceived his own conception of the seemingly imminent Second World War to be markedly 'different' from his youthful response to the early stages of the First World War in 1914. In 1914, Jones had conceived of the war through the refracting lens of his 'thoroughly romantic' imagination, an imagination that produced highly idealized pieces of both writing and illustration that sought to anachronistically reaffirm chivalric notions regarding the virtue of honourable and pious conflict in order to demonstrate the morality of the Allied cause. Moreover, we have also seen how Jones used his Malorian allusions in *In Parenthesis* to partially recant

[103] McDonough, *Neville Chamberlain, Appeasement, and the British Road to War*, 64.
[104] McDonough, *Neville Chamberlain, Appeasement, and the British Road to War*, 65.
[105] David Jones, letter to Harman Grisewood, 24 September 1938, in Jones, *Dai Greatcoat*, 87–8.

this former naive outlook. But in the above letter, he also seems to condemn the socialist 'Left' and the 'League [of Nations] and Co.' as holding similarly reductive and dangerous 'idealisms', a term that in this context not only evokes both the revolutionary utopianism of Russian communism and the League of Nations' emphasis on collective security and disarmament in the wake of the punitive Treaty of Versailles, but also, with regret, the naive imperial patriotism of Jones's youth. Such 'idealisms' were terrifying for Jones in regard to the issue of Hitler's acquisition of the Sudetenland. If the League of Nations, of which the Soviet Union was then a member state, chose to intervene in this matter, then it could provoke another world war.

It is important to note that Jones cites as a possible cause for such a conflict not German aggression but instead the unwillingness of the League of Nations to accede to Hitler's demands for territorial expansion. In the wake of the First World War, Jones believed that the economic sanctions placed upon the defeated Germany by the Treaty of Versailles had been too severe. The seemingly idealistic goals of the League of Nations were hypocritical, in his view, because they had been inaugurated and promoted at the expense of German economic stability. Jones was always conscious of the way in which Germany had been overly vilified by English propaganda during the First World War, and so during the 1930s he simply refused to believe that Hitler's intentions were fundamentally malign.[106] Marina MacKay has observed that this was far from a unique perspective during the interwar period, pointing out that during the 1930s

> the overblown demonising of the Kaiser's Germany in the First World War made it impossible for public figures to describe the Nazi agenda, in years when its enormities might have beggared the imagination of the First World War's infamously gothic propagandists, without being discredited as a warmonger of the Great War stripe.[107]

In contrast, in September 1938, Chamberlain's conciliatory attitude towards Germany was not without support. *The Times* describes the adulation that met him at the airport when he returned from his first meeting with Hitler on 15 September: 'People thronged the roads leading to the air park and filled all the available space on the roof of the booking offices. As Mr. Chamberlain descended smiling from the aeroplane he bowed and raised his hat in acknowledgement of the cheers.'[108] Moreover, the article in *The Times* on 23 September that Jones in the same letter refers to as 'masterly and unanswerable' is most probably the one entitled 'Mr. Chamberlain's Mission'.[109] The writer of this article sums up the intention behind Chamberlain's diplomatic meetings with Hitler in one sentence: 'the Prime Minister has set himself to get the work of a peace conference done before the next war not after it'. The writer praises Chamberlain's actions and condemns his detractors: 'Grandiose charges of cowardice, defeatism and betrayal, abusive and mischievous generalities about "democracies on the run," will serve no longer.' In particular, the writer critiques Winston Churchill: 'Mr. Churchill preaches the preventative war, while the Prime Minister practices preventative diplomacy.'

In the early hours of 30 September, six days after Jones wrote to Grisewood, Chamberlain's attempts at 'preventative diplomacy' appeared to have borne fruit. After a

---

[106] See the edition by Tom Villis, pp. 53–99 below in this volume, of Jones's 1939 essay on Hitler.
[107] Marina MacKay, *Modernism and World War II* (Cambridge: Cambridge University Press, 2007), 11.
[108] 'The Return to London: Mr. Chamberlain at No. 10', *The Times*, 17 September 1938, 10.
[109] 'Mr. Chamberlain's Mission', *The Times*, 23 September 1938, 13.

last-minute conference in Munich, a diplomatic agreement was reached that forced Czechoslovakia to accede to Hitler's demands. This agreement effectively handed Hitler a bloodless victory, and Chamberlain was its chief architect. Moreover, during the conference, Chamberlain had met with Hitler in private and had persuaded him to sign a document that stated that Britain and Germany would not go to war with one another. With this piece of paper in hand, Chamberlain arrived back in Britain and famously declared that he had achieved 'peace for our time'. In response, he was greeted by many as a hero. McDonough describes the sort of mass adulation that Chamberlain received in the wake of his perceived victory:

> For his energetic efforts to secure the Munich Agreement Chamberlain received over 20,000 letters and telegrams of praise, and numerous gifts from people at home and abroad. 'No conqueror returning from victory of the battlefield,' wrote *The Times* on 2 October, 'had come adorned with greater laurels'. A popular record was produced at the time entitled 'God Bless You, Mr. Chamberlain', which contained the line: 'We're all mighty proud of you'. Quite clearly, there was overwhelming relief that war had been averted.[110]

In the wake of this mass outpouring of relief and adulation, Jones sent his letter to Chamberlain. Not all those who supported Chamberlain's diplomatic policies or celebrated his seeming success shared Jones's interest in the ideology of National Socialism, of course, an issue more directly addressed in Tom Villis's essay in this volume.[111] There were certainly those, including Winston Churchill, who considered the Munich Agreement a shameful acquiescence to Hitler's increasingly unreasonable demands. Nevertheless, we can see that Jones's positive response to the cause of appeasement during the late 1930s is not without precedent. Although unpalatable in hindsight, Jones's attitude may well have been shaped by the same reappraisal of his own youthful idealism discernible in the Malorian allusions in *In Parenthesis*.

Jones's letter to Chamberlain, dated 18 December 1938, opens with his indication that his gift of *In Parenthesis* should be seen as 'an expression of gratitude for all you have done and are continuing to do to mend things in Europe and to save us from the worst'. Jones immediately goes on to praise Chamberlain's recent success at the Munich Conference by saying that, 'What you have already managed to effect by your forbearance, imagination, and very great courage, gives reason to hope still for the future – in spite of the misunderstanding, prejudice and stupidity in this country and the unhelpful and difficult behaviour elsewhere.'[112] After briefly expressing his disbelief '[t]hat so many of our countrymen should be blind to what you've done for them and to the absolute sanity of your continued attempt', Jones makes the first of his Malorian allusions:

> [B]ut on the other hand there are those who will always remember, in remembering you, the words that Malory, in book xx. ch.1 of the Morte D'Arthur, makes Gawain say to those who would make mischief:

[110] McDonough, *Neville Chamberlain, Appeasement, and the British Road to War*, 72.

[111] See pp. 45–53.

[112] David Jones, letter to Neville Chamberlain, 18 December 1938, box 3, folder 1, Harman Grisewood Papers 1, Booth Family Center for Special Collections, Lauinger Library, Georgetown University Libraries, Georgetown University, Washington, DC. See page 1 of 3 of this letter in this volume, pp. 38–9 below.

The best of us all had been full cold at the heart root
had not Launcelot been better than we & that hath he proved
himself full oft.[113]

These lines describe Sir Agravaine and Sir Mordred's attempts to expose the illicit love of Lancelot for Guinevere, which, once revealed, will lead to civil war and the societal breakdown of the Arthurian realm. Two allusions to this chapter of *Le Morte* appear in *In Parenthesis*. The first concerns Brân's head in Dai's boast in 'Part 4'; the second occurs in 'Part 6', where it relates to the disintegration of the Round Table. In this chapter of *Le Morte* Sir Gawain reminds Agravaine and Mordred that civil war will surely break out if they reveal Lancelot's affair to the king. Here Gawain is reminding the traitorous pair that Lancelot has saved all their lives many times. Jones refers to Lancelot in a heroic light in order to compare Chamberlain to him. It is Chamberlain, in Jones's view, who has saved the lives of both his supporters and detractors through his appeasement of Hitler. Those, such as Churchill, who criticized Chamberlain for signing the Munich Agreement and advocated a firmer response to Germany, are cast in the role of the warmongering Agravaine and Mordred. In addition, we might suggest that Gawain's practical stance, which would conceal Lancelot's crime in order to preserve the integrity and stability of the brotherhood of the Round Table, would seem to be Jones's own view of the impending crisis of war during 1938.

We have observed how Jones's dedication of *In Parenthesis* '[t]o the enemy front-fighters' in the wake of Hitler's remilitarization of the Rhineland in 1936 suggests a partially propagandist intervention in the tumultuous political climate of the mid-1930s. This same sentiment of soldierly solidarity with Germany reoccurs in Jones's letter to Chamberlain almost directly after its first Malorian allusion, where Jones writes:

> When, during the [First World] War, we looked across to the other entrenchments, I know that at least for some of us, one thought was uppermost: we looked to the day when those opposite would be our friends again – indeed that & perhaps that friendship might be the greater & more intimate because of our mutual hardship. It was an instinctive aspiration & one natural to soldiers – but since those days our hopes have been less than unfulfilled – no-man's-land has remained with us – our soldierly fraternization has not borne to us the common unity we wished.[114]

We can once again sense Jones's feelings of regret and disillusionment regarding the First World War, and, in this context, it also reaffirms our notion of Jones's entrenched desire to avoid such conflict with Germany in the future. However, when deployed as a response to Chamberlain's appeasement of Hitler over Germany's territorial acquisition of large parts of Czechoslovakia, it reveals an inability, or unwillingness, to discern the difference between the causes of the First World War and the contemporary political situation. Earlier in the letter, Jones makes references to 'our common European unity', an idea that has both historical overtones and also links to the 'common unity' that Jones felt for the German soldiers against whom he had fought. In the face of the rise of the fascist states during the 1930s, such a conception seems highly idealistic and may strike the contemporary reader as naive.

---

[113] Jones, letter to Neville Chamberlain, 2 of 3. See pp. 40–1. Quoted from Malory, *Le Morte d'Arthur*, book xx, ch. 1, 340.

[114] Jones, letter to Neville Chamberlain, 2–3 of 3. See pp. 40–1 and 42–3 below.

After closing his letter to Chamberlain with the line 'I dearly hope that your leadership may yet engender among us all that same persistence that you have shown in seeking the way to peace by attempting to understand other nations, rather than by abusing them', Jones uses another Malorian allusion as a postscript:

> P.S. There is another passage in the Morte D'Arthur which your critics might do well to remember:
>
> > 'Lo ye all Englishmen, see ye not what a mischief here was . . . . by him they were all upholden, now might not those Englishmen hold them content with him . . . . Alas this is a great default in us Englishmen for there may no thing please us no term'.[115]

These lines are taken from the first chapter of the twenty-first book of *Le Morte*, which describes Mordred's attempts to marry Guinevere. References to this chapter also occur at the beginning of 'Part 6' of *In Parenthesis*, where Mordred's siege of the Tower in London is used to serve as an analogue for trench warfare perpetrated for selfish and dishonourable ends. The lines that Jones cites in his letter to Chamberlain come after Mordred's siege of the tower has failed. Subsequently, on hearing that King Arthur is returning to England to reclaim the throne, Mordred calls 'all the barony of this land' to him.[116] Despite Mordred's villainy, many of the barons pledge their allegiance to him. Malory explains their inexplicable loyalty to the pretender in this way:

> For then was the common voice among them that with Arthur was none other life but war and strife, and with Sir Mordred was great joy and bliss. Thus was Sir Arthur depraved and evil said of. And many there were that King Arthur had brought up of nought, and given them lands, might not then say him a good word.[117]

The lines that Jones quotes in his letter to Chamberlain come immediately after these. In full, the section reads:

> Lo ye all Englishmen, see ye not what a mischief here was*! for he that was the most kind and noblest knight of the world, and most loved the fellowship of noble knights, and* by him they were all upholden, now might not those Englishmen hold them content with him. *Lo, thus was the old custom and usages of this land; and men say that we of this land have not yet lost that custom.* Alas, this is a great default in us Englishmen for there may no thing please us no term.[118]

Anthony Goodman argues that these lines question 'the unstable temperament of the English' as revealed by extreme partisan violence perpetrated during the War of the Roses, a conflict that Malory himself most probably participated in.[119] For Jones, the quotation

---

[115] Jones, letter to Neville Chamberlain, pp. 42–3.

[116] Malory, *Le Morte d'Arthur*, book xxi, ch. 1, 379–81.

[117] Malory, *Le Morte d'Arthur*, book xxi, ch. 1, 380–1.

[118] Malory, *Le Morte d'Arthur*, book xxi, ch. 1, 381. Italics here mark Malory's words that Jones replaces with '. . .' in his quotation. Jones later quotes this passage from Malory in his essay 'The Myth of Arthur', written in 1940–1 and first published in 1942. See David Jones, 'The Myth of Arthur', in Douglas Woodruff (ed.), *For Hilaire Belloc: Essays in Honour of His 71st Birthday* (London: Sheed & Ward, 1942), 208–9, and David Jones, *Epoch and Artist*, ed. Harman Grisewood (London: Faber & Faber, 1959), 251.

[119] Anthony Goodman, *The War of the Roses: Military Activity and English Society, 1452–97* (London: Routledge, 2002), 213.

conveys a sense of exasperation and disgust at those who opposed Chamberlain's policy of appeasement.

Jones's allusions in his letter are subtly different from those we find in *In Parenthesis*. Although the allusions to Malory's work in *In Parenthesis* might suggest an anti-war stance that is indebted to both Jones's sense of personal regret and his conception of the First World War having been brought about by the manipulation of 'youthful innocence', the allusions to Malory in his letter to Chamberlain imply a more explicit level of political engagement. In the context of the First World War, Jones's mining of Malory's images of fratricidal civil war affords a poignant retrospective appraisal of his own participation in such a conflict. However, the same images, when deployed in the letter to suggest that a war between Germany and Britain in 1938 would be fratricidal, reveal how little Jones understood the fundamental virulence of fascism. By focusing on Lancelot's heroic deeds in the first allusion, Jones takes a literary device that was utilized effectively in *In Parenthesis* to reveal a range of seemingly unheroic psychological states and deploys it to praise Chamberlain's achievements in a considerably less complex manner. The tone with which he refers to those who disagreed with Chamberlain's policy of appeasement as prejudiced, stupid, and blind demonstrates a self-congratulatory attitude that is further implied by Jones's allusions to the faults of Englishmen in the second Malorian allusion.

Conclusion

In summary, it is evident that the use of Malorian allusions in *In Parenthesis* often reveals Jones's personal sense of regret and disillusionment concerning his early idealization of the First World War. In particular, his depiction of the figure of Lancelot suggests an unheroic conception of that conflict and emphasizes the inner turmoil of those men who were forced to fight against one another through 'misadventure'. Considered in this way, such imagery does not seem to glorify the war or to view its connection to Malory's text as ironic, but implies a sincere attempt to capture elements of Jones's war experience that could only be articulated through this complex framework of literary and cultural associations. Overall, when read in their wider Malorian context, the allusions to *Le Morte d'Arthur* in Jones's first book suggest an anti-war stance that continually questions the root causes of warfare and seeks to uncover the duplicitous means by which it may be brought about. However, when such a stance is considered in relation to the political events that surround the text's date of publication (1937), it exposes an inflexible and entrenched opinion regarding Germany at that moment. This reluctance to concede that there was any difference between the Germany of 1914 and the fascist state the country had become by the late 1930s led Jones to believe that the anti-war stance to be discerned within the Malorian allusions of *In Parenthesis* was an equally apt response to the seemingly imminent Second World War as it had been for the First, as evidenced by the allusions to Malory and Jones's description of his feelings of comradeship for the German soldiers against whom he fought to be found in his letter to Chamberlain of 1938. In the context of the letter, the Malorian allusions become little more than the most overt kind of appeasement propaganda. The first allusion is used to glorify Chamberlain's actions and the second to condemn those who would disagree with him as traitors and to reveal Jones's own disinclination towards the British public and its opinions regarding Nazi Germany.

ANNOTATED TRANSCRIPTION

Provenance

David Jones, 'Correspondence: Jones to Chamberlain, Neville' (18 December 1938), 'Correspondence IV: Sent/Rec'd by David Jones', Harman Grisewood Papers 1, box 3, folder 1, in the Booth Family Center for Special Collections, Lauinger Library, Georgetown University Libraries, Georgetown University, Washington, DC. Component unique identifier: 42201. Finding aid available online: http://findingaids.library.georgetown.edu/repositories/15/archival_objects/1169824.

Copy

3, Glebe Place.
Chelsea S.W. 3
Flax 0829,
Dec 18th 38

The Right Hon Neville Chamberlain.

Dear Sir,

Would you accept this copy of my book, "In Parenthesis". I send it to you as a token of my respect, as an expression of gratitude for all you have done & are continuing to do to mend things in Europe & to save us from the worst. What you have already managed to effect by your forbearance, imagination, & very great courage, gives reason to hope still for the future – in spite of the misunderstanding, prejudice & stupidity in this country & the unhelpful & difficult behaviour elsewhere. I am sure you must have received many letters of this sort, but I did wish to contribute to those expressions of gratefulness, & I thought that to send you my book was one way of doing so – if you would accept it. That so many of our Countrymen should be blind to what you've done for them & to the absolute sanity of your continued attempt, makes me perplexed

[*Page 1 of 3*]

Copy[120]

3, Glebe Place,

Chelsea S.W. 3

Flat 0829,[121]

Dec 18th 38

The Right Hon Neville Chamberlain.[122]

Dear Sir,

Would you accept this copy of my book, 'In Parenthesis'.[123] I send it to you as a token of my respect, as an expression of gratitude for all you have done & are continuing to do to mend things in Europe & to save us from the worst. What you have already managed to effect by your forbearance, imagination, & very great courage, gives reason to hope still for the future – in spite of the misunderstanding, prejudice & stupidity in this country & the unhelpful & difficult behaviour elsewhere. I am sure you must have received many letters of this sort,[124] but I did wish to contribute to those expressions of gratefulness, & I thought that to send you my book was one way of doing so – if you would accept it. That so many of our countrymen should be blind to what you've done for them & to the absolute sanity of your continued attempt, makes me perplexed

---

[120] In his unpublished notes on his edition of Jones's correspondence, *A Self-portrait of David Jones in his Letters* (London: Faber & Faber, 1980) – which can be found in folder CD2/7 of the David Jones Papers, National Library of Wales, Aberystwyth – René Hague writes that Jones 'preserved a careful copy of his letter to Chamberlain'. The document reproduced here appears to be this 'careful copy'. It is held in box 3, folder 1, of part 1 of the Harman Grisewood Papers at the Booth Family Center for Special Collections, Lauinger Library, Georgetown University Library, Georgetown University, Washington, DC. Hague preserved a typed copy of the letter; this typescript is held in folder CD2/7 of the David Jones Papers, National Library of Wales, Aberystwyth.

[121] This flat belonged to Jones's friend the Catholic publisher Tom Burns (1906–95). Judging from the letters reproduced in *Dai Greatcoat*, Jones lived in Burns's flat for various periods between 7 July 1938 and 21 June 1941, on which latter date he appears to have been staying with his friends Arthur and Daphne Pollen at 57 Onslow Square. Burns himself was working at the British Embassy in Madrid as a press attaché for the majority of the war. For a detailed account of Burns's life during the Second World War, see Jimmy Burns, *Papa Spy: Love, Faith, and Betrayal in Wartime Spain* (London: Bloomsbury, 2009).

[122] Chamberlain (1869–1940) was a British Conservative politician who served as Prime Minister between May 1937 and May 1940. For a discussion of Chamberlain's life, see Robert Self, *Neville Chamberlain: A Biography* (Aldershot: Ashgate, 2006).

[123] *In Parenthesis* was first published, in London, by Faber & Faber in 1937. It won the prestigious Hawthornden Prize in 1938. For a transcript of Jones's acceptance speech, see 'The Hawthornden Prize: 1938', *The Tablet*, 2 July 1938, 18–19.

[124] Chamberlain did indeed receive many letters of congratulations and other gifts from the public after the Munich Conference. These letters and gifts are held among the Papers of Neville Chamberlain, Cadbury Research Library, University of Birmingham, Edgbaston, Birmingham, UK. For a brief account of these letters and gifts, see Frank McDonough, *Neville Chamberlain, Appeasement, and the British Road to War* (Manchester: Manchester University Press, 1998), 72.

& angered — but on the other hand, there are those who will always remember, in remembering you, the words that Malory, in Book XX. Ch. 1. of the Morte D'Arthur, makes Gawain say to those who would make mischief:

"The best of us all had been full cold at the heart root had not Launcelot been better than we & that hath he proved himself full oft"

I pray that in spite of them all you will see some realisation of your Christian & courteous Effort. I hope this for all our sakes — as also for the saving of ~~our European~~ our common European unity, whose custodian you are, in this country.

When, during the war, we looked across to the other entrenchments, I know that at least for some of us, one thought was uppermost: we looked to the day when those opposite would be our friends again — indeed that & perhaps that friendship might be the greater & more intimate because of our mutual hardship. It was an instinctive aspiration & one natural to soldiers — but since those days our hopes have been less than unfulfilled — no-man's-land has remained with us — our soldierly

[*Page 2 of 3*]

& angered – but on the other hand, there are those who will always remember, in remembering you, the words that Malory, in Book XX. Ch.1. of the Morte D'Arthur, makes Gawain say to those who would make mischief:[125]

> 'The best of us all had been full cold at the heart root
> had not Launcelot been better than we & that hath he proved
> himself full oft'

I pray that in spite of them all you will see some realisation of your Christian & courteous effort. I hope this for all our sakes – as also for the saving of ~~our European~~ our common European unity, whose custodian you are, in this country.

When, during the war, we looked across to the other entrenchments,[126] I know that at least for some of us, one thought was uppermost: we looked to the day when those opposite would be our friends again – indeed that & perhaps that friendship might be the greater & more intimate because of our mutual hardship. It was an instinctive aspiration & one natural to soldiers – but since those days our hopes have been less than unfulfilled – no-man's-land has remained with us – our soldierly

[125] This section of *Le Morte d'Arthur* describes the machinations of the knights Mordred and Agravaine, who are intent upon revealing Lancelot's illicit love affair with Guinevere to Arthur. Gawain speaks to forestall what he thinks will be the end of the brotherhood of the Knights of the Round Table upon the revelation of this crime to Arthur. See Thomas Malory, *Le Morte d'Arthur*, ed. Ernest Rhys (London: Dent, 1933), book xx, ch. 1, 340.

[126] Jones served as a private in the Royal Welch Fusiliers during the First World War. For a detailed account of Jones's wartime experiences, see Thomas Dilworth, *David Jones in the Great War* (London: Enitharmon, 2012).

fraternization has not borne to us the common unity we wished.

You, sir, have seen that the first necessity in Europe is such an understanding as we hoped for on the West Front. You have said so in clear words, & you have given bodily expression to your words, in difficult & worsening circumstances – for that alone you deserve our abiding gratitude.

I dearly hope that your leadership may yet engender among us all that same persistence that you have shown, ~~in the avoidance of the recrimination of,~~ ~~& the desire to understand the aspirations of other nations.~~

in seeking the way to peace by attempting to understand the other nations, rather than by abusing them.

I ask you & Mrs Chamberlain to accept my sincere good wishes

I have the honour to be,

Sir,

Your faithful servant

David Jones

P.S.

There is another passage in the Morte D'Arthur which your critics might do well to remember:

"Lo ye all Englishmen, see ye not what a mischief here was. . . . by him were they all upholden, now might not these Englishmen hold them content with him . . . . Alas this is a great default in us Englishmen for there may no thing please us no term"

[*Page 3 of 3*]

fraternization has not borne to us the common unity we wished. You, sir, have seen that the first necessity in Europe is such an understanding as we hoped for on the West Front. You have said so in clear words, & you have given bodily expression to your words, in difficult & worsening circumstances – for that alone you deserve our abiding gratitude.

I dearly hope that your leadership may yet engender among us all that same persistence that you have shown, ~~in the avoidance of the recriminations of, & the desire to understand the aspirations of, other nations~~.

[*Correction inserted in left-hand margin:* in seeking the way to peace by attempting to understand other nations, rather than by abusing them.]

I ask you & Mrs Chamberlain[127] to accept my sincere good wishes.

I have the honour to be,

Sir.

Your faithful servant

David Jones

P.S.

There is another passage in the Morte D'Arthur which your critics might do well to remember:

> 'Lo ye all Englishmen, see ye not what a mischief here was . . . . by him were they all upholden, now might not those Englishmen hold them content with him . . . . Alas this is a great default in us Englishmen for there may no thing please us no term'[128]

---

[127] Anne de Vere Chamberlain (née Cole, 1883–1967) was married to Chamberlain from 1911 until his death in May 1940. See Self, *Neville Chamberlain*, 33–7.

[128] This section of *Le Morte d'Arthur* runs in full:

> Lo ye all Englishmen, see ye not what a mischief here was*! for he that was the most kind and noblest knight of the world, and most loved the fellowship of noble knights, and* by him they were all upholden, now might not those Englishmen hold them content with him. *Lo, thus was the old custom and usages of this land; and men say that we of this land have not yet lost that custom.* Alas, this is a great default in us Englishmen for there may no thing please us no term.

Malory refers to the traitorous barons of England who gave their allegiance to Mordred in Arthur's absence. See Thomas Malory, *Le Morte d'Arthur*, book xxi, ch. 1, 379–81. Italics here indicate words that Jones omits. Jones received a response from Chamberlain on 9 January 1939. This letter is held in folder CT2/1 of the David Jones Papers, National Library of Wales, Aberystwyth. It reads in full:

[*typed script*]

> Dear Sir,
>
> I received yesterday at the hands of Miss Jelly d'Aranyi your letter of the 16th December and your book, 'In Parenthesis', which you have been kind enough to send me.
>
> I shall have great pleasure in accepting your gift and shall hope to find time in due course to read it. In the meanwhile however I should like to express my warm thanks for your understanding and sympathetic letter and to assure you that it has given me much pleasure.
>
> [*autograph script*]
>
> Yours sincerely
>
> Neville Chamberlain
>
> [*typed script*]
>
> David Jones, Esq.

Jelly d'Aranyi was a Hungarian violinist who lived in London during the late 1930s. In his unpublished notes made as editor of *Dai Greatcoat* (folder CD2/7 of the David Jones Papers, National Library of Wales, Aberystwyth), René Hague suggests that Jones met d'Aranyi at some point while staying at Rock Hall, the Northumberland estate of Helen Sutherland, in the early 1930s. For a brief discussion of Sutherland's connection to d'Aranyi, see Nicolete Gray (ed.), *Helen Sutherland Collection: A Pioneer Collection of the 1930s* (London: Lund Humphries, 1970), 22–3.

CHAPTER TWO

David Jones, Essay on Adolf Hitler, 11 May 1939

TOM VILLIS

INTRODUCTION

David Jones's attitudes to fascism have long been controversial. In her 1983 book, *David Jones, Mythmaker*, Elizabeth Ward suggests that Jones expressed sympathy for the fascist and Nazi revolutions and that some of his thinking shows affinities with fascism.[1] These claims have been vigorously rejected by Thomas Dilworth and others.[2] Much of the evidence for Jones's attitudes comes from a previously unpublished typescript written in May 1939, versions of which are deposited in the John J. Burns Library, Boston College, and in the Booth Family Center for Special Collections at the Lauinger Library of Georgetown University Libraries. A good portion of it has been quoted in Thomas Dilworth's 1986 article 'David Jones and Fascism' in the *Journal of Modern Literature*, revised and expanded for republication in an edited collection of 1989.[3] Dilworth summarizes the first six pages and then, in his words, presents an 'edited version' with 'ellipses marking elisions' which 'shorten the text without distorting its meaning'.[4] Dilworth then presents the essay alongside his commentary, which fiercely rejects the claim that Jones demonstrated anything but limited sympathy for fascism. Interest in this subject is now such to justify publishing an unexpurgated text, so as to allow David Jones scholars and general readers the chance to make up their own minds. In a typed note dated 12 June 1975, attached to the copy of the typescript of the essay in box 2, folder 6, in the Burns Library's David Jones Papers, Jones's friend Harman Grisewood suggests that he had considered publishing the piece in *Epoch and Artist* (1959) but decided against it for the same reason that David Jones had decided against publishing it in 1939: that it would be misinterpreted as being overly sympathetic to Hitler. Grisewood also suggests that Jones realized that the extent of the piece made it far too long for any newspaper. In the 1970s, Grisewood felt it would be less difficult to publish the essay, as long as it was accompanied by a note stressing that the article did not approve

[1] Elizabeth Ward, *David Jones, Mythmaker* (Manchester: Manchester University Press, 1983).

[2] Thomas Dilworth, 'David Jones and Fascism', *Journal of Modern Literature* 13, no. 1 (March 1986): 149–62; Paul Robichaud, 'David Jones, Christopher Dawson, and the Meaning of History', *Logos: A Journal of Catholic Thought and Culture* 6, no. 3 (Summer 2003): 68–85.

[3] Thomas Dilworth, 'David Jones and Fascism', in John Matthias (ed.), *David Jones: Man and Poet* (Orono, ME: National Poetry Foundation, University of Maine, 1989), 143–59. This is the version cited here.

[4] Dilworth, 'David Jones and Fascism', 148.

of Hitler's methods.[5] Debates about Jones's views on Hitler can easily become accusatory or defensive. It is hoped that the publication of this typescript in full will help move the debate away from such polarized views towards a more nuanced understanding of how Jones's views fitted into the wider cultural and political context.

Jones's article was written in May 1939, between the failure of appeasement and the outbreak of the Second World War. Many felt that allowing Hitler to annex the Sudetenland in the Munich Agreement of September 1938 had averted war. However, when, in March 1939, German troops marched into Prague and occupied the rest of Czechoslovakia, it seemed that territorial appeasement had finally been discredited. Previous supporters of appeasement and apologists for Hitler, including the Marquis of Clydesdale, Francis Yeats-Brown, Lord Esher and G. Ward Price of the *Daily Mail*, publically repudiated the policy.[6] The public and the mainstream press became increasingly reconciled to war. In this context, those who wanted to avoid war at any cost were pushed into more and more extreme arguments. After declining since its peak in 1934, membership of Oswald Mosley's British Union of Fascists started to grow rapidly again after the failure of the Munich Agreement as those who wanted peace at any price were drawn to them.[7] David Jones was therefore writing in a context in which war looked increasingly inevitable to many people and where putting the opposing argument might have seemed to require extra effort and independence of mind. Before it became too long, Jones had intended to publish this piece as a letter to *The Tablet,* a Catholic periodical which, as Jones puts it, had 'done service to the truth by emphasising the complexity of international issues, which the press too often attempts to resolve into some simple right and wrong'.[8] *The Tablet* had certainly been prepared to be open-minded about fascism throughout the interwar period and is a good place to start contextualizing the way in which Jones's views in this typescript reflect broader Catholic thinking in the period. Under Douglas Woodruff's editorship, from 1936, the paper's sales nearly doubled in a year, and it was rapidly becoming, in Michael Walsh's words, 'part of the furniture of Catholic middle-class households'.[9] Woodruff's mission for the paper was 'to endeavour to interpret not only the Church to the outside world but the outside world to those members of the Church who need a general survey'.[10]

The Tablet is a useful source of some of the views and opinions of upper and middle class Catholics on the rise of fascism and Nazism in the interwar period. Evelyn Waugh, acting as the paper's 'special correspondent in Addis Ababa' provided a pro-Italian reading of the Abyssinian war.[11] *The Tablet*'s view on Italy's victory was that it was 'quite certain that in terms of human happiness the conquest will mean for most of the Abyssinians the exchange of a more humane for a less humane overlord'.[12] In common with most of the rest of the Catholic press in Britain and abroad, *The Tablet* was an enthusiastic supporter of the Nationalists in the Spanish Civil War. It was particularly sensitive about the way in

---

[5] Note by Harman Grisewood, dated 12 June 1975, enclosed with the 'Hitler Essay', David Jones Papers, John J. Burns Library, Boston College, MS 86–1, series II, subseries 1, box 2, folder 6.

[6] Martin Pugh, *'Hurrah for the Blackshirts!' Fascists and Fascism in Britain Between the Wars* (London: Jonathan Cape, 2005), 284.

[7] Roger Thurlow, *Fascism in Britain: From Oswald Mosley's Blackshirts to the National Front* (London: I.B. Tauris, 1998), 92.

[8] Hitler Typescripts, p. 57 below.

[9] Michael J. Walsh, *The Tablet, 1840–1990: A Commemorative History* (London: The Tablet Publishing Company, 1990), 50.

[10] Walsh, *The Tablet, 1840–1990*, 49.

[11] 'Italy in Abyssinia', *The Tablet*, 13 June 1936, 750–1.

[12] 'The Abyssinian Record', *The Tablet*, 2 May 1936, 546.

which this isolated it from much of the rest of the British press and population, and, in common with many on the right, tried to separate support for Franco from support for fascism in general.[13] Nevertheless, if faced with the choice, Woodruff stated that '[n]o sane and instructed man would hesitate to prefer Fascism to Communism'.[14] With regard to Nazism, the editorial line was much more hostile: like many other Catholic publications, the paper criticized the paganism and state-worship of Nazi ideology and condemned Nazi persecution. The correspondence columns of the paper, however, contain numerous expressions of support for Hitler's regime, including, for example, a claim that 'the Jews "wax remarkably fat" in spite of the "great persecution"'.[15] The worst examples were often censored by an editorial comment. *The Tablet* was, nevertheless, a firm supporter of appeasement, believing it was the 'duty of the rest of Europe to maintain all the contacts it can with the Germans'.[16] Jones had good reason to believe, therefore, that his views would not be particularly out of place in this paper and might get a fair hearing.

Similar ambivalence with regard to fascism and Nazism can be found in many other quarters of the Catholic press and in Catholic literary society.[17] The *Catholic Herald*[18] was reluctant to criticize Hitler even when his anti-Catholicism became obvious, claiming in an editorial that '[w]e have every desire to put the best interpretation on the acts and words of a government that has undoubtedly dealt atheistic Communism some heavy blows both at home and abroad' even if 'it is not really possible to rely on its intentions'.[19] The *Catholic Herald* was also a strong supporter of appeasement and featured contributions from major Catholic authors to make the case.[20] In September 1939 the paper admitted that '[o]nly at the very end have we allowed ourselves to be satisfied that the evil genius and stupidity of Hitler preponderated over the qualities which enabled him to render so many services to his great country'.[21] The *Catholic Herald* even granted an interview to Oswald Mosley in July 1939.[22]

A number of prominent Catholic writers and thinkers also expressed some sympathy for European fascism. G. K. Chesterton expressed limited admiration for Mussolini in his 1930 book *The Resurrection of Rome*, as did Hilaire Belloc in a number of contexts.[23] Neither writer was in favour of Nazism, which they saw as a continuation of Prussian authoritarianism. Belloc's anti-communism occasionally tempered his anti-Nazism, however. In one article of 1937 he writes that even if 'Berlin' is 'the basest of the modern absolute governments; it is still a symbol of resistance to chaos and destruction, and sooner or later England must, in the nature of things take part in that resistance'.[24] Turning to a younger generation of Catholic

[13] See, for example, 'Fascism as Cant Phrase', *The Tablet*, 3 October 1936, 438.

[14] Quoted in Walsh, *The Tablet, 1840–1990*, 55.

[15] Anthony Gittens, 'Mussolini and Hitler', *The Tablet*, 29 September 1934, 409.

[16] 'The Germans in Europe', *The Tablet*, 1 October 1938, 421.

[17] For a fuller discussion, see Tom Villis, *British Catholics and Fascism: Religious Identity and Political Extremism Between the Wars* (Basingstoke: Palgrave Macmillan, 2013).

[18] The *Catholic Herald* is a British weekly, founded in 1884 as a radical newspaper for the Catholic working class. Under the editorship of Michael de la Bédoyère from 1934 it gained more middle-class readers and its editorial line became more conservative.

[19] 'Germany and Europe', *Catholic Herald*, 5 February 1937, 8.

[20] See the *Catholic Herald*, 7 October 1938: Douglas Jerrold, 'Stop Those War Mongers!', 2; Arnold Lunn, 'Bellicose Pacifism Is Not New', 5; Christopher Dawson, 'If the Dictators Seek War, Then We Must Seek Peace', 9; Robert Sencourt, 'These Are the Facts', 7.

[21] 'Hitler's Responsibility', *Catholic Herald*, 8 September 1939, 6.

[22] 'Catholics–BUF: Mosley Discusses their Relations', *Catholic Herald*, 21 July 1939, 1.

[23] G. K. Chesterton, *The Resurrection of Rome* (London: Hodder & Stoughton, 1930), 226–86. For a fuller discussion of the attitude of Chesterton and Belloc to fascism, see Villis, *British Catholics and Fascism*, chapter 4.

[24] Hilaire Belloc, 'Moscow or Berlin', *G. K.'s Weekly*, 14 January 1937, 367.

writers, Bernard Wall's review *Colosseum* contains a number of articles sympathetic to fascism that, while mostly anti-Nazi, are sometimes prepared to give it a fair hearing against the perceived unthinking criticism of the left. At one point, for example, Wall posits a bizarre moral equivalence between anti-Semitism and anti-Nazism.[25] Elsewhere, on what might be described as the Catholic literary right,[26] writers such as Douglas Jerrold and Sir Charles Petrie expressed pro-fascist views in the *English Review*, a periodical that became a forum where pro-Nazis could conduct an 'open' discussion of the benefits of the regime to counter the hostility shown in much of the rest of the press.[27] The Catholic converts Christopher Hollis and Arnold Lunn, too, tried to remain open-minded about Nazism and expressed limited support for fascism in Italy, which led to them being accused of pro-fascism.[28]

Jones's views expressed in this article, therefore, are to an extent reflected in the general Catholic literary community of the late 1930s. His immediate cultural circle, however, had sought to dissociate themselves from what they saw as the more integralist line of older writers such as Hilaire Belloc and the views of the Catholic literary right such as Jerrold or Petrie. When Jones writes in his essay of the views he heard discussed 'by various groups of Catholics', he is probably referring particularly to the circle which gathered around the Catholic publisher Tom Burns.[29] In the late 1920s Burns ran an informal salon in his home at 40 St. Leonard's Terrace, Chelsea, which attracted many young Catholic writers and intellectuals, including Alick Dru, Francis Howard, Harman Grisewood, Bernard Wall, and Robert Speaight as well as Jones. The subjects of discussion were a deliberate contrast to the political and economic concerns of earlier Catholic writers such as Belloc or Chesterton: Burns later remarked that 'it astonishes me now what little attention my group – with the exception of Christopher Dawson – paid to politics as such'.[30] Instead, as Harman Grisewood put it, political matters were only discussed in so far as they 'arose as an inference from aesthetic and philosophical beliefs'.[31] As such, fascism was not their primary interest. Burns had rejected the ideas of the Action Française as a young man in Paris[32] and claimed that the ideas of his circle 'had nothing to do with the New Order of German or Italian nationalism emerging at that time'.[33] Nevertheless, the group developed a critique of the culture of liberalism. They sought a spiritual transcendentalism that echoed aspects of the European right while criticizing its political authoritarianism. Burns's interpretation of English history had much in common with the reactionary tradition that he supposedly rejected:

> It seemed to us that the Reformation, the Age of Revolution and Industrialism had eroded the territory of the sacral in daily living: modern man was losing a vital

[25] Bernard Wall, 'Germany and Racism', *Colosseum* 5, no. 20 (January 1939): 32–3.
[26] See Villis, *British Catholics and Fascism*, 136–74.
[27] See, for example, J. D. Gregory, 'Germany', *English Review*, May 1934, 621–5, or E. T. S. Dugdale, 'National Socialism in Germany', *English Review*, October 1931, 569.
[28] See, for example, Christopher Hollis, *Foreigners Aren't Knaves* (London: Longmans, 1939), and Arnold Lunn, *Spanish Rehearsal* (London: Hutchinson, 1937).
[29] Tom Burns was an influential Catholic publisher and editor who worked for Sheed & Ward and Longmans as a young man. In 1936, he helped buy out *The Tablet* and served as its editor from 1967 to 1982. For more on Burns's life, see his autobiography, *The Use of Memory: Publishing and Further Pursuits* (London: Sheed & Ward, 1993).
[30] Burns, *The Use of Memory*, 46.
[31] James R. Lothian, *The Making and Unmaking of the English Catholic Intellectual Community, 1910–1950* (Notre Dame, IN: University of Notre Dame Press, 2009), 239.
[32] Burns, *The Use of Memory*, 26.
[33] Burns, *The Use of Memory*, 46.

> dimension of his life, the utilitarian motive was self-sufficient; a culture without religion was no culture – and scarcely civilized.[34]

Burns's salon was also consciously right-wing and rejected what they saw as the fashionably secular liberalism of the rest of the literary establishment. As Harman Grisewood put it:

> Bloomsbury was fashionable and trendy; we were relatively unknown and espoused unpopular causes. Bloomsbury was leftist; we were decidedly rightist. Bloomsbury was late Victorian English; we were twentieth-century European. We were tenaciously Catholic; Bloomsbury was confidently agnostic. In the words of Samuel Butler, they regarded the end of Christianity as 'virtually settled'; we looked forward to a renaissance.[35]

One of the products of Burns's Chelsea salon was a short-lived publication entitled *Order*. This periodical was not widely read: its original print run was 500 copies, but it eventually sold 2,000 copies of the first issue.[36] *Order* was very critical of the perceived authoritarian politics of Hilaire Belloc. An anonymous article which Burns later attributed to Denis Brogan doubted whether Belloc's immense influence had always been positive. In particular, Brogan took issue with the way in which his views 'are regarded as a new Catholic orthodoxy'.[37] In fact, as the European situation increasingly radicalized throughout the 1930s, writers like Tom Burns did not wholly reject the Bellocian line. In the late 1930s, Burns was a reader for Eyre & Spottiswoode, where he became friends with key figures on the Catholic right such as Douglas Jerrold and Charles Petrie, attending informal board meetings near the Garrick Club.[38] He became a supporter of the Nationalist side in the Spanish Civil War, even driving an ambulance bought by charitable donations to Burgos, the Nationalist headquarters.[39]

Jones and many of the writers who later wrote for *Order* and *Colosseum* were more interested in art and culture than in politics. Nevertheless, they all shared the view that the organic society of the past had been destroyed by a variety of historical processes including the Reformation, the rise of liberalism and nationalism, and secularization, the Industrial Revolution, and capitalism. Jones describes this as 'the Break'.[40] Like many of his fellow Catholic intellectuals, Jones was concerned about the effects of technological progress on the bonds of human fellowship: the contrast between the traditional and the modern is one of the most important themes in his art and poetry. Jones and the *Order* circle felt that religion could help alleviate the deadening materialism of contemporary culture. This echoes the long-standing Catholic view of English history that suggests that the Merrie England of the late Middle Ages was destroyed by the Protestant Reformation, and it mirrors, with slightly different emphases, the view shared by both the radical right and left that industrial capitalism had destroyed the community of an earlier period.[41] While such views might not necessarily lead to a particular political position, they can have political ramifications.

---

[34] Burns, *The Use of Memory*, 52; also quoted in Lothian, *Making and Unmaking*, 248.

[35] Quoted in Lothian, *Making and Unmaking*, 249.

[36] Lothian, *Making and Unmaking*, 263–4.

[37] 'On the Teaching of Mr Belloc', *Order: An Occasional Catholic Review* 1, no. 4 (November 1929): 120.

[38] Burns, *The Use of Memory*, 59.

[39] Burns, *The Use of Memory*, 80.

[40] See Jones's preface to *The Anathemata* (London: Faber & Faber, 1952), 15.

[41] See, for example, Hilaire Belloc, *A History of England*, 4 vols (London: Methuen, 1925–31); Christopher Hollis, *The Two Nations: A Financial Study of English History* (London: Routledge, 1935); Douglas Jerrold, *England* (Bristol: Arrowsmith, 1935).

One of the most significant of these political ramifications is not the positive embrace of fascism or any other reactionary or revolutionary system but the rejection of the assumptions of contemporary liberalism. Christopher Dawson felt that the 'liberal and humanitarian ideals that inspired the civilization of the last two centuries are dead or dying and there is nothing left to take their place'.[42] Bernard Wall, editor of *Colosseum*, felt the world was 'sick of the old liberal muddle'[43] and by 1936 was writing that 'Liberal democracy in Europe is bankrupt.'[44]

Equally significant, this meant a rejection of the materialist left. For Dawson both liberal capitalism and Marxist socialism 'were vitiated by a bias towards materialism which rendered them unbalanced and morally unsatisfying'.[45] Communism was the ultimate evil, therefore, described by Dawson as the first time in the world's history where the 'kingdom of the Antichrist has acquired political form and social substance'.[46] Anti-communism was so significant for Jones that he considered enlisting to fight against the Reds in the Russian Civil War.[47]

Putting these two commonly held beliefs together could lead to the view that fascism was wrong but the least of many evils. More interestingly, however, such views suggest that Catholic thinkers were variously attracted and repulsed by the extent to which fascism was an anti-materialist ideology which sought to repudiate the spiritual emptiness of either liberal or materialist views of the world. This, too, was the limit of their attraction in that this spiritual revolt was animated by the wrong spirit and directed towards the wrong ends.

The views that David Jones expresses in his essay reflect these broader concerns in a number of ways. Jones clearly felt that the things Hitler was against were very similar to what he, and other Catholic thinkers like him, were against such as the 'chain store', the 'banking system' and 'capitalist exploitation'. Jones even mentions, for the only time in his writings, 'international Jewry' and 'alien finance' in a way which echoes some of the worst prejudices of the period. Harman Grisewood has suggested that Jones's Nazi sympathies were 'with the portrayal of injustice in *Mein Kampf*, not with the brutal means taken to correct it'.[48] However, some readers of this typescript may feel that he goes a little further than this, in the way he uses the imagery of 'the sword'; in the view that even 'the terrible aspects of those regimes, the brutality and suppression of individual freedom, must at least be considered in relation to the nature and malignancy of the particular conditions and evils that those regimes set out to correct'. Jones echoes many of his Catholic contemporaries, too, in viewing Nazism as the lesser of many evils. There is a suggestion that Nazism is not only a lesser evil than communism, but also a lesser evil than liberal capitalism: 'If the Axis Powers are said to display the marks of the dragon, what, after all, can be said for the Champion, or association of Champions and their hangers-on, who are represented as defending civilization against the dragon?' His eventual tentative conclusion is that 'For the Catholic, if it come [sic] to deciding in penny catechism terms of virtues and vices, as between dragon and champion, the dragon does not come off altogether badly. He seems anyway patient of baptism.' Jones, too, shares many of his Catholic contemporaries' scepticism

[42] Christopher Dawson, *Religion and the Modern State* (London: Sheed & Ward, 1938), 152.
[43] 'Commentary', *Colosseum* 1, no. 20 (June 1934): 7.
[44] 'Editorial', *Colosseum* 3, no. 12 (December 1936): 245.
[45] Dawson, *Religion and the Modern State*, 43.
[46] Dawson, *Religion and the Modern State*, 58.
[47] Thomas Dilworth, *David Jones in the Great War* (London: Enitharmon, 2012), 206.
[48] Quoted in Dilworth, 'David Jones and Fascism', 154.

about the virtues of Britain, particularly its liberal myths about non-violence, tolerance and civilization. Jones writes of the 'gangster-work and breaking of heads and hearts to rear the stately homes of England' and suggests that Hitler's designs on Czechoslovakia were no worse than some of the liberal powers' actions in the past: a similar argument could hypothetically be made, so Jones argues, about England absorbing Wales.

David Jones's fascination with *Mein Kampf* can also be traced through his private correspondence. In a letter to Harman Grisewood of 24 April 1939 he writes of rereading Hitler's book:

> I am deeply impressed by it, it is amazingly interesting in all kinds of ways – but pretty terrifying too. God, he's nearly right – but this hate thing mars his whole thing, I feel. I mean, it just misses getting over the frontier into the saint thing . . . but, having got so far, the conception of the world in terms of race-struggle (that's what it boils down to) will hardly do . . . Anyway, I back him still against all this currish, leftish, money thing.[49]

All in all, '[c]ompared with his opponents he is grand, but compared with the saints he is bloody'.[50] This reflects the suggestion expressed in the typescript about Hitler being on the verge of sainthood and taking the plunge into 'John of the Cross's tunnel'. To be fair to Jones, though, this letter was him at his most extreme and he showed some awareness of this fact. In a postscript he apologized to Grisewood: 'I've written this very late at night and after some whisky – so forgive it's horrible balls.'[51]

This typescript is evidence that even when sober Jones saw something to admire in Nazism, if only for a limited period. In some ways, though, his flirtation with fascism was less about ideas than about identity. Jones and many of his Catholic contemporaries felt alienated from aspects of British culture that could lead to a kind of wilful contrariness. Burns described in his autobiography his impression of Catholic literary society as less of a 'sub-culture' than a 'super-culture . . . inhabiting a fortress rather than a ghetto'.[52] Unfashionable views on European politics could be a mark of identity for members of this 'super-culture'. Harman Grisewood, also an attendee at the Chelsea salon, described the atmosphere of the time in London as 'narrowminded and suspicious towards an Englishman who questioned the assumptions of the English culture'.[53] Grisewood claimed that he opened himself up to accusations of being a traitor merely for reading *Mein Kampf*, and he clearly admired Jones for 'speaking his mind' in the face of disapproval.[54]

Jones believed that Hitler was *both* a rebuke to the decadence of the Western world and a horrific dictator. Stanley Honeyman felt that Jones remained convinced that the Nazi attack on Western decadence was on to something: Hitler had the right diagnosis but the wrong medicine.[55] Jones's interest in Hitler did not remain at this level of intensity for long, however, and in a letter to Grisewood in June 1939 he was already saying that '[o]ver all that political stuff, I believe I've altered a bit – I feel less interested in it somehow

---

[49] Quoted in Joseph Pearce, *Literary Converts: Spiritual Inspiration in an Age of Unbelief* (London: HarperCollins, 1999), 211.

[50] From the same letter, quoted in Dilworth, 'David Jones and Fascism', 152.

[51] David Jones to Harman Grisewood, 24 April 1939, in the Booth Family Center for Special Collections, Lauinger Library, Georgetown University Libraries, Harman Grisewood Papers 1, box 2, folder 6.

[52] Burns, *The Use of Memory*, 120.

[53] Harman Grisewood, *One Thing at a Time: An Autobiography* (London: Hutchinson, 1968), 116.

[54] Quoted in Dilworth, 'David Jones and Fascism', 155.

[55] Stanley Honeyman to Harman Grisewood, 25 September 1984, in the Georgetown University Library's Harman Grisewood Papers 1, box 5, folder 23.

at the moment'.[56] That Jones was sympathetic to aspects of Hitler's revolt in the 1930s did not diminish his horror at the events of the 1940s.[57] Similarly, there is no suggestion that Jones's views of Nazism define his cultural or artistic vision: It is unhelpful to reduce the richness and ambiguity of poetry to one political or cultural viewpoint. No doubt, too, this typescript will be read in different ways: as a reminder of just how far sympathy with fascism could go in the late 1930s, as a sophisticated critique of liberal materialism, as a plea for peace, or as an indication of the complexity of the cultural and political debates of the period.

Note on the transcription

The following edition of Jones's essay on Hitler collates four versions of the typescript, two of which are held in the David Jones Papers of the John J. Burns Library at Boston College, and the two others in the Harman Grisewood Papers and the Michael Richey Papers in the Booth Family Center for Special Collections, Lauinger Library, Georgetown University Libraries. I transcribe here the version in the Michael Richey Papers at Georgetown, which is twenty pages long (5,440 words) and almost the same as one of the copies at Boston College (referred to here as 'BC 1'). Harman Grisewood's copy at Georgetown is identical to Michael Richey's copy at Georgetown, except that Grisewood's copy bears a title, added in his handwriting: 'The Pursuit of Peace'. 'BC 1' bears a number of handwritten amendments, which I have indicated with either a strikethrough or brackets. The second typescript at Boston College (here referred to as 'BC 2') is probably an earlier draft, as it contains spelling mistakes which are corrected in the other copies, but it is still, like the others, dated 11 May 1939. 'BC 2' occupies thirty instead of twenty pages, but, at 5,697 words, it contains only 257 more words than the other versions. There are, however, some significant differences, particularly at the end of the essay, where many of the additional words make their appearance. I have not indicated every difference among the four versions of spelling, punctuation, and word order, but where the wording is significantly different or where passages have been removed, I have given and labelled the alternative version in a footnote. While Jones did not publish any version of the essay, he had the twenty-page version duplicated and circulated among some of his friends,[58] hence its survival among the papers of Harman Grisewood and Michael Richey

[56] David Jones to Harman Grisewood, 23 June 1939, in David Jones, *Dai Greatcoat: A Self-portrait of David Jones in his Letters*, ed. René Hague (London: Faber & Faber), 93.

[57] There is some evidence to suggest, however, that Jones continued to feel that the popular view of Hitler was too simplistic even as the war progressed. In an unpublished letter to the *Catholic Herald*, dated 15 August 1941, Jones complains about the depiction of Adolf Hitler as the man nailing Christ to the cross in Jaroslav Krechler's *Stations of the Cross* (1941) at Our Lady of Mount Carmel Church in Lampeter, Wales. Jones feels that this depiction suggests 'an identification satisfying only to the very natural anger of a particular epoch or society, to the eclipse of dogma'. In particular, Jones feels that this image prevents meditation on the shared guilt for the crucifixion and therefore crudely overinterprets one of the central mysteries of the Christian religion. He therefore describes it as 'vulgarian' and 'propagandist'. Jones suggests towards the end of the letter that Hitler is generally being treated in the Britain of the 1940s without the proper restraint and sense of proportion. See folder CF2/13 of the David Jones Papers, National Library of Wales, Aberystwyth. Many thanks to Oliver Bevington for bringing this letter to my attention.

[58] Typescript note by Harman Grisewood, dated 12 June 1975, enclosed with the 'Hitler Essay', David Jones Papers, John J. Burns Library, Boston College, MS 86–1, box 2, folder 6.

at Georgetown, as well as at Boston College.[59] This is the version that can therefore be considered the final statement of Jones's argument. The copy in the Michael Richey Papers at Georgetown is reproduced in facing-page facsimile with a transcription, variants indicated in-line and in the notes, below.

ANNOTATED TRANSCRIPTION

Provenance

David Jones, '"Hitler Essay", 20-page typescript intended for *The Tablet*', John J. Burns Library, Boston College, David Jones Papers, MS 86–1, series II, subseries 1, box 2, folder 5.

Note: This twenty-page, 5,440-word folio typescript is identified in the notes below as 'BC 1'. Handwritten amendments on this typescript are indicated in this edition with brackets and strikethroughs.

David Jones, '"Hitler Essay", second typescript', John J. Burns Library, Boston College, David Jones Papers, MS 86–1, series II, subseries 1, box 2, folder 6.

Note: This thirty-page, 5,697-word quarto typescript is identified in the notes below as 'BC 2'. Variant and additional text from this typescript is given in the notes to this edition. This typescript is accompanied in the folder by a typescript note signed by Grisewood and dated 12 June 1975. See the discussion of this note in the Introduction to this chapter by Tom Villis, pp. 45–6.

David Jones, 'The Pursuit of Peace', Harman Grisewood Papers 1, 'David Jones Manuscripts', box 5, folder 22, in the Booth Family Center for Special Collections, Lauinger Library, Georgetown University Libraries. Component unique identifier 42307. Finding aid available online: http://findingaids.library.georgetown.edu/repositories/15/archival_objects/1169933.

Note: This twenty-page, 5,440-word folio typescript in the Grisewood Papers, Georgetown University Library, uniquely among the four typescripts bears the following title, added in Grisewood's hand in pencil at the top of the first page: 'The Pursuit of Peace'.

David Jones, 'Paper re Peace' (11 May 1939), Michael Richey Papers 1, Booth Family Center for Special Collections, Lauinger Library, Georgetown University Libraries, box 1, folder 43. Unique component identifier: 65734. Finding aid available online: http://findingaids.library.georgetown.edu/repositories/15/archival_objects/1192657.

Note: This twenty-page, 5,440-word folio typescript in the Richey Papers, Georgetown University Library, is the primary source of the edition of the essay given below. Differing and additional text appearing in 'BC 2' is indicated in the notes. In-line insertions and deletions indicated in this edition by brackets and strikethroughs are transcribed from 'BC 1'. This copy includes a cover page inscribed 'M. Richey. 1939.'.

---

[59] The Englishman Michael Richey (1917–2009) had become friends with Jones when they were both working with Eric Gill at Pigotts, Gill's Buckinghamshire farmstead, in the late 1930s. See Thomas Dilworth, *David Jones: Engraver, Soldier, Painter, Poet* (London: Jonathan Cape, 2017), 193.

[*Cover page*]

M. Richey. 1939.

Letters appearing in the last few issues of "The Tablet" from M. Korostovetz, Mr. Sencourt, Mr. Hayes and others all give expression, in their respective ways, to the misgivings, questions and hopes that are prominent in the minds of many people in this country. "The Tablet" itself has done service to the truth by emphasising the complexity of international issues, which the press too often attempts to resolve into some simple right and wrong.

Nothing is so necessary to the preservation of peace, as insistence on this complexity; for calamities usually come, in both private and public affairs when people find a generalization to their liking and act precipitately upon it; thereafter, as the truth emerges, is rage and disillusionment. In the present state of affairs, when false premises and untrue deductions will most certainly bring ruin to us all, this necessity of probing every appeal made to us, in the name of various ideals becomes terribly urgent. None of us can escape the responsibility of testing every link in that chain of arguments which is being forged to enslave our intelligences (that it may utilize our bodies), by those whose one simple cry is : "Stop the Dictators". As Catholics we are, in a special way, concerned for the truth about Europe and civilization and mankind. There is no excuse for us, as there is to a certain degree, for some other Englishmen who have been accustomed to think in terms of the English Weltanschauung

Letters appearing in the last few issues of 'The Tablet' from M. Korostovetz,[60] Mr. Sencourt,[61] Mr. Hayes[62] and others all give expression, in their respective ways, to the misgivings, questions and hopes that are prominent in the minds of many people in this country. 'The Tablet' itself has done service to the truth by emphasising[63] the complexity of international issues, which the press too often attempts to resolve into some simple right and wrong.

Nothing is so necessary to the preservation of peace, as insistence on this complexity; for calamities usually come, in both private and public affairs when people find a generalization to their liking and act precipitately upon it; thereafter, as the truth emerges, is rage and disillusionment. In the present state of affairs, when false premises and untrue deductions will most certainly bring ruin to us all, this necessity of probing every appeal made to us, in the name of various ideals becomes terribly urgent. None of us can escape the responsibility of testing every link in that chain of arguments which is being forged to enslave our intelligences (that it may utilize our bodies), by those whose one simple cry is: 'Stop the Dictators'. As Catholics we are, in a special way, concerned for the truth about Europe and civilization and mankind. There is no excuse for us, as there is to a certain degree, for some other Englishmen who have been accustomed to think in terms of the English Weltanschauung

[60] Vladimir Korostovetz (1888–1953) was the Ukrainian Hetman's representative in the UK in 1939. Hetmanites wanted the restoration of the Monarchist Hetman Ukrainian state that existed between 1648 and 1782 and briefly in 1918. Korostovetz was in touch with a number of German officials and under review by the British security services. See National Archives, KV 2/2574, and Thomas Dilworth, *David Jones: Engraver, Soldier, Painter, Poet* (London: Jonathan Cape, 2017), 201. In his letter to *The Tablet* (29 April 1939, 21–22), Korostovetz criticizes the Front Populaire in France and Soviet actions in Spain and China.

[61] Robert Sencourt (1890–1969) was a devout Roman Catholic and author of books on Newman, T. S. Eliot and Churchill. In his letter to *The Tablet* (22 April 1939, 20–1) he writes that 'Dictators are, of course, dangerous: but so, in their ignorance, are democracies.' He also writes about the power of Soviet-inspired left-wing propaganda, which he believes has been particularly influential in Britain, France, and the United States with regard to the Spanish Civil War.

[62] Mr K. (Kevin) Hayes (of 16 St John Street, Oxford) in a letter to *The Tablet* (22 April 1939, 21–2) argues strongly against an Anglo-Soviet alliance.

[63] In BC 2: 'great service to the truth by constantly'.

2.

almost exclusively, (although it is difficult to excuse their blindness when they are prepared to regard Charlie Napier's great bear as a safe guardian of our English World Order). At the present moment, so far has this poison of false simplification worked in peoples' minds, by means of the press, the wireless and political partisans, that even to suggest in a pub, that, after all, there is something to be said for the Dictators, arouses doubts as to one's loyalty, or even one's sanity. Those of us who fought in the last war are by this time very conscious that our heads were filled with a good deal of nonsense as to the nature and need of that struggle. That war may have been politically "unavoidable" - that makes the exploitation of our youthful innocence even more a matter for anger. There are few things more ignominious than being given bogus reasons for doing highly distasteful and boring feats. The qualities that the doing of these feats called up in men is quite beside the point - although it is constantly used to cover up all kinds of tomfoolery by sentimental or interested parties. It is, then, especially for us ex-service men, a matter for concern that in any future call upon the heroic qualities of men in this country, the false cries should be silenced so that what is strictly the end to which this heroism proceeds is defined and clear.

The things at stake are so grave that only a lunatic would be prepared to accept any of the appeals that have hitherto passed as excuses for war. Of course this is admitted by everybody and must indeed be a constant and terrible thought in the minds of

almost exclusively, (although it is difficult to excuse
their blindness when they are prepared to regard Charlie
Napier's great bear as a safe guardian of our English
World Order).[64] At the present moment, so far has this
poison of false simplification worked in peoples'
minds, by means of the press, the wireless and political
partisans,[65] that even to suggest in a pub, that, after
all, there is something to be said for the Dictators,
arouses doubts as to one's loyalty, or even one's
sanity. Those of us who fought in the last war are by
this time very[66] conscious that our heads were filled
with a good deal of nonsense as to the nature and need
of that struggle. That war may have been politically
'unavoidable' – that makes the exploitation of our
youthful innocence even more a matter for anger. There
are few things more ignominious than being given bogus
reasons for doing highly distasteful and boring feats.
The qualities that the doing of these facts called
up in men is quite beside the point – although it is
constantly used to cover up all kinds of tomfoolery
by sentimental or interested parties. It is, then,
especially for us ex-service men,[67] a matter for concern[68]
that in any future call upon the heroic qualities of
men in this country, the false cries should be silenced
so that what is strictly the end to which this heroism
proceeds is defined and clear.

The things at stake are so grave that only
a lunatic would be prepared to accept any of the appeals
that have hitherto passed as excuses for war. Of
course this is admitted by everybody and must indeed
be ~~a~~ constant[ly] ~~and terrible thought~~ in the minds of

[64] By 'Charlie Napier's great bear', Jones probably means Russia. The bear is a common symbol of Russia. Sir Charles John Napier (1786–1860) was a vice-admiral in the Crimean War, in command of the Royal Navy's fleet in the Baltic Sea. A reference to Russia makes sense in the context of the rest of the passage, which suggests that people used to thinking in terms of the English *Weltanshauung* were nevertheless content to lend unthinking support to the USSR against Germany.

[65] In BC 2: 'political agitators and the rest'.

[66] In BC 2: 'painfully'.

[67] For an account of David Jones's experience in the First World War, see Thomas Dilworth, *David Jones in the Great War* (London: Enitharmon, 2012).

[68] In BC 2: 'for us, ex-service men, very especially, a matter for concern'.

3.

those in office, nevertheless, it must be said, the most questionable arguments are daily being put forward by those who regard war with the Dictators as inevitable or necessary, and accepted without scepticism by the mass of people. The supreme patriotic act, at the moment, it seems to me, is to question every argument put forward that presupposes the need of such a war. It is necessary to look with what Herr Hitler, in another connection, calls "eyes of ice" upon all remotely bellicose arguments. The best of us require dope on certain occasions, but the hour is when even the legitimate opiates must be thrust aside. There is no "necessity" now but one - and that is the avoidance of the suicide of Europe by the inception of a major war. I would say, at "whatever cost" - because I have yet to be absolutely convinced that "the things more precious than peace" are other than hypothetically threatened. But even admitting that an attempt to "dominate the world by force" (somebody else's force, of course) was imminent, and must "be resisted come what may" - even so, it would be important to examine what is indicated in "come what may". It does not require any great imagination to be aware that there are possible, conceivable evils, more atrocious even than this domination. It would still be important to know, beyond any shadow of doubt that this feared domination was absolutely certain and absolutely the worst fate, otherwise the argument is invalid - we shall destroy ourselves and our supposed enemies owing to a misunderstanding. And seeing that many of the arguments used, even by very responsible persons, in defence of war, are very

those in office, nevertheless, it must be said, the
most questionable arguments are daily being put forward
by those who regard war with the Dictators as inevitable
or necessary, and accepted without scepticism[69] by the
mass of people. The supreme patriotic act, at the
moment, it seems to me, is to question every argument
put forward that presupposes the need of such a war.
It is necessary to look with what Herr Hitler, in
another connection, calls 'eyes of ice' upon all remotely
bellicose arguments.[70] The best of us require dope on
certain occasions, but the hour is when even the
legitimate opiates must be thrust aside. There is no
'necessity' now but one – and that is the avoidance of
the suicide of Europe by the inception of a major war.
I would say, at 'whatever cost' – because I have yet to
be absolutely convinced that 'the things more precious
than peace' are other than hypothetically threatened.[71]
But even admitting that an attempt to 'dominate the
world by force'[72] (somebody else's force, of course) was
imminent, and must 'be resisted come what may' – even
so, it would be important to examine what is indicated
in 'come what may'. It does not require any great
imagination to be aware that there are possible, con-
ceivable evils, more atrocious even than this domination.
It would still be important to know, beyond any shadow
of doubt that this feared domination was absolutely
certain and absolutely the worst fate, otherwise the
argument is invalid – we shall destroy ourselves and
our supposed enemies owing to a misunderstanding.
And seeing that many of the arguments used, even by
very responsible persons, in defence of [the last] war, are very

---

[69] In BC 2: 'accepted with a singular lack of scepticism'.

[70] *Eiskalt* ('ice-cold') was a favourite word of Hitler's. See Professor Dr Percy Ernst Schramm, 'Adolf Hitler: Anatomie eines Diktators', *Der Spiegel* 5, 29 January 1964, 40–61, available at http://www.spiegel.de/spiegel/print/d-46162899.html (accessed 22 January 2016). See also Percy E. Schramm, *Hitler: The Man and the Military Leader*, trans. Donald S. Detwiler (London: Allen Lane, 1972), 93.

[71] In BC 2: 'hypothetically threatened and anyway the phrase is high falutin''. The best-known use of the phrase 'more precious than peace' is in Woodrow Wilson's 'Address to a Joint Session of Congress Requesting a Declaration of War Against Germany' of 2 April 1917. Wilson says there that 'the right is more precious than peace', but it is probable that Jones is quoting this phrase from memory. See https://www.ourdocuments.gov/doc.php?doc=61&page=transcript (accessed 21 May 2017).

[72] This phrase is used by Neville Chamberlain in a speech in Birmingham of 17 March 1939. For the full text, see http://avalon.law.yale.edu/wwii/blbk09.asp (accessed 27 May 2016).

4.

much open to question, one may be reasonably in doubt about the arguments, from whosoever they come, that seem so compelling today.

It is significant that when the Prime Minister was pursuing his earlier tactics in the pursuit of peace, he was constantly abused, and his efforts shamefully unsupported. It was said that he was pursuing a largely personal policy, that he was undemocratic, and all that could be done to cancel his good will was done, by sections of the press, and by public men. Now that, at all events, in appearance, he is attempting a method less conciliatory, he is at last said to "have the country behind him" (I imagine this must be the most hard of all for the man himself).

Had England - that is to say the press of England and <u>all</u> her public men - fanatically supported that earlier policy, things might stand now other than they do. It is disturbing that those men and those newspapers and those cartoonists who were so hostile to him when he more obviously sought conciliation, should not, feeling themselves happily free of constraint, settle down to what can only be called War Propaganda. That this grim change of direction (even if in the mind of the Prime Minister, the goal is the same) should be the cause of satisfaction, whereas the more plainly hopeful and reasonable policy had to be pursued in the teeth of continual criticism, is extremely depressing, and suggests anything but a solid will to peace in this country.

A glance at the English press today is sufficient to make clear, that all the bellicosity, all

much open to question, one may be reasonably in doubt about the arguments, from whosoever they come, that seem so compelling today.

It is significant that when the Prime Minister was pursuing his earlier tactics in the pursuit of peace, he was constantly abused, and his efforts shamefully unsupported.[73] It was said that he was pursuing a largely personal policy, that he was undemocratic, and all that could be done to cancel his good will was done, by sections of the press, and by public men. Now that, at all events, in appearance, he is attempting a method less conciliatory, he is at last said to 'have the country behind him' (I imagine this must be the most hard of all for the man himself).

Had England – that is to say the press of England and all her public men – fanatically supported that earlier policy, things might stand now other than they do. It is disturbing that those men and those newspapers and those cartoonists who were so hostile[74] to him when he more obviously sought conciliation, should ~~not~~ [now], feeling themselves happily free of constraint, settle down to what can only be called War Propaganda. That this grim change of direction (even if in the mind of the Prime Minister, the goal is the same) should be the cause of satisfaction, whereas the more plainly hopeful and reasonable policy had to be pursued in the teeth of continual criticism, is extremely depressing, and suggests anything but a solid will to peace in this country.

A glance[75] at the English press today is sufficient to make clear, that all the bellicosity, all

---

[73] A reference to Neville Chamberlain's policy of appeasement. David Jones had sent Neville Chamberlain a copy of *In Parenthesis* with an accompanying note expressing 'gratitude for all you have done and are continuing to do to mend things in Europe and to save us from the worst'. David Jones to Neville Chamberlain, letter dated 18 December 1938, in the Booth Family Center for Special Collections, Lauinger Library, in Georgetown University Libraries, Harman Grisewood Papers 1, box 3, folder 1. See Oliver Bevington's edition of the letter in this volume, pp. 37–43.

[74] In BC 2: 'cartoonists who were so disloyal'.

[75] In BC 2: 'mere glance'.

5.

the ill-will, all the guile, all the unreason and presumption, in short, all the threat to peace, is by no means confined to the Axis Powers.

The simplification has been effected: morals, policy, self-interest, religion, all are seen as demanding one course of action and one only - the Beast is named. God wills the destruction of the Beast. What could be more easy - and what more unhelpful ? There is a story related of a French painter, that during the siege of Paris in 1871, he being something of a recluse, at the sound of the first gun-fire, opened his door and asked a passer-by what the noise was about. She said, "The bombardment, old man". He said, "Whose bombardment ?" She said, "The Prussians, old fool". He said, "Well, there are other nations".

It is important to remember that "there are other nations", and that though the Prussians bombard, the opening of that cannonade is not to be attributed to the particular wickedness of one nation, but rather a state of things for which all are responsible. While there is yet a semblance of peace, that truth is paramount, and we are under an obligation to give voice to this truth especially when it is being so commonly neglected, even by people who are themselves partly responsible for the evils of the last 20 years. If the Axis Powers are said to display the marks of the dragon, what, after all, can be said for the Champion, or association of Champions and their hangers-on, who are represented as defending civilization against the dragon ?

If we think we can see in that company the true defenders of liberty of conscience, civil freedom,

the ill-will, all the guile, all the unreason and presumption, in short, all the threat to peace, is by no means confined to the Axis Powers.[76]

The simplification has been effected: morals, policy, self-interest, religion, all are seen as demanding one course of action and one only – the Beast is named. God wills the destruction of the Beast. What could be more easy – and what more unhelpful? There is a story[77] related of a French painter, that during the siege of Paris in 1871, he being something of a recluse, at the sound of the first gun-fire, opened his door and asked a passer-by what the noise was about. She said, 'The bombardment, old man'. He said, 'Whose bombardment?' She said, 'The Prussians, old fool'. He said, 'Well, there are other nations'.

It is important to remember that 'there are other nations', and that though the Prussians bombard, the opening of that cannonade is not to be attributed to the particular wickedness of one nation, but rather a state of things for which all are responsible. While there is yet a semblance of peace, that truth is paramount, and we are under an obligation to give voice to this truth especially when it is being so commonly neglected, even by people who are themselves partly responsible for the evils of the last 20 years. If the Axis Powers are said to display the marks of the dragon, what, after all, can be said for the Champion, or association of Champions and their hangers-on, who are represented as defending civilization against the dragon?

If we think we can see[78] in that company the true defenders of liberty of conscience, civil freedom,

[76] The 'Axis Powers' refers to Germany and Italy (and sometimes, colloquially, to Japan, which was part of the Anti-Comintern Pact but not at this point a military ally). Jones is writing a few days before the 'Rome–Berlin Axis' between Italy and Germany became a military alliance in the 'Pact of Steel', on 22 May 1939.

[77] In BC 2: 'There is a legend'.

[78] In BC 2: 'If we can see'.

6.

humane living, human progress, the reign of law, and the rest, what of those less agreeable figures who seem most loud in urging the destruction of the dragon ? They sound ugly enough too, when they cry against the beast, they too seem to know the persuasion of brute force not a little. Those mysterious figures that we have heard condemned so often, and of whom men say that they fight invisible. The instruments or creators of capitalist exploitation, of imperialist necessity, the unamed forces that control commidities, and gold and the instigators of world revolution ... As James Joyce says :

"My colonial, wardha bagful ! ... All that and more under one crinoline envelope if you dare to break the porkbarrel seal. No wonder they'd run from her pison plague".

It is the strangest combination - how come these to be united in a common quest ? It makes you rub your eyes when you see Pte. Garvin lending his pull-through to Pte. Stalin, and dapper Pte. Cooper sharing his button-stick with a Bloomsbury rooky. What common urge caused these boys to enlist in the same mob ? One would hardly be surprised if the favourite record at Berchtesgaden should prove to be :

"Oh my name it is Sam Hall
And I hate you one and all".

I confess I have only the vaguest notion as to what constitutes these forces of international capitalism, etc. or how they operate. The "hidden hand" argument is usually unconvincing and there are so many contrary theories about where the evil

humane living, human progress, the reign of law, and the rest, what of those less agreeable figures who seem most loud in urging the destruction of the dragon? They sound ugly enough too, when they cry against the beast, they too seem to know the persuasion of brute force not a little. Those mysterious figures that we have heard condemned so often, and of whom men say that they fight invisible. The instruments or creators of capitalist exploitation, of imperialist necessity, the unnamed forces that control commodities, and gold[,] and the instigators of world revolution . . . As James Joyce says :

'My colonel, wardha bagful! . . . All that and more under one crinoline envelope if you dare to break the porkbarrel seal. No wonder they'd run from her pison plague'.[79]

It is the strangest combination – how come these to be united in a common quest? It makes you rub your eyes when you see Pte. Garvin lending his pull-through to Pte. Stalin, and dapper Pte. Cooper sharing his button-stick with a Bloomsbury rooky.[80] What common urge caused these boys to enlist in the same mob? One would hardly be surprised if the favourite record at Berchtesgaden[81] should prove to be :

'Oh my name it is Sam Hall
And I hate you one and all'.[82]

I confess I have only the vaguest notion as to what constitutes these forces of international capitalism, etc. or how they operate. The 'hidden hand' argument is usually unconvincing[83] and there are so many contrary theories about where the evil

---

[79] Jones is quoting James Joyce, *Finnegans Wake* (London: Faber & Faber, 1939), 212, line 20 (from the 'Anna Livia Plurabelle' section, first published in Paris in 1925). A copy of the Faber first edition, which had just been published on 4 May 1939, survives in Jones's personal library, where it is dated 27 May 1948. See Huw Ceiriog Jones (ed.), *The Library of David Jones (1895–1974): A Catalogue* (Aberystwyth: National Library of Wales, 1995), 159. Jones repeats Joyce's phrase 'My colonel, wardha bagful!' in his preface to *Epoch and Artist*, ed. Harman Grisewood (London: Faber & Faber, 1959), 18.

[80] James Louis Garvin (1868–1947) was the editor of the *Observer*, an idiosyncratic Conservative, and a prominent supporter of rearmament. (Alfred) Duff Cooper (1890–1954), 1st Viscount Norwich, was First Lord of the Admiralty when he resigned over the Munich Agreement with Hitler in 1938. Neither had much in common with either Stalin or a Bloomsbury intellectual except for their support for military action against Germany. Jones is using an image of these various people as soldiers on the front line of an ideological war. 'Pte.' is an abbreviation of 'private', the lowest rank in the army; a 'pull-through' is a rag attached to weigh on a cord which is used to clean a rifle; and a 'button-stick' is a device used to protect the fabric of a uniform when cleaning buttons.

[81] Berchtesgaden is an area in the German Alps and location of Hitler's Berghof (residence) where he spent much of his time and of the Kehlsteinhaus, known in English speaking countries as the Eagle's Nest.

[82] 'My name it is Sam Hall' is an English folksong about an unrepentant criminal. In BC 2 the lines are given as 'Oh my name is Sam Hall, Sam Hall / And I hate you one and all, one and all'. The ironic implication is that Hitler is a criminal who is spurned by the world but who remains defiant. For more on the song and its various forms see Bertrand H. Bronson, 'Samuel Hall's Family Tree', *California Folklore Quarterly* 1, no. 1 (January 1942): 47–64.

[83] In BC 2: 'argument is usually boring'. *The Hidden Hand* (London: Grant Richards, 1917) is a book by Arnold White that suggests that Britain was being secretly infiltrated by German sympathizers. Jones is using the phrase as a synonym for 'conspiracy theories'. In White's work and in others on the radical right of British politics, the 'Hidden Hand' behind international capitalism often had anti-Semitic connotations. See Colin Holmes, *Anti-Semitism in British Society, 1876–1939* (London: Edward Arnold, 1979).

7.

chiefly lies, but my point is, that <u>if</u> these forces are an invented bogey, all one can say is that it was not the Dictators who invented that bogey. For many years now, those mysterious powers and their menace to mankind have been taken for granted, have been the main topic of those concerned with social, cultural, economic and religious matters - whether Right, Left, Christian, Agnostic or whatever.

In reading "Mein Kampf" I was often reminded of the problems I used to hear discussed continuously by various groups of Catholic people concerning the recovery of social justice : how to break the "chain store", how to live uncorrupted by the "banking system", how to free men from the many and great evils of "capitalist exploitation", how to effect some real and just relationship between the price of things and the labour expended. Sincere and idealistic men all had theories of how best to resolve these problems because they said that if these problems were dealt with, men would live more justly and more fully as men, and more responsibly as workmen, and much more besides. All took it for granted that there existed powers inimical to a humane way of life who were the enemy of any attempt at a solution, because of money interest and one thing and another. The whole system was said to be corrupt, unChristian, intolerable. Now one did not have to be extra aware to agree with most of this. But what to do ? The solutions varied, especially in emphasis. In the main, however, there was the idea that some sort of return to the Land was of great importance. Some hoped that it might be possible for

[*Page 7 of 20*]

chiefly lies, but my point is, that if these forces are an invented bogey, all one can say is that it was not the Dictators who invented that bogey. For many years now, those mysterious powers and their menace to mankind have been taken for granted, have been the main topic of those concerned with social, cultural, economic and religious matters – whether Right, Left, Christian, Agnostic or whatever.

In reading 'Mein Kampf' I was often reminded[84] of the problems I used to hear discussed continuously ~~by various groups of~~ [among] Catholic[s] ~~people~~[85] concerning the recovery of social justice : how to break the 'chain store', how to live uncorrupted by the 'banking system', how to free men from the many and great evils of 'capitalist exploitation', how to effect some real and just relationship between the price of things and the labour expended.[86] Sincere and idealistic men all had theories of how best to resolve these problems because they said that if these problems were dealt with, men would live more justly and more fully as men, and more responsibly as workmen, and much more besides. All took it for granted that there existed powers inimical to a humane way of life who were the enemy of any attempt at a solution, because of money interest and one thing and another. The whole system was said to be corrupt, unChristian, intolerable. Now one did

---

[84] In BC 2: 'In perusing Mein Kampf I was continually reminded . . .'. It is likely that Jones had been reading the full translation into English which had appeared in March of that year: Adolf Hitler, *Mein Kampf*, trans. J. V. Murphy (London: Hurst and Blackett, 1939). In a letter to Harman Grisewood of 24 April 1939 Jones writes, 'I'm reading the full edition of *Mein Kampf*, and it is so different from the miserable cut-about edition I read previously.' See David Jones, *Dai Greatcoat: A Self-portrait of David Jones in his Letters*, ed. René Hague (London: Faber & Faber, 1980), 92–3. The 'cut-about edition' was the abridgment translated by E. T. S. Dugdale that appeared in 1933, also from Hurst and Blackett. See James J. Barnes and Patience P. Barnes, *Hitler's* Mein Kampf *in Britain and America: A Publishing History, 1930–39* (Cambridge: Cambridge University Press, 1980). Neither edition appears in the catalogue of Jones's library.

[85] In BC 2, also 'among Catholics' instead of 'by various groups of Catholic people.'

[86] In BC 2: 'the labour expended and all the rest of it'. Jones would have discussed these ideas with a number of Catholic writers who attended the informal salons organized by the Catholic publisher Tom Burns at his home at 40 St Leonard's Terrace, Chelsea. Attendees included Alick Dru, Francis Howard, Harman Grisewood, Bernard Wall, and Robert Speaight. One of the products of these meetings was a short-lived periodical entitled *Order* (1928–9), for which Jones designed the cover. Jones also was introduced to many of the ruralist ideas in Catholic thought in the early 1920s when he worked with Eric Gill at Ditchling in Sussex and at Capel-y-ffin in the Black Mountains on the Welsh border. For more on the *Order* group, see James R. Lothian, *The Making and Unmaking of the Catholic Intellectual Community* (Notre Dame, IN: University of Notre Dame Press), 260–5. For more on Eric Gill, see Fiona MacCarthy, *Eric Gill* (London: Faber & Faber, 1989).

7.

chiefly lies, but my point is, that <u>if</u> these forces are an invented bogey, all one can say is that it was not the Dictators who invented that bogey. For many years now, those mysterious powers and their menace to mankind have been taken for granted, have been the main topic of those concerned with social, cultural, economic and religious matters - whether Right, Left, Christian, Agnostic or whatever.

In reading "Mein Kampf" I was often reminded of the problems I used to hear discussed continuously by various groups of Catholic people concerning the recovery of social justice : how to break the "chain store", how to live uncorrupted by the "banking system", how to free men from the many and great evils of "capitalist exploitation", how to effect some real and just relationship between the price of things and the labour expended. Sincere and idealistic men all had theories of how best to resolve these problems because they said that if these problems were dealt with, men would live more justly and more fully as men, and more responsibly as workmen, and much more besides. All took it for granted that there existed powers inimical to a humane way of life who were the enemy of any attempt at a solution, because of money interest and one thing and another. The whole system was said to be corrupt, unChristian, intolerable. Now one did not have to be extra aware to agree with most of this. But what to do ? The solutions varied, especially in emphasis. In the main, however, there was the idea that some sort of return to the Land was of great importance. Some hoped that it might be possible for

[*Page 7 of 20*] (continued)

not have to be extra aware to agree with most of this. But what to do? The solutions varied, especially in emphasis. In the main, however, there was the idea that some sort of return to the Land was of great importance.[87] Some hoped it might be possible for

[87] Ideas about returning to the land have a long pedigree in British culture stretching back at least to the anti-industrialism of William Cobbett (1763–1835), John Ruskin (1819–1900), and William Morris (1834–96). Idealized rural patriotism had been part of the political mainstream in Edwardian Britain, not least in Lloyd George's Land Movement. In Catholic thinking, arguably the most influential statement of these ideas can be found in Hilaire Belloc and G. K. Chesterton's theory of 'distributism'. Partly inspired by Catholic social teaching, distributists were opposed equally to capitalism and socialism and advocated widespread property ownership. In the early twentieth century, 'back to the land' ideas inspired a number of local associations under the umbrella of the Catholic Land Association and numerous craft communities like the ones in Ditchling and Capel-y-ffin led by Eric Gill. For more on Catholic 'back to the land' ideas, see Kester Aspden, *Fortress Church: The English Roman Catholic Bishops and Politics, 1903–63* (Leominster: Gracewing, 2003), 183–4.

8.

small units to live more humane, responsible lives as small-holders of one sort or another, or as independent craftsmen of some kind. Some of this may be said to have partly succeeded by the efforts of heroic individuals, but in the main, I do not think it unfair to say, in terms of a War Communique coming from Enemy H.Q: "The attempt to penetrate our system by infiltration has failed".

That there is something radically wrong, seems by now obvious to all. The cure, not so obvious. Now the writer of "Mein Kampf" shared this conviction with so many of our friends, he even names the same supposed evils. (He was also concerned with matters they happily have no conception of, a nation defeated and starving, not only, so to say accidentally exploited by the machinations of the "system" but wilfully and purposely being punished by victorious enemies - but that is another matter). He too, looked about and said "something must be done", just as our best friends have said in one way or another. Just like the ex-officer who "took a small farm" or the man who fled from Brum, or even the typist who sang a folk-song on Saturday, in Sussex, or the art student who railed against Windsor and Newton and made his own paints out of "earth" pigment, even though they cracked and scaled, not to mention the beloved originator, or rather the most notorious user of, that phrase. The man whom our newspapers, with unspeakable vulgarity and class-consciousness, talk of as "The Austrian ex-house painter" also said, something must be done, about the exploitation of the citizen, "chain-stores", alien financial control, small units to live more humane, responsible lives as small-holders of one sort or another, or as independent craftsmen of some kind. Some of this may be said to have partly succeeded by the efforts of heroic individuals, but in the main, I do not think it unfair to say, in terms of a War Communique coming from Enemy H.Q.:[88] 'The attempt to penetrate our system by infiltration has failed'.

That there is something radically wrong, seems by now obvious to all.[89] The cure, not so obvious. Now the writer of 'Mein Kampf' shared this conviction with so many of our friends, he even names the same supposed evils. (He was also concerned with matters they happily have no conception of, a nation defeated and starving, not only, so to say accidentally exploited by the machinations of the 'system' but wilfully and purposely being punished by victorious enemies – but that is another matter). He too, looked about and said 'something must be done', just as our best friends[90] have said in one way or another. Just like the ex-officer who 'took a small farm' or the man who fled from Brum, or even the typist who sang a folk-song on Saturday, in Sussex, or the art student who railed against Windsor and Newton[91] and made his own paints out of 'earth' pigment, even though they cracked and scaled, not to mention the beloved originator, or rather the most notorious user of, that phrase. The man whom our newspapers, with unspeakable vulgarity and class-consciousness, talk of as 'the Austrian ex-house painter'[92] also said, [']something must be done['] about the exploitation of the citizen, 'chain-stores', alien financial control,

---

[88] In BC 2: 'a War Communique coming for Query H.Q.'.

[89] In BC 2 there is another section at the beginning of this paragraph: 'In parenthesis, if [sic] should be said that if such a communique were issued it would only be for very secret circulation among the enemy chiefs of staff, for, of course, in this particular "war" the whole concern of the enemy is to officially take the line that there <u>is</u> no war and that nothing is so nice and cultural as to have "picturesque" people on the land, or "quaint" people plying their crafts, or "interesting" people expounding their theories in public houses, or monks building their own monasteries "like the middle ages", it all goes to show that there is no such thing as regimentation in a pluto-democratic state, that all the talk of control and suppression and exploitation is only a fanatical illusion, everybody can do precisely what they please in the kindest of possible systems. But that there is something radically wrong, seems by now obvious to all.'

[90] In BC 2: 'just as so many of our dearest and best friends'.

[91] Windsor and Newton is a well-known British manufacturer of artists' paints and other fine art materials.

[92] Hitler was commonly misrepresented as a 'house-painter' when in fact he was an easel painter of landscapes. Leon Surette has suggested that Wyndham Lewis might be the original source of this erroneous claim in his *Dreams of a Totalitarian Utopia: Literary Modernism and Politics* (London: McGill-Queen's University Press, 2009), 329, n. 13. This is unlikely, as he is referred to as such in the Montréal *Gazette* for 24 March 1933, 3. Winston Churchill refers to Hitler as a 'former Austrian house-painter' in 1935. See Winston Churchill, *Great Contemporaries* (London: Butterworth, 1937), 262.

9.

lands going waste. He came to the conclusion that only one thing was potent enough to deal with these evils and that thing was the sword.

He came to the conclusion that the intelligent goodwill of artists, writers, land-reformers, poets, men of religion, was too frail an instrument for such a brute task. Such a conclusion, if acted upon, meant a rough house for most, and a hell on earth for many (whether innocent or guilty could be of no consequence).

I am far from saying that he was right, but that was his conclusion; but again to quote Joyce, his conclusion may only result in

"Out of the paunschaup on to the pyre".

The necessary conditioning of a whole people for such a task, means the temporary subordination of almost all the virtues to the virtue of courage. From most of our points of view this would simply mean that the sticky tyranny of Commercialism, money, etc., was replaced by the harsh and boring tyranny of the sword and all those new evils which as usual leap up where the old ones die - at all events temporarily. I think he shows an understanding of this. He seems to cast his glance forward, even if it be eight hundred years; but, I admit, in the main his general conception of the destiny of the world is a pretty steely one. Certainly that is easily explainable, for we are apt, all of us, to form our philosophies according to the accidents of our lives. Perhaps there is only one thing left for Adolf Hitler, and that is for him to become a saint - for if a man has looked so steadfastly and with such passion upon the deplorable and cruel

lands going waste. He came to the conclusion that only one thing was potent enough to deal with these evils and that thing was the sword.[93]

He came to the conclusion that the intelligent goodwill of artists, writers, land-reformers, poets, men of religion, was too frail an instrument for such a brute task. Such a conclusion, if acted upon, meant a rough house for most, and a hell on earth for many (whether innocent or guilty could be of no consequence).

I am far from saying that he was right, but that was his conclusion; but again to quote Joyce, his conclusion may only result in[94]

'Out of the paunschaup on to the pyre'.[95]

The necessary conditioning of a whole people for such a task, means the temporary subordination of almost all the virtues to the virtue of courage. From most of our points of view this would simply mean that the sticky tyranny of Commercialism, money, etc., was replaced by the harsh and boring tyranny of the sword and all those new evils which as usual leap up where the old ones die – at all events temporarily. I think he shows an understanding of this.[96] He seems to cast his glance forward, even if it is to be eight hundred years; but, I admit, in the main his general conception of the destiny of the world is a pretty steely one. Certainly that is easily explainable, for we are apt, all of us, to form our philosophies according to the accidents of our lives.[97] Perhaps there is only one thing left for Adolf Hitler, and that is for him to become a saint – for if a man has looked so steadfastly and with such passion[98] upon the deplorable and cruel

---

[93] In BC 2: 'also said, something must be done, about "chain-stores", financial control, lands going waste, and all the rest of it. He came to the conclusion that only one thing was potent and violent enough to break this (admitted by so many of our friends) "evil", and that one thing was the sword.'

[94] In BC 2: 'I am far from saying that he was right, but that was his conclusion; but again to quote Joyce, very happily I think, his conclusion may only result in . . .'.

[95] Joyce, *Finnegans Wake*, 209, line 31. In BC 2, Jones gives the source of this quote as '(A.L.P., p.23. [sic])'. He refers to the thirty-two-page pamphlet *Anna Livia Plurabelle: Fragment of Work in Progress* (London: Faber & Faber, 1930), 23.

[96] In BC 2: 'tyranny of the sword and all that, new evils, as usual, leap up where the old ones died – at all events temporarily. I think somewhere he shows some understanding of this.'

[97] The phrase 'for we are apt, all of us, to form our philosophies according to the accidents of our lives' is present in BC 2 but not in BC 1.

[98] The phrase 'and with such passion' is absent from BC 2.

10.

truths of this world and this world-order, then no compromise is possible, the next plunge is into John of the Cross's tunnel.

At all events, those people who, in this country, have said strong things about the iniquities of the capitalist exploitation and money power and international Jewry and the need for a return to the land and to a more healthy and normal way of life in all spheres must never forget that the conditions they find brutal and barbarous under Herr Hitler are largely the price paid for daring to deal arbitrarily, physically and directly, with some of those very problems. I must say it is difficult to see how other than by very severe and grim methods various vested interests and organized and powerful controls can be shattered, if one thinks they need shattering. It is one thing to talk about this and that evil, but to do something about it always means, in practice, the letting loose of forces that are in themselves partly evil. It is a question of what you can stick and what is most intolerable to the human spirit.

To return from this digression, one is tempted to say of the dragon what Perceval said of the lion, that it appears "the more natural beast of the two" in this battle. For the Catholic, if it come to deciding in penny catechism terms of virtues and vices, as between dragon and champion, the dragon does not come off altogether badly. He seems anyway patient of baptism.

What then is necessary is to discount all attempt to state this crisis in terms of vice and virtue - and any appeal to religion must be excluded. It is unconvinc-

truths of this world and this world-order, then no compromise is possible, the next plunge is into John of the Cross's tunnel.[99]

At all events, those people who, in this country, have said strong things about the iniquities of the capitalist exploitation and money power and international Jewry[100] and the need for a return to the land and to a more healthy and normal way of life in all spheres must never forget that the conditions they find brutal and barbarous under Herr Hitler are largely the price paid for daring to deal arbitrarily, physically and directly, with some of these very problems. I must say it is difficult to see how other than by very severe and grim methods various vested interests and organized and powerful controls can be shattered, if one thinks they need shattering. It is one thing to talk about this and that evil, but to do something about it always means, in practice, the letting loose of forces that are in themselves partly evil. It is a question of what you can stick and what is most intolerable to the human spirit.[101]

To return from this digression, one is tempted to say of the dragon what Perceval said of the lion, that it appears 'the more natural beast of the two' in this battle.[102] For the Catholic, if it come [sic] to deciding in penny catechism terms of virtues and vices, as between dragon and champion, the dragon does not come off altogether badly. He seems anyway patient of baptism.

What then is necessary is to discount all attempt[s] to state this crisis in terms of vice and virtue – and any appeal to religion must be excluded. It is unconvinc-

---

[99] In BC 2: 'the next plunge is right slap into John of the Cross's tunnel.' This is a reference to St John of the Cross's sixteenth-century poem *The Dark Night of the Soul* (*La Noche Oscura Del Alma*). The use of the word 'tunnel' may come from Edgar Allison Peers's introduction to his 1934 translation: 'In order to reach the Union of Light, the soul must pass through the Dark Night – that is to say, through a series of purifications, during which it is walking, as it were, through a tunnel of impenetrable obscurity and from which it emerges to bask in the sunshine of grace to enjoy the Divine intimacy.' See *The Complete Works of Saint John of the Cross, Doctor of the Church*, Vol. 1 (London: Burns, Oates & Washbourne, 1934–5), 2.

[100] This is one of the few references in Jones's writings to the anti-Semitic canard that cosmopolitan Jews are behind the forces of international capitalism. He mentions it here in the context of 'those people who . . . have said' rather than in relation to his own views. Similar sentiments were widespread in Catholic literary circles and there are hints in some of David Jones's unpublished letters that he associated Jews with the negative aspects of international finance. According to Thomas Dilworth, this bias was 'unknown to most of his friends and not present in his published writing (or 99.99% of his unpublished writing) . . .' See Thomas Dilworth. *David Jones: Engraver, Solider, Painter, Poet* (London: Jonathan Cape, 2017), 201.

[101] In BC 2: 'what is most intolerable to the human spirit, and all that.'

[102] In Malory's *Le Morte d'Arthur* Sir Percival comes across a serpent fighting with a lion. Percival kills the serpent, whereupon the lion 'made him all the cheer that a beast might make a man'. Sir Thomas Malory, *Le Morte d'Arthur*, ed. Ernest Rhys (London: J. M. Dent & Sons, 1933), book 14, chapter 6, 199. See Huw Ceiriog Jones, *The Library of David Jones*, 189.

ing, for instance, when too much is made of the paganization of Germany by persons who have hitherto seemed to regard the historic church as inimical to human progress - and I suspect considerable political bias in the kind words said recently of the Holy See - one feels that these kind words may turn to venom any time. What it boils down to is that there is much in both the Fascist and Nazi revolutions that demand our understanding and sympathy. They represent, for all their alarming characteristics an heroic attempt to cope with certain admitted corruptions in our civilization. Even the terrible aspects of those regimes, the brutality and suppression of individual freedom, must at least be considered in relation to the nature and malignancy of the particular conditions and evils that those regimes set out to correct. We can, in this country, only vaguely imagine what happens when a person, regardless of consequences, actually does something to radically change the society for which he is responsible. We have to look back into our lost history to get some idea of the nature and necessities, the grimness and relentlessness of such struggles. We are rather apt to whitewash in one case and blacken in the other. The historical person who tackles great matters with ruthlessness and energy is apt to be excused his excesses as the implement of God, or the scourge that cleansed the city - but the contemporary person can only be seen as a gangster, a blackguard. But apart from this, his ruthlessness will also be excused or magnified according to individual preferences. Thus, the more clear-headed Left person

ing, for instance, when too much is made of the paganization of Germany by persons who have hitherto seemed to regard the historic church as inimical to human progress – and I suspect considerable political bias in the kind words said recently of the Holy See[103] – one feels that these kind words may turn to venom any time. What it boils down to is that there is much in both the Fascist and Nazi revolutions that demand our understanding and sympathy. They represent, for all their alarming characteristics an heroic attempt to cope with certain admitted corruptions in our civilization. Even the terrible aspects of those regimes, the brutality and suppression of individual freedom, must at least be considered in relation to the nature and malignancy of the particular conditions and evils that those regimes set out to correct. We can, in this county, only vaguely imagine what happens when a person, regardless of consequences, actually does something to radically change the society for which he is responsible. We have to look back into our lost history to get some idea of the nature and necessities, the grimness and relentlessness of such struggles. We are rather apt to whitewash in one case and blacken in the other. The historical person who tackles great matters with ruthlessness and energy is apt to be excused his excesses as the implement of God, or the scourge that cleansed the city – but the contemporary person can only be seen as a gangster, a blackguard. But apart from this, his ruthlessness will also be excused or magnified according to individual preferences. Thus, the more clear-headed Left person

[103] Pope Pius XII (Eugenio Pacelli) had been elected to the papacy on 2 March 1939 to largely favourable press attention. See, for example, *The Times* for 3 March 1939, 6 and 14; and for 6 March 1939, 14.

12.

will excuse all the horrors connected with the establishment of the Soviet regime as necessary and is prepared to admit the necessity of such horrors in this country or elsewhere, for the realization of the Marxist dream.

So that we can reasonably reject the argument that the Axis Powers must be broken on account of their resort to violence and suppression. The truth seems to be that the kingdoms of this world use, mathematically almost, that amount of violence and suppression that is necessary to the establishment and defence of their particular Weltanschauung, at any given time. This is a hard saying, and one would gladly have it disproved, but the facts seem to me to point to this conclusion. The text, so often quoted wich such disgusting satisfaction by your "serve God and honour the King" type of Catholic, in refuting the honest pacifist; "the strong man armed" etc. has obviously this meaning, as also it complementary text, "they who take to the sword" etc. What is forgotten is that we all have taken to the sword in as far as we are national or cultural groups - it is a condition of our terrestrial existence. The throwing of stones is entirely ruled out. The whole lot of us live in houses made exclusively of glass.

If some of us in this country, being of a certain kind or class, are "free" in so many ways, and enjoy a humane and tolerant existence, are able to pursue our individual preferences to a remarkable degree, it is largely because our ancestors so

will excuse all the horrors connected with the establishment of the Soviet regime as necessary and is prepared to admit the necessity of such horrors in this country or elsewhere, for the realization of the Marxist dream.

So that we can reasonably reject the argument that the Axis Powers must be broken on account of their resort to violence and suppression. The truth seems to be that the kingdoms of this world use, mathematically almost, that amount of violence and suppression that is necessary to the establishment and defence of their particular Weltanschauung, at any given time. This is a hard saying, and one would gladly have it disproved, but the facts seem to me to point to this conclusion. The text, so often quoted with such disgusting satisfaction by your 'serve God and honour the King'[104] type of Catholic, in refuting the honest pacifist; 'the strong man armed' etc.[105] has obviously this meaning, as also it [sic] complementary text, 'they who take to the sword'[106] etc. What is forgotten is that we all have taken to the sword in as far as we are national or cultural groups – it is a condition of our territorial existence. The throwing of stones is entirely ruled out. The whole lot of us live in houses made exclusively of glass.

If some of us in this country, being of a certain kind or class, are 'free' in so many ways, and enjoy a humane and tolerant existence, are able to pursue our individual preferences to a remarkable degree, it is largely because our ancestors so

[104] A reference to both the Royal Navy's motto and its New Testament source, 1 Pet. 2.17.

[105] 'When the strong man fully armed guardeth his own court, his goods are in peace' (Lk. 11.21, KJV).

[106] 'Then saith Jesus unto him, Put up again thy sword into its place: for all they that take the sword shall perish with the sword' (Mt. 26.52, KJV).

13.

gathered the world's wealth, so established, by the application of armed and economic pressure, the British thing in the world, so set a bulwark of power round our pax - that we who can live, almost, the lives of pure spirits and have almost forgotten the hard, brutal, realistic, unscrupulous, spade-work that has made our humane and tolernnt virtues possible of growth. Within that established order it has been possible for the flowers of sophistication and refinement to grow. All this of the highest value, beauties otherwise unobtainable, and truths otherwise hidden have thus been discovered, but it would be extremely unintelligent of us (and a breach of the intelligence is the worst crime a sophisticated person can commit - intelligence is the one virtue such a person must possess, or lose all the purpose of his existence) not to see clearly that this "emancipated" world of ours has been historically made possible by acts of brutality and aggression, the destruction of cultures, the infliction of wrong. Impregnable defences have to be reared and brute force applied, it would seem, before the amiable, sensitized, individual, appreciative, humane type of human being, we regard as normal to our society, can begin to exit. It took a lot of gangster-work and breaking of heads and hearts to rear the stately homes of England, and you have to have a fairly large police force, I imagine, before it is possible for a neurotic aesthete, like myself, to exist at all. An incredible number of wolves heads have to be brought in tribute before the

gathered the world's wealth, so established,[107] by the application of armed and economic pressure, the British thing in the world, so set a bulwark of power round our pax – that we who can live, almost, the lives of pure sprits and have almost forgotten the hard, brutal, realistic, unscrupulous, spade-work that has made our humane and tolerant virtues possible of growth. Within that established order it has been possible for the flowers of sophistication and refinement to grow. All this of the highest value, beauties[108] otherwise unobtainable, and truths otherwise hidden have thus been discovered, but it would be extremely unintelligent of us (and a breach of the intelligence is the worst crime a sophisticated person can commit – intelligence is the one virtue such a person must possess, or lose all the purpose of his existence) not to see clearly that this 'emancipated' world of ours has been historically made possible by acts of brutality and aggression, the destruction of cultures, the infliction of wrong. Impregnable defences have to be reared and brute force applied, it would seem,[109] before the amiable, sensitized, individual, appreciative, humane type of human being, we regard as normal to our society, can begin to exit [sic]. It took a lot of gangster-work and breaking of heads and hearts to rear the stately homes of England, and you have to have a fairly large police force, I imagine, before it is possible for a neurotic aesthete, like myself, to exist at all. An incredible number of wolves heads have to be brought in tribute before the

[107] In BC 2: 'because our ancestors so gathered the world! Wealth, so established . . .'.
[108] In BC 2: 'Now, I regard all this of the highest value. Beauties . . .'.
[109] In BC 2: 'it would seem, in this world of ours, before'.

14.

S.P.C.A. can begin to prosecute. This is all obvious I expect, but so obvious as to be forgotten, the forgetting tends to self-righteousness and that to indignation and that to interference and disastrous action.

If one is aware, as is the writer of this letter, that one would quickly cease to exist in any but an highly sophisticated, sheltered, intelligent, and if you like, decadent, society; if one has a loathing for any other society, either Left or Right, that need not prevent one having one's eyes open to the real nature, the stark actualities that govern the kingdoms of this world and the glory of them. There remains the Kingdom of God. It is temerarious to judge, in that Kingdom, between the vices and virtues of the Frankish chiefs and virtues and vices of the citizens of Lutetia. Not that the present alignment in Europe correspond to civilized and uncivilized - it is far more complicated than that - but even if it were so, it would be well to pipe down as to the moral issue.

We are all "aggressive" or "peace-loving" as the necessity dictates. This is indicated in our time and among our friends, by those large number of sincere believers in peace pledges who now have changed their attitude as to the need for brute force. Should this conflict come, it will not be an affair of morals, or the defence of civilization or the punishment of an aggressor, but rather an affair of supposed necessity and struggle for survival. That is why a sceptical

S.P.C.A.[110] can begin to prosecute. This is all obvious I expect, but so obvious as to be forgotten, the forgetting tends to self-righteousness and that to indignation and that to interference and disastrous action.

If one is aware, as is the writer of this letter, that one would quickly cease to exist in any but an [sic] highly sophisticated, sheltered, intelligent, and if you like, decadent, society;[111] if one has a loathing for any other society, either Left or Right, that need not prevent one having one's eyes open to the real nature, the stark actualities[112] that govern the kingdoms of this world and the glory of them. There remains the Kingdom of God. It is temerarious to judge, in that Kingdom, between the vices and virtues of the Frankish chiefs and[113] [the] virtues and vices of the citizens of Lutetia.[114] Not that the present alignment in Europe correspond[s] to civilized and uncivilized – it is far more complicated than that – but even if it were so, it would be well to pipe down as to the moral issue.

We are all 'aggressive' or 'peace-loving' as the necessity dictates. This is indicated in our time and among our friends, by those large number of sincere believers in peace pledges who now have changed their attitude as to the need for brute force. Should this conflict come, it will not be an affair of morals, or the defence of civilization or the punishment of an aggressor, but rather an affair of supposed necessity and struggle for survival. That is why a sceptical

[110] Jones presumably means the R.S.P.C.A. (Royal Society for the Prevention of Cruelty to Animals). It was originally (1824) the S.P.C.A. but was granted royal status by Queen Victoria in 1840.

[111] In BC 2: 'If one is painfully aware, as is the writer of this letter, that one would quickly cease to exist in any other but a highly sophisticated, humane, sheltered, intelligent, if you like – decadent, society, and if . . .'.

[112] In BC 2: 'stark, brutal, necessities'.

[113] In BC 2 this phrase reads 'between the vices and virtues of the citizens of Lutetia'. The reference to the Frankish chiefs is absent from BC 2.

[114] Lutetia was a Gallo-Roman city that later became Paris. The Franks were a confederation of German tribes in Late Antiquity. Jones is suggesting that in the eyes of God there is no difference between the Germans (the Frankish chiefs) and the French (the citizens of Lutetia).

15.

attitude is necessary when any uplift is dragged into the argument. For any evil that war apologists can fling at the Axis Powers the Axis Powers can easily and justly retaliate.

If this catastrophe should occur with its miseries, and futilities, at least let us, sophisticated persons, not allow ourselves to suffer the final ignominy of being fooled as to the nature of it. If we are clerks, let us not commit the treason of clerks, who should bring even their own intelligences into subjection by allotting praise and blame when there is no conceivable means of examining the data upon which alone such judgment can rest - so vast and intricate and outside human volition is the whole thing. Heaven knows, "encouragement" will be necessary and dope in vast quantities, should it occur. But even those who are most fond of saying "Honour is more important than Peace" will admit that the greatest conceivable honour is to be found in that integrity of the mind, which stubbornly refuses to allot blame to either the bomb-droppers or those responsible for the bomb-dropping, when the causes of it all are as deep and complex and tangled as are the causes of all the great historic culture-struggles. And, as I say, the only consolation a miserable intellectual has is this possibility of refusing to allow the mind to be doped, whatever he may find is necessary or right to do with his body. It will no doubt be said that it would be more to the point to preach this kind of detachment in the dictator countries - and see where it landed one.

attitude is necessary when any uplift is dragged into the argument. For any evil that war apologists can fling at the Axis Powers the Axis Powers can easily and justly retaliate.

If this catastrophe should occur with its miseries, and futilities, at least let us, sophisticated persons, not allow ourselves to suffer the final ignominy of being fooled as to the nature of it.[115] If we are clerks, let us not commit the treason of clerks,[116] who should bring even their own intelligences into subjection by allotting praise and blame when there is no conceivable means of examining the data upon which alone such judgement can rest – so vast and intricate and outside human volition is the whole thing. Heaven knows, 'encouragement' will be necessary and dope in vast quantities, should it occur. But even those who are most fond of saying 'Honour is more important than Peace' will admit that the greatest conceivable honour is to be found in that integrity of the mind, which stubbornly refuses to allot blame to either the bomb-droppers or those responsible for the bomb-dropping, when the causes of it all are as deep and complex and tangled as are the causes of all the great historic culture-struggles. And, as I say, the only consolation a miserable intellectual has is this possibility of refusing to allow the mind to be doped, whatever he may find is necessary or right to do with his body. It will no doubt be said that it would be more to the point to preach this kind of detachment in the dictator countries – and see where it landed one.

---

[115] In BC 2: 'the nature of the affair'.

[116] A reference to the title of Julien Benda's book *La Trahison des Clercs* (Paris: Bernard Grasset, 1927), translated by Richard Aldington as *The Treason of the Intellectuals* (New York: William Morrow, 1928) and as *The Great Betrayal* (London: Routledge, 1928). Benda argued that French intellectuals of the day had betrayed the principles of reason and entered the political fray to support nationalism and militarism. Benda's work is often referred to in support of the opposite conclusion: that intellectuals have betrayed their calling by *not* entering the political fray and remaining locked in their ivory towers. Jones seems to be using the analogy in the sense originally intended by Benda. See Stefan Collini, *Absent Minds: Intellectuals in Britain* (Oxford: Oxford University Press, 2006), 279–300.

16.

But after all one can only properly understand the weaknesses of one's own group and is in any case only responsible to one's own group, and if free expression is as yet allowed us here, it is necessary to take advantage of it, moreover, the particular kind of attitude I am concerned with, is, I think it is true to say, actually more evident in the democracies than elsewhere. Herr Hitler, for instance, in his writings, for all his contempt of the "intellectual", less often offends the intelligence by giving uplift reasons for his political actions, than do his critics. His propaganda is easily recognisable as propaganda. His words constantly have an authentic ring, and correspond to the beastly actualities of this world and this world-order. Some say that that is because he is in league with the "cosmocrats of the dark aeon" and can make guile sound like the words of life. That apocalyptic view appears too partizan, too easy. I prefer : "Germany must export or die, Germany will not die" to: "Honour is above peace" - if it comes to knowing why one must be blown up.

The dictators use their own brands of high-falutin', bombastic, speciously idealistic language when they are up to their propaganda - but I think when they are seriously analysing a situation and formulating demands they are commonly more down to facts than is usually granted. Herr Hitler, certainly, in his last two important speeches has been very clear and intelligible, and considerate of historic realities (and also extremely interesting) in a way that is rarely known to our political leaders. For instance,

But after all one can only properly understand the weakness of one's own group and is in any case only responsible to one's own group, and if free expression is as yet allowed us here, it is necessary to take advantage of it, moreover, the particular[117] kind of attitude I am concerned with, is, I think it is true to say, actually more evident in the democracies than elsewhere. Herr Hitler, for instance, in his writings, for all his contempt of the 'intellectual', less often offends the intelligence by giving uplift [sic] reasons for his political actions, than do his critics. His propaganda is easily recognisable as propaganda.[118] His words constantly have an authentic ring, and correspond to the beastly actualities of this world and this world-order. Some say that that is because he is in league with the 'cosmocrats of the dark aeon'[119] and can make guile sound like the worlds of life. That apocalyptic view appears too partizan, too easy. I prefer :[120] 'Germany must export or die, Germany will not die' to: 'Honour is above peace' – if it comes to knowing why one must be blown up.

The dictators use their own brands of high-falutin', bombastic, speciously idealistic language[121] when they are up to their propaganda – but I think when they are seriously analysing a situation and formulating demands they are commonly more down to facts than is usually granted. Herr Hitler, certainly, in his last two important speeches has been very clear and intelligible, and considerate of historic realities (and also extremely interesting) in a way that is rarely known[122] to our political leaders. For instance,

---

[117] In BC 2, 'particular' is underlined.

[118] In BC 2 this sentence reads: 'His propaganda is not easily recognised as propaganda.' This is presumably a mistake, corrected for BC 1.

[119] 'Cosmocrats of the dark aeon' (Eph. 6.12) refers to powers which rule the world. Jones uses the phrase in his poem of 1941 (first published in 1973), 'The Narrows': 'Still more, and internecine too / when the cosmocrats of the dark aeon / find themselves / wholly at a loss / in the meandered labyrinth of / their own monopolies.' See David Jones, *The Roman Quarry and Other Sequences*, ed. Harman Grisewoood and René Hague (New York: Sheep Meadow Press, 1981), 62. The Catholic historian Christopher Dawson, a friend of Jones's, uses the phrase in a similar way in his book *The Dynamics of World History* (London: Sheed & Ward, 1956), 262–3: 'Human life is essentially a warfare against unknown powers — not merely against flesh and blood, which are themselves irrational enough, but against principalities and powers, against "the Cosmocrats of the Dark Aeon," to use St. Paul's strange and disturbing expression, powers which are more than rational and which make use of lower things, things below reason, in order to conquer and rule the world of man.' For more on Jones's and Dawson's use of the phrase, see Christine Pagnoulle, *David Jones: A Commentary on Some Poetic Fragments* (Cardiff: University of Wales Press, 1987), 33–4, where she quotes an essay by Dawson of 1930 that contains the phrase 'the world-rulers of the dark aeon'.

[120] In BC 2: 'too partizan, too easy, too self-righteous. I confess I prefer . . .'.

[121] In BC 2: 'No one would suggest that the dictators are backward in using their own brand of high falutin', bombastic, bogusly idealistic language . . .'.

[122] In BC 2: 'unknown'.

his elucidation of the position of Teutonic-Celtic peoples of the East Mark, from which he springs, in relation to the dynastic division called Austria, was of great interest, and explains, at least to me, a lot of things concerning the Anschluss. Similarly his explanation of the incorporation of Moravia and Bohemia in the Reich seemed reasonable enough, taking a long view. If the Welsh, for instance, can be said to be geographically, historically, economically, and politically part of the English sphere of control, the Czechs can equally be said to be, by the same accidents, part of the German sphere of control. If this seems far-fetched, it is only because we choose to apply different standards over this "sacredness of small nationalities" principle according to how it suits us and according to all kinds of necessities and accidents. That being so, we must not at the same moment be too shocked, as contemporary history makes itself, to find the pattern changing in accordance with changing actualities, as it did in the past.

To continue the analogy, had the Welsh preserved their Catholic religion, and some vestige of political integrity, and had they established a contact with Ireland, and some sort of connection with a continehtal power, France for instance, then, even today it might be necessary for England to argue that this situation must be liquidated (especially if there was a Skoda munition works at Neath and turbulent and discontended minorities appealing for

his elucidation of the position of Teutonic-Celtic peoples of the East Mark, from which he springs, in relation to the dynastic division called Austria, was of great interest, and explains, at least to me, a lot of things concerning the Anschluss. Similarly his explanation of the incorporation of Moravia and Bohemia in the Reich seemed reasonable enough, taking the long view. If the Welsh, for instance, can be said to be geographically, historically, economically, and politically part of the English sphere of control,[123] the Czechs can equally be said to be, by the same accidents, part of the German sphere of control. If this seems far-fetched, it is only because we choose to apply different standards over this 'sacredness of small nationalities' principle according to how it suits us and according to all kinds of necessities and accidents. That being so, we must not at the same moment be too shocked, as contemporary history makes itself, to find the pattern changing in accordance with changing actualities, as it did in the past.

To continue the analogy, had the Welsh preserved their Catholic religion, and some vestige of political integrity, and had they established a contact with Ireland, and some sort of connection with a continental power, France for instance, then, even today it might be necessary for England to argue that this situation must be liquidated (especially if there was a Skoda munition works at Neath[124] and turbulent and discontented minorities appealing for

[123] In BC 2: 'If the Welsh, for instance, are geographically, historically, economically, and politically part of the English sphere of control, as they undoubtedly are . . .'.

[124] The Skoda munitions works in Pilsen (Plzeň) was one of the largest in Europe and close to the border of the Sudentenland, the area of Czechoslovakia that Germany was allowed to annex under the terms of the Munich Agreement. Neath is a town in South Wales, at that time associated with heavy industry.

18.

protection against the Cardiff Government, in the Lleyn Peninsular and Anglesey, as there certainly would be. Geographical, historical, cultural, economic, political arguments would soon be found by the London Administration to explain the necessity of incorporating the Welsh people within the English lebensraum andsphere of control, and no amount of talk about the sacredness of nationality, coming, let us say, from an Italian theorist, would stop the English Government from acting according to the political and strategic necessities of the situation, more especially would this be so if the Welsh State were being used by the Irish, backed by the French, to undermine the prestige of England. It seems only by some such imaginary situation, in countries that we know as we know the palms of our own hands, can we be fair to foreign governments dealing with a state of affairs that we can at best only guess at, for all the broadcast talks on what it feels like to be a Pole or a Ukrainian, and for all the journalists who travel in, and report from, far countries, or for all the diplomats whose business it is to keep an eye on strategic positions, whether it be in Europe, Asia or the antipodes, nor for all the leaderwriters who would drag in Owain Glyndwr as easily as they dragged in Wenceslaus, and forgot them as easily as it suited their book. My point again is that it is unwise and irrelevant to raise the moral issue.

It is interesting to compare the contents of the telegram sent by the President of the United States with the reply to it from the Chancellor of the Reich. Even granting goodwill in the former, the latter disturbs the intelligence far less. One finds it difficult to know how

protection against the Cardiff Government, in the Lleyn Peninsular [sic] and Anglesey, as there certainly would be.)[125] Geographical, historical, cultural, economic, political arguments would soon be found by the London Administration to explain the necessity of incorporating the Welsh people within the English lebensraum and sphere of control, and no amount of talk about the sacredness of nationality, coming, let us say, from an Italian theorist, would stop the English Government from acting according to the political and strategic necessities of the situation, more especially would this be so if the Welsh State were being used by the Irish, backed by the French, to undermine the prestige of England. It seems only by some such imaginary situation, in countries that we know as we know the palms of our own hands, can we be fair to foreign governments dealing with a state of affairs that we can at best only guess at, for all the broadcast talks on what it feels like to be a Pole or a Ukrainian, and for all the journalists who travel in, and report from, far countries, or for all the diplomats whose business it is to keep an eye on strategic positions, whether it be in Europe, Asia or the antipodes, nor for all the leaderwriters who would drag in Owain Glyndwr as easily as they dragged in Wenceslaus, and forget them as easily as it suited their book.[126] My point again is that it is unwise and irrelevant to raise the moral issue.[127]

It is interesting to compare the contents of the telegram sent by the President of the United States with the reply to it from the Chancellor of the Reich.[128] Even granting goodwill in the former, the latter disturbs the intelligence far less. One finds it difficult to know how

[125] In BC 2: 'as there certainly would be!)'. I have added the right parenthesis, which is absent from BC 1 but present in BC 2. The Llyn (less commonly referred to as Lleyn) Peninsula and Anglesey are areas of north-west Wales, home to many who count Welsh as their first language.

[126] In BC 2: 'suited their work'. Owain Glyndwr (c. 1359–c. 1416) was the leader of a revolt against English authority in Wales. King Wenceslaus, often anglicized as Wenceslas, was referred to in British newspapers to underline the historical pedigree of Czechoslovakian national identity. There were a number of kings and dukes of Bohemia named Wenceslas or Wenceslaus and it is unclear which in particular either Jones or the newspapers were referring to. See, for example, 'Future of Bohemia', *The Times*, 17 March 1939, 18.

[127] In BC 2: 'fatal and stupid to raise the moral issue.'

[128] Roosevelt's telegram to Hitler, dated 14 April 1939, asks for assurances that Germany will not invade 'Finland, Estonia, Latvia, Lithuania, Sweden, Norway, Denmark, The Netherlands, Belgium, Great Britain and Ireland, France, Portugal, Spain, Switzerland, Liechtenstein, Luxemburg [sic], Poland, Hungary, Rumania, Yugoslavia, Russia, Bulgaria, Greece, Turkey, Iraq, the Arabias, Syria, Palestine, Egypt and Iran'. A reproduction of the original telegram is available online: http://www.fdrlibrary.marist.edu/daybyday/resource/april-1939-7/ (accessed 6 June 2017). The reply to which Jones refers is Hitler's speech to the Reichstag of 28 April 1939. A translated extract is available online: http://avalon.law.yale.edu/wwii/blbk13.asp (accessed 6 June 2017). This is the speech in which Hitler renounced the Anglo-German Naval Agreement of 18 June 1935.

19.

much the President's message was a truly genuine gesture of goodwill and desire for agreement and how much it was a veiled threat. Certainly it was a rebuke, even if it was a well-intentioned one, and to rebuke is seldom the best method of reaching reconciliation. However, one good thing has issued from this famous message and that is the extremely interesting, able, clear and reasoned reply from the Fuhrer; as Mr. Charles Roden Buxton points out in The Times of May 10th, that speech "quite obviously needs to be studied".

The press reception of it, and indeed the official reception of it, as far as one can judge from the remarks of ministers, has been profoundly disappointing. The press comments on the whole, after expressing some relief that "war was no nearer", confined themselves to generalization about "deeds not words" and how, anyway, it was useless to listen to what dictators had to say. There was no attempt whatever, that I saw, to carefully consider the Fuhrer's arguments, or even to pay proper tribute to mastery of the thing as a thing. You may say that this is no time to appreciate art works, and that if it was, that would have no bearing on the contents. I think that is a great mistake, for where there is order and sequence and power of expression there is probably something worth expressing - even if it comes from an enemy, and in this instance so far from being an enemy, the artist in question, protested, and has always protested, as clearly as a man could, his desire to be our friend (unless, of course, words mean absolutely nothing and white <u>is</u> black, once you have determined to give your whitish dog a black name, then, even a streak of grey is hardly admitted). That is the tragedy now. By a sort of

much the President's message was a truly genuine gesture of goodwill and desire for agreement and how much it was a veiled threat. Certainly it was a rebuke, even if it was a well-intentioned one, and to rebuke is seldom the best method of reaching reconciliation.[129] However, one good thing has issued from this famous message and that is the extremely interesting, able, clear and reasoned reply from the Fuhrer; as Mr. Charles Roden Buxton points out in The Times of May 10th, that speech 'quite obviously needs to be studied'.[130]

The press reception of it, and indeed the official reception of it, as far as one can judge from the remarks of ministers, has been profoundly disappointing. The press comments on the whole, after expressing some relief that 'war was no nearer', confined themselves to generalization about 'deeds not words' and how, anyway, it was useless to listen to what dictators had to say. There was no attempt whatever, that I saw, to carefully consider the Fuhrer's arguments, or even to pay proper tribute to mastery of the thing as a thing. You may say that this is no time to appreciate art works, and that if it was, that would have no bearing on the contents. I think that is a great mistake, for where there is order and sequence and power of expression there is probably something worth expressing – even if it comes from an enemy, and in this instance so far from being an enemy, the artist in question, protested, and has always protested, as clearly as a man could, his desire to be our friend (unless of course, words mean absolutely nothing and white <u>is</u> black, once you have determined to give your whitish dog a black name, then, even a streak of grey is hardly admitted). That is the tragedy now. By a sort of

[129] In BC 2: 'And to rebuke is hardly the best way of breaking a deadlock.'

[130] Charles Roden Buxton (1875–1942) was a Labour MP and advisor on foreign and imperial affairs. He was a campaigner for peace and believer that efforts should be made to answer German grievances. He was still campaigning for this as late as August 1939. Charles Roden Buxton's letter to *The Times* (Wednesday, 10 May 1939, 17) contains interesting echoes of Jones's arguments: 'Indeed, merely to wish to understand the Nazi attitude is to be called a "pro-Nazi." The charge is unpleasant, but that is a small sacrifice to make, when we consider the greatness of the cause we are serving – the cause of peace, the cause for which our friends died in the Great War.' According to Buxton's letter, the main reason Hitler's speech 'needs to be studied' is that 'it defines, in particular, more clearly than before, his conception of the German living space or *Lebensraum*. This is the vital issue, because on this depends the question whether German aims are limited or unlimited; and if the former, where the limit lies.'

alchemy of prejudice and fear every word and every deed, good, bad or indifferent, coming from the supposed enemy, is transmuted into a base thing. To question and mistrust the works of such alchemists is surely our duty.

In Miss Weston's book "From Ritual to Romance", where she is dealing with the Peredur story and the Waste Land, she says :

> "... the misfortunes and wasting of the land are the result of war, and directly caused by the hero's failure to ask the question".

"The Question" - the questions that need asking are many and urgent. Some of those questions are being asked in letters to "The Tablet" and in "The Tablet" Editorials. Mr. Christopher Dawson has asked them in full in his short but very important collection of writings called "Beyond Politics" (how differently might the public understand the present situation if they would read those essays) Viscount Lymington, Lord Ponsonby, Lord Rushcliffe, all in their own way are asking "the question".

It is to be hoped that more and more Englishmen will ask it so as, if possible to avoid the consequences of Peredur's silence at the court of the Lame King, in the presence of the dripping spear, so that all be not waste and ruin for lack of enquiry into causes.

David Jones.

May 11th, 1939.

alchemy of prejudice and fear every word and every deed, good, bad or indifferent, coming from the supposed enemy, is transmuted into a base thing. To question and mistrust the works of alchemists is surely our duty.

In Miss Weston's book 'From Ritual to Romance', where she is dealing with the Peredur story and the Waste Land, she says :

> '. . . the misfortunes and wasting of the land are the result of war, and directly caused by the hero's failure to ask the question'.[131]

'The Question' – the questions that need asking are many and urgent. Some of those questions are being asked in letters to 'The Tablet' and in 'The Tablet' Editorials. Mr. Christopher Dawson has asked them in full in his short but very important collection of writings called 'Beyond Politics'[132] (how differently might the public understand the present situation if they would read those essays) Viscount Lymington,[133] Lord Ponsonby,[134] Lord Rushcliffe,[135] all in their own way are asking 'the question'.

---

[131] Jessie L. Weston, *From Ritual to Romance* (Cambridge: Cambridge University Press, 1920), 21. Jones's copy of this edition, dated 1930, survives in his library. See Huw Ceiriog Jones, *The Library of David Jones*, 306.

[132] Christopher Dawson (1889–1970) was a cultural historian, friend of Jones, and author of many books, including *Progress and Religion* (London: Sheed & Ward, 1929) and *Religion and Culture* (London, Sheed & Ward, 1948). *Beyond Politics* (London: Sheed & Ward, 1939) is a critique of both democratic liberalism and the excesses of fascism. For a full discussion, see Tom Villis, *British Catholics and Fascism: Religious Identity and Political Extremism Between the Wars* (Basingstoke: Palgrave Macmillan, 2013), 114–16.

[133] Viscount Lymington (1898–1984), born Gerard Vernon Wallop, was a Conservative MP for Basingstoke (1929–34) and the head of two 'back to the land' English nationalist movements: the English Mistery (1930–6) and, from 1936, its successor, the English Array. He was also editor of the anti-Semitic and pro-German periodical the *New Pioneer* (1938–40). He founded the British Council Against European Commitments after the Munich crisis in 1938.

[134] Arthur Augustus William Harry Ponsonby (1871–1946), 1st Baron Ponsonby of Shulbrede, was a politician and peace campaigner. He was the Labour leader in the House of Lords from 1931 to 1935 and a prominent advocate of disarmament and supporter of appeasement.

[135] Henry Bucknall Betterton, Baron Rushcliffe (1872–1949), was a Conservative politician. He was appointed Minster for Labour in Ramsay MacDonald's National government in 1931. He held this post for three years and opposed Chamberlain's reform of unemployment relief (when Chamberlain was serving his second term as Chancellor of the Exchequer). He was on good terms with many in the Labour Party.

20.

alchemy of prejudice and fear every word and every deed, good, bad or indifferent, coming from the supposed enemy, is transmuted into a base thing. To question and mistrust the works of such alchemists is surely our duty.

In Miss Weston's book "From Ritual to Romance", where she is dealing with the Peredur story and the Waste Land, she says :

> "... the misfortunes and wasting of the land are the result of war, and directly caused by the hero's failure to ask the question".

"The Question" - the questions that need asking are many and urgent. Some of those questions are being asked in letters to "The Tablet" and in "The Tablet" Editorials. Mr. Christopher Dawson has asked them in full in his short but very important collection of writings called "Beyond Politics" (how differently might the public understand the present situation if they would read those essays) Viscount Lymington, Lord Ponsonby, Lord Rushcliffe, all in their own way are asking "the question".

It is to be hoped that more and more Englishmen will ask it so as, if possible to avoid the consequences of Peredur's silence at the court of the Lame King, in the presence of the dripping spear, so that all be not waste and ruin for lack of enquiry into causes.

David Jones.

May 11th, 1939.

[*Page 20 of 20*] (continued)

It is to be hoped that more and more Englishmen will ask it so as, if possible to avoid the consequences of Peredur's silence at the court of the Lame King, in the presence of the dripping spear, so that all be not waste and ruin for lack of enquiry into causes.[136]

David Jones.

May 11th, 1939.

[136] In BC 2 the final paragraph reads: 'It is to be hoped that more and more Englishmen will ask it so as, if possible, to avoid the consequences of Peredur's silence at the court of the Lame King, in the presence of the dripping shear [sic], so that all be not waste and ruin for lack of enquiry into causes. It might be well, in conclusion, to notice that the Holy Father, and indeed a succession of Pontiffs, has "asked the question". It is necessary in any quarrel, to be Socratic in this, to enquire all the time, to probe, to sabotage action, for men being what they are usually act with the utmost folly, and none so foolishly as those who think in themselves that they are righteous and despise others.' Peredur is the Welsh name of the Percival of Arthurian legend, possibly based on the unfinished Old French poem *Perceval* (c. 1181) by Chrétien de Troyes. According to the medieval romance story, Peredur must 'ask the question' that heals the land. In 'King Pellam's Launde', part four of *In Parenthesis*, Jones refers to the same episode at the end of the boast of Dai Greatcoat: 'You ought to ask: Why, / what is this, / what's the meaning of this. / Because you don't ask, / although the spear-shaft / drips, / there's neither steading – not a roof-tree[M].' See David Jones, *In Parenthesis* (London: Faber & Faber, 1937), 84. Jones adds an endnote which includes a quote from Lady Guest's 1877 edition of *The Mabinogion*: 'Cf. the Welsh *Percivale* story, *Peredur ap Evrawc:* "Peredur, I greet thee not, seeing that thou dost not merit it. Blind was fate in giving thee fame and favour. When thou wast in the Court of the Lame King, and didst see there the youth bearing the streaming spear, from the points of which were drops of blood flowing in streams, even to the hand of the youth, and many other wonders likewise, thou didst not enquire their meaning nor their cause. Hadst thou done so, the King would have been restored to health, and his dominions to peace. Whereas from henceforth, he will have to endure battles and conflicts, and his knights will perish, and wives will be widowed, and maidens will be left portionless, and all this is because of thee." See also Jessie Weston, *From Ritual to Romance*, ch. ii.' See Jones, *In Parenthesis*, 210. Jones refers to the same story in a footnote in the *The Anathemata*, 226, n. 1, this time quoting the 1949 translation of *The Mabinogion* by Gwyn Jones and Thomas Jones. The question refers to the cause of suffering: Jones believes that asking the right question can help restore life to the Waste Land and, by analogy, help avoid war in Europe.

CHAPTER THREE

David Jones, Essay on Gerard Manley Hopkins, c. 1968

THOMAS BERENATO

INTRODUCTION

A 're-cognition' in 'the exact sense of that word'

—David Jones's Unfinished Essay on Gerard Manley Hopkins

On 8 March, 1968, the British Jesuit journal *The Month* commissioned an essay from David Jones to join, in its July–August 1968 issue, a set of poems and prose-pieces commemorating the poet Gerard Manley Hopkins (1844–89) on the centenary of his entry into the Society of Jesus.[1] In his column introducing the issue, Peter Hebblethwaite, SJ, *The Month*'s editor, notes an additional anniversary that prompted the decision to give 'Homage to Hopkins' on this occasion: December 1968 was to mark the half-century since the publication of the first edition of Hopkins's *Poems*.[2] A search of *The Month*'s archive in London has failed to recover any further correspondence between Jones and its editors about his essay's origins or fate; in any case, no essay by Jones on Hopkins ever appeared

[1] *The Month*, New Series, 40, nos 1–2 (July–August 1968). A 'Homage to Hopkins' (the title on the cover) feature runs from p. 37 to p. 65, with contributions by Paul L. Mariani, Jean Mambrino, SJ (on whose association with Jones see below), Philip Hobsbaum, Elizabeth Jennings, John L'Heureux, SJ, and Ralph Wright, OSB. A copy of this issue is in David Jones's personal library now held at the National Library of Wales, Aberystwyth. See Huw Ceiriog Jones, *The Library of David Jones (1895–1974): A Catalogue* (Aberystwyth: National Library of Wales, 1995), 334. In a letter dated 8 March 1968, Peter Hebblethwaite, S.J., *The Month*'s editor, invited Jones to contribute 'a poem on this occasion or possibly a few paragraphs saying what Hopkins has meant to you. It does not have to be all incense.' He gives Jones the due-date of 15 May 1968. 'The fee would be a modest one of five guineas per poem or per page. This does not exclude subsequent publication of the Homage in pamphlet form.' Such 'subsequent publication' does not appear to have occurred. (See David Jones Papers, National Library of Wales, Aberystwyth, folder CT4/16, item 109.)

[2] *The Month*, 3. Hebblethwaite's 'Letter from the Editor' is the issue's opening item, 3–4: 'A hundred years after Hopkins' entry into the Society of Jesus, our contributors pay tribute to him. The range is wide, from meticulous scholarship to personal, uninhibited response.' Famously, *The Month* had in 1876 rejected Hopkins's ode *The Wreck of the Deutschland*. Robert Bridges, born in Walmer, Kent, in 1844, was a friend of Hopkins's since their Oxford days. As Hopkins's de facto literary executor and, from 25 July 1913 to his death on 21 April 1930, Britain's Poet Laureate, Bridges took charge of Hopkins's posthumous publication, culminating in *Poems of Gerard Manley Hopkins, now first published, Edited with notes by Robert Bridges, Poet Laureate* (London: Humphrey Milford, printed at the Oxford University Press, 1918). This book was published in December 1918 in an edition of 750 copies, which did not sell out until 1928. See Tom Dunne, *Gerard Manley Hopkins: A Comprehensive Bibliography* (London: Oxford University Press at the Clarendon Press, 1976), 14.

in *The Month*.[3] The magazine's summer double number did include a nine-line lyric by the French poet Jean Mambrino, SJ, 'Le Coeur de Temps', accompanied by an English version attributed there to Jones, who is also the poem's dedicatee.[4] The issue's leading book review was of Pierre Teilhard de Chardin's *Writings in Time of War* (London: Collins, 1968), a volume translated by Jones's friend René Hague.[5] Thomas Corbishley, SJ, another of *The Month*'s editors, is the author of this review, in which he draws particular attention to Teilhard's essay therein on a subject of intense interest to Jones: 'The Eternal Feminine', written in Verzy, France, near Reims, in late March 1918, within days of both the beginning of the German Spring Offensive and the end of Jones's combat service.[6] Jamie Callison has uncovered a manuscript fair copy of Jones's translation of Mambrino's 'The Heart of Time' that, unlike *The Month*'s version (whose French title is not rendered into English), includes acute accent-marks over certain syllables – a practice that Jones had introduced into his printed poetry with *The Anathemata* (1952) and may well have picked up from Hopkins, a few of whose own manuscript accents are reproduced in the second edition of his *Poems*, prepared by the Inkling Charles Williams for Oxford University Press in November 1930, a book that Jones received that year for Christmas from his father.[7]

---

[3] Thanks to Rebecca Somerset, Province Archivist at the Archives of the Jesuits in Britain, 114 Mount Street, London W1K 3AH, for performing the search on site, 1–7 July 2016. In a letter to Jones dated 4 June 1968, Gilbert Inglefield, the Lord Mayor of London, notified Jones that he had been awarded the first Midsummer Prize of the City of London. In a draft reply of 8 June 1968, Jones declined to receive the prize in person at the ceremony scheduled for 25 June: 'There is one thing which I must mention, though not easy to say. It is that I may be unable to be present at the Midsummer Banquet at the Mansion House. For many years I have suffered from what used to be called "nervous breakdown". I've been a very great deal better over the last ten years but quite latterly I've had something of a return of it. Not anything like as bad as it once was, but I'm in the doctor's hands and never know how I shall be. It is an awful nuisance and embarrassment and prevents my doing many things – but I had to mention this to you.' See David Jones Papers, National Library of Wales, Aberystwyth, folder CT4/17. A letter from Jones to Jim Ede dated 21 February 1970 confirms that he did not attend the Mansion House Banquet: 'No, I wasn't up to that, they most kindly sent me the prize and indeed were extremely understanding about my not being there to receive it in person – though I felt pretty awful about not being able to go.' See Papers of Harold Stanley 'Jim' Ede, Kettle's Yard Museum and Art Gallery, University of Cambridge, GB 1759 KY/EDE/1/8/1/119, and David Jones, 'Letters to H. S. Ede', selected and ed. John Matthias, *PN Review* 22, vol. 8, no. 2 (November–December 1981): 16. Thanks to Oliver Bevington for providing this information from the archive (email of 4 July 2016). One of the 'many things' which the state of Jones's health at this time may have prevented him from completing is the essay on Hopkins for *The Month*.

[4] *The Month*, 45. Mambrino's three-stanza, nine-line poem, 'Le Coeur du Temps', is tagged under its title here 'à David Jones'. Below the poem, which is in French, is a three-stanza, nine-line English version printed in italic type. At the bottom of this is the label '*Translated by* DAVID JONES'. See below for more information about this curious page, across the footer of which awkwardly spill the notes from the previous page's scholarly article by Paul Mariani on Hopkins's sonnet 'Harry Ploughman'.

[5] *The Month*, 86–7. Three years later Hague would publish an English translation of Henri de Lubac's book-length study of Teilhard's text 'The Eternal Feminine': Henri de Lubac, *The Eternal Feminine: A Study on the Text of Teilhard de Chardin, followed by Teilhard and the Problems of Today*, trans. René Hague (London: Collins, 1971).

[6] Pierre Teilhard de Chardin, *Writings in a Time of War* (London: Collins, 1968), 191 and 202, where the text is datelined '*Verzy – 19–25 March 1918*'. Thomas Dilworth, in his *David Jones in the Great War* (London: Enitharmon, 2012), 187, gives the approximate date of Jones's final departure from the French front: '21 March [1918], a few days after his evacuation to England' (to recover from a debilitating fever he had developed in mid-February) from his position near Armentières, about 150 miles north-west of Verzy. See Dilworth, *David Jones in the Great War*, 185.

[7] See Jamie Callison, '"The Heart of Time" Revisited: A New Translation by David Jones', *PN Review* 42, no. 2 (November–December 2015): 11–14. Callison's transcription of the manuscript (reproduced in facsimile in his report) follows the lineation that Jones indicates there with red solidi, but it does not include or otherwise account for Jones's accent-marks. For an instance of accent-marks typographically reproduced in the earliest edition of Hopkins's poems known to belong to Jones, see *Poems of Gerard Manley Hopkins, edited with notes*

Manuscript drafts of Jones's essay on Hopkins survive on fifty-four unlined foolscap folio sheets (8.0 x 13.0 inches) now on deposit in the John J. Burns Library at Boston College, Chestnut Hill, Massachusetts.[8] Internal evidence suggests that Jones still had his drafts of the essay to hand in late May 1968. At the bottom of the same page of the manuscript on which he compares Hopkins's poems to a time-fused hand grenade, Jones drafts a letter in reply to one 'Mr. Billcliffe', who had written to ask about a watercolour drawing of Jones's from 1931.[9] The addressee is Roger Billcliffe, at the time of Jones's writing Assistant Keeper of British Art at the Walker Art Gallery, Liverpool, which owned the artwork.[10] The Walker's archive holds the letter Jones sent; it is dated 22 May 1968. On another page of the manuscript Jones has drafted what he labels a 'Greetings telegram' to a 'Mrs George Hyne', his older sister Alice (1891–1974).[11] 'Happy Day', Jones writes there. If he was composing a birthday greeting, this page, at least, can be dated to on or about 29 April – of which year, it remains uncertain.[12] The bottom of another page

---

by Robert Bridges, second edition, with an index of additional poems, and a critical introduction by Charles Williams (London: Humphrey Milford, Oxford University Press, 1930), 30–1. Jones uses accent-marks to guide recitation notably in *The Anathemata* (London: Faber & Faber, 1952), 103, lines 13–17. Page 238, n. 6 of *The Anathemata* cites a word, inflected by an umlaut, from line 2 of Hopkins's 'terrible' sonnet of 1885, 'I wake and feel the fell of dark not day': 'hoürs'. This diacritic appears over this vowel in the second edition of Hopkins's *Poems*, 65, to which Jones probably referred when writing his poem. In a letter to his friend Harman Grisewood of Christmas Day 1930, addressed from his parents' home at 115 Howson Road, Brockley, Kent, Jones writes: 'My father gave me Gerard Manley Hopkins's poems for Christmas – for which I am delighted.' See David Jones, *Dai Greatcoat: A Self-portrait of David Jones in his Letters*, ed. René Hague (London: Faber & Faber, 1980), 47. Jones refers there to Charles Williams's second edition of Hopkins's *Poems*, published in November 1930. See Huw Ceiriog Jones, *The Library of David Jones*, 140, which reports that one of the two copies of this book in Jones's library is dated 'Christmas 1930' and that it bears an 'autograph dedication to David Jones from his father'.

[8] 'Hopkins Essay Draft', Box 2, Folder 2/7, David Jones Papers (MS1986.001), John J. Burns Library, Boston College. On most sheets of the manuscript is clearly visible the watermark 'DEVON VALLEY / PARCHMENT'. The Burns Library's finding aid for the David Jones Papers, revised in July 1994 by Mark Roskoski, gives the accession date of the Jones collection as 'prior to 1986'. The now-defunct Serendipity Books, Berkeley, California, is listed as the collection's 'source'. No other information about its provenance is indicated. The cataloguers do not attempt to date the composition of Jones's Hopkins essay drafts in this finding aid. Thanks to Katherine Fox, the Burns Library's Head of Public Services and Engagement, and the other members of the Library's staff, especially Andrew Isidoro.

[9] See the manuscript facsimile in the edition p. 202 below. Jones refers there to the 'Mark I Hopkins grenade'. Compare Jones's letter to Saunders Lewis of 23 April 1971, published in *Agenda* 11, no. 4–12, no. 1 (Autumn–Winter 1973–4): 24: 'things, maybe happening or places or things said, hardly register at the time, but rather like projectiles that penetrate the earth but are fused to explode some time after, so things I've chanced to experience or gaze upon don't *usually* move me at the time, but sometime afterwards, I find, continuously occupy my thoughts.'

[10] Thanks to Alex Patterson, Assistant Curator (Fine Art), Art Galleries, National Museums Liverpool, Walker Art Gallery, William Brown Street, Liverpool L3 8EL, for locating the letters (search conducted 14–15 July 2016). The letters are held in the Walker's object file for Jones's *Panthers*, pencil and watercolour on paper, signed 1931 (Walker inventory number 1253). Thanks also to Roger Billcliffe, now of Roger Billcliffe Gallery, Blythswood Street, Glasgow G2 4EL, UK, for confirmation in an email of 29 June 2016 of his 1968 correspondence with Jones.

[11] See the manuscript facsimile, p. 186 below. Thanks to Sarah Williams, granddaughter of Alice Mary Hyne (née Jones) and a trustee of the David Jones Estate, for confirming information about the Jones and Hyne families.

[12] See the manuscript facsimile, p. 186 below. Alice Mary Jones was born on 29 April 1891. In his biography of Jones, Thomas Dilworth reports that on 14 April 1967 Jones attended a party for Alice's fiftieth wedding anniversary (George and Alice married on 14 April 1917 at St James' Hatcham). See Thomas Dilworth, *David Jones: Engraver, Soldier, Painter, Poet* (London: Jonathan Cape, 2017), 337.

contains a greeting, in Welsh, 'to the Lord and Lady Rhŷs from David Jones'.[13] Just below this, apparently associated with it, is a date, also in Welsh: Thursday, 16 May 1968. (Jones gives the year in Roman numerals.)[14] Next to a grocery list on another page of the manuscript Jones has written another date: 17 December 1968.[15] It would seem that six months later he had these drafts ready to hand among his papers in his room at the Monksdene Hotel, Harrow, where he had been lodging since April 1964.[16]

Part of a draft or copy of a letter, very probably to Jones's friend and patron the art historian and curator Kenneth Clark (1903–83), is also included in the manuscript.[17] The fragment opens with a brief remark about Hopkins's small but consistently impressive corpus. Jones compares it to the 'vast output' of the painter J. M. W. Turner, of whom he conceives, in contrast to the supremely 'vocational' artist Hopkins, as a consummate 'professional'.[18] After a digression on Dürer, Jones brings up 'that forthcoming issue of *Agenda*', by which, it soon becomes clear, he refers to the Spring–Summer 1967 special issue devoted to his own work.[19] In a draft letter to Clark in the archive at the National Library of Wales dated 3 April 1967, Jones writes that he has just submitted corrections to the proofs of the 1967 special issue and that it is now in the hands of the printers.[20] In

[13] Thanks to Thomas Dilworth and Paul Robichaud for fielding inquiries about the appearance of these names here and to Paul Robichaud for translations of Jones's Welsh. 'Lord and Lady Rhŷs' could designate the Welsh prince Rhys ap Gruffydd (1132–97), traditionally referred to as 'the Lord Rhys', and his wife Gwenllian ferch Madog. Rhys ap Gruffydd was ruler of the southern Welsh kingdom of Deheubarth and, from 1163, ally of Henry II of England until the latter's death in 1189. See John Davies, *A History of Wales*, rev. edn (London: Penguin, 2007), 122–5. Davies, 125, notes that 'Rhys ap Gruffydd was referred to on occasion as *proprietarius princeps Sudwalliae* (the proprietory [sic] prince of south Wales)'. 'Lord and Lady Rhŷs' could also refer to Richard Charles Uryan Rhys, 9th Baron Dynevor (19 June 1935–12 November 2008) and his wife, Lucy Catherine King Rothenstein (16 October 1934–). They wed on 7 January 1959, and she was styled Lady Dynevor of Dynevor from 1962 until the marriage was dissolved in 1978. The couple's only son, Hugo Griffith Uryan Rhys, 10th Baron Dynevor, was born on 19 November 1966. Richard Rhys's Black Raven Press published Peter Levi's poetry collection *Fresh Water, Sea Water* in 1966 with Jones's painted inscription *Extensis manibus* (made for Levi's ordination in 1964) reproduced on its cover. Thanks to Sarah Rhys and Ceridwen Lloyd-Morgan for this information.

[14] See the manuscript facsimile, p. 252 below.

[15] See the manuscript facsimile, p. 250 below.

[16] See Hague's note on Jones's lodgings, *Dai Greatcoat*, 201.

[17] See the manuscript facsimile, pp. 258–66 below. Thanks to Paul Hills for help identifying Clark as the addressee of this letter.

[18] See the manuscript facsimile, pp. 258–60 below. Jones esteemed Turner highest among British painters. See David Jones, *David Jones: Letters to a Friend*, ed. Aneirin Talfan Davies (Swansea: Triskele, 1980), 15.

[19] *Agenda* 5, nos 1–3 (Spring–Summer 1967). This was *Agenda*'s first 'David Jones Special Issue'. A second appeared during Jones's lifetime: *Agenda* 11, no. 4–12, no. 1 (Autumn–Winter 1973–4). For a history of Jones's association with *Agenda*, see Tom Dilworth, 'William Cookson, David Jones, and *Agenda*', *Agenda* 48, nos 3–4 (11 November 2014): 9–12.

[20] David Jones Papers, National Library of Wales, Aberystwyth, folder CF1/5. The final version of this letter, the one Jones sent, is in the Clark papers at the Tate Gallery Archive, London. For an annotated transcription, see Thomas Dilworth, 'Letters from David Jones to Kenneth Clark', *Burlington Magazine* 142, no. 1165 (April 2000): 215–25, where this letter of 3 April 1967 appears on pp. 224–5. On p. 225, at the end of his transcription of the letter, Dilworth notes, 'Here the letter breaks off, presumably before a last page on which Jones would have signed off, as usual, "Yours ever David".' The three pages of the unaddressed, unsigned, undated, and incomplete draft letter preserved with the Hopkins essay drafts are almost certainly Jones's draft or copy of the missing 'last page' that Dilworth presumes here. On p. 225, at the end of the letter as Dilworth has transcribed it, Jones is discussing 'how *terribly few* works by *some* artists are right on the bull's eye – the rest are "outers" or not on the target at all. And this *seems* to be true of some really great artists as well as lesser ones. Consider Coleridge – precious little, considering his greatness, apart from the *Ancient Mariner*, *Christobel* [sic] (& that not complete), the tiny fragment *Kubla Khan* & a few others but considering how great he was, it's a bit surprising there is not more of what the Welsh call *O'r gorau* – meaning "indisputably O.K". [sic] literally "of the best".' The draft letter included with the Hopkins essay manuscript opens, 'Then there's the other sort of chap, of which, I (personally) think G. M. Hopkins is a shining example. Not a large output, but practically *all* bloody good.' See the manuscript facsimile, pp. 258–60 below.

another letter in the National Library, dated 9 October 1966, Jones thanks Clark for agreeing to write 'a thing about my stuff' for the *Agenda* issue (which 'thing' was to be published there as an essay entitled 'Some Recent Paintings of David Jones')[21] and for sending him a copy of his new book *Rembrandt and the Italian Renaissance*.[22] 'Perhaps, as with Rembrandt, you may be able to help me appreciate him, Dürer, better,' Jones writes in the draft letter included with the Hopkins manuscript.[23] If Jones refers here to Clark's 1966 book on Rembrandt – based on lectures he delivered at the Metropolitan Museum of Art, New York, in April 1964 – this page of the manuscript must have been written between the autumn of 1966, when Clark's book was published, and early June 1967, when the *Agenda* issue had been printed.[24]

The draft letter's chronological relationship to the rest of the manuscript is more difficult to determine. Jones may have written it before he began the essay on Hopkins and have returned to it for inspiration when he accepted the assignment from *The Month*, or he may have worked on the essay and letter simultaneously. The letter includes in its margins a sidebar, inserted in green ink, retailing 'a rather amusing anecdote touching Hopkins'.[25] It is a tale that Jones had also told to his friend the Welsh poet and critic Aneirin Talfan Davies (1909–80) in a letter of November 1962.[26] Its upshot is that on his very first hearing of Hopkins's verse, around 1926 or 1927, Jones had intuited an affinity in it with the Welsh language and Welsh prosody.[27] Nowhere in this letter does Jones mention his essay for *The Month*, which very well may not yet have been solicited. But the 'amusing anecdote' also appears in the body of the essay draft itself.[28] William Blissett records the outlines of a conversation of 25 September 1970 in which Jones retells the anecdote, and Thomas Dilworth, writing in 1985, reports hearing it as well, although he does not say when.[29]

Between November 1966 and April 1967 Jones was sweating over 'The Sleeping Lord', which he raced to finish in time for the *Agenda* special issue.[30] His idea of Hopkins

---

[21] See *Agenda* 5, nos 1–3 (Spring–Summer 1967): 97–100.

[22] David Jones Papers, National Library of Wales, Aberystwyth, folder CF1/5. See Kenneth Clark, *Rembrandt and the Italian Renaissance* (London: Murray, 1966). On the biographical context of this book, see James Stourton, *Kenneth Clark: Life, Art, Civilisation* (London: Collins, 2016), 267–8.

[23] See the manuscript facsimile, p. 260 below.

[24] See William Blissett, *The Long Conversation: A Memoir of David Jones* (London: Oxford University Press, 1981), 47, which quotes a letter from Jones dated 11–12 June 1967 and postmarked 18 June 1967: 'The issue of *Agenda* is just, this day, ready all printed & fixed for distribution – so you'll see a copy soon, all being well.'

[25] See the manuscript facsimile, p. 262 below.

[26] Jones, *David Jones: Letters to a Friend*, 79.

[27] On Hopkins's endeavour to learn Welsh language and prosody, see Norman White, *Gerard Manley Hopkins in Wales* (Bridgend: Seren, 1998). In his essay 'David Jones and Gerard Manley Hopkins', in Richard F. Giles (ed.), *Hopkins Among the Poets: Studies in Modern Responses to Gerard Manley Hopkins* (Hamilton, Ontario: International Hopkins Association, 1985), 54, Thomas Dilworth reports that when Jones first encountered Hopkins's work he, Jones, 'was already familiar with the Middle Welsh and later Welsh poetry that had strongly influenced Hopkins' and that Jones had started teaching himself Welsh 'in 1910, at the age of sixteen'. See also the letter to Aneirin Talfan Davies of 27 November 1962, in Jones, *David Jones: Letters to a Friend*, 78–91, which constitutes perhaps the most sustained treatment in prose of the ideas that Jones would return to in the Hopkins essay a few years later.

[28] See the manuscript facsimile, pp. 174, 176, 196, 198, 228, and 234 below.

[29] Blissett, *The Long Conversation*, 59; Dilworth, 'David Jones and Gerard Manley Hopkins', 54.

[30] In a letter to William Blissett dated 16 May 1967, reproduced in Blissett, *The Long Conversation*, 40, Jones writes of 'a new and longer fragment which I've been working on during most of the time from last November to this March or April'. This is 'The Sleeping Lord', his headnote to the first publication of which in the first *Agenda* special issue Jones dates 'April the 1st, 1967'. See *Agenda* 5, nos 1–3 (Spring–Summer 1967): 28. On p. 54 of this issue Jones dates the poem itself in a tag following its final line: '1966–7 incorporating a small proportion of earlier material'.

as it emerges in the essay for *The Month* over the following year corresponds to the Christ–Arthur archetype elaborated in this latest poetic fragment. The poem – rhetorically interrogative throughout – ends with the question, 'Does the land wait the sleeping lord / or is the wasted land / that very lord who sleeps?'[31] This is of course a leading question. The parallelism of 'the sleeping lord' and 'the wasted land' formally enforces the equation in question. But the solution is premature as long as the slant rhyme of 'wait' and 'waste' remains unresolved. The question as posed hangs on the page, giving rise to the unprinted, perhaps unprintable, question of what is to be done until 'land' and 'lord' awake as one. Jones does in fact print this question elsewhere, in the first line of his poem 'A, a, a, Domine Deus', first published in a partial and at the time still untitled version (designated by Jones as 'fragments of a fragment abandoned in *c.* 1938') at the end of his major essay of 1953–4, 'Art and Sacrament',[32] and then as the first item in the 1967 *Agenda* special issue, where it has acquired a coda in prose and the additional date of 1966.[33] The question in both places runs, 'what shall I write?'[34] In these four words lies coiled a series of questions concerning what Jones was fond of calling his 'situation' as a poet.[35] 'In my view the most we can do is to ask questions concerning a situation' Jones writes near the end of 'Art and Sacrament'.[36] The 'most' for Jones is also a 'must', and it is a big ask. The situation is one of 'divorce', 'dichotomy', and 'dilemma'.[37] Man is himself the 'wedding' of what Jones terms the 'utile' and the 'sacramental', but this marriage is, in the modern age, on the rocks.[38] The state of the union is, in other words, now open to question, and it is the artist's particular task to take charge of the interrogation in the interest of its object's health. To shirk the question is to forfeit the opportunity of officiating a remarriage on which the very survival of human culture depends.

The high stakes of the question – 'what shall I write?' – are indicated by Karl Barth in an address delivered in July 1922 under the title 'The Need and Promise of Christian Preaching'.[39] There Barth poses what he calls 'the minister's question' before an audience

---

[31] *Agenda* 5, nos 1–3 (Spring–Summer 1967): 54.

[32] David Jones, 'Art and Sacrament: An Enquiry Concerning the Arts of Man and the Christian Commitment to Sacrament in Relation to Contemporary Technocracy', in Elizabeth Pakenham (ed.), *Catholic Approaches* (London: Weidenfeld & Nicolson, 1955), 181. On p. 182 of this volume Jones dates the composition of his essay 'Oct. 1953–Jan. 1954'. A revised version appears in David Jones, *Epoch and Artist* (London: Faber & Faber, 1959), 143–79. This is Jones's major prose statement of his theological aesthetics. Compare the end of Jones's broadcast talk dated 24 March 1962, 'Use and Sign', in David Jones, *The Dying Gaul and Other Writings*, ed. Harman Grisewood (London: Faber & Faber, 1978), 184: 'And what little I have said here is meant as a kind of question. A question to which I do not know the answer and which perturbs me all the day long.' On the following page Jones goes on to compare the consequences of Peredur's failure to ask the question to the psychoanalytic 'commonplace . . . that the obsessions of the fathers condition the children'. This suggests that for Jones the scene of interrogation is analogous to the analytic situation.

[33] *Agenda* 5, nos 1–3 (Spring–Summer 1967): 5. This page presents the first item of the special issue after the front matter, a version of Jones's short lyric '*A, a, a, DOMINE DEUS*', as he entitles it here. What Douglas Cleverdon calls 'the first complete printing' of this poem appeared in a sixteen-page Christmas (1966) supplement of the Poetry Book Society edited by Eric W. White. For a description of this item see Douglas Cleverdon (ed.), *Word and Image IV: David Jones* (London: National Book League, 1972), 57.

[34] *Agenda* 5, nos 1–3 (Spring–Summer 1967): 5.

[35] Jones, 'Art and Sacrament', *Catholic Approaches*, 179.

[36] Jones, 'Art and Sacrament', *Catholic Approaches*, 179.

[37] Jones, 'Art and Sacrament', *Catholic Approaches*, 178–9.

[38] Jones, 'Art and Sacrament', *Catholic Approaches*, 179.

[39] Karl Barth, 'The Need and Promise of Christian Preaching', in Karl Barth, *The Word of God and the Word of Man*, trans. with a new foreword by Douglas Horton (New York: Harper & Row, 1957), 97–135. A footnote on p. 97 reports, 'This address was delivered at a Ministers' Meeting in Schulpforta in July, 1922.'

of clergymen: 'What is preaching? – not How *does* one do it? but How *can* one do it?'[40] Along Barth's lines Jones's question might be reformulated: not *what* shall I write, but *what can it mean* to write in an age for which the very possibility of the meaningfulness of any act of signification is no longer to be taken for granted?[41] This is the 'meaning' of the question the demand for which Jones puts in the mouth of Dai Greatcoat at the end of his long boast in 'Part 4' of *In Parenthesis*: 'You ought to ask: Why, / what is this, what's the meaning of this.'[42] And it is the question that the editors of *The Month* apparently asked Jones to ask apropos of Gerard Manley Hopkins, under the sign of 'homage'. Jones meets this challenge on etymological grounds. To pay homage (the Old English *manred*)[43] to someone means, for Jones, to acknowledge his essential 'manliness', and in the case of the *makar* (as Jones dubs him here)[44] Manley Hopkins, 'manley-ness' means one's life in art, or, as Jones puts it, in *poiesis*.[45] What does it mean for man – a man – to be a maker? To ask this question is, like the making of homage, an obligation. 'You ought to ask' it because the meaningfulness of all you do or say owes everything to the fact that you *can* ask it in the first place and, in the act of asking it, make meaning at all.

Jones admits as much on the first page of his manuscript when he warns that we must not 'take Hopkins for granted'.[46] To do so 'would be most unfortunate; it would indeed make void and cancell [sic] out his ever having become accepted and made available'.[47] To avoid asking the question ever anew – to take it always as already asked – is to fail to do homage to the memory of making that constitutes culture. To ask a question in this sense is what Martin Heidegger means when, at the end of an essay first published in 1954, he calls questioning 'the piety of thought'.[48] The 'piety' in question is in the nature of an obeisance, and what is to be obeyed is the call to questioning that a work of art or a life in art issues. Charles O. Hartman has defined a poem as 'the language of an act of attention'.[49] A poem is a 'matrix' in which a poet's act of attention occasions a

---

[40] Barth, 'The Need and Promise of Christian Preaching', 103.

[41] In a letter to Harman Grisewood of 4 September 1971, in Jones, *Dai Greatcoat*, 232–3, Jones writes of 'this extremely difficult question concerning man's innate and million-years' habit of making inutile acts': 'Do you think, the main reason for any lack of comprehension of our question is that it is so taken for granted that men make *signa* that it's futile to say, for instance, that the Church can't have seven Sacraments with a cap "S" unless man is a user of sign and sacrament with a small "s" – they say, Well, of course man is a maker and user of *signa* with a small "s" – but they *don't seem to have grasped the actual situational fact* that technological man is fast losing that habit of thought, or at *every* level the capacity to understand what one is talking about.' See below for a discussion of Jones's phrase 'taken for granted'.

[42] David Jones, *In Parenthesis* (London: Faber & Faber, 1937), 84.

[43] See 'manred, n.', *OED Online*, Oxford University Press. Available at http://www.oed.com/Entry/113639 (accessed 13 December 2016).

[44] See for instance the manuscript facsimile, p. 126 below.

[45] See for instance the manuscript facsimile, p. 166 below.

[46] See the manuscript facsimile, p. 126 below.

[47] See the manuscript facsimile, p. 126 below.

[48] Martin Heidegger, 'The Question Concerning Technology', in Martin Heidegger, *The Question Concerning Technology and Other Essays*, trans. and intro. William Lovitt (New York and London: Garland, 1977), 35. Heidegger's essay, whose origins lie in a series of lectures first delivered in Bremen in December 1949, was first published in German in 1954, in English in 1977. See Albert Borgmann, 'Technology', in Hubert L. Dreyfus and Mark A. Wrathall (eds), *A Companion to Heidegger* (Oxford: Blackwell, 2005), 428. The connection between Jones's 'question' and Heidegger's deserves fuller treatment than possible here, as does the resonance of Heidegger's concept of 'the turning' (*Die Kehre*) with Jones's notion that the artist in making an effective sign 'turns a hard corner', on which see Jones, *Dai Greatcoat*, 233, n. 9.

[49] Charles O. Hartman, *Free Verse: An Essay on Prosody* (Princeton, NJ: Princeton University Press, 1980), 12. Hartman discusses the relationship of Hopkins's 'sprung rhythm' to 'free verse' but does not mention Jones.

reader's corresponding act of attention.[50] Jones's act of homage strives to illuminate the lineaments of that poetic matrix in which he discovers himself to be Hopkins's sibling. The matrix – *poiesis* as such – is a historical 'situation'. It exists in time as well as space, and its unique configuration along these two axes is Jones's chief object of attention in this essay.

Jones writes that Hopkins's lifework 'is of that sort which prompts, goads, alerts'.[51] It 'requires us to "ask the question"', he says, recurring to a favorite motif of his from one account of the Fisher King tale, the *Peredur* story of the *Mabinogion* as told, perhaps, by Jessie Weston in the second chapter of *From Ritual to Romance*, a book that Jones later claimed to have known before he read *The Waste Land*.[52] Weston understands the hero's failure to ask the question ('to enquire the meaning of what he sees') to be, in *Peredur ap Evrawc*, the direct cause of the general vastation that ensues upon the hero's visit to the Castle of Wonders, whereas before the encounter misfortune had been restricted to the body of the king.[53] By 'asking the question' Jones unmistakably means the initiation of a diagnostic process. He concedes that posing a question does not amount to arriving at a cure – he 'does not suppose that in asking the question the land can be "restored"' – but it is a necessary first move if such restoration is to be seriously pursued and soberly hoped for.[54] Articulating the question can inspire others to ask it in turn, and 'if all the world asked the question perhaps there might be some fructification – or some "sea-change"'.[55] When Jones says that 'Hopkins requires us to "ask the question"' he has this catalytic quality of Hopkins's work in mind.[56]

Finding the right words for this phenomenon is one of Jones's preoccupations in these drafts. In one of the more fully realized movements of the manuscript he adduces the testimony of a contemporary: 'He [Hopkins] chanced to be one of those sorts of "makaris" whose making has a quality which conditions the works of those who come after them. By this I do not mean imitation. As I think Mr Steven [sic] Spender rightly said some years back, Hopkins is inimitable, but that one can see in later poets the vivifying effects of Hopkins [sic] immense labours.'[57] Spender had remarked, in a review of the first (1944) volume of W. H. Gardner's major study of Hopkins, that 'He [Hopkins] ferments in other

---

[50] Hartman, *Free Verse*, 12.

[51] See the manuscript facsimile, pp. 126, 138, 140, and 144 below.

[52] See the manuscript facsimile, p. 126 below; Jessie L. Weston, 'The Task of the Hero', chapter two of *From Ritual to Romance* (Cambridge: Cambridge University Press, 1920), 11–22. See especially p. 16. Jones dates the copy of this edition of Weston's book in his personal library '1930'. See Huw Ceiriog Jones, *The Library of David Jones*, 306. David Jones refers his readers to the second chapter of Weston's book in his note M to 'Part Four' of *In Parenthesis*. See Jones, *In Parenthesis*, 210. On 19 August 1972 David Jones surprised William Blissett with the disclosure that 'he knew the books of both [Sir James G.] Frazer and Jessie L. Weston before he knew or had heard of *The Waste Land* [1922].' See Blissett, *The Long Conversation*, 96. In a letter to Jim Ede of 24 October 1929 Jones reports, 'I'm reading a very interesting book, called *From Ritual to Romance*, a learned book about the Grail legend – very *Golden Boughish* but I think, in the main, sound, by a woman called Jessie Weston – a bit trying in places. It's very interesting to me at the moment, with this Arthur business in my head.' See Jones, *Dai Greatcoat*, 26. In a letter of 22 May 1962 to Harman Grisewood, Jones writes, 'Certainly the impact on me of reading *The Waste Land* in *circa* 1926 or 1927 was considerable.' See Jones, *Dai Greatcoat*, 188.

[53] Weston, *From Ritual to Romance*, 16.

[54] David Jones, 'Art in Relation to War', *The Dying Gaul*, 123. This long essay, first published here, is dated on p. 166: '1942–3, 1946'.

[55] 'Art in Relation to War', *The Dying Gaul*, 122.

[56] See the manuscript facsimile, p. 126 below.

[57] See the manuscript facsimile, p. 140 below.

poets, but he is not an influence.'[58] Jones probably read this at second hand: Gardner himself quotes it at the end of his introduction to his Penguin edition of Hopkins's *Poems and Prose*, a 1967 reprint of which Jones kept in his personal library.[59]

The distinction between 'imitation' and 'influence' is a crucial one for Jones, and drawing it is another of his essay's main concerns. At issue is the operation of the 'vivifying' (or, as he puts it elsewhere in the manuscript, 'adjuvant' or 'confirmatory') mechanism of an irresistible leavening agent like Hopkins.[60] The 'question of influences' is how Jones phrases the problem in a letter of 24 February 1954 to W. H. Auden.[61] It is a 'jolly tricky . . . business', he admits there.[62] Jones formulates this sensitive question frequently in his correspondence, but nowhere more succinctly than in a letter of 2 May 1962 to the critic John H. Johnston: 'What one is "influenced" by is the *absolute* necessity to find a "form" that "fits" the contemporary situation.'[63] Jones elaborates the argument in a letter of 12 July 1961 to William Hayward: '[T]he truth is that a given civilisational situation will, necessarily, produce the same problems for people of certain sorts of perception, and that therefore, both in form and content, their work will show an affinity that looks like direct borrowing but which is, in reality, a similar response to an identical "situation" on the part of persons of similar perception.'[64]

The timing of the publication of Robert Bridges' first edition of Hopkins's *Poems* – in December 1918, almost thirty years after the latter's death in June 1889 – is at least as important to Jones as the 'form and content' of the poems themselves.[65] Five times in

---

[58] Stephen Spender, 'A Jesuit Poet', *Tribune*, 17 November 1944, 16. (Thanks to Benjamin Kohlmann for the reference.) This is a review of W. H. Gardner, *Gerard Manley Hopkins (1844–1889): A Study of Poetic Idiosyncrasy in Relation to Poetic Tradition* [Volume 1 of 2] (London: Martin Secker & Warburg, 1944). A copy of this book, dated 7 August 1953, appears in the catalogue of Jones's personal library, Huw Ceiriog Jones, *The Library of David Jones*, 109. Jones's copy of Gardner's second volume (first published 1949) is dated 1955. See Huw Ceiriog Jones, *The Library of David Jones*, 109.

[59] *Poems and Prose of Gerard Manley Hopkins*, selected with an introduction and notes by W. H. Gardner (Harmondsworth: Penguin, 1967 [revision of an edition first published 1953]), xxxvi. Gardner's introduction is dated August 1952 and ends, on p. xxxvi: 'Though he is inimitable, Hopkins (as Mr Stephen Spender has said) "ferments in other poets". No one can really know him without acquiring a higher standard of poetic beauty, a sharper vision of the world, and a deeper sense of the underlying spiritual reality.'

[60] For Jones on 'the vivifying effects of Hopkins [sic] immense labours', see the manuscript facsimile, p. 140 below. For their 'positively adjuvant' and 'confirmatory' effects, see the cancelled passages in the manuscript facsimile, p. 146 below.

[61] Jones, *Dai Greatcoat*, 163.

[62] Jones, *Dai Greatcoat*, 160.

[63] John H. Johnston, *English Poetry of the First World War* (Princeton, NJ: Princeton University Press, 1964), 322.

[64] David Jones, *Letters to William Hayward*, ed. Colin Wilcockson (London: Agenda Editions, 1979), 58.

[65] Bridges reports in a letter of 8 December 1918 to Mrs. F. C. Glover (his sister), 'This morning had the very first copy of my edition of Gerard Hopkin's [sic] poems.' See Robert Bridges, *The Selected Letters of Robert Bridges*, Vol. 1, ed. Donald E. Stanford (Newark: DE University of Delaware Press, 1983), 819. Bridges' first edition of Hopkins's poems was published on or around this date. The first traced review appeared on 2 January 1919. See Dunne, *Gerard Manley Hopkins: A Comprehensive Bibliography*, 14. Jones was 'disembodied' (transferred to Reserve), at Wimbledon, on 18 December 1918. See Dilworth, *David Jones in the Great War*, 203. The art historian Paul Hills noted in a diary entry of late June 1969 (entered after 23 June but before the end of the month) the following recollection from a recent phone conversation with Jones: 'DJ returned from Wales and stayed with Tom Burns in the spring of 1927. There he saw the journals and papers of Hopkins.' See Paul Hills, 'The Romantic Tradition in David Jones', *Malahat Review* 27 (July 1973): 51–2. In his article Hills suggests an affinity between Jones's drawings and watercolours of the late 1920s and the journals of Hopkins, which were not first published until a decade later, as *Notebooks and Papers of Gerard Manley Hopkins, edited with notes and a preface by Humphry House* (London and New York: Oxford University Press, 1937). Tom Burns (1906–95), the

these drafts Jones refers to 1918 as '"the acceptable year"'.[66] He is quoting Lk. 4.19, in which Jesus himself cites Isa. 61.2 in order to establish his appearance on the scene as the fulfillment of Old Testament prophecy.[67] The year 1918 is to be celebrated as a Jubilee year, therefore, and the end of the war that November forms a fortuitous coincidence not lost on Jones's historical imagination.[68] Exploding into consciousness at this kairotic moment, the Hopkins time bomb sent out shock waves the force of whose initial impact, Jones insists over and over, must not be made subject to 'appreciation' (down which road the 'taking-for-granted', the normalization, of Hopkins's astonishing achievement lies) but rather felt afresh in their full 'relevance'.[69]

English Catholic publisher, editor, and friend of Jones, had been given a trunk of Hopkins's papers to store. 'David Jones well remembers his fascination when he first dipped into this trunk', Hills writes on p. 52 of his essay. Thanks to Paul Hills for sharing the quotation from his diary (email of 1 July 2016). In his biography of Jones, Thomas Dilworth reports that Martin D'Arcy, SJ, then of Campion Hall, Oxford, had lent the unpublished journals to Burns, who, in 1932, stored them at his Chelsea residence, 10 Jubilee Place. See Dilworth, *David Jones: Engraver, Soldier, Painter, Poet*, 152: 'There, "on one or two occasions", Jones had "a look at" the unpublished notebooks of Gerard Manley Hopkins, loaned to Burns by D'Arcy. Although Burns remembered him as showing only "mild interest", so they may have been no influence, the descriptive language of *In Parenthesis* has striking affinity with Hopkins's visually vivid and acoustically rich lyrical notebook descriptions.' Dilworth here quotes a letter from Jones to John H. Johnston of 24 August 1962 and his own interview with Tom Burns of 20 June 1986. For an account of Bridges' delay to publish until 1918 a first edition of Hopkins's poems, see Catherine L. Phillips, 'Robert Bridges and the First Edition of Gerard Manley Hopkins's Poems', in Eugene Hollahan (ed.), *Gerard Manley Hopkins and Critical Discourse* (New York: AMS Press, 1993), 293–307. On p. 296 of her essay Phillips argues that Bridges delayed publication of Hopkins's poems in the first instance (in 1889, the year of Hopkins's death) out of a sincere 'desire to win acceptance for sprung rhythm' before unleashing the full battery of Hopkins's innovations upon the reading public.

[66] See for instance the manuscript facsimile, p. 134 below.

[67] See also 2 Cor. 6.2: '(For he saith, I have heard thee in a time accepted, and in the day of salvation have I succoured thee: behold, now *is* the accepted time; behold, now *is* the day of salvation.)' (KJV).

[68] An unspoken question hovers between the lines of the whole essay: Had Bridges published Hopkins's poems before 1918, could the course of war have been altered? Had he published them before 1914, could the war itself have been averted? See the manuscript facsimile, p. 150 below, where Jones hesitates to indulge in counterfactual history: 'Such suppositions are not very helpfull [sic]; they pose too many imponderables, it is more rewarding to consider the ~~sequence~~ actual sequence of events & the effects as we know them to be.'

[69] For Jones on ineffective 'appreciation' and the phenomenon of 'relevance', see the manuscript facsimile, p. 128 below. Tom Dunne shows that 'one of the most durable myths about Hopkins suggests that his immediate impact on English poetry resembled an exploding bomb'. See Dunne, *Gerard Manley Hopkins: A Comprehensive Bibliography*, xvi. In a conversation with Peter Orr of 24 November 1964, Jones repeats this 'myth', on which he doubles down in the Hopkins essay drafts. Orr has asked Jones if he, Jones, sees his work as 'renewing the past'. Jones replies, 'Renewing is a *very* good word because, you see, that has always been so. The past takes on a new form because of the changed situation. I think one of the most interesting examples in modern times, in the English-speaking world anyhow, is Hopkins, because he was not consciously trying to do a new thing; one of his great influences was this mediaeval, incredibly intricate Welsh metric and yet, you see, it was almost like a time-fused bomb. It wasn't until 1918 that people in general have now accepted him as part of the corpus of English literature.' See Peter Orr (ed.), *The Poet Speaks* (London: Routledge & Kegan Paul, 1966), 98–9. On the 'fascination' of Hopkins for later poets, see Laurence Binyon, 'Gerard Manley Hopkins and His Influence', *University of Toronto Quarterly* 8, no. 3 (April 1939): 265: 'We all know what fascination the poetry of Hopkins has had for the younger generation of poets and poetry-readers. Fascination is the word; for it is a strange kind of spell that it exerts, once it has been yielded to, causing one to forgive the startling singularities, the often-contorted syntax, the queer words and queer uses of words; one is fascinated into accepting them, because it is manifest that the poet is so passionately sincere, and because it is equally manifest that he is an artist unusually learned in his art.' For a different but relevant approach to the release-mechanism of the Hopkins grenade, compare Charles Williams, 'Gerard Hopkins', *Time and Tide* 26, no. 5 (3 February 1945): 102–3, a review of the first volume of W. H. Gardner's 1944 study discussed above, reprinted in Charles Williams, *The Image of the City*, ed. and intro. Anne Ridler (London and New York: Oxford University Press, 1958), 48–51. On pp. 50–1 of this volume, Williams writes, 'We may come to see that Hopkins does not belong to our time (in so far as we can properly talk

In a letter to *The Times* of 11 June 1958 Jones writes of Hopkins's own ability to recognize the 'relevance' of tradition for his own practice: 'A decade ago, in a now famous analytical study, Dr. W. H. Gardner made it plain that certain intricate metrical forms of specifically Welsh medieval development had quite a lot to do with the present joy which twentieth-century Englishmen get from the unique poetry of a nineteenth-century and very English Jesuit. The older and obscurer things of any great, complex heritage tend to be like that: they suddenly have fresh relevance and become newly requisite in some quite unexpected way.'[70] Jones recalls here his resonant phrase 'requisite now-ness' that appears, as a criterion of the 'validity' of signs, in his preface to *The Anathemata*, an essay he dates to July 1951.[71] He had put the term 'now-ness' in print four years before the publication of *The Anathemata*, in a critique of Charles Williams's literary engagement with the figure of Arthur.[72] 'Now-ness', Jones judges, is both the one thing needful in art and just what Williams's work lacks. He glosses his coinage, 'now-ness', as 'a sense of the contemporary', which he says 'escapes' Williams.[73]

To enjoy continued 'relevance', in Jones's sense, an artwork must have met its own age head on. This is the paradox on which Jones's reception of Hopkins turns, and which his essay attempts to elucidate. Lasting 'influence' comes not from an artwork's 'transcendence' of its native time and place but rather its utter absorption in the milieu of its making. If the poet has failed to integrate the conditions of production into the finished product, the latter is doomed to depreciate upon arrival, and no amount or degree of posterior 'appreciation' can salvage it from 'the time-factor affecting' this process.[74] The poet must

about "time" and poetry) as much as we had supposed. The more the Victorian age is examined, the more native to it Hopkins seems. He was indeed, in some sense, its corrective within it; as the Augustans carried Charles Wesley, and the Romantics Byron. Dr. Gardner's second volume proposes to discuss Hopkins's "real status as a poet". The sooner the more welcome. He prepares Hopkins so for posterity. But the one thing we cannot do instead of posterity is to remember. I will permit myself to say that those of us who in our youth came across those poems and fragments [before they were collected in Bridges' first edition of 1918] are more like posterity than the great students of the *Poems* [Bridges' first edition]. Tradition lives in such moments, and Hopkins was now, in that verse, part of our own poetic youth.' See also the fourteen-page letter of 11 April 1962 from Jones to the Welsh poet Vernon Watkins (1906–67), pp. 55–65 in David Jones, *Letters to Vernon Watkins*, ed. and notes Ruth Pryor (Cardiff: University of Wales Press, 1976), in which Jones argues that Hopkins did 'envigorate the English language by his study of Welsh metrical forms . . . It was an astounding achievement. The implications of which are still barely understood – perhaps less understood now than 20 years ago'. (59) For a biographical account, roughly contemporary with this letter, of the influence of Wales and Welsh on Hopkins, see Alfred Thomas, SJ, 'Hopkins, Welsh and Wales', *Transactions of the Honourable Society of Cymmrodorion*, Session 1965, Part II (1966), 272–85. A copy of this publication is in Jones's personal library. See Huw Ceiriog Jones, *The Library of David Jones*, 341. For a brief discussion of the place of Welsh language and literature between Hopkins and Jones, see Samuel Rees, *David Jones* (Boston: Twayne, 1978), 133–5. Rees, 134, claims that Jones 'read all of Hopkins in 1928' and that 'in a very real sense Jones's "anathemata" is a redefinition of [Hopkins's] "inscape"' (135).

[70] David Jones, 'Welsh Wales', *Epoch and Artist*, 54–5.

[71] 'The Preface to *The Anathemata*', in *Epoch and Artist*, 112. *The Anathemata* was first published, with its preface, by Faber in 1952. Both the table of contents (p. 9) to *Epoch and Artist* (1959), where the preface is reprinted in a revised version, and the last page of the preface as it appears at the beginning of the 1952 volume date the preface to 1951. See David Jones, *The Anathemata* (London: Faber & Faber, 1952), 43, where he datelines the prefatory essay '*Harrow-on-the-Hill / July* 1951'.

[72] David Jones, 'The Arthurian Legend', *Epoch and Artist*, 209. This essay is a review, first published in *The Tablet* on 25 December 1948, of Charles Williams, *Arthurian Torso* (London: Oxford University Press, 1948), the posthumous publication of Charles Williams's unfinished essay on 'The Figure of Arthur', with a commentary by C. S. Lewis on Williams's Arthurian poems. For Lewis on the idea of what he calls 'Unshared Background', see *Arthurian Torso*, 189: 'An example of difficulties arising from Unshared Background would be *The Waste Land*.'

[73] Jones, 'The Arthurian Legend', *Epoch and Artist*, 209.

[74] Jones, 'The Preface to *The Anathemata*', *Epoch and Artist*, 112.

perform the metamorphosis of interrogation into integration without losing the force of the inaugurating interrogative impulse. Discussing the hazards of this process, Jones adopts the idea of 'unshared backgrounds' from C. S. Lewis's commentary on Williams's 'Arthuriad'.[75] Jones understands artists and audiences to face each other across a widening abyss in which the dream, once the reality, of mutual recognition threatens to be wholly swallowed up. He proclaims his hope in the 'Zeitgeist' as a medium of communion even as he condemns the reckless ghostbusters of his own time who have set their sights on the spirits of the age.[76]

The demand to 'ask the question' arises from the need to share a background that has all but withdrawn from view, and it compels the artist who accepts it to reset the foreground in relief. A background shared by itself is just as incomprehensible as a foreground that has floated free of its background. Art's special office is to offer 'comprehension' as composition – a composition that comprehends both foreground and background, past and future, on the same plane, from which might be read off a vision of the future. Jones often cites to this effect an image of the Virgin's womb that appears in a distich from the Gradual from the Mass of the Eve of the Assumption: 'That which the whole world cannot contain, is contained.'[77] In his essay on Hopkins Jones quotes the Vulgate's Ps. 121, v. 3, to make an adjacent point: '*cujus participatio ejus in idipsum*'.[78] This phrase describes Jerusalem as a city 'whose parts are united in one', as Jones translates it in a 1940 essay in appreciation of the recently deceased Eric Gill, who, Jones writes there, as he would of Hopkins later, took it to heart as a paradigm of aesthetic integrity.[79] Like the Theotokos, the artist must brood if what hatches is to hold together as a 'whole', which, Jones insists in a letter of 27 November 1962, 'has to be shown forth within the confined conditions which *any* artform necessarily imposes'.[80]

Jones finds the 'struggle' to 'comprehend', in this sense, palpable in the verse and prose of Hopkins.[81] These drafts afford a glimpse, as if into a nest or an incubation chamber, of Jones's own struggle to comprehend this poet in the only way he knows how – by creating a composition in which the Jesuit's quest for the whole might coincide with his own, taking up its position in and as the background of one ongoing argosy. René Hague has memorably compared Jones's method (such as it is)[82] of composition to the recursive

---

[75] 'The Preface to *The Anathemata*', *Epoch and Artist*, 112, n. 1: 'See commentary by C. S. Lewis, "Williams and the Arthuriad", in *Arthurian Torso*, 1948.'

[76] On the *Zeitgeist*, see Jones, *Dai Greatcoat*, 160, and Jones, *Letters to Vernon Watkins*, 20. In the letter in the former volume Jones trails the word with a parenthetical '(if that's the right word)'. In the letter in the latter volume the word appears in quotation marks, in the phrase 'the "common tongue of the Zeitgeist"'. Compare Jones's use of the word *Weltanschauung* in the Hitler essay, in Tom Villis's edition in this volume, pp. 57 and 81 above.

[77] 'Art in Relation to War', *The Dying Gaul*, 142.

[78] See the manuscript facsimile, p. 226 below.

[79] 'Eric Gill, *an Appreciation* [italics thus in table of contents, p. 10]', *Epoch and Artist*, 301. This essay was first published in *The Tablet* on 10 November 1940, 'that is to say almost immediately upon Mr. Gill's death', Jones writes in a footnote on p. 296. Gill died on 17 November, having entered hospital on 4 November. See the biography by Fiona MacCarthy, *Eric Gill* (London: Faber & Faber, 1989), 292. For another use of this verse of Ps. 121, a Jonesian motto, see Jones, *David Jones: Letters to a Friend*, 18 and 81.

[80] Jones, *David Jones: Letters to a Friend*, 82.

[81] See the manuscript facsimile, p. 226 below.

[82] In a letter to Desmond Chute of 29 December 1952 Jones admitted his writing '"method"' to be 'merely to arse around with such words as are available to me until the passage in question takes on something of the shape I think it requires & invokes the image I want.' See David Jones, *Inner Necessities: The Letters of David Jones to Desmond Chute*, ed. Thomas Dilworth (Toronto: Anson-Cartwright Editions, 1984), 24.

movement of a long-jumper 'constantly returning to the starting point of his run because, as he was about to take off, he found that he had missed his step'.[83] This characterization of Jones's manuscript practice at large, as a lifework of *reculer pour mieux sauter*, applies to these drafts in particular: 'A passage will be written out again and again and again, with perhaps one or two verbal changes.'[84]

Kathleen Henderson Staudt has distilled the drafts' 15,000 words to a little over four pages in her *Agenda* article of 1993 about the abandoned essay.[85] In her headnote she discerns in the drafts two distinct 'directions of inquiry'.[86] The first is the idea of 'influence', the second what Staudt calls the 'significance' of Hopkins 'as a poet'.[87] The latter investigation she summarizes as being pursued by Jones along a pair of parallel 'lines of argument': that the Victorian Hopkins was received as a 'contemporary' by Jones and his friends of the two decades after the First World War; and that Hopkins exerts, perhaps embodies, artistic 'influence' as such.[88] As the folds and creases of Staudt's analysis expose, in the meaning of 'influence' lies the rub.

The Month had requested a personal reminiscence: what has Hopkins meant to Jones – where, when, and how? In what he seems to have intended as the essay's first paragraph, Jones at once introduces the 'far from simple' implications of this apparently innocent question.[89] Seven times in the drafts he claims that the miracle of delayed 'relevance', however common an occurrence in cultural reception-history, remains to him a 'mystery'.[90] 'I loathe the word mystic – it might mean anything – ' Jones had written in a letter of 4 November 1927.[91] Deploying the word 'mystery' in his essay on Hopkins, Jones evokes the, for him, quite unmystical mystery of the Eucharist, the real presence of Christ in the Blessed Sacrament. This is of course the central mystery around which his theological aesthetics turns, the mastery of which mystery Jones arrogates – perhaps most perplexedly at the end of his essay 'Art and Sacrament' – to the 'intransitive activity' of the artist.[92]

'Not, needless to say', he says there, is the shrimp girl of Hogarth's eponymous eighteenth-century portrait '"really present"' under the species of oil and canvas, 'but in a certain analogous sense' to that employed by theologians.[93] 'All art "re-presents",' Jones writes on the previous page.[94] He goes on to justify his odd hyphenation in the following discussion of *The Shrimp Girl*, but he avoids any mention of his equally anomalous use of 'scare-quotes' there. These quotation marks reappear around an analogous coinage in the

---

[83] Jones, *Dai Greatcoat*, 145. In his biography of Jones, Thomas Dilworth claims that Jones's prescription medications affected his writing habits adversely. See Dilworth, *David Jones: Engraver, Soldier, Painter, Poet*, 335: 'Evidence of the effect of drugs is his composing in November thirteen drafts of a letter thanking Bernard Bergonzi for publishing a chapter on *In Parenthesis* in *Heroes' Twilight* (1965).' For a record of Jones's prescriptions, see Dilworth's biography, 314–15.

[84] Jones, *Dai Greatcoat*, 145. Jones progressed through the drafts of *The Anathemata* by means of such textured repetition – likely a translation of basic sketching technique. See Dilworth, *David Jones: Engraver, Soldier, Painter, Poet*, 260.

[85] See Kathleen Henderson Staudt, 'An Unpublished Appreciation of Gerard Manley Hopkins', *Agenda* 31, no. 3 (Autumn 1993): 172–80. See the Appendix to this volume, pp. 321–5 below.

[86] Staudt, 'An Unpublished Appreciation of Gerard Manley Hopkins', 72 (p. 321 below).

[87] Staudt, 'An Unpublished Appreciation of Gerard Manley Hopkins', 72 (p. 321–2 below).

[88] Staudt, 'An Unpublished Appreciation of Gerard Manley Hopkins', 73 (p. 322 below).

[89] See the manuscript facsimile, p. 122 below.

[90] See the manuscript facsimile, p. 126 below.

[91] Jones, *Dai Greatcoat*, 45.

[92] Jones, *Epoch and Artist*, 175.

[93] Jones, *Epoch and Artist*, 175.

[94] Jones, *Epoch and Artist*, 174.

Hopkins essay: '"re-cognition"'.[95] By hyphenating and setting off in quotation marks this rather ordinary word (which appears, unhyphenated and typographically unhedged, a total of twenty-one times in the Hopkins manuscript drafts), Jones means to specify what he calls there its 'exact sense'.[96] And what is that sense exactly? 'This is not quite the same thing as what is usually meant ~~by~~ <when literary and art-critics [the next seven words added in left-hand margin] speak of the work of Mr X> ~~the work of Mr Mr X. so & so~~ being "influenced" by the work of ~~Mr A,~~ <"y"> ~~B~~ [*overwritten by* Q], <"Q"> or <or> "C." It is something more inevitable and beyond choice that is involved. Something more to do with the situation, than with ~~a~~ personal predilections.'[97] This is an especially heavily worked-over version of the manuscript's much-repeated passage about the relationship between the non-recognition of Hopkins by his own contemporaries and his posthumous recognition by Jones and his. As Staudt's version consommes it, 'But few men of this sort can have experienced more isolation and less recognition during their life days than Hopkins, to be recognized a few decades after their deaths as not only of singular genius but as harbingers whose work would have a special relevance for the poets, artists, makers, call them what you will, of those few decades later.'[98]

From Jones's perspective, Hopkins's double vocation as poet and priest ('*poeta-sacerdos*') is his leading feature.[99] Protestations that an 'analogy' obtains between writing a poem and uttering the Words of Institution bounce off this poet-priest, '(whose *poiesis* is that which is made at the altar)'.[100] Or so Jones implies to be his premise. What is striking about this essay is the steadfastness with which Jones demurs to get down to the brass tacks, in the conventional terms of literary criticism, of Hopkins's poetic achievement, let alone speculate on the ways in which Hopkins's innovative diction and prosody (for instance) might have 'influenced' his own. This is, however, consistent with Jones's approach elsewhere to what he calls here 'written poetry'.[101] Nowhere does he reveal himself to be on speaking terms with the ins and outs of 'metric' (unless it happens to be a Welsh metric, which he knows when he hears it).[102]

Except for William Dunbar (with his concern for the *makar*), Jones associates Hopkins not with other metrists but with painters: Piero della Francesca, El Greco, Blake, Turner, Constable – each, like Hopkins, introduced to Jones in his art-student youth '"as one born out of due time"'.[103] It is not a coincidence that all of them enjoyed belated 're-cognition' by the tastemakers of Jones's art-school days. Eliot and Joyce, Jones's highest priest of *poiesis*, are admitted into the discussion, but for narrow reasons. Eliot's Tiresias

---

[95] See the manuscript facsimile, p. 202 below.

[96] See the manuscript facsimile, p. 202 below.

[97] See the manuscript facsimile, p. 202 below.

[98] Staudt, 'An Unpublished Appreciation of Gerard Manley Hopkins', 75 (p. 323 below).

[99] See the manuscript facsimile, pp. 122 and 136 below.

[100] See the manuscript facsimile, p. 170 below.

[101] See the manuscript facsimile, pp. 160, 170, and 248 below.

[102] See the manuscript facsimile, pp. 228 and 262 below. For a harsh view of Jones's professed ignorance of 'metric', see Donald Davie, 'A Grandeur of Insularity', *Times Literary Supplement*, issue 4039, 22 August 1980, 935. Davie discusses a letter of 4 July 1945 from Jones to Harman Grisewood reporting a dinner conversation with W. F. Jackson Knight about prosody: 'These chaps are awfully interested in the metre thing, aren't they?' See Jones, *Dai Greatcoat*, 129.

[103] Jones, 'The Preface to *The Anathemata*', *Epoch and Artist*, 122. Jones is quoting 1 Cor. 15.8 (KJV). For Jones on Dunbar's 'Lament for the Makaris', see the manuscript facsimile, p. 126 below. For Piero della Francesca, El Greco, and Blake, see the manuscript facsimile, p. 200 below; for Turner, see the manuscript facsimile, pp. 258 and 260 below; for Constable, see the manuscript facsimile, pp. 214 and 216 below.

reprises the prophetic role he played in the preface to *The Anathemata*, foresuffering all, like Hopkins, all over again.[104] And Hopkins is to Duns Scotus, he of 'the *haeccietas*' [sic], as Joyce is to Aquinas, whose 'school' had 'steeled' him.[105] Jones knows himself to be untempered in (and in any case out of temperament with) the school of 'close reading' that has long dined out on Hopkins's poems, and so he sidesteps its strictures here to pursue a kind of homespun *Strukturanalyse* instead.[106]

Jones 'painted not from where he stood but from a point about 20 feet up in the air,' recalled the wood-engraver Philip Hagreen, who had known him at Ditchling, Capel-y-ffin, and Lourdes in the 1920s.[107] This is also the altitude from which Jones tends to write. (The vantage is reversed when he is building a nest of footnotes under the nose of his reader.) It is a particular, if not so peculiar, image of Hopkins that matters most to Jones, and this essay is his attempt to bring it forth anew in the mode of personal-historical reminiscence, or 're-cognition'. In this it resembles nothing in Jones's voluminous prose so much as the opening section of his long essay on *The Rime of the Ancient Mariner*, published in 1964 to introduce, or rather reintroduce, his set of copperplate engravings executed in 1928–9 to illuminate Coleridge's poem.[108] As in the Hopkins essay, where he acknowledges but does not engage in detail with Hopkins's critical history, Jones assumes the attitude of an amateur with respect to *The Rime*: 'I must emphasize that what I say is entirely the subjective impression of a layman. My intention here (as throughout this foreword) is to record my personal impressions, and largely those of some decades back.'[109] The foreword in its full extent, first published in 1972, runs to thirty-nine pages.[110] Yet there is on none of them any mark of 'mugging-up'; Jones's lavish display of autodidacticism is awash in 'what is actually loved and known'.[111] What Jones has managed to do here – and what he set out to do in his Hopkins essay – is weave the weft of autobiography into the warp of history so tightly that tradition and the individual talent emerge as one 'pure myth' (one 'devoid of the fictitious'), in which the voices of David and the Sibyl, subjective and objective, blend.[112] With Hopkins, however, Jones

---

[104] For Jones on the 'foresuffering' of Tiresias in Eliot's *The Waste Land* (l. 243), see the manuscript facsimile, pp. 132 and 142 below, and 'The Preface to *The Anathemata*', *Epoch and Artist*, 122.

[105] See the manuscript facsimile, p. 172 below. See annotations on the facing page for details on Dun Scotus's term *haecceitas* and Jones's quotation from Joyce's 1904 broadside 'THE HOLY OFFICE'.

[106] See Christopher S. Wood, *The Vienna School Reader: Politics and Art Historical Method in the 1930s* (New York: Zone Books, 2000), 51: '*Strukturanalyse* managed to coordinate historical and contemporary art more successfully than other art historical methods because it converted every work, in effect, into a modernist work.'

[107] See the letter of 28 January 1978 from Philip Hagreen to Stella Wright quoted in Lottie Hoare, *Philip Hagreen: A Sceptic and a Craftsman* (Winchester: Ritchie Press, 2009), 94. See https://www3.nd.edu/~jsherman/hagreen/Hagreen-13Dec2012.pdf (accessed 20 December 2016).

[108] See Dilworth's preface to David Jones, *The Rime of the Ancient Mariner*, ed., with preface and afterword by Thomas Dilworth (London: Enitharmon, 2005), 11. In his introduction to Coleridge's poem, included in Dilworth's edition, Jones quotes lines from Hopkins's pair of shipwreck poems: 'The Loss of the Eurydice', stanza 15, and *The Wreck of the Deutschland*, stanza 19. See Jones, 'An Introduction to in Jones, *The Rime of the Ancient Mariner*', 15. In a conversation with William Blissett of 9 September 1972 Jones identifies Hopkins's 'love of shipwrecks' as something 'very Victorian'. See Blissett, *The Long Conversation*, 111.

[109] Jones, 'An Introduction to *The Rime of the Ancient Mariner*', 17.

[110] See Dilworth's preface to his edition of Jones, *The Rime of the Ancient Mariner*, 11.

[111] 'The Preface to *The Anathemata*', *Epoch and Artist*, 120.

[112] 'The Preface to *The Anathemata*', *Epoch and Artist*, 134, n. 2. For Jones on 'a theme that runs like a thread through the whole mysterious weft and warp of *The Rime of the Ancient Mariner*', see his 'An Introduction to *The Rime of the Ancient Mariner*', 42. In the manuscript facsimile, pp. 224 and 226 below, Jones apologizes for dwelling 'too much on matters of an autobiographical nature', but he goes on to argue for their necessary inclusion in the essay. A version of this apology appears four times in the manuscript.

seems to have lost the thread, or else realized in time that the thread he had found was too thin or too short to manipulate at length.

In Hopkins's poetry Jones prided himself on detecting an 'undercurrent' not of Welsh 'traditions' per se but one of Welsh 'technique and inward feeling'.[113] The implied analogy with Jones's own Welsh affinities could not be clearer. It is precisely in order to accent Hopkins's imaginative identification with Welshness as such that Jones is so keen to emphasize the extent to which Hopkins was a 'Victorian Englishman (and *how* Victorian!)'.[114] 'Wales' is the imagined community in which the Victorian Englishmen Jones and Hopkins commune. Hopkins 'influences' or 'conditions' Jones only by this proxy. In his only other essay on a writer of English verse, Jones notes that Christopher Smart, too, was of Welsh extraction.[115] But for all his congenial qualities, Smart is felled, in Jones's estimation, by a fatal flaw: an unexpected 'fear of "embodiment"'.[116] Jones quotes Smart's conviction that 'painting is a species of idolatry' as evidence of his 'muddled head'.[117] This proscription serves to set off Smart's 'serious wrongheadedness' against the *analogia entis* to which Jones's art-making adheres: 'as through and by the Son, all creation came into existence and is by that same agency redeemed, so we, who are co-heirs with the Son, extend, in a way, creative and redeeming influences upon the dead works of nature, when we fashion material to our hearts' desire'.[118]

The question – and it is the question of the Hopkins essay – remains: how to 'extend' this 'influence'? Jessie Weston's research programme models this question for Jones. In *From Ritual to Romance* Weston goes in search of what she calls 'a genuine *Elucidation* of the Grail problem'.[119] She assumes from the outset 'the possibility of identifying two objects' – pagan and Christian 'Grail' motifs – 'which, apparently, lie at the very opposite poles of intellectual conception'.[120] This hypothesis allows her to initiate her inquiry: 'What brought them together? Where shall we seek a connecting link?'[121] Jones, likewise, presumes the presence of an anterior affinity: there is no question that between Hopkins and himself an aboriginal 'influence' abides. 'You smell a rat or two pretty early on,' he remarks of his earliest influences.[122] 'For it is axiomatic that the origin of things conditions their ends, in however obscure, roundabout, mutated, or even quite contradictory a manner.'[123] Jones's

---

[113] Jones, 'Welsh Culture', an unsent letter to the editor of the *Catholic Herald* dated 9 September 1948, in *The Dying Gaul*, 122.

[114] See the manuscript facsimile, p. 134 below.

[115] 'Christopher Smart', first published in *The Tablet* as a review of Christopher Smart, *Rejoice in the Lamb*, ed. W. Force Stead (London: Cape, 1939), *Epoch and Artist*, 282. This is Jones's only other essay on the verse of an English writer except that of Coleridge and himself. (His review of Charles Williams's *Arthurian Torso* centres on the prose. For Jones's brief assessment of Williams's poems, which C. S. Lewis discusses in the volume under review, see 'The Arthurian Legend', *Epoch and Artist*, 210.) Jones doesn't go so far as to turn Coleridge into a Welshman, but he does compare the imagery of *The Rime* to 'the shape-shifting figures in Celtic mythology'. See Jones, 'An Introduction to *The Rime of the Ancient Mariner*', 16.

[116] 'Christopher Smart', *Epoch and Artist*, 287.

[117] 'Christopher Smart', *Epoch and Artist*, 286.

[118] 'Christopher Smart', *Epoch and Artist*, 286. On Jones's understanding of 'analogy', see his remark in a review of Herbert Read's *Poetry and Anarchism* (London: Faber & Faber, 1938): 'an art-work is a similitude of the Kingdom of God'. See Jones, 'Poetry and Anarchy', *The Tablet*, 16 July 1938, 77.

[119] Weston, *From Ritual to Romance*, 1.

[120] Weston, *From Ritual to Romance*, 132.

[121] Weston, *From Ritual to Romance*, 132.

[122] 'The Preface to *The Anathemata*', *Epoch and Artist*, 135.

[123] Jones, 'Wales and the Crown', *Epoch and Artist*, 45. This is a transcript of a radio broadcast of 23 July 1953. For a discussion of Jones's 'axiom', see Kathleen Raine, *David Jones: Solitary Perfectionist* (Ipswich: Golgonooza, 1974), 7.

poetic project tackles the task of turning the 'intransitive activity' of *ars* to account in an age in thrall to *prudentia*.[124] To 'ask the question' to which 'influence' stands already answerable is Jones's prescribed *praxis*. Such inquiry is less a transitive than it is a transitional activity – one whose end is not progress but praise, for '"art" *as such* is "heaven" . . . analogous not to faith but to charity'.[125]

ANNOTATED TRANSCRIPTION

Provenance

David Jones, 'Gerard Manley Hopkins, essay on, manuscript draft', John J. Burns Library, Boston College, Chestnut Hill, MA, David Jones Papers, MS 86–1, series II, subseries 1, box 2, folder 7.

Note on the transcription

This transcription takes the occasion of an extended example, rare among Jones's papers, of an early-stage essay draft to illuminate the process by which the writer, here in his final decade, painstakingly laboured – in his own phrase – 'to make a shape in words'.[126] Each page of the transcription below complements a facing-page facsimile of its corresponding page in the manuscript, so many of the latter's unique features (elaborate doodles and designs, arithmetic problems, tea stains, tears or holes, and cigarette burns) require no further 're-presentation', as Jones might put it. Certain recurring marks, however, call for transcription. One is the middle dot (·) with which the writer rests his pen at the end of a line. Neither a period nor a comma, it scores the rhythm of the writer's train of thought. Often Jones pauses to switch his writing utensil from his regular pen to the more tentative or at least more forgiving pencil, whose marks he might later erase and overwrite in ink.

Another notable, and notated, feature is the author's sometimes unsystematic two-tiered page-numbering system that unfolds in the top centre and right corner of the manuscript pages. Jones's unit of composition is a single side of a foolscap sheet. He collects a sequence of numbered sheets under a symbol, here variously a red-brown crossed check-mark, a black uncrossed check-mark, a red-brown asterisk, a green asterisk, 'XX' (in pencil), 'XXX' (in pencil or pen), and 'XXXX' (in pen, enclosed by a rectangle). Some sheets bear no such symbol but do bear the circled Arabic numerals ('1' to '4', and, in one instance, '5') that Jones uses to order the sheets within his sheaves of sheets. (This transcription re-presents the circles around these numerals with parentheses.) This transcription presents the sheets in the order in which they appear in the archive, last arranged – as slips of paper among the sheets included in the facsimile indicate – by

---

[124] 'Art and Sacrament', *Epoch and Artist*, 149. Inside his inverted commas Jones paraphrases Aristotle's *Nicomachean Ethics*, VI, iv, 1140a. For a discussion of the origins of this phrase, see Paul Robichaud, *Making the Past Present: David Jones, the Middle Ages, and Modernism* (Washington, DC: Catholic University of America Press, 2007), 143.

[125] Jones, 'Art in Relation to War', *The Dying Gaul*, 164. For a discussion of this startling conjunction of equation and analogy, see W. David Soud, *Divine Cartographies: God, History, and* Poiesis *in W. B. Yeats, David Jones, and T. S. Eliot* (New York and Oxford: Oxford University Press, 2016), 101.

[126] David Jones, *In Parenthesis* (London: Faber & Faber, 1937), x.

Kathleen Henderson Staudt in the late 1980s and early 1990s. (See Staudt's redaction of the drafts, reprinted in this volume, pp. 321-5 below.) The pencilled numbers in the left-hand margins of some sheets are in the hand of someone other than either Jones or Staudt – perhaps that of an archivist. The staff at the John J. Burns Library, Boston College, which holds this manuscript, do not know who added them or when. The numerals do not seem to correspond to the sequence of sheets as either Jones or Staudt after him suggests.

The transcription practice in play here takes its point of departure from that summarized by David L. Vander Meulen and G. Thomas Tanselle in their article 'A System of Manuscript Transcription', *Studies in Bibliography* 52 (1999): 201–12. The latter seeks to provide a set of conventions that might simplify the task of producing an 'inclusive' text (one in which textual events appear along the line rather than in appended notes) that relies on words rather than symbols to convey information about the look of the manuscript. This transcription adopts the principles of this system as first principles but departs from them notably in re-presenting, with a few exceptions, Jones's numerous cancellations with a single line struck through the cancelled text. Where Jones has struck through whole passages in which he had earlier cancelled only certain words, phrases, or lines, in-line commentary explains the local complication. Unless noted, Jones writes in ink, a ballpoint pen.

In-line commentary appears in italic type inside brackets or – on only two occasions – in braces, when an expansion of Jones's abbreviations does not merit a footnote. No attempt has been made to alter Jones's often idiosyncratic or inconsistent spelling. Words between guillemets re-present Jones's insertions above the line, which Jones sometimes indicates with a caret, duly re-presented by a caret. Underlining follows Jones's own, italics being reserved for commentary.

[*Cover page*]

Essay on Hopkins ·

Hopkins (1)

To contribute something in homage to Hopkins in this centenary year of his entry into the Noviciate of the Society of Jesus might appear a not only congenial but fairly simple task in that there is so much which the name 'Hopkins' has evoked for many of us over the half-century. But when comes to actually making some such contribution, the task, at least for the present writer, is very far from simple.

For one thing, so much has been written in appraisment of this remarkable man and his works: studies of every sort ~~assessing~~ seeking to assess every aspect of the ~~works~~ writings of this great metrist and of their author. The range and depth of what has been written ~~is~~ varies from the comprehensive and intensive two volume study by Dr W. H. Gardner, published in 1944 and 1949 back to innumerable ~~articles articles~~ articles & a number of books written in the nineteen-thirties & 'twenties and forward to books and articles written in the 'fifties and 'sixties, some making available additional material, some concentrating ~~and~~ on a particular facet or aspect of this poeta-sacerdos.

So that to-day, exactly fifty years since the first appearance of Poems of Gerard Manley Hopkins edited with notes by Robert Bridges, and seventy-nine years since the poet's death, Hopkins stands indisputably within the received canon of English poetry. He was by some literary critics and by the general public regarded for some time as, at the most, deuterocanonical, but gradually a protocanonical status has been allowed him.

His poetry has become 'accepted', so much so, that it is difficult to imagine any anthology of English verse that did not include at least one poem by G. M. Hopkins.

But, with 'acceptance', there not infrequently comes a 'taking-for-granted,'

[*page 1*]

[*crossed check in red-brown ink or pencil in top right-hand corner*]

11

Hopkins (1)

To contribute something in homage to Hopkins in this centenary year of his entry into the Noviciate of the Society of Jesus might appear a not only congenial but fairly simple task in that there is so much which the name 'Hopkins' has evoked for many of us over the half-century.[127] But when comes to actually making some such contribution, the task, at least for the present writer, is very far from simple.

For one thing, so much has been written in appraisment of this remarkable man and his works: studies of every sort ~~assessing~~ seeking to assess every aspect of the writings of this great metrist and of their author. The range and depth of what has been written varies from the comprehensive and intensive two volume study by Dr W. H. Gardner, published in 1944 and 1949[128] back to innumerable articles & a number of books written in the nineteen-thirties & 'twenties and forward to books and articles written in the 'fifties and 'sixties, some making available additional material, some concentrating on a particular facet or aspect of this poeta-sacerdos.[129]

---

[127] A 'noviciate' (or novitiate) is a training college for the novices of the Jesuit order. The term also refers to the two-year probationary period between a candidate's 'Entrance Day', upon which he is named a 'novice', and his progression to 'First Studies' (three years of graduate-level work in philosophy and theology). At the end of the novitiate the novice pronounces his 'first vows' of poverty, chastity, and obedience. The English poet Gerard Manley Hopkins was born on 28 July 1844, in Stratford, Essex, the eldest of nine children of Manley Hopkins, an average adjuster in marine insurance, and his wife Kate Hopkins, née Smith. Raised in a High-Church Anglican household, Hopkins became a Catholic on 21 October 1866, while still a student at Balliol College, Oxford. After taking First Class Honours in 'Greats' in June of the following year, Hopkins assumed a teaching post at the school of the Birmingham Oratory, founded by John Henry Newman, who had received him into the Church there. In May of 1868 Hopkins decided to become a priest and destroyed all of his verse. On 7 September 1868, he entered the Jesuit novitiate at Manresa House, Roehampton, south London. After completing his studies at St Beuno's College, north Wales, he was ordained a priest in September 1877 and taught and ministered in locations around England and Scotland until his transfer to University College Dublin in February 1884, where he served as professor of Classics until his death there, of typhoid, on 8 June 1889. Hopkins published no major poetry during his lifetime, although in 1876 he submitted his ode *The Wreck of the Deutschland*, written in Wales in 1875–6, to the London-based Jesuit journal *The Month*, whose editor eventually rejected it. The physician Robert Bridges (1844–1930), Hopkins's friend from their undergraduate days, became Poet Laureate in 1913 and prepared the first edition of Hopkins's *Poems* for publication by Humphrey Milford at the Oxford University Press in December 1918. This first impression of 750 copies took ten years to sell out. Bridges died on 21 April 1930, and the second edition of Hopkins's poems was prepared by the Inkling and Oxford University Press employee Charles Williams for publication, by Milford again, in November of that year. Jones received a copy of this second edition as a gift from his father, dated Christmas 1930. The most authoritative biography of Hopkins to date is Norman White, *Hopkins: A Literary Biography* (Oxford: Oxford University Press at the Clarendon Press, 1992). See also Alfred Thomas, SJ, *Hopkins the Jesuit: The Years of Training* (London: Oxford University Press, 1969). For the books by Hopkins owned by Jones, see Huw Ceiriog Jones, *The Library of David Jones (1895–1974): A Catalogue* (Aberystwyth: National Library of Wales, 1995), 140.

[128] W. H. Gardner, *Gerard Manley Hopkins (1844–1889): A Study of Poetic Idiosyncrasy in Relation to Poetic Tradition* (London: Martin Secker & Warburg, 1944). A copy of volume one of this two-volume book, dated 7 August 1953, appears in the catalogue of Jones's personal library, *The Library of David Jones*, 109. Jones's copy of Gardner's second volume (first published 1949) is dated 1955. See Huw Ceiriog Jones, *The Library of David Jones*, 109. On Gardner's seminal study and all of the other English-language secondary literature on Hopkins up to 1970, see part two of Tom Dunne, *Gerard Manley Hopkins: A Comprehensive Bibliography* (London: Oxford University Press at the Clarendon Press, 1976), 101–325.

[129] *Sacerdos* is the Latin word for 'priest'. The *OED*'s entry cites editions of Ezra Pound's *Cantos* dated 1930 and 1949. For editions of Pound's *Cantos* owned by Jones, see Huw Ceiriog Jones, *The Library of David Jones*, 230–1.

Hopkins (1)

To contribute something in homage to Hopkins in this centenary year of his entry into the Noviciate of the Society of Jesus might appear a not only congenial but fairly simple task in that there is so much which the name 'Hopkins' has evoked for many of us over the half-century. But when comes to actually making some such contribution, the task, at least for the present writer, is very far from simple.

For one thing, so much has been written in appraisment of this remarkable man and his works: studies of every sort seeking to assess every aspect of the writings of this great metrist and of their author. The range and depth of what has been written varies from the comprehensive and intensive two volume study by Dr W. H. Gardner, published in 1944 and 1949 back to innumerable articles & a number of books written in the nineteen-thirties & 'twenties and forward to books and articles written in the 'fifties and 'sixties, some making available additional material, some concentrating on a particular facet or aspect of this poeta-sacerdos.

So that to-day, exactly fifty years since the first appearance of Poems of Gerard Manley Hopkins edited with notes by Robert Bridges, and seventy-nine years since the poet's death, Hopkins stands indisputably within the received canon of English poetry. He was by some literary critics and by the general public regarded for some time as, at the most, deuterocanonical, but gradually [illegible] protocanonical status has been allowed him.

His poetry has become 'accepted', so much so, that it is difficult to imagine any anthology of English verse that did not include at least one poem by G. M. Hopkins.

But, with 'acceptance', there not infrequently comes a 'taking-for-granted,'

[*page 1*] (continued)

So that today, exactly fifty years since the first appearance of <u>Poems of Gerard Manly Hopkins</u> edited with notes by Robert Bridges, and seventy-nine years since the poet's death, Hopkins stands indisputably within the~~, so to say,~~ ~~‘~~received canon~~’~~ of English poetry.

He was by some literary critics and by the general public regarded for some time as, at the most, deuterocanonical, but [*the next eight words inserted in pencil*] gradually a protocanonical status has been allowed him.[130]

His poetry has become ‘accepted’, so much so, that ~~this~~ it is difficult to imagine any anthology of English verse that did not include at least one poem by G. M. Hopkins.[131]

But, with ‘acceptance’, there not infrequently comes a ‘taking-for-granted’,

[130] The prefixes ‘deutero-’ and ‘proto-’ derive from the Greek words for ‘second’ and ‘first’ respectively.

[131] For an annotated list of anthologies, see Tom Dunne, *Gerard Manley Hopkins: A Comprehensive Bibliography*. Notably, the editions (published in 1915 and 1930) of *The Oxford Book of English Verse, 1250–1900*, ed. Arthur Quiller-Couch, in Jones's personal library do not contain any poems by Hopkins. One anthology that Jones owned, Edith Sitwell's two-volume *The Atlantic Books of British and American Poetry* (London: Victor Gollancz, 1959), contains poetry by both Jones (part of *The Anathemata*) and Hopkins (including *The Wreck of the Deutschland*). See Huw Ceiriog Jones, *The Library of David Jones*, 268, and Tom Dunne, *Gerard Manley Hopkins: A Comprehensive Bibliography*, 90. A favourite anthology of Jones's, W. H. Auden and John Garrett, *The Poet's Tongue* (London: George Bell & Sons, 1935), contains three poems by Hopkins: ‘The Leaden Echo’, the late sonnet ‘I wake and feel the fell of dark, not day’, and stanzas 12–16 of *The Wreck of the Deutschland*. See Huw Ceiriog Jones, *The Library of David Jones*, 12, for details of the 1946 edition in Jones's personal library, dated by Jones 1952. Jones praises the anthology in a letter to Auden of 24 February 1954, calling it ‘one of my constant companions’. See David Jones, *Dai Greatcoat: A Self-portrait of David Jones in his Letters*, ed. René Hague (London: Faber & Faber, 1980), 162.

(2)

never a good thing either with regard to works or persons—and to take Hopkins for granted would be most unfortunate; it would indeed make void and cancel out his ever having become accepted and made available.

I say this because of the particular nature of his contribution (the poems, notes, diaries, letters, etc.) is of that sort which prompts, goads, alerts. To borrow from an important motif in the medieval romance-tale of Peredur (Perceval), Hopkins requires us to 'ask the question'—or rather a complex of questions. Should we fail in this, no amount of appreciation of the beauty of this or that poem will suffice against the danger of our taking him for granted.

Hopkins chanced to be one of those sorts of 'makaris' whose making has the quality to condition in a certain way the works of those who come after them.

This, in itself, is no unfamiliar thing, such artists crop up from time to time in any medium you like to name. But few men of this sort can have experienced more isolation and less recognition during their life days than Hopkins, to be recognized a few decades after their deaths as not only of singular genius but as harbingers whose work would have a special relevance for the poets, artists, makers, call them what you will, of those few decades later.

[*page 2*]

[*crossed check in red-brown ink or pencil in top right-hand corner*]

12

(2)

never a good thing either with regard to works or persons and to take Hopkins for granted would be most unfortunate; it would indeed make void and cancell out his ever having become accepted and made available.

I say this because of the particular nature of his contribution ~~(this actual~~ (the poems, notes, diaries, letters, etc.) ~~is of that~~ is of that sort which prompts, goads, alerts. ~~To borrow from the medieval Perad Peredur (Perceval) romance-tale, Hopkins~~

~~To borrow <^from>~~ To borrow from an important motif in the medieval romance-tale of Peredur (Perceval), Hopkins requires us to 'ask the question' – or rather a complex of questions. Should <^we> fail in this, no amount of ~~the~~ appreciation of the beauty of this or that poem will suffice against the danger of our taking him for granted.[132]

Hopkins chanced to be one of those sorts of 'makaris' whose making ~~has destined~~ has the quality to condition in a [*the next ten words and period inserted in pencil*] certain way the works of those who come after them.[133]

This, in itself, is no unfamiliar thing, such artists crop up from time to time in any medium you like to name.

But few men of this sort can have experienced more isolation and less recognition during their life days than Hopkins, to be recognized a few decades after their deaths as not only of singular genius but as harbingers whose work would have a special relevance for the poets, artists, makers, call them what you will, of those few decades later.

~~Though this matter of sudden recognition of relevance by artists of our age~~ ·

---

[132] On Peredur, see David Jones, *In Parenthesis* (London: Faber & Faber, 1937), 210, his endnote 'M' to Dai Greatcoat's boast. Jones cites there the second chapter of Jessie Weston, *From Ritual to Romance* (Cambridge: Cambridge University Press, 1920). See also David Jones, *The Anathemata* (London: Faber & Faber, 1952), 226 n. 1.

[133] *Makar* is the Scots word for 'maker'. The Scots poet William Dunbar (1460?–died by 1530) refers to himself as a *makar*, and Jones, citing the title of Dunbar's poem 'Lament for the Makaris', employs the term here as a literal translation of the Greek ποιητής. Jones's copy of *The Poems of William Dunbar*, ed. W. Mackay Mackenzie (Edinburgh: Porpoise Press, 1932) is dated Christmas 1933 and has 'few notes' by David Jones, according to Huw Ceiriog Jones, *The Library of David Jones*, 91. 'Lament for the Makaris: "Quhen He Wes Sek"', composed c. 1508, is poem seven in Mackenzie's edition, 20–3. It lists and elegizes the great poets of Scotland up to Dunbar's day. In the introduction to his edition, Mackenzie writes, xxxiii–iv, 'Over all, then, Dunbar is one of the poets who illuminate the life of their time but do not idealistically transform it. Robert Browning in an essay distinguishes the class of poet as "fashioner", or as the Scots, after the Greeks, would say, "makar", from that of the poet as "seer" – the objective from the subjective type. Dunbar is of the former class; he does not proffer "intuitions" as reflections of an "absolute mind", as Browning held himself to do. Poetry was for him a social art, not the functioning of a seer or diviner, the latter being an assumption which by now as surely dates itself as does Dunbar's "mellifluate" diction.' Mackenzie refers here to Browning's famous distinction in his 1851 'Essay on Shelley'. Shelley is Browning's type of the 'subjective' poet, Shakespeare of the 'objective'. For a recent scholarly edition of Browning's essay, see 'Appendix A' in John Woolford, Daniel Karlin, and Joseph Phelan (eds), *Robert Browning: Selected Poems* (London and New York: Routledge, 2013), 851–77. Jones quotes lines 46–8 of Dunbar's 'Lament' at the end of his February 1941 essay 'Eric Gill as Sculptor', in *Epoch and Artist* (London: Faber & Faber, 1959), 295. Of Gill, Jones writes there, 'All said and done, he was a great worker in stone, he was a great maker.' Jones quotes lines 26–7, 29–30, and 77–9 of Dunbar's 'Lament' in *In Parenthesis*, 95, probably from the version in *The Oxford Book of English Verse*, of which the 1915 (dated by Jones 9 September 1916) and 1930 (dated November 1937 in Jones's copy) editions survive in his personal library. See Huw Ceiriog Jones, *The Library of David Jones*, 235.

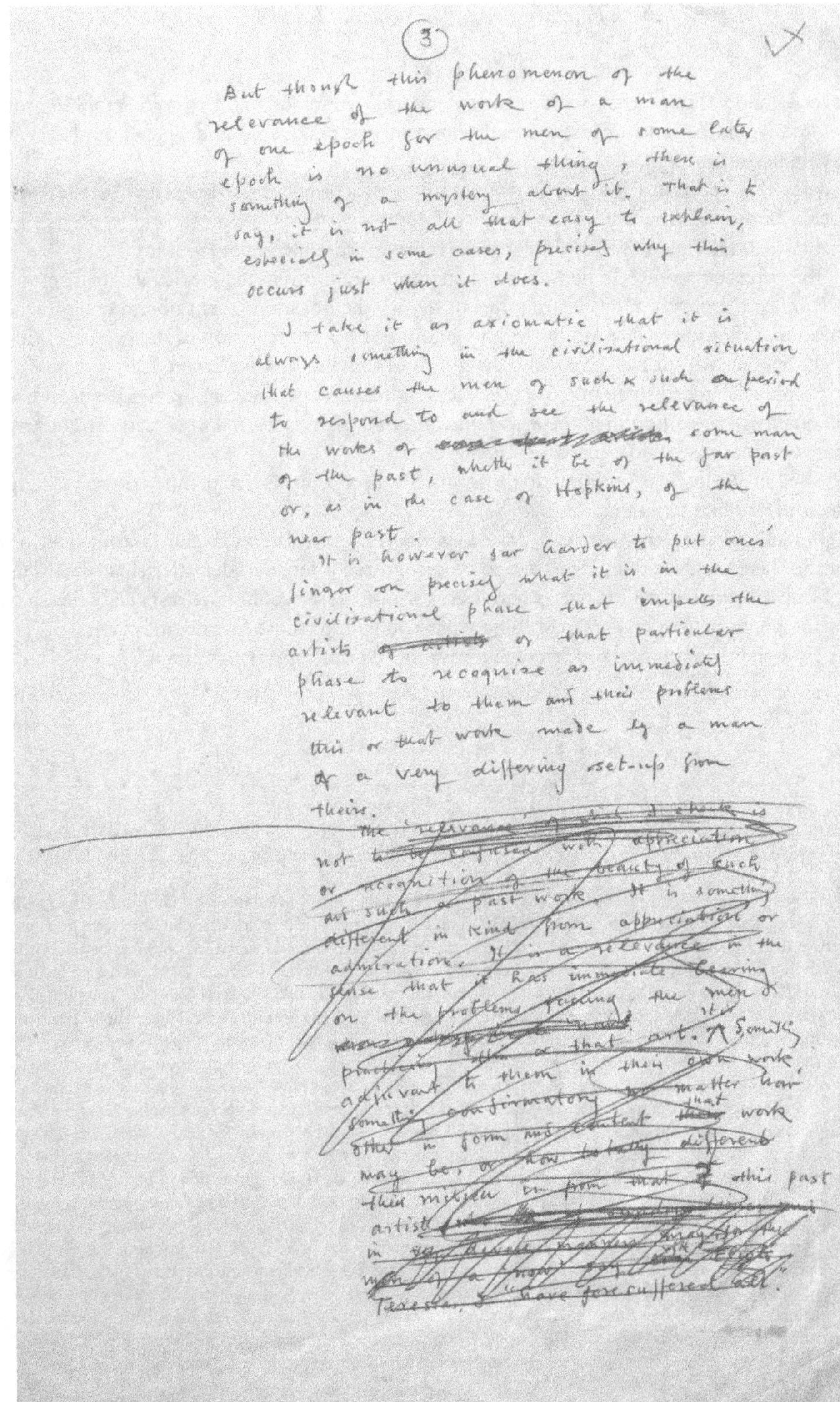

(3)

But though this phenomenon of the relevance of the work of a man of one epoch for the men of some later epoch is no unusual thing, there is something of a mystery about it. That is to say, it is not all that easy to explain, especially in some cases, precisely why this occurs just when it does.

I take it as axiomatic that it is always something in the civilisational situation that causes the men of such & such a period to respond to and see the relevance of the works of some man of the past, whether it be of the far past or, as in the case of Hopkins, of the near past.

It is however far harder to put one's finger on precisely what it is in the civilisational phase that impels the artists of that particular phase to recognize as immediately relevant to them and their problems this or that work made by a man of a very differing set-up from theirs.

[*page 3*]

[*crossed check in red-brown ink or pencil in top right-hand corner*]

36

(3)

But though this phenomenon of the relevance of the work of a man of one epoch for the men of some later epoch is no unusual thing, there is something of a mystery about it. That is to say, it is not all that easy to explain, especially in some cases, precisely why this occurs just when it does.

I take it as axiomatic that it is always something in the civilizational situation that causes the men of such & such a period to respond to and see the relevance of the works of ~~some past artist~~ some man of the past, whether it be of the far past or, as in the case of Hopkins, of the near past.[134]

It is however far harder to put one's finger on precisely what it is in the civilizational phase that impells the artists ~~of artists~~ of that particular phase to recognise as immediately relevant to them and their problems this or that work made by a man of a very differing set-up from theirs.

~~The 'relevance' of which I speak is not to be confused with appreciation or recognition of the beauty of such and such a past work. It is something different in kind from appreciation or admiration. It is a relevance in the sense that it has immediate bearing on the problems facing the men [whose making is of a 'now'.] practicing this or that art. <^it is.> Something adjuvant to them in their own work, something confirmatory no matter how other in form and content <^that>~~ [*the next word cancelled*] ~~their work may be, or how totally different their milieu is from that <^of>~~ [*the next word cancelled*] ~~of this past artist who at sundry times and in diverse manners may, for the men of a 'now' say <^with>~~ [*the next word cancelled*] ~~like Eliot's Teresias, I "have foresuffered all".~~[135]

[134] Influenced partly by his reading of Spengler, Jones often asserts the specific gravity of a civilization's 'situation' in both time and space. See for instance 'The Preface to *The Anathemata*', in *Epoch and Artist*, 119: 'The poet is born into a given historic situation and it follows that his problems – i.e. his problems as a poet – will be what might be called "situational problems".'

[135] See *The Waste Land* (1922), l. 243, in *The Poems of T. S. Eliot: Volume 1: Collected and Uncollected Poems*, ed. Christopher Ricks and Jim McCue (Baltimore, MD, and London: Johns Hopkins University Press and Faber & Faber, 2015), 64. Jones quotes this line in 'The Preface to *The Anathemata*', *Epoch and Artist*, 122, and elsewhere in his prose.

[*page 4*]

[*in red-brown ink or pencil in top left-hand corner*]

226-0880

(4)

This relevance of which I speak is not to be confused with appreciation of the beauty or admiration for the skill of such & such a past work. It is something different in kind from such admiration. It is a relevance in the sense of having an immediate bearing on problems facing the men practicing this or that art at a given time, something adjuvant to them in their own work, something confirmatory no matter how other in form, content or intention their work may be or how totally different their civilizational milieu.

It is something which, whether it comes to them from across many centuries or from over a few decades, says to them, in the words of Eliot's Tiresias-figure: and I have foresuffered all.

Away back in the mid nineteen twenties when I first became aware of Hopkins it was not infrequently complained that Bridges was much to blame for not getting published the Hopkins MSS long before 1918.

I can make no claims to have gone into the reasons why Bridges delayed throughout the eighteen-nineties or why he turned down the request of Fr. Joseph Keating S.J. that a complete edition of the poems should be published in 1909. But if the true reason was that he felt the climate of opinion was not propitious and that an adverse reception was certain, well, perhaps he was right — it is impossible to be sure of what might have been the effect of something that did not happen.

[*page 5*]

[*crossed check in red-brown ink or pencil in top right-hand corner*]

48

(4)

This relevance of which I speak is not to be confused with appreciation of the beauty or admiration for the skill of such & such a past work. It is something <^different> in kind from such admiration. It is a relevance in the sense of having an immediate bearing on problems facing the men practicing this or that art at a given time, something adjuvant to them in their own work, something confirmatory no matter how other in form, content <^and intention> their work may be or how totally different their <^civilizational> milieu.

[*The following sentence inserted in pencil*] It is something which, whether it comes to them from across many centuries or from over a few decades, says to them, in the words of Eliot's Tiresias-figure: I have foresuffered all.

Away back in the mid nineteen twenties [*the next word overwrites an illegible word*] when I first became aware of Hopkins it was not infrequently complained that Bridges was much to blame for not getting published the Hopkins MSS long before 1918.

~~I can make~~ [*the next word inserted above an illegible word]* ~~<no> claims whatever to <^have> gone into the reasons why Bridges delayed throughout the eighteen-nineties or why he turned down the request of Fr Joseph Keating S.J. that a complete edition of the poems should be published in 1909. But if, in his judgement, 1909 or any previous date back to 1890 was inauspicious for anything but an adverse reception~~[136]

I can make no claims to have gone into the reasons why Bridges delayed throughout the eighteen-nineties or why he turned down the request of Fr. Joseph Keating S.J. that a complete edition of the poems should be published in 1909. But if the true <^reason> was that he felt ~~that~~ the climate of opinion was not propitious and that an adverse reception was certain, well, perhaps he was right – it is impossible to <^be> sure ~~about things that never happened~~. of what might have been the effect of something that did not happen.

---

[136] See Joseph Keating, SJ, 'Impressions of Father Gerard Hopkins, S.J. I.', *The Month* 114, no. 541 (July 1909): 60: 'it would seem that that time has now come for Father Hopkins' poems to appear in a collected form as a distinct and valuable addition to the literary heritage of the Catholic Church.' The second and third instalments of Keating's 'Impressions' appeared in *The Month* in August and September 1909. See Dunne, *Gerard Manley Hopkins: A Comprehensive Bibliography*, 112. On Bridges' hostility to Keating's suggestion, see White, *Hopkins: A Literary Biography*, 463.

(5)

But if Bridges did indeed see clearly that 1918 was 'the acceptable year', then his prescience was remarkable. I don't know what auspex or auspices he consulted but the determining formula Aves admittunt would seem to me to have been declaimed just about on time.

That a Victorian Englishman (and how Victorian!) of Liddon's Oxford, received into the Church by Newman, a priest of the Society of Jesus, who wrote poetry and who in notes, diaries, letters discoursed in great detail upon his theory of metrics, who observed cloud formations, trees, flowers, the behaviour of streams, the stratification of rocks and whose sensitive drawings of these natural phenomena remind one of Ruskin, should have turned out to be of the greatest interest to the men who had either served in, or had come to manhood during, the 1914–18 war is hardly what one supposed most likely. Yet such was in fact the case; so much so that any conversation of the nineteen twenties or 'thirties which chanced to turn on a discussion of some living writers, St.-J. Perse, Joyce, Eliot, would sooner or later, almost certainly involve Hopkins. Indeed it required a conscious effort of some sort to remember that the work of Hopkins was made in Victoria's England and that he was born ten years before the Crimean War and was dead a decade before the earliest motor-car would "unseeve the sweet especial scene" whether where Binsey's poplars once were felled or in Benno's wilder land. For we discussed him as though his contribution was contemporary. I can't think, off hand, of any other artist of the past of whom this could said in quite the same way.

[*page 6*]

[*crossed check in red-brown ink or pencil in top right-hand corner*]

50

(5)

But if Bridges did indeed see clearly that 1918 was 'the acceptable year', then [*two illegible words cancelled*] his prescience was remarkable. I don't know what ~~aup.~~ auspex or auspices he consulted but the determining formula Aves admittunt would seem to have ~~declaimed~~ been declaimed just about on time.[137]

That a Victorian Englishman (and how Victorian!) of Liddon's Oxford, received into the Church by Newman, a priest of the Society of Jesus who wrote poetry and who in notes, diaries, letters discoursed in great detail upon his theory of metrics, who observed [*one cancelled word illegible*] cloud-formations, trees, flowers, the behaviour of streams, the [*one cancelled word illegible*] stratification of rocks and whose sensitive drawings of these natural phenomena remind one of Ruskin, should have turned out to be of the greatest interest to the men who had either served in, or had come to manhood during, the 1914–18 war is hardly what one suppose most likely. Yet such was in fact the case; so much so that any conversation of the nineteen twenties or 'thirties which chanced to turn on a discussion of some living writers, St.-J. Perse, Joyce, Eliot, would sooner or later, almost certainly involve Hopkins. [*The next word cancelled.*] ~~Indeed It was, indeed, only by a conscious effort that~~[138]

Indeed it required a conscious effort of some sort to remember that the work of Hopkins was made in Victoria's England and that he ~~had been dead~~ was born ten years before the Crimean War and was dead a decade before the earliest motor-car would 'unselve the sweet especial scene' whether where Binsey's poplars once were felled or in Beuno's wilder land.[139]

For we discussed him as though [*the next word changed from* he] his
~~was a contemporary figure~~

contribution was contemporary. I can't think, ~~of any~~ off hand, of any other artist of the past of whom this could said in quite the same way.

---

[137] Five times in these drafts Jones refers to 1918 as '"the acceptable year"'. He is quoting Lk. 4.19, in which Jesus himself cites Isa. 61.2 in order to establish his appearance on the scene as the fulfilment of Old Testament prophecy. See also 2 Cor. 6.2: '(For he saith, I have heard thee in a time accepted, and in the day of salvation have I succoured thee: behold, now *is* the accepted time; behold, now *is* the day of salvation.)' (KJV). Compare David Jones, *The Anathemata*, 58: 'at the turn of time / not at any time, but / at this acceptable time'. *Aves admittunt* is the favourable report of the Roman augur or auspex: 'the birds allow it'. For a reproduction of an extant sketch by Jones of a Roman *templum*, see Jonathan Miles, *Backgrounds to David Jones: A Study in Sources and Drafts* (Cardiff: University of Wales Press, 1990), 132.

[138] On the influence on Hopkins of the High-Church (Anglican) theologian and preacher Henry Parry Liddon (1829–90), see White, *Hopkins: A Literary Biography*, 52 and 61–3. On the influence of Ruskin on Hopkins's sketching technique, see White, *Hopkins: A Literary Biography*, 75–7. On the influence on Jones of James Joyce and of T. S. Eliot's 1930 translation of *Anabasis*, the long poem first published in 1924 as *Anabase* by the French poet Alexis Leger (1887–1975) under the pseudonym Saint-John Perse, see Thomas Dilworth, *David Jones: Engraver, Soldier, Painter, Poet* (London: Jonathan Cape, 2017), 129.

[139] Jones quotes lines 21–2 of Hopkins's 1879 poem 'Binsey Poplars'. For an edition of the text that Jones owned (a gift from *Agenda* editor William Cookson dated Christmas 1967), see *The Poems of Gerard Manley Hopkins*, 4th edn, ed. W. H. Gardner and N. H. MacKenzie (London: Oxford University Press, 1967), 78–9.

(1) Hopkins

To contribute something in homage to Hopkins in this centenary year of his entry into the Novitiate of the Society of Jesus might appear ~~to~~ not only congenial but fairly simple a task in that there is so much which the name Hopkins has evoked for many of us over the last half century.
But when it comes to actually making some such contribution the task, at least for the present writer, is far from simple.

For one thing so much has been written ~~[illegible]~~ ~~[illegible]~~ in appraisal of the works and the man: studies of every sort seeking to assess every aspect of ~~the~~ ~~[illegible]~~ the writings of this great metrist and of their author.
The range and depth of what has been written extends from Dr W. H. Gardner's comprehensive and intensive ~~volume~~ work, the first volume of which appeared in 1944 and the second in 1949, back to ~~the~~ articles and books published in the nineteen-thirties and 'twenties and forward to works published in the 'fifties and 'sixties, some of which have made available additional material, some concentrating on a particular facet or aspect of this poeta-sacerdos.

So that to-day, exactly fifty years since the appearance of Poems of Gerard Manley Hopkins edited by Bridges and seventy-nine years since the poet's death, Hopkins stands indisputably within the, so to say, 'received canon' of English poetry.

His poetry has become 'accepted', so much so that it is now difficult to imagine any anthology of English verse which did not include at least one poem by Hopkins.
But with 'acceptance' there not infrequently comes a 'taking for granted';

[*page 7*]

[*crossed check in red-brown ink or pencil in top right-hand corner*]

5

(1) [*the next word in red ink or pencil*] Hopkins

To contribute something in homage to Hopkins in this centenary year of his entry into the Novitiate of the Society of Jesus might appear ~~a~~ not only congenial but fairly simple a task in that there is so much which the name Hopkins has evoked for many of us over the last half century.

But when it comes to actually making some such contribution the task, at least for the present writer, is far from simple.

For one thing so much has been written ~~in appraisment of the man and his works seeking to make~~ in appraisal of the works and the man: studies of every sort seeking to assess every aspect of ~~this great metrist~~ the writings of this great metrist and of their author.

The range and depth of what has been written extends from Dr W. H. Gardner's comprehensive and intensive ~~volumes~~ <work,> the first volume of which appeared in 1944 and the second in [*the following number changed from* 1944] 1949, back to ~~in~~ articles and books published in the nineteen-thirties and 'twenties and forward to works published in the 'fifties and 'sixties, Some of which have made available additional material, some concentrating on a particular facet or aspect of this poeta-sacerdos.

So that to-day, exactly fifty years since the appearance of Poems of Gerard Manly Hopkins edited by Bridges and seventy-nine years since the poet's death, Hopkins stands indisputably within the, so to say, 'received canon' of English poetry.

His poetry has become 'accepted', so much so that it is now difficult to imagine any anthology of English verse which did not include at least one poem by Hopkins.

But with 'acceptance' there not infrequently comes a 'taking for granted';

(2)

never a good thing either with regard to works or persons and to take Hopkins for granted would be most unfortunate. ~~It would indeed make void or cancell out~~ It would indeed, in an important sense, make void or cancell out his ever having become accepted and available.

I say this because the particular nature of ~~the~~ his contribution (the poems, notes, diaries, letters, etc.) is of that sort which prompts, goads, alerts. To borrow from a motif in the medieval romance-tale of Peredur (Perceval) ~~and~~ in which the land is waste, the maimed king unhealed the wives ~~barren~~ widowed, all creatures barren because of the failure of the hero to 'ask the question',

[*crossed check in red-brown ink or pencil in top right-hand corner, followed by a dot (·)*]

13

(2)

never a good thing either with regard to works or persons and to take Hopkins for granted would be most unfortunate. ~~It would indeed make void or cancell out~~

It would indeed, in an important sense, make void or cancell out his ever having become accepted and available.

I say this because ~~of~~ the particular nature of ~~th~~ his contribution (the poems, notes, diaries, letters, etc.) is of that sort which prompts, goads, alerts. To borrow from a motif in the medieval romance-tale of Peredur (Perceval) ~~and~~ in which the land is waste, the maimed king unhealed the wives ~~barren~~ widowed, all creatures barren because of the failure of the hero to 'ask the question', ·

(2)

never a good thing either with regard to works or persons and to take Hopkins for granted would be most unfortunate. It would indeed, in an important sense, make void or cancell out his ever having become accepted and available.

I say this because the particular nature of his contribution (the poems, notes, diaries, letters, etc.) is of that sort which prompts, goads & alerts. To borrow from a motif in the romance-tale of Peredur (Perceval) in which everything hangs on the asking of a question, Hopkins requires us to 'ask the question' or rather a complex of questions. Should we fail in this, no amount of appreciation of the beauty of this or that of his poems will suffice against the danger of our taking him for granted.

He chanced to be one of those sorts of 'makaris' whose making has a quality which conditions the works of those who come after them.

By this I do not mean imitation, as I think Mr Stephen Spender rightly said some years back, Hopkins is inimitable, but that we can see in later poets the vivifying effects of Hopkins immense labours.

Because he himself subjected himself to a most rigorous asking of the question, he did 'free the waters' what is perhaps his greatest contribution [illegible] the [illegible] & exacting the discipline the more we may become [illegible] the

[*crossed check in red-brown ink or pencil in top right-hand corner*]

19

(2)

never a good thing either with regard to works or persons and to take Hopkins for granted would be most unfortunate. It would indeed, in an important sense, make void or cancell out his ever having become accepted and available.

I say this because the particular nature of his contribution (the poems, ~~the~~ notes, diaries, letters, etc.) is of that sort which prompts, goads & alerts.

To borrow from a motif in the romance-tale of Peredur (Perceval) in which everything hangs on the asking of a question, Hopkins requires us to 'ask the question' or rather a complex of questions. Should we fail in this, no amount of appreciation of the beauty of this or that of his poems will suffice against the danger of our taking him for granted.

He chanced to be one of those sorts of 'makaris' whose making has a quality which conditions ~~the~~ the works of those who come after them.

[*The rest of the script on this page inserted in pencil*]

By this I do not mean imitation, As I think Mr Steven Spender rightly said some years back, Hopkins is inimitable, but that one can see in later poets the vivifying effects of Hopkins immense labours.[140]

Because he himself subjected himself to a most rigorous asking of the question, he did 'free the waters'. That is perhaps his greatest contribution that the more arduous & exacting the disciplina the more we may come to the[141]

[140] Spender had remarked, in a review of the first (1944) volume of W. H. Gardner's two-volume study of Hopkins, that 'He [Hopkins] ferments in other poets, but he is not an influence.' See Stephen Spender, 'A Jesuit Poet', *Tribune*, 17 November 1944, 16. Jones probably read this remark at second hand: Gardner himself quotes it at the end of his introduction to his Penguin edition of Hopkins's *Poems and Prose*, a 1967 reprint of which Jones kept in his personal library. See *Poems and Prose of Gerard Manley Hopkins*, selected with an introduction and notes by W. H. Gardner (Harmondsworth: Penguin, 1967 [a revision of an edition first published in 1953]), xxxvi. Gardner's introduction is dated August 1952 and ends, 'Though he is inimitable, Hopkins (as Mr Stephen Spender has said) "ferments in other poets". No one can really know him without acquiring a higher standard of poetic beauty, a sharper vision of the world, and a deeper sense of the underlying spiritual reality' (xxxvi). Thanks to Benjamin Kohlmann for the reference.

[141] On the 'freeing of the waters', see Jones, *The Anathemata*, 225 and 235–8, and the commentary in Jonathan Miles, *Backgrounds*, 171–2. For a discussion of Jones's idea of 'discipline', see Adrian Poole, 'The Disciplines of War, Memory, and Writing: Shakespeare's *Henry V* and David Jones's *In Parenthesis*', *Critical Survey* 22, no. 2 (2010): 91–104. See Jones's capacious definition of *disciplinae* in 'The Preface to *The Anathemata*', *Epoch and Artist*, 129, n. 1.

It is something which whether across the centuries or across but a few decades, that, like Eliot's Tiresias, says to them 'I have foresuffered all'

Away back in the mid nineteen-twenties when I first became aware of Hopkins it was not infrequently complained that Bridges was much to be blamed for not getting published the Hopkins MSS long before 1918.

While I can make no claim to have studied the reasons for Bridges' delay, I feel that *if* the true reason was that he judged the 1890s, —or the year 1909 (the year in which Fr Keating S.J desired him to publish a complete edition of Hopkins poems) to be too soon for anything but adverse reception.

[*page 10*]

[*crossed check in red-brown ink or pencil in top right-hand corner*]

47

(4)

~~Somet~~

It is something which whether across the centuries or across but a few decades, that, ~~which,~~ like Eliot's Tiresias, says to them 'I have foresuffered all'

Away back in the mid ~~1920's I~~ nineteen-twenties when I first became aware of Hopkins it was not infrequently complained that Bridges was much to be blamed for not getting published the Hopkins MSS long before 1918.[142]

While I can make no claim to have studied the reasons for Bridges' delay I feel that if the true reason was that he judged the 1890s, or the year 1909 (the year in which Fr Keating S. J desired him to publish a complete edition of Hopkins poems) to be too soon for anything but adverse reception.

[142] For an account of Bridges' delay to publish until 1918 a first edition of Hopkins's poems see Catherine L. Phillips, 'Robert Bridges and the First Edition of Gerard Manley Hopkins's Poems', in Eugene Hollahan (ed.), *Gerard Manley Hopkins and Critical Discourse* (New York: AMS Press, 1993), 293–307. Phillips shows that Bridges delayed publication of Hopkins's poems in the first instance (in 1889, the year of Hopkins's death) out of a sincere 'desire to win acceptance for sprung rhythm' before unleashing the full battery of Hopkins's innovations upon the reading public (296).

(2)

But with 'acceptance' there not infrequently comes a 'taking for granted', never a good thing, either with regard to works or persons and to take Hopkins for granted would be most unfortunate; it would indeed make void and cancel out his having been accepted and made available.

The particular nature of his contribution (his actual poems, notes, diaries, letters) is of that sort which prompts, goads, alerts and to borrow from the Peredur (Perceval) romance 'asks the question' – the complex of questions, which is perennially with us which we shall fail to ask if, in spite of our appreciation of the beauty of Hopkins poems, we take them & their author 'for granted'.

1901 1889 1899 -10 1900 1901

Hopkins chanced to be one of those sorts of 'makaris' whose making is destined to condition in various ways the works of those who come after them.

This, in itself, is no unfamiliar thing, such artists crop up from time to time working in any medium you care to mention. But few artists of this sort can have experienced more isolation and less recognition during their life days than Hopkins, to be seen a few decades after their deaths as not only of great and singular genius but harbingers whose work would have a special sort of relevance for other poets, artists, makers, call them what you will, of those few decades later.

Though this matter of sudden recognition of some past artist by those of a later date is so well known and common a phenomenon there is something of a mystery about it. It is not all that easy to explain, especially in some cases, precisely why this occurs just when it does.

[*page 11*]

[*crossed check in black ink in top right-hand corner*]

17

(2)

But with 'acceptance' there not infrequently comes a 'taking for granted', never a good thing, either with regard to works or persons and to take Hopkins for granted would be most unfortunate; it would indeed make void and cancell out his having been accepted and made available.

The particular nature of his contribution ([*the next word either overwrites or is overwritten by* the] his actual poems, notes, ~~diar~~ diaries, letters) is of that sort which ~~which~~ prompts, goads, alerts and ~~(~~[*the next word overwrites an illegible word*] to borrow from the Peredur (Perceval) romance 'asks the question' – the complex of questions, which is perennially with us [*the next word overwrites* and] but which we shall fail to ask if, in spite of our appreciation of the beauty of Hopkins poems, we take them & their author 'for granted.'

[*Dates written in left-hand margin:* 1901 [/] 1889 [/] 1899–10 [/] 1900 [/] 1901]

Hopkins chanced to be one of those sorts of 'makaris' whose making ~~was~~ is destined to condition in various ways the works of those who come after ~~him~~ them.

This, in itself, is no unfamiliar thing, such artists crop up from time to time <^working> in any medium you care to mention. But few ~~men~~ artists of this sort can have experienced more isolation and less recognition during their life days than Hopkins, to be seen a few decades after their deaths as not only of great and singular genius but as ~~harbin~~ harbingers whose work would have a special sort of relevance for other poets, artists, makers, call them what you will, of those few decades later.

Though this matter of sudden recognition of some past artist by [*the next word inserted in the left-hand margin*] those ~~by artists~~ of a later date is so well known and common a phenomenon there is something of a mystery about it. It is not all that easy to explain, especially in some cases, precisely why this occurs just when it does.

(3)

I take it as axiomatic that it is always something in the civilizational situation that causes the artists of such & such a period to respond to, and see the relevance of, the works of some artist of the past, whether it be the far past or as in the case of Hopkins, of but a century back. It is however far harder to put one's finger on precisely what it is in the civilizational phase that conditions the artists of that phase to recognize as immediately relevant to them and to their problems, this or that work made by a man of a very differing civilizational set-up from theirs.

This 'relevance' of the works of some past artist for the artists of 'now' is not the same thing as their appreciation of the skill, competence or even the great beauty evident in past works of every period, it is the immediate relevance itself, something adjuvant to them in their own work, something confirmatory – no matter how different the form and content or how other their milieu may be from that of the past work which at their moment in history chances to say to them I "have foresuffered all."

Away back in the mid 1920s when I first became aware of Hopkins it was frequently complained that Bridges was much to blame for not getting published the Hopkins MSS long before 1918.

[*page 12*]

[*crossed check in black ink in top right-hand corner*]

35

(3)

I take it <^as> axiomatic that it <^is> always something in the civilizational situation that causes the artists of such & such a period to respond to, and see the relevance of, the works of some artist of the past, whether it be the far past or ~~the~~ as in the case of Hopkins, of but a ~~few decades~~ <century> back. ~~It is far harder to~~

It is however far harder to put one's finger on precisely what it is in ~~the works of~~ the civilizational phase that conditions the artists of that phase to [*one cancelled word illegible*] recognize as immediately relevant to them and to their problems, this or that [*one cancelled word or beginning of a word illegible*] work made by a man of a very differing civilizational set-up from theirs. ~~I~~

~~This 'relevance' that makes the works of such & such a figure from the past~~ [*the next two words cancelled*] ~~adjuvant, vivifying significant,~~ [*the next word cancelled*] ~~and confirmatory,~~ [*the next word cancelled*] ~~of positively adjuvant to this or that later generation of artists is not the same thing as their appreciation of the skill, competence~~ [*the next seven words cancelled*] ~~or~~ [*the next two words inserted above two illegible words*] <~~even the~~> [*the next word cancelled*] ~~evident~~ [*the next word cancelled*] ~~beauty beauty of and evident beauty of other works of the past it is~~ ·

This 'relevance' of the works of some past artist for the artists of 'now' is not the same thing as their appreciation of <^the> skill, competence or even the great beauty evident in ~~works~~ past works of every period, it is the immediate relevance itself, ~~something confirmatory and adjuvant to them~~ adjuvant to ~~their~~ them in their own work, something confirmatory – no matter how different the form and content or how their ~~civilizational milieu~~ milieu may be from that of ~~the~~ of the past work which at their moment in history chances to say to them I 'have foresuffered all'

Away back in the mid 1920s when I first became aware of Hopkins it was frequently complained that Bridges was much to blame for not getting published the Hopkins MSS long before 1918. ~~While I do not pretend to know~~

(4)

While I can make no claim to any detailed study of the reasons for Bridges' delay, I feel that if the true reason was that he judged the 1890s or the year 1909 (when Fr. Keating S.J. desired him to publish Hopkins poems complete) to be too soon for anything but an adverse reception but sensed that 1918 was 'the acceptable year', then I think Bridges prescience was remarkable — ~~the aves admittent of whatever anger he consulted was said just about on time.~~

~~A Victorian~~

~~That the [illegible] prosody of the poet [illegible] to any concerning it~~

That a mid Victorian Englishman, a convert to the Catholic Church in the days of Liddon's & Pusey's Oxford a priest of the Society of Jesus who wrote poetry and in notes and letters discussed his theories of metrics at great length should have turned out to be of the greatest possible interest & appeal to the men who had either served in, or had come to manhood during, the 1914–18 war is about the last thing that might be expected. Yet such was the case. So much so that any conversation in the 1920s or 30s that chanced to turn discussing some living writer — St Jean Perse or Joyce or Eliot was ~~bound to~~ would sooner or later be sure to turn on Hopkins. In fact it was

[*crossed check in black ink in top right-hand corner*]

45

(4)

~~The~~

While I can make no claim to any detailed study of the reasons for Bridges' delay, I feel that if the true reason was that he judged the 1890s ~~and~~ <or the year> 1909 (when Fr. Keating S.J. desired him to publish Hopkins poems complete) to be too soon for anything but an adverse reception. but sensed that 1918 was 'the acceptable year', then I think Bridges prescience was remarkable – [*the next fourteen words and period inserted in pencil over erasures*] the <u>aves admittunt</u> of whatever augur he consulted was said just about on time.

~~A Victorian~~ ··

~~That the~~ [*the next word cancelled*] ~~prosody prosody and what the poet had to say concerning it~~

[*The next word overwrites* of] That a mid Victorian Englishman, ~~who~~ a convert to the Catholic Church in the days of Liddon's & Pusey's[143] Oxford a priest of the Society of Jesus ~~should have~~ who wrote poetry and ~~in~~ notes and letters ~~be~~ discussed ~~metrics~~ his ~~metrics~~ theories of metrics ~~is very~~ at great length should have ~~be~~ turned out to be of the greatest possible interest ~~to~~ & appeal to the men who had either served in, or had ~~gown~~ come to manhood during, the 1914–1918 war is about ~~thing~~ the last thing that might be expected. Yet such was the case. So much so that any ~~chance~~ conversation in the [*one cancelled part-word illegible*] 1920s or '30s that chanced to turn ~~on~~ to discussing some living writer – St Jean Perse or Joyce or Eliot was ~~bound to~~ would sooner or later be sure to turn on Hopkins. In fact it was

[143] Edward Bouverie Pusey (1800–82), a leader of the Oxford Movement and, during Hopkins's years at Balliol College, Regius Professor of Hebrew at the University of Oxford. For Pusey's reaction to Hopkins's conversion, see Norman White, *Hopkins: A Literary Biography*, 139: 'Those who will gain by what you have determined to do, will be the unbelievers.'

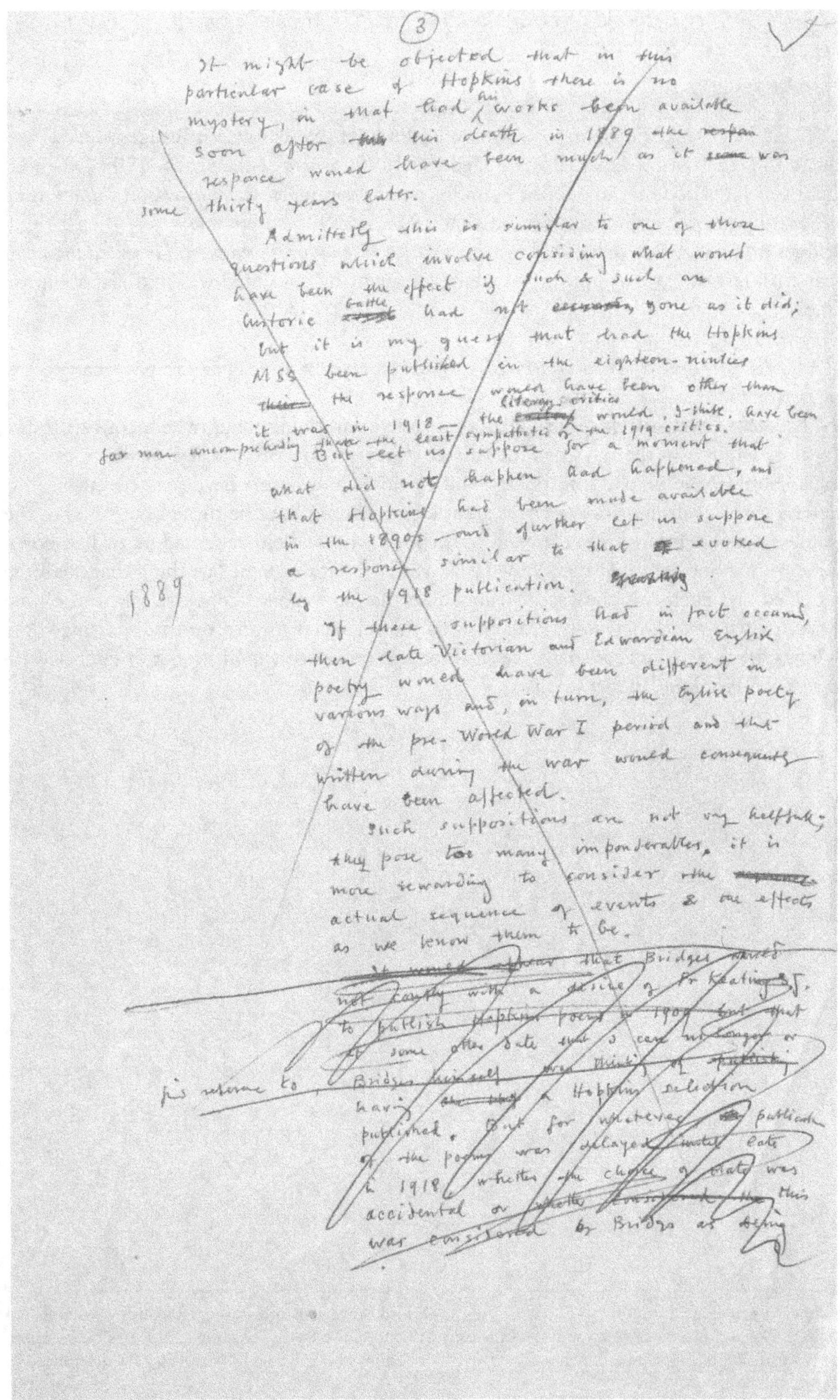

(3)

It might be objected that in this particular case of Hopkins there is no mystery, in that had his works been available soon after ~~the~~ his death in 1889 ~~the respon~~ the response would have been much as it ~~was~~ was some thirty years later.

Admittedly this is similar to one of those questions which involve considering what would have been the effect if such & such an historic battle had not ~~occurred~~ gone as it did; but it is my guess that had the Hopkins MSS been published in the eighteen-nineties ~~the~~ the response would have been other than it was in 1918 — the literary critics would, I think, have been far more uncomprehending than the least sympathetic of the 1919 critics. But let us suppose for a moment that what did not happen had happened, and that Hopkins had been made available in the 1890s and further let us suppose a response similar to that evoked by the 1918 publication.

1889

If these suppositions had in fact occurred, then late Victorian and Edwardian English poetry would have been different in various ways and, in turn, the English poetry of the pre-World War I period and that written during the war would consequently have been affected.

Such suppositions are not very helpful; they pose too many imponderables, it is more rewarding to consider the actual sequence of events & the effects as we know them to be.

~~It would appear that Bridges [illegible] not [illegible] with a desire of Fr Keating S.J. to publish Hopkins poems in 1909 but that at some other date which I can no longer recall Bridges himself was thinking of~~ his reference to, ~~having a Hopkins selection published. But for whatever publication of the poems was delayed until late in 1918 whether the choice of date was accidental or whether this was considered by Bridges as being~~

[*page 14*]

[*crossed check in black ink in top right-hand corner*]
[*entire page cancelled with an* X]

27

(3)

It might be objected that in this particular case of Hopkins there is no mystery, in that had <^his> works been available soon after ~~his~~ his death in 1889 the ~~respon~~ response would have been much as it ~~some~~ was [*the next word inserted in left-hand margin*] some thirty years later.

Admittedly this is similar to one of those questions which involve considing what would have been the effect if such & such an historic ~~event~~ <battle> had not [*one cancelled word illegible*] gone as it did; but it is my guess that had the Hopkins MSS been published in the eighteen-ninties ~~their~~ the response would have been other than it was in 1918 – the ~~critics~~ <^literary critics> would, I think, have been far more uncomprehending than the least sympathetic of the 1919 critics.

But let us suppose for a moment that what did not happen had happened, and that Hopkins had been made available in the 1890s and further let us suppose a response similar to that ~~of~~ evoked by the 1918 publication. [*one cancelled word illegible*] ·

[*written in left-hand margin:* 1889]

If these suppositions had in fact occurred, then late Victorian and Edwardian English poetry would have been different in various ways and, in turn, the English poetry of the pre-World War I period and that written during the war would consequently have been affected.

Such suppositions are not very helpfull; they pose too many imponderables, it is more rewarding to consider the ~~sequence.~~ actual sequence of events & the effects as we know them to be.

[*The rest of the script on this page is struck-through*]

It would appear that Bridges would not comply with a desire of Fr Keating S.J. to publish Hopkins poems in 1909 but that at some other date that I can no longer or find reference to, Bridges himself was thinking of ~~publishing~~ having ~~the~~ [*one cancelled word illegible*] a Hopkins selection published. But for whatever [*one cancelled word illegible*] publication of the poems was delayed until late in 1918, whether the choice of date was accidental or whether considered the this was considered by Bridges as being

(3)

It may be objected that in this particular
case of Hopkins there is no mystery, in
that had his works been available soon after
his death in 1889 the response would have
been much as it was some thirty years
later.

Such a view raises all sorts of
unanswerable questions similar to those
raised by some such query as to what
might have happened had such and such
a decisive battle gone other than it did.

My guess is that had the Hopkins MSS
been published in the 1890s the response
would have been very other than it was
in 1918 — the literary critics would I
think have been far less comprehending
than the most unsympathetic of
the 1919 critics.

But let's pretend for a moment that
what did not happen had happened and
that Hopkins had been made available
in the 1890s, and, further, let us suppose
a response similar to that evoked
by the 1918 publication.

If these suppositions had in fact
occurred then late Victorian and
Edwardian poetry would have different
in various ways and in turn the English
poetry of the immediately pre-War I period
and that written during the war would
consequently have been affected

Such suppositions are not very
helpful — they pose too many
imponderables, it is more rewarding
to consider the actual sequence
of events & the effects as we
know them it be.

[*crossed check in black ink in top right-hand corner*]

33

(3)

It may be objected that in this particular case of Hopkins there is no mystery, in that had his works been available soon after his death in 1889 the response would have been much as it was some thirty years later.

~~Admittedly this raises the sort of question~~

Such a view raises all sorts of ~~questions~~ unanswerable questions similar to those raised by some such a query as to what might have happened [*the rest of this sentence and the next inserted in pencil*] had such and such a decisive battle gone other than it did.

My guess is that had the Hopkins MSS been published in the 1890s the response would have <^been> very other than it was in 1918 – the literary critics would I think have been far less comprehending than the most unsympathetic of the 1919 critics.

But let's pretend for a moment that what did not happen had happened and that Hopkins had been made available in the 1890s, and, further, let us suppose a response similar to that evoked by the 1918 publication.

If these suppositions had in fact occurred then late Victorian and Edwardian poetry would have different in various ways and in turn the English poetry of the immediately pre-War I period and that written during the war would consequently have been affected

Such suppositions are not very helpfull – they pose too many imponderables, it is more rewarding to consider the actual sequence of events and other effects as we know them it be.

④

Whether the publication of Hopkins poems was delayed until late in 1918 by various accidents or whether Bridges judged the ~~[illegible]~~ moment now opportune (he appears to have turned down the notion in 1909 when F. Keating S.J. ~~[illegible]~~ wished for their publication) ~~or indeed whether for what reasons Bridges considered this date auspicious —~~ or indeed for what reasons Bridges found 1918 an appropriate date — I mean whether convenient in various ways, or whether he truly sensed that this was 'the acceptable year', and that the literary climate was just about right to appreciate the very particular contribution this thirty years dead ~~[illegible]~~ friend had made to the greater glory of English letters, I do not know. ~~But whether Bridges, with clear placement or not [illegible] deliberation timed to a nicety the release of Hopkins' highly charged material, I fancy it was the right moment.~~

~~But whether Bridges with clear placement and deliberately timed to a nicety the release of Hopkins' highly charged material or whether it the timing was largely accidental, there are reasons for thinking the date to have been fortunate.~~

But deliberate or not, there are reasons for thinking the date of the release of Hopkins' highly charged material was auspicious.

[*page 16*]

[*uncrossed check in black ink in top right-hand corner*]

46

(4)

Whether the publication of Hopkins poems was delayed until late in 1918 by various accidents. or whether Bridges judged the ~~mome~~ moment now opportune (he appears to have turned down the notion <^in> 1909 when Fr. Keating S.J. wished for their publication) ~~or indeed whether for what reasons Bridges considered this date auspicious~~ –

Or indeed for what reasons Bridges found 1918 an appropriate date – I mean whether convenient in various ways, or whether he truly sensed that this was 'the acceptable year' and that the literary climate was just about right <^to> appreciate the very particular ~~contribution~~ <contribution> his thirty years dead ~~poet-priest friend~~ friend had made to the greater glory of English letters, I do not know. ~~But whether or not this was Bridges, with <^clear> discernment~~ [*the next word cancelled*] ~~great deliberation had timed to a nicety the release of Hopkins' highly charged materiel, I fancy it was the right moment~~

~~But whether Bridges with clear discernment~~ [*the next two words cancelled*] ~~and a deliberately timed to <^a> nicety the release of Hopkins' highly charged materiel or whether~~ [*the next two words cancelled*] ~~it was the timing was largely accidental, there are reasons for thinking the date to have been fortunate.~~

But deliberate or not, these are reasons for thinking the date of the release of Hopkins' highly charged <u>materiel</u> was auspicious.

(4)

✓

Whether Bridges delayed the publication
of Hopkins poems until late in 1918

[*page 17*]

[*uncrossed check in black ink in top right-hand corner*]

(4)

Whether Bridges delayed the publication of Hopkins poems until late in 1918

(1)

The invitation to write something as a tribute to or recalling of Gerard Manley Hopkins in this Centenary year of his entry into the Novitiate of the Society of Jesus might appear ~~[illegible]~~ a not only congenial but fairly simple task in that there is so much which, over the years, the name 'Hopkins' has evoked.

But it becomes, at least in my case, a far from simple matter, once one tries to write down a tribute. For one thing so much has been written in appraisement of Hopkins and his works. ~~these~~ Studies ranging from the intensive two volume work by Dr W. H. Gardner published in 1944 and 1949 to the various books and articles of the nineteen-twenties and thirties and those written since 1949 making available additional material as well as concentrating on some particular aspect of the man and his works.

Anyway, to-day, exactly half a century since the first publication of a collection of his poems and seventy-nine years since the poet's death, Hopkins is part of the canon of English poetry; he is 'accepted'. Once his works became known it was inevitable that, sooner or later, this acceptance would follow. But what is 'accepted' is always in danger of being taken for granted, and while, in any context, a taking for granted whether of works or of persons is never a good thing, it would, for a number of self-evident reasons, be particularly unfortunate in the case of Hopkins.

As is noted above so much has been written [illegible] of Fr Hopkins and his poetry [illegible] perhaps my contribution to this collection might take the form of attempting to recall [illegible] personal [illegible] first coming into contact with Hopkins' work [illegible] Society of Jesus [illegible] poetry.

[*page 18*]

[*circled number in top centre and asterisk in top right-hand corner in red-brown ink or pencil*]

6

[*The next two words in faint grey pencil*]

Hopkins (Month) (1)

The invitation to write something as <^a> tribute to or recalling of Gerard Manley Hopkins in this centenary year of his entry into the Novitiate of the Society of Jesus might appear ~~seem~~ a not only congenial but fairly simple task in that there is so much which, over the years, the name 'Hopkins' has evoked.

But it becomes, at least in my case, a far from simple matter, once one tries to write down a tribute. For one thing so much has been written in appraisement of Hopkins and his works. [*The next word cancelled in pencil*] ~~These~~ [*The first letter of the next word overwritten in upper case in pencil*] Studies [*the next word changed from* range *to* ranging *by, in pencil, turning the final* e *into an* i *and adding* ng] ranging from the intensive two volume work by Dr W. H. Gardner published in 1944 and 1949 to the various books and articles of the nineteen-twenties and 'thirties and those written since 1949 making available additional material as well <^as> concentrating on some particular aspect of the man and his works.

Anyway, to-day, exactly half a century since the first publication of a collection of his poems and seventy-nine years since the poet's death, Hopkins [*the rest of the script on this page inserted in pencil*] is part of the canon of English poetry; he is 'accepted'.

Once his works became known it was inevitable that, sooner or later, this acceptance would follow. But what is 'accepted' is always in danger of being taken for granted, and while, in any context, a taking for granted whether or works or of persons is never a good thing, it would, for a number of interrelated reasons, be particularly unfortunate in the case of Hopkins.

As is noted above so much has been written touching every aspect of Fr Hopkins and his poetry it occurred to me that perhaps my contribution to this collection might take the form of attempting to recall a few personal reactions when first coming into contact with Hopkins work and hearing a good deal about him from friends who chanced to have much interest in him as a priest of the Society of Jesus as well as in his poetry.

(2)

When Bridges published the first edition of Hopkins poems I was away in the army and wholly unaware of this important event. And when December 1918 I was demobilized I returned at once to my studies at an art school which had been interrupted three years and more back. My preoccupation was then, with certain of the visual arts, as indeed it had been from childhood. That preoccupation did not, of course, preclude an interest in other of the arts, such as written poetry, but as a student one's mind was occupied pretty closely with the problems of the art one was trying to practice so that contemporaneous events in other of the arts might easily be unknown or barely known to one.

At all events Hopkins was little more than a name to me for some while.

In 1917, in the trenches of the West Front, I became aware that I belonged to the Catholic tradition but it was not until 1921 that I was formally received into the Church. Without doubt this decisive step was brought about by my having certain art-student friends who were Catholics and unless my memory is playing me false (which is very likely) I first heard of Hopkins with reference to a poem by Walt Whitman which one of these friends chanced to mention. But however that may be, various strands were drawing together and it was in that art-school at Westminster between 1919 & 1922 that I became conditioned toward that kind of thought which

[*asterisk in red-brown ink or pencil in top right-hand corner*]

20

(2) [*overwrites* (3)]

When Bridges published the first edition of Hopkins poems I was away in the army and wholly unaware of this important event. And when ~~on the~~ December 1918 I was demobilized I returned at once to my studies at an art school which had been interrupted three years and more back. My preoccupation was then ~~what it had been from childhood~~ with certain of the visual arts, as indeed it had been from childhood. The preoccupation did not, of course, preclude an interest in other of the arts, such as written poetry, but, as a student one's mind was occupied pretty closely with the problems of the art one was trying to practice so that contemporaneous events in other of the arts might easily be unknown or barely known to one.[144]

At all events Hopkins was little more than a name to me for some while.

~~As far as my memory can disentangle things of forty-eight or so years ago, I first heard of Fr Hopkins referred to by a fellow art student in relation to Walt Whitman a poem of Walt Whitman~~[145]

In 1917, in the trenches of the West Front, I became aware that I belonged to the Catholic tradition but it was not until 1921 that I was formally received into the Church.[146] Without doubt this decisive step was brought about by my having certain art-student friends who were Catholics and unless my memory is playing me false (which is very likely) I first heard of Hopkins with reference to a poem of Walt Whitman which one of these friends chanced to mention. But however that may be, various strands were drawing together and it was in that art-school at Westminster between 1919 & 1922 that I became conditioned toward that habit of thought which ~~later on a few years time made me respond~~

---

[144] Jones was 'disembodied' (transferred to Reserve), at Wimbledon, on 18 December 1918. See Thomas Dilworth, *David Jones in the Great War* (London: Enitharmon, 2012), 203. In 1919, on a government grant, Jones re-enrolled in the School of Arts and Crafts in Peckham Road, Camberwell, London, where he had studied from 1909 to 1914. See Dilworth, *David Jones: Engraver, Soldier, Painter, Poet*, 58. Following his instructor Walter Bayes, Jones transferred to the Westminster School of Art in Vincent Square in March 1921 (see Dilworth, *David Jones: Engraver, Soldier, Painter, Poet*, 60) and studied there until joining Hilary Pepler, Eric Gill, and the Guild of Saints Joseph and Dominic at Ditchling, Sussex, later that year (see Dilworth, *David Jones: Engraver, Soldier, Painter, Poet*, 67). He formally withdrew from Westminster in early January 1922 (see Dilworth, *David Jones: Engraver, Soldier, Painter, Poet*, 71).

[145] Hopkins wrote to Robert Bridges in a letter of 18–19 October 1882, 'I always knew in my heart Walt Whitman's mind to be more like my own than any other man's living. As he is a very great scoundrel this is not a pleasant confession.' See Gerard Manley Hopkins, *The Collected Works of Gerard Manley Hopkins, Volume II: Correspondence 1882–1889*, ed. R. K. R. Thornton and Catherine Phillips (London: Oxford University Press, 2013), 542–3.

[146] Jones was received into the Roman Catholic Church by John O'Connor (G. K. Chesterton's model for Father Brown) on 7 September 1921. See Dilworth, *David Jones: Engraver, Soldier, Painter, Poet*, 68. By late 1917 Jones had felt 'inside, a Catholic' (see Dilworth, *David Jones: Engraver, Soldier, Painter, Poet*, 51).

Hopkins ① ✱

The invitation to contribute something to this 'Homage to Hopkins' issue of The Month in the centenary year of the poet's entry into the Noviciate of the Society of Jesus might appear a not only congenial but fairly simple task, in that over the years the name Hopkins as evoked so much.

But when it comes to actually making a contribution of some sort, the task, at all events in my case, becomes far from simple.

For one thing so much has been written in appraisement of this man and his works: studies ranging from the intensive and thorough two volume work of Dr W. H. Gardner, published in 1944 and 1949, to the various articles & books of the nineteen thirties and twenties and those publications since 1949, perhaps making available additional material or concentrating on some particular aspect of the poetry or the poet.

To-day, exactly half a century since Bridges' publication of a selection of his friend's poems & seventy-nine years since the poet's death, Hopkins has become fully 'accepted' – his work unquestionably part of the canon of English poetry.

With the 'acceptance' of anything there is the danger of that thing being taken for granted. This taking for granted is never a good, whether with regard to works or persons, in the case of Hopkins, such a taking for granted would be analogous to never having heard of him at all.

I think my contribution to this collection of tributes can only take the form of an attempt to recall something of the impact of Hopkins in the nineteen-twenties among my friends and acquaintances and on myself.

When Bridges published the first edition of Hopkins poems I was away in the army & wholly unaware of this important event. In 1919 I resumed my studies as an art-student and

[*page 20*]

[*asterisk in green ink in top right-hand corner*]

Hopkins (1)

The invitation to contribute something to his 'Homage to Hopkins' issue of The Month in this centenary year of the poet's entry into the Novitiate of the Society of Jesus might appear a not only congenial but fairly simple task, in that over the years the name Hopkins as evoked so much.

But when it comes to <^actually> making a contribution of some sort, the task, at all events in my case, becomes far from simple.

For one thing so much has been written in appraisement of this man and his works: studies ranging ^from^ the intensive and thorough two volume work by Dr W. H. Gardner, published in 1944 and 1949, to the various articles & books of the nintine thirties and twenties and those ~~written~~ <publications> since 1949, ~~some~~ <perhaps> making available additional material or concentrating on some particular aspect of the poetry or the poet.

To-day, exactly half a century since Bridges' ~~publ~~ publication of a selection of ~~Hopkins~~ <his friend's> poems & seventy-nine years since the poet's death, Hopkins has become fully 'accepted' – his work unquestionably part of the canon of English poetry.

With <^the> 'acceptance' of anything there is the danger of that thing being taken for granted. This taking for granted is never a good, ~~thing~~ whether with regard to ~~their~~ works or persons. [*The previous full-stop changed from a comma, and the following word changed from* and] But, in the case of Hopkins, such a taking for granted would ~~by~~ be analogous to never having heard of him at all.

I think my contribution to this collection of tributes can only take the form of an attempt to recall something of the impact of Hopkins in the nineteen-twenties among my friends and acquaintances and on myself.

When Bridges published the first edition of Hopkins poems I was away in the army & wholly unaware of this important event. In 1919 I resumed my studies as an art-student and

The invitation to contribute a brief recalling for this Homage to Hopkins' issue of The Month would appear not only a congenial but a simple task,

[*page 21*]

[*all script on this page cancelled*]

The invitation to contribute a ~~few~~ brief recalling for this ~~the~~ 'Homage to Hopkins' issue of The Month would appear not only a congenial but a fairly simple task.

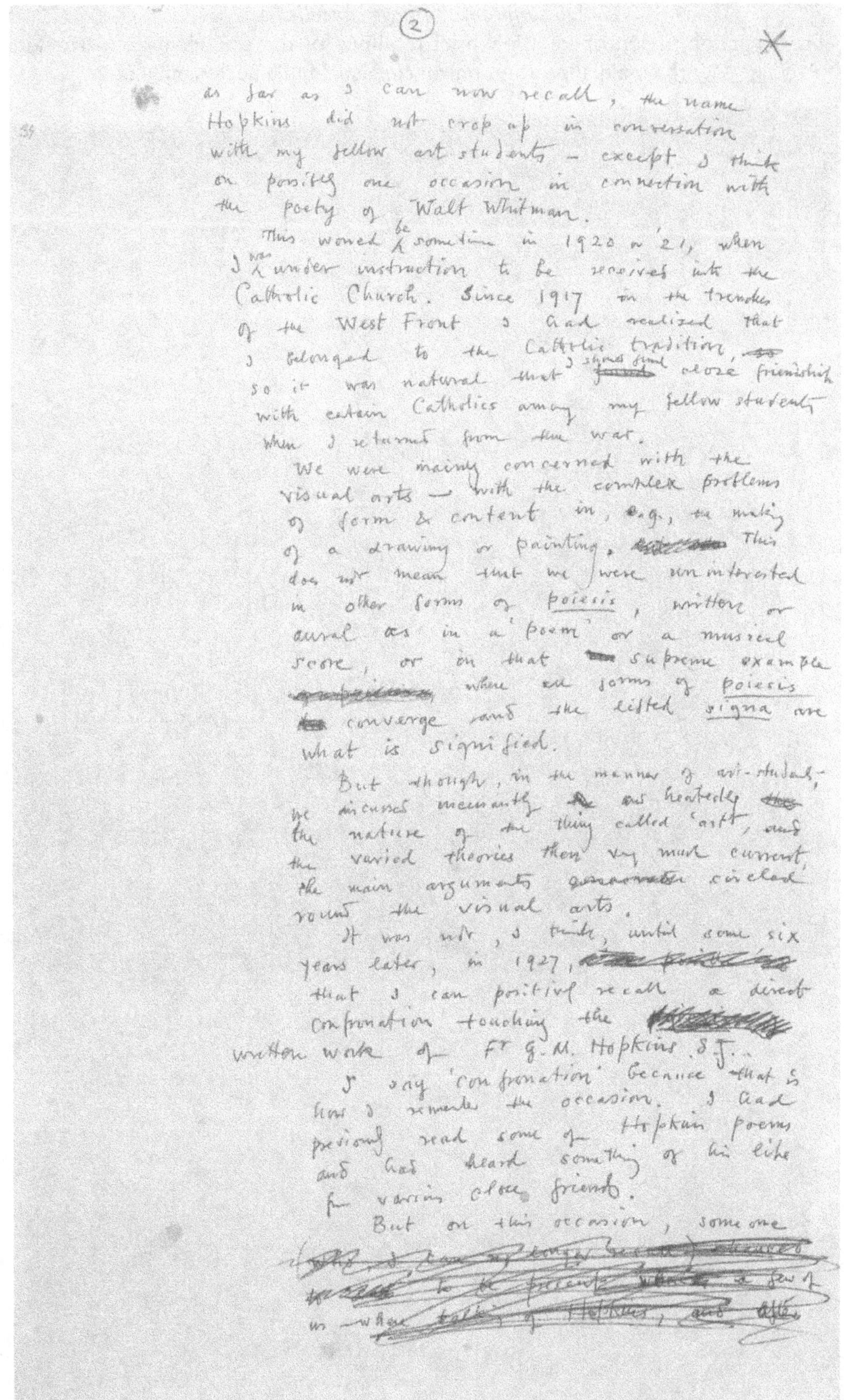

(2)

as far as I can now recall, the name Hopkins did not crop up in conversation with my fellow art students – except I think on possibly one occasion in connection with the poetry of Walt Whitman.

This would be sometime in 1920 or '21, when I was under instruction to be received into the Catholic Church. Since 1917 in the trenches of the West Front I had realized that I belonged to the Catholic tradition, so it was natural that I should find close friendship with certain Catholics among my fellow students when I returned from the war.

We were mainly concerned with the visual arts – with the complex problems of form & content in, e.g., the making of a drawing or painting. This does not mean that we were uninterested in other forms of *poiesis*, written or aural as in a 'poem' or a musical score, or in that supreme example where all forms of *poiesis* converge and the lifted *signa* are what is signified.

But though, in the manner of art-students, we discussed incessantly and heatedly the nature of the thing called 'art', and the varied theories then very much current, the main arguments circled round the visual arts.

It was not, I think, until some six years later, in 1927, that I can positively recall a direct confrontation touching the written work of Fr G. M. Hopkins, S.J.

I say 'confrontation' because that is how I remember the occasion. I had previously read some of Hopkins poems and had heard something of his life from various close friends.

But on this occasion, someone

[*page 22*]

[*asterisk in green pen in top right-hand corner*]

39

as far as I can now recall, the name Hopkins did not crop up in conversation with my fellow art students – except I think on possibly one occasion in connection with the poetry of Walt Whitman.

This would <^be> sometime in 1920 or '21, when I <^was> under instruction to be received in to the Catholic Church. Since 1917 in the trenches of the West Front I had realized that I belonged to the Catholic tradition, ~~so~~ so it was natural that ~~found~~ <I should find> close friendships with certain Catholics among my fellow students when I returned from the war.

We were mainly concerned with the visual arts – with the complex problems of form & content in, e.g., the making of a drawing or painting. ~~but~~ [*one cancelled word illegible*] This does not mean that we were uninterested in other forms of poieisis, written or aural as in a 'poem' or a musical score, or in that [*one cancelled word illegible*] supreme example ~~of poiesis~~ where all forms of poiesis [*one cancelled word illegible*] converge and the lifted signa are what is signified.[147]

But though, in the manner of art-students, we discussed incessantly ~~the~~ and heatedly ~~the~~ the nature of the thing called 'art', and the varied theories then very much current, the main arguments [*one or two cancelled words illegible*] circled round the visual arts.

It was not, I think, until some six years later, in 1927, ~~or else possibly '28~~ that I can positively recall a direct confronation touching the ~~poiesis of~~ [*the next word added in the left-hand margin*] written work of F^r^ G. M. Hopkins. S.J. .

I say 'confronation' because that is how I remember the occasion. I had previously read some of Hopkins poems and had heard something of his life from various close friends.

[*The next sentence cancelled in black ink and red ink or pencil*]

But on this occasion, someone (who, I can no longer recall) chanced ~~to call~~ to be present when [*one cancelled word illegible*] a few of us where talking of Hopkins, and after

[147] The 'supreme example' of *poiesis* in Jones's estimation is the Roman Catholic Mass, as he makes clear elsewhere in these drafts.

[*page 23*]

(3)

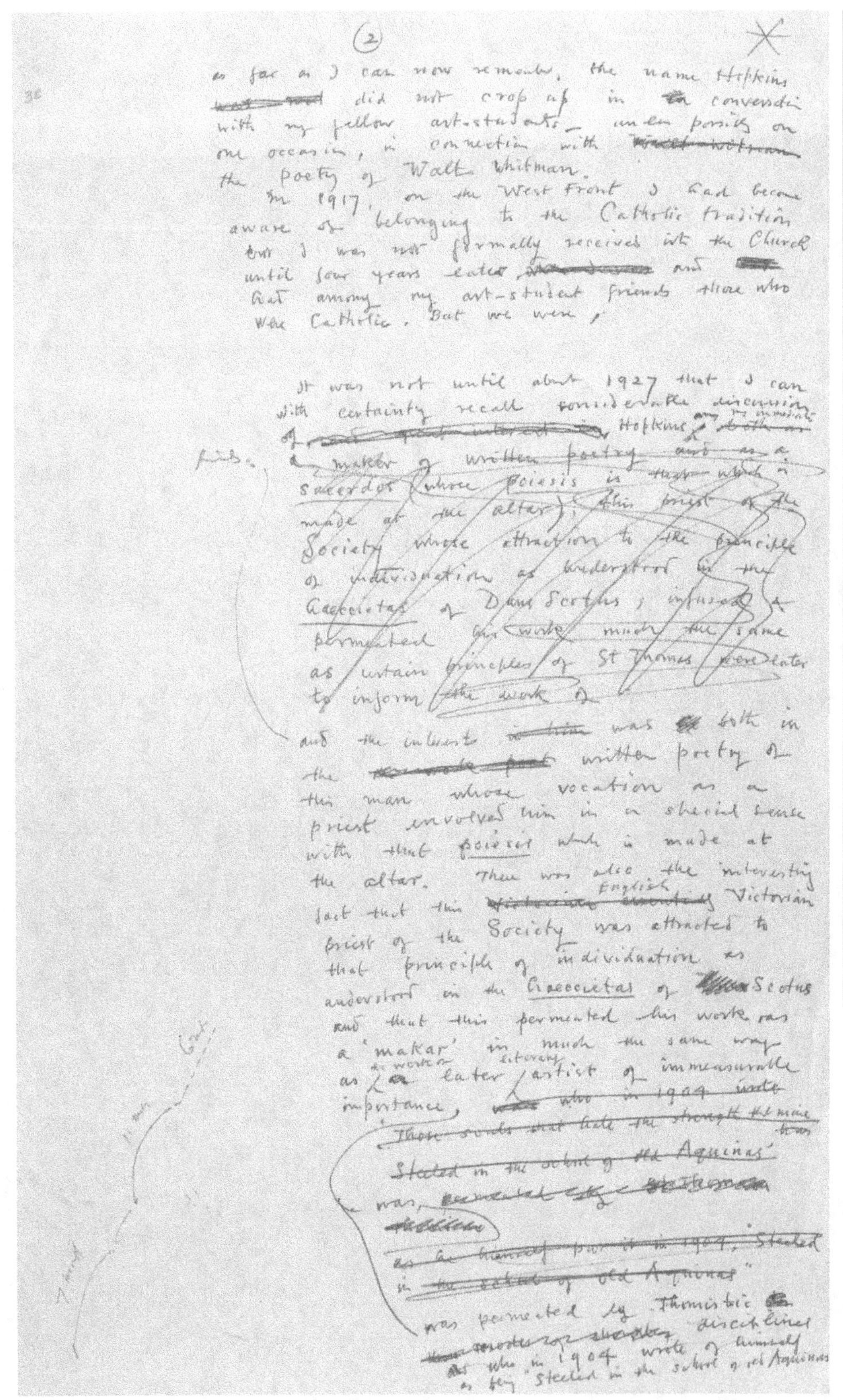

(2)

as far as I can now remember, the name Hopkins did not crop up in conversation with my fellow art-students – unless possibly on one occasion, in connection with the poetry of Walt Whitman.

In 1917, on the West Front I had become aware of belonging to the Catholic tradition but I was not formally received into the Church until four years later, and that among my art-student friends those who were Catholic. But we were,

It was not until about 1927 that I can with certainty recall considerable discussion of Hopkins ~~both as a maker of written poetry and as a sacerdos (whose poiesis is that which is made at the altar); this priest of the Society whose attraction to the principle of individuation as understood in the haecceitas of Duns Scotus, infused & permeated his work much the same as certain principles of St Thomas were later to inform the work of~~

and the interest was both in the written poetry of this man whose vocation as a priest involved him in a special sense with that poiesis which is made at the altar. There was also the interesting fact that this English Victorian priest of the Society was attracted to that principle of individuation as understood in the haecceitas of Scotus and that this permeated his work as a 'makar' in much the same way as a later literary artist of immeasurable importance, ~~who in 1904 wrote Those words that hold the strength ... Steeled in the school of old Aquinas' was, ... as he himself put it in 1904, "Steeled in the school of old Aquinas"~~ was permeated by Thomistic disciplines who in 1904 wrote of himself as being "Steeled in the school of old Aquinas"

[*page 24*]

[*asterisk in green ink in top right-hand corner*]

38

(2)

as far as I can now remember, the name Hopkins ~~was not~~ did not crop up in ~~in~~ conversation with my fellow art-students – unless possibly on one occasion, in connection with ~~Walt Whitman~~ the poetry of Walt Whitman.

In 1917, on the West Front I had become aware of belonging to the Catholic tradition but I was not formally received into the Church until four years later ~~when I was~~ and ~~had~~ had among my art-student friends those who were Catholic. But we were,

It was not until about 1927[148] that I can with certainty recall considerable discussion of ~~and great interest in~~ Hopkins <^among my immediate [*the next word inserted in the left-hand margin*] friends.> ~~both as a maker of written poetry and as a sacerdos (whose poiesis is that which is made at the altar), this priest of the Society whose attraction to the principle of individuation as understood in the haeccietas of Duns Scotus, infused & permeated his work much the same as certain principles of St Thomas were later to inform the work of~~[149]

and the interest ~~in him~~ was [*one cancelled word illegible*] both in the ~~the work poet~~ written poetry of this man whose vocation as a priest involved him in a special sense with that poiesis which is made at the altar. There was also the interesting fact that this ~~Victorian~~ <English> ~~essentially~~ Victorian priest of the Society was attracted to that principle of individuation as understood in the haeccietas of ~~Duns~~ Scotus

[*In the left-hand margin here: a timeline in red ink marking* 7 months, 11 months, 6 months]

---

[148] The art historian Paul Hills noted in a diary entry of late June 1969 (entered after 23 June but before the end of the month) the following recollection from a recent phone conversation with Jones: 'DJ returned from Wales and stayed with Tom Burns in the spring of 1927. There he saw the journals and papers of Hopkins.' See Paul Hills, 'The Romantic Tradition in David Jones', *Malahat Review* 27 (July 1973): 51–2. In this article Hills suggests an affinity between Jones's drawings and watercolours of the late 1920s and the journals of Hopkins, which were not first published until a decade later, as *Notebooks and Papers of Gerard Manley Hopkins*, ed. Humphry House (London and New York: Oxford University Press, 1937). Tom Burns (1906–95), the English Catholic publisher, editor, and friend of Jones, had been given a trunk of Hopkins's papers to store. 'David Jones well remembers his fascination when he first dipped into this trunk', Hills writes (52). Thanks to Paul Hills for sharing the quotation from his diary (email of 1 July 2016). In his biography of Jones, Thomas Dilworth reports that Martin D'Arcy, SJ, then of Campion Hall, Oxford, had lent the unpublished journals to Burns, who, in 1932, stored them at his Chelsea residence, 10 Jubilee Place. See Dilworth, *David Jones: Engraver, Soldier, Painter, Poet*, 152: 'There, "on one or two occasions", Jones had "a look at" the unpublished notebooks of Gerard Manley Hopkins, loaned to Burns by D'Arcy. Although Burns remembered him as showing only "mild interest", so they may have been no influence, the descriptive language of *In Parenthesis* has striking affinity with Hopkins's visually vivid and acoustically rich lyrical notebook descriptions.' Dilworth here quotes a letter from Jones to John H. Johnston of 24 August 1962 and his own interview with Tom Burns of 20 June 1986.

[149] John Duns Scotus, c. 1265–1308, Franciscan friar and theologian born in the Scottish borders, posited a principle of individuation, which he called *haecceitas* ('this-ness'), that Jones in a BBC broadcast of 23 July 1953 defines as 'that which makes a thing essentially other from some other thing'. See 'Wales and the Crown', in *Epoch and Artist*, 46. For a concise, authoritative account of Hopkins's appropriation of this term and suggestions for further reading, see Norman H. MacKenzie, *A Reader's Guide to Gerard Manley Hopkins*, 2nd edn (Philadelphia: Saint Joseph's University Press, 2008), 240–1. For a brief account of Jones's formative encounter with Neo-Thomist thought in his intellectual circles of the 1920s and 1930s, see Dilworth, *David Jones: Engraver, Soldier, Painter, Poet*, 126.

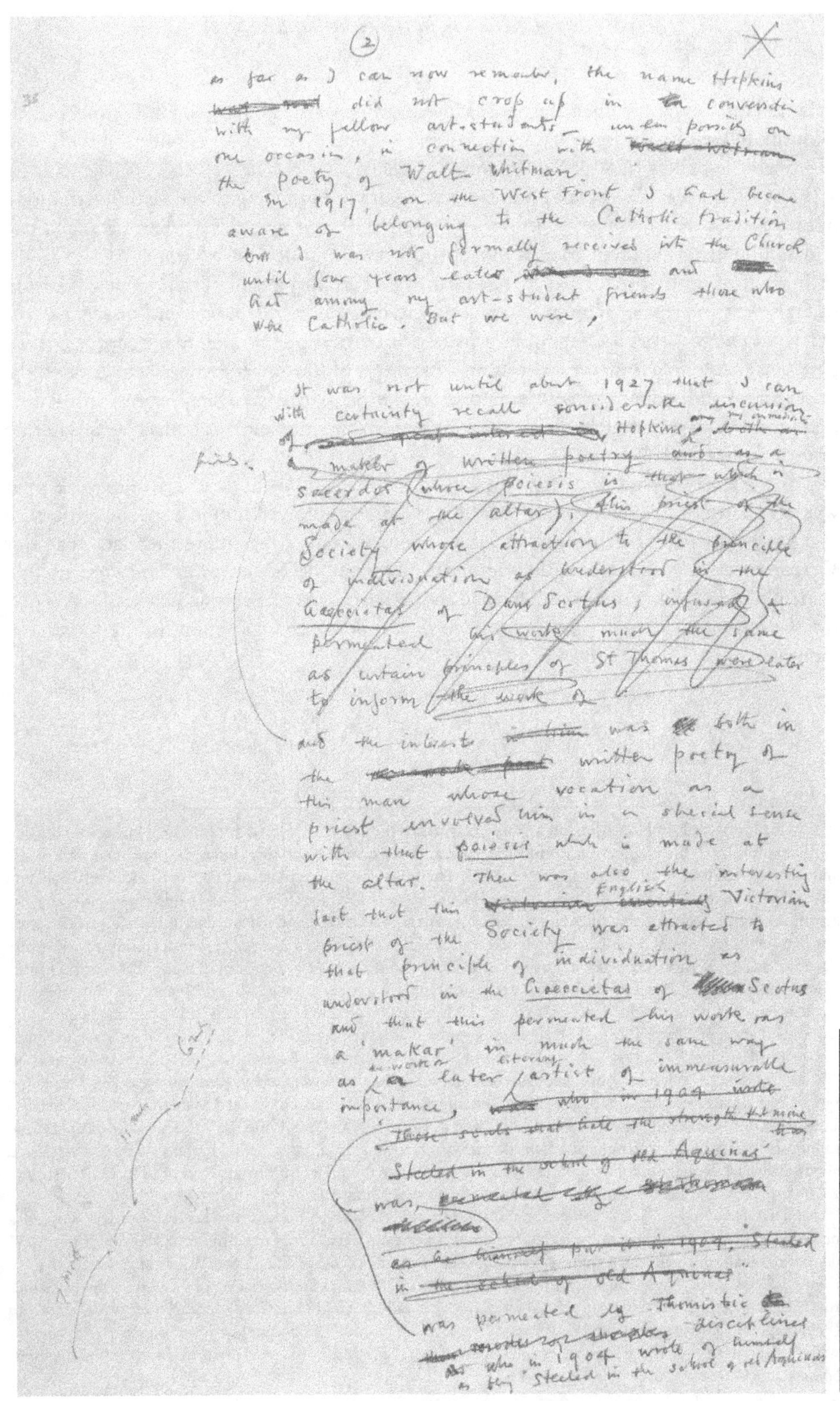
(2)

as far as I can now remember, the name Hopkins did not crop up in conversation with my fellow art-students — unless possibly on one occasion, in connection with the poetry of Walt Whitman.

In 1917, on the West Front I had become aware of belonging to the Catholic tradition but I was not formally received into the Church until four years later and that among my art-student friends those who were Catholics. But we were,

It was not until about 1927 that I can with certainty recall considerable discussion of Hopkins,

and the interests was both in the written poetry of this man whose vocation as a priest involved him in a special sense with that *poiesis* which is made at the altar. There was also the interesting fact that this English Victorian priest of the Society was attracted to that principle of individuation as understood in the Haecceitas of Scotus and that this permeated his work as a 'makar' in much the same way as a writer literary a later artist of immeasurable importance, was permeated by Thomistic disciplines who in 1904 wrote of himself as being "Steeled in the school of old Aquinas"

[*page 24*] (continued)

and that this permeated his work as a 'makar' in much the same way as <^the work of> a later <^literary> artist of immeasurable importance ~~was who in 1904 wrote 'Those souls that hate the strength that mine has steeled in the school of old Aquinas' was permeated by St Thomas Aquinas~~

~~Thomistic~~

~~as he himself put it in 1904 "Steeled in the school of old Aquinas"~~

was permeated by Thomistic [*once cancelled word illegible*] ~~thou modes of thought~~ disciplines [*once cancelled word illegible*] who in 1904 wrote of himself as being 'steeled in the school of old Aquinas'.[150]

[150] Jones is quoting line 82 of James Joyce's satirical broadside poem 'The Holy Office', written in August 1904: 'So distantly I turn to view / The shamblings of that motley crew, / Those souls that hate the strength that mine has / Steeled in the school of old Aquinas' (ll. 79–82). See James Joyce, *Poems and Shorter Writings*, ed. Richard Ellmann, A. Walton Litz, and John Whittier-Ferguson (London: Faber & Faber, 2001), 99. Joyce lampoons the Irish literati, the 'crew' of Yeats and George Russell among them, just before his departure in October 1904 for self-imposed exile on the continent. Joyce was 'schooled' in the Jesuit *ratio studiorum* at Clongowes Wood College in County Kildare and Belvedere College in Dublin and attended the inaugural meeting of a Thomas Aquinas Society while an undergraduate at University College Dublin. See Richard Ellmann, *James Joyce*, new and rev. edn (London: Oxford University Press, 1982), 65. William T. Noon, SJ, for the endpapers of whose 1967 book *Poetry and Prayer* Jones supplied lettering, suggests that in fact Joyce 'made little formal study of St. Thomas' works during his student days', his 'steeling' being a mainly extracurricular affair. See William T. Noon, *Joyce and Aquinas* (New Haven, CT, and London: Yale University Press, 1963), 9. The first chapter of Noon's monograph on Joyce takes its title and epigraph from the lines of the poem by Joyce that Jones quotes. Jones's personal copy of this book is dated 1 October 1965. See Huw Ceiriog Jones, *The Library of David Jones*, 211.

(3)

read aloud one or two of Hopkins poems.

But my suggestion that I thought the poet must of been of Welsh affinity and certainly.

[*page 25*]

[*asterisk in green ink in top right-hand corner*]

(3)

42

read aloud one or two of Hopkins poems.

~~I ventured to ask is it known to what degree Hopkins was Welsh, but the opinion seemed to be that~~ [*once cancelled word illegible*] ~~there was no ground for supposing any Welshness at all.~~[151]

But my suggestion that I thought ~~Hopk~~ the poet must of been of Welsh affinity and certainly ·

[151] Throughout his essays and correspondence Jones consistently emphasizes Hopkins's affinity with the Welsh nation, language, and culture. See for example Jones's marginal note in his copy of Wyn Griffith, *The Welsh* (Harmondsworth: Penguin, 1950), 103: 'The influence of Hopkins is here very understated. Also I should have thought there was something very Welsh in "his turn of mind", Cf. e.g. ~~The~~ Vaughan, Traherne, Donne, Herbert, all of Welsh affinities.' On Hopkins's Welsh connection to the Metaphysical poets ('who were so largely Welsh'), see Jones's letter to the Welsh poet Vernon Watkins of 17 April 1962 in Kathleen Henderson Staudt, 'David Jones: Eight Previously Unpublished Letters to Vernon Watkins', *Anglo-Welsh Review* 87 (1987): 81–2. See also Jones's 1958 'Preface by the Author', *Epoch and Artist*, where he refers to Hopkins as 'an English Jesuit in a house of studies in that part of North Wales properly called Gwynedd-below-the-Conwy, and not uninfluenced by the strict metrical ingenuities of the old poetry of the land in which he was living' (15).

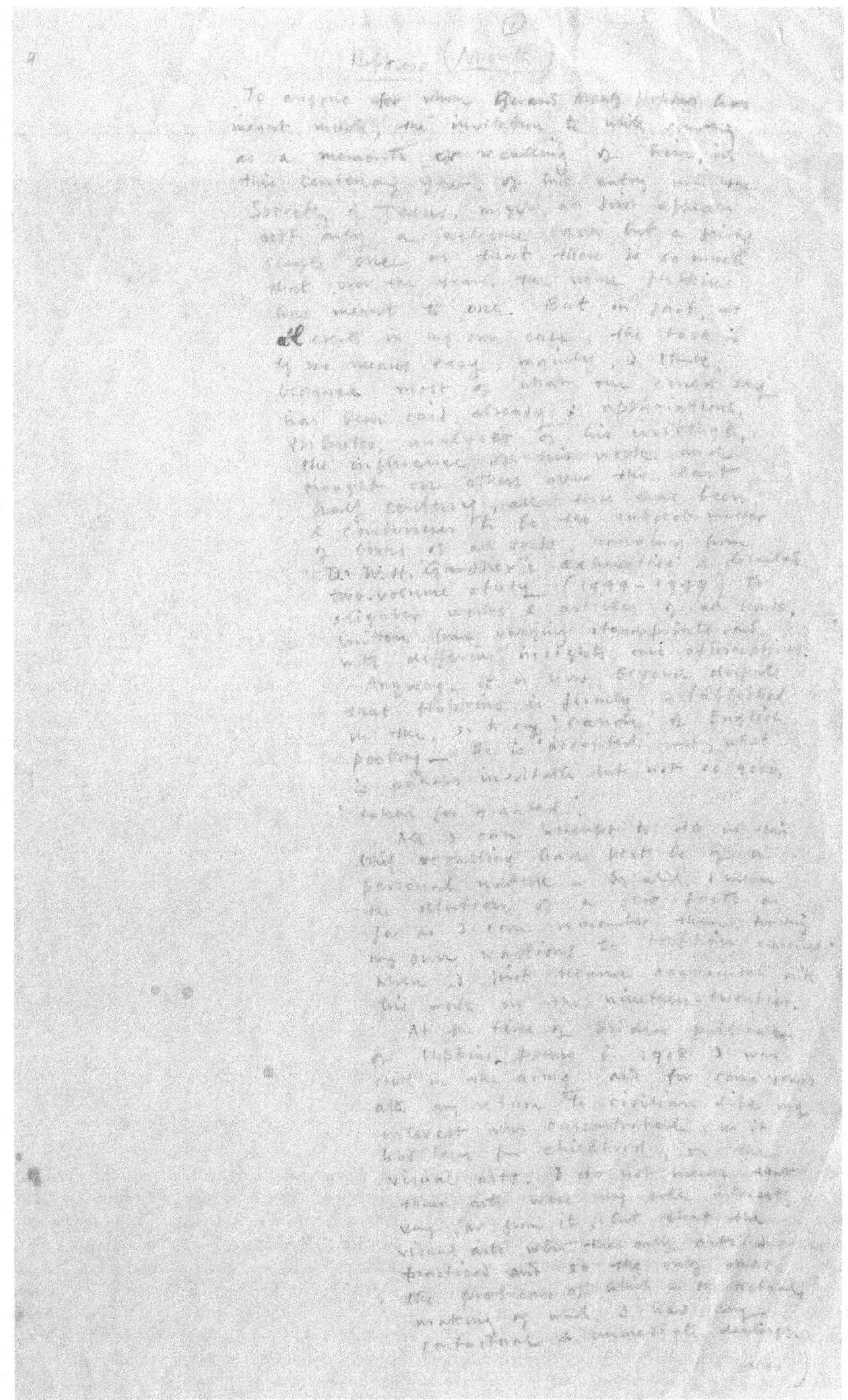

Hopkins (Month)

To anyone for whom Gerard Manley Hopkins has meant much, the invitation to write something as a memento or recalling of him, in this centenary year of his entry into the Society of Jesus, might at first appear not only a welcome task but a fairly simple one in that there is so much that over the years the name Hopkins has meant to one. But in fact, at least in my own case, the task is by no means easy, mainly, I think, because most of what one would say has been said already & appreciations, tributes, analyses of his writings, the influence of his work and thought on others over the last half century, all this have been & continue to be the subject-matter of books of all sorts, ranging from Dr W. H. Gardner's exhaustive & detailed two-volume study (1944–1949) to slighter works & articles & ad hocs, written from varying standpoints and with differing insights and attributions. Anyway, it is now beyond dispute that Hopkins is firmly established in the, so to say, 'canon' of English poetry — he is 'accepted' and, what is perhaps inevitable but not so good, 'taken for granted'.

All I can attempt to do in this [illegible] recalling [illegible] best be by a personal note [illegible] by which I mean the relation of a few facts as far as I can remember them, having my own reactions to Hopkins's [illegible] when I first became acquainted with his work in the nineteen-twenties.

At the time of Bridges' publication of Hopkins's poems in 1918 I was still in the army and for some years after my return to civilian life my interest was concentrated, as it had been from childhood, on the visual arts. I do not mean that those arts were my sole interest, very far from it, but since the visual arts were the only arts I [illegible] practised and so the only ones the practice of which [illegible] making of [illegible], I had [illegible] contextual & [illegible] dealings [illegible]

[*page 26*]

[*this page in pencil*]
(1)
<u>Hopkins</u> (<u>Month</u>)

4

To anyone for [*overwrites* whom] whom [*the following* G *overwrites* H] Gerard Manly Hopkins has meant much, the invitation to write something as a memento or [*overwrites* of] recalling of him, in this centenary year of his entry into the Society of Jesus, might at first appear not only a welcome task but a fairly simple one in that there is so much that over the years the name Hopkins has meant to one. But, in fact, at all events in my own case, the task is by no means easy, mainly, I think, because most of what one could say has been said already: appreciations, tributes, analyses of his writings, the influence of his work and thought on others over the last half century, all this has been & continues to be the subject-matter of books of all sorts, ranging from Dr W. H. Gardner's exhaustive & detailed two-volume study (1944–1949) to slighter works & articles of all kinds, written from varying standpoints and with differing insights and apperceptions.

Anyway, it is now beyond dispute that Hopkins is firmly established in the, so to say, 'canon' of English poetry – he is 'accepted' and, what is perhaps inevitable but not so good, 'taken for granted'.

All I can attempt to do in this brief recalling had best be of a personal nature – by which I mean the relation of a few facts as far as I can remember them, touching my own reactions to Hopkins especially when I first became acquainted with his work in the nineteen-twenties.

At the time of Bridges publication of Hopkins poems in 1918 I was still in the army and for some years after my return to civilian life my interest was concentrated, as it had been from childhood, on the visual arts. I do not mean that those arts were my sole interest, very far from it, but that the visual arts were the only arts I practiced and so the only ones the problems of which – the actual making of which, I had any contractual & immediate dealings.

(over)

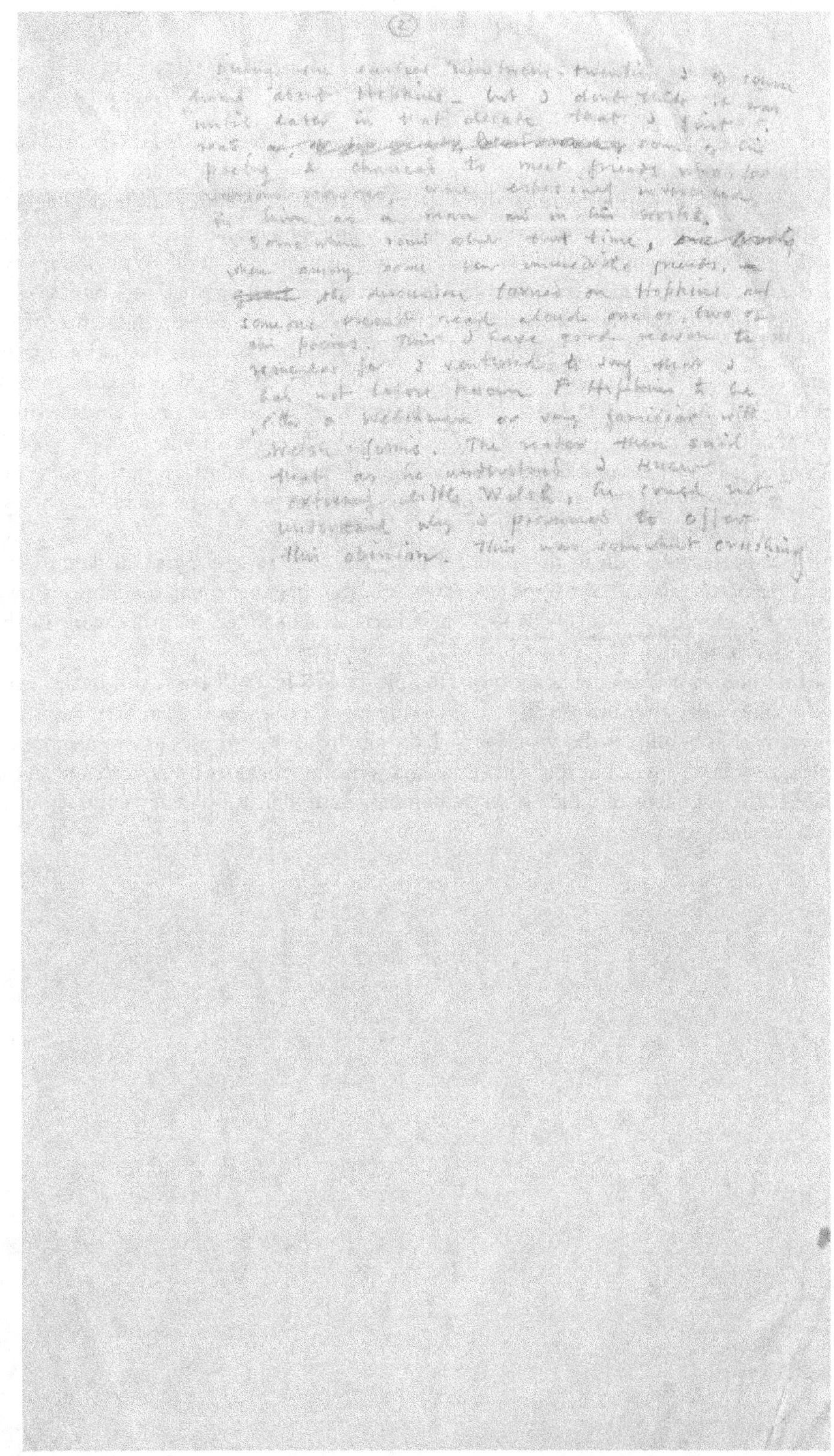

(2)

During the earliest nineteen-twenties I of course heard about Hopkins – but I don't think it was until later in that decade that I first read, or [illegible] some of the poetry & chanced to meet friends who, for various reasons, were especially interested in him as a man and in his works.

Some while round about that time, one evening when among some few immediate friends, the discussion turned on Hopkins and someone present read aloud one or two of his poems. This I have good reason to remember for I ventured to say that I had not before known Fr Hopkins to be either a Welshman or very familiar with Welsh forms. The reader then said that as he understood I knew extremely little Welsh, he could not understand why I presumed to offer this opinion. This was somewhat crushing

[*page 27*]

[this page in pencil]

(2)

During the earlier nineteen-twenties I of course heard about Hopkins – but I dont think it was until later in that decade that I first read~~, or, to be exact, heard read,~~ some of his poetry & chanced to meet friends who, for various reasons, were especially interested in him. as a man and in his works.

Somewhere round about that time, [*two illegible words cancelled*] when among some few immediate friends, ~~a guest~~ the discussion turned on Hopkins and someone present read aloud one or two of his poems. This I have good reason to remember for I ventured to say that I had not before known Fr Hopkins to be either a Welshman or very familiar with Welsh forms. The reader then said that as he understood I knew extremely little Welsh, he could not understand why I presumed to offer this opinion. This was somewhat crushing.

[Four lines of erasures follow]

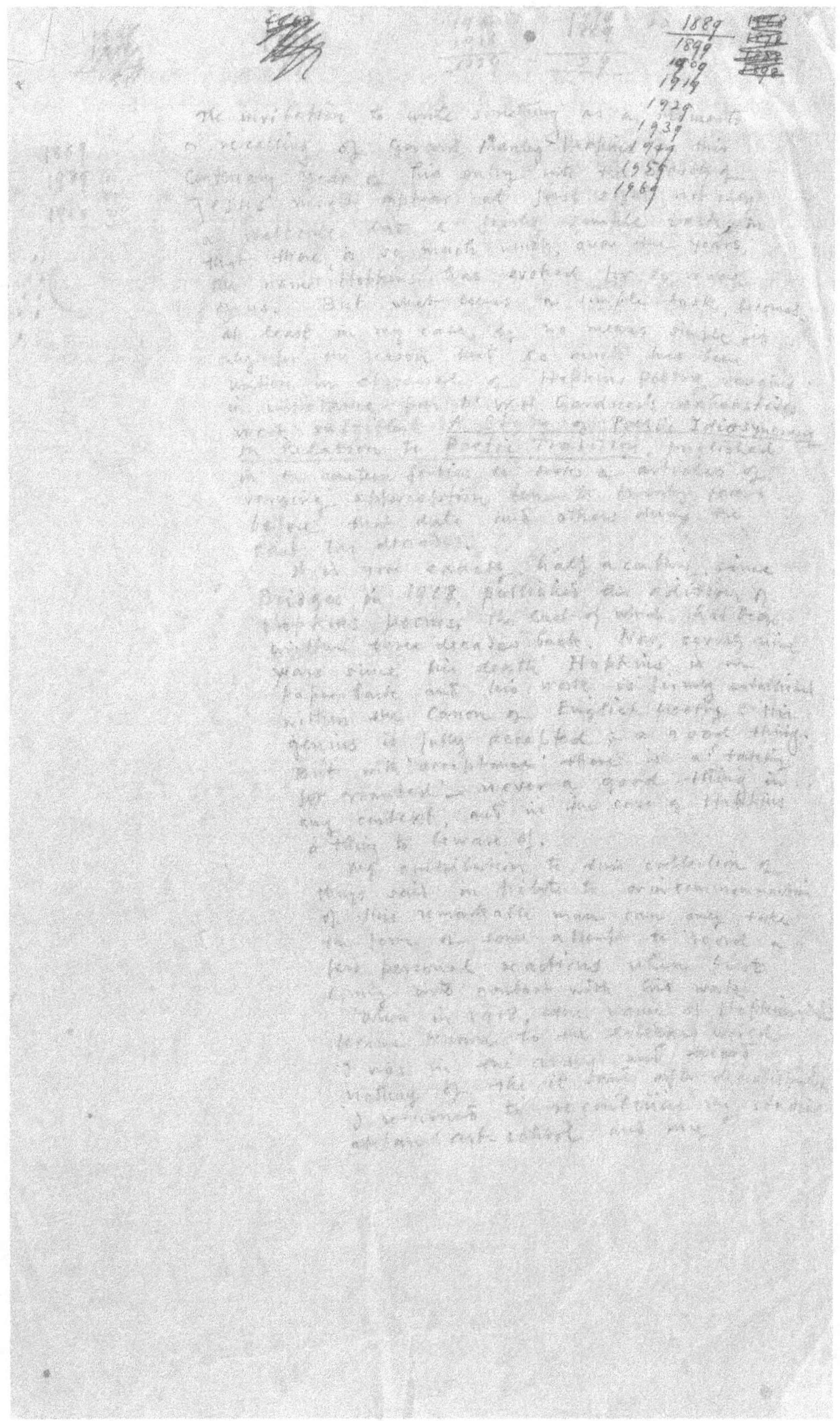

[*page 28*]

[*sums and differences of dates written at top and in the left-hand margin in both pencil and pen, three of them cancelled; the rest of this page in pencil*]

8

The invitation to write something as a memento or recalling of Gerard Manley Hopkins in this centenary year of his entry into the Society of Jesus might appear at first sight not only a welcome but a fairly simple task, in that there is so much which, over the years, the name 'Hopkins' has evoked for so many of us. But what seems a simple task, becomes, at least in my case, by no means simple if only for the reason that so much has been written in appraisal of Hopkins poetry ranging in importance from Dr W. H. Gardner's exhaustive work subtitled A Study of Poetic Idiosyncrasy in Relation to Poetic Tradition, published in the nineteen forties to books & articles of varying apperception ten to twenty years before that date and others during the last two decades.

It is now exactly half a century since Bridges, in 1918, published his edition of Hopkins poems, the last of which had been written three decades back. Now, seventy-nine years since his death Hopkins is in paper-back and his work is firmly established within the canon of English poetry. His genius is fully accepted; a good thing. But with 'acceptance' there is a 'taking for granted' – never a good thing in any context, and in the case of Hopkins a thing to beware of.[152]

My contribution to this collection of things said in tribute to or in commemoration of this remarkable man can only take the form of some attempt to record a few personal reactions when first coming into contact with his work.

When in 1918, the name of Hopkins became known to the literary world I was in the army and heard nothing of the it and after demobilization I returned to recontinue my studies at an art-school and my

[152] Jones owned the first (1953) Oxford University Press edition of John Pick (ed.), *A Hopkins Reader*, which was published in a revised and enlarged paperback edition as a Doubleday Image Book in February 1966. He also owned the tenth impression of Gerard Manley Hopkins, *Poems and Prose of Gerard Manley Hopkins*, ed. W. H. Gardner (Harmondsworth: Penguin, 1967), a paperback first published in 1953. For further publication details, see Huw Ceiriog Jones, *The Library of David Jones*, 140, and Tom Dunne, *Gerard Manley Hopkins: A Comprehensive Bibliography*, 34.

(2)

This recalling of personal reactions of some decades back may seem too autobiographic for which I apologize.

In 1918 when Bridges published the first edition of *Poems of Gerard Manley Hopkins* I was away in the army and heard nothing of this important 'literary' event and so have no first hand knowledge of its immediate effect. After demobilization in December 1918 I resumed my studies at an art-school. My main concern was with the visual arts, as indeed it had been since childhood, so that speaking in very general terms the people I most mixed with were more aware of the contemporary [illegible] to do with those visual arts than with the written or aural arts. I do not mean that these arts were neglected by us but merely that we were involved in a continual, immediate manual problem with the intractable problems of the making of a drawing or a painting as distinct from the same problems in the making of a written work, a poem or a musical score.

Sometime in 1917 while on the West Front I became aware of belonging to the Catholic tradition though I was not formally received into the Church until four years later. At Westminster Art School where I was from 1919 to 1921, I had student friends who were Catholic and who—apart from obvious influences—unwittingly and in ways that they themselves least imagined turned my thoughts to the whole complex matter of *poiesis*, of 'making', of *signa* and of the *signum*-making proclivity of man. It was clear that the Catholic religion took it for granted that this sign-making was not peripheral but central to man, so central indeed that the Church's central act was not only an act of *poiesis*.

[*this page in pencil*]
(2)

22

This recalling of personal reactions of some decades back may seem too autobiographic for which I apologize.

In 1918 when Bridges published the first edition of Poems of Gerard Manley Hopkins I was away in the army and, heard nothing of this important 'literary event' and so have no firsthand knowledge of its immediate effect.

After demobilization in December 1918 I resumed my studies at an art-school. My main concern was with the visual arts, as indeed it had been since childhood, so that speaking in very general terms the people I most mixt with were more aware of the contemporary problems to do with those visual arts than with the written or aural arts. I do not mean that these arts were neglected by us but merely that we were involved in a contactual, immediate, manual fashion with the intractable problems of the making of a drawing or a painting as distinct from the same problems in the making of a written work, a poem or a musical score.

Sometime in 1917 while on the West Front I became aware of belonging to the Catholic tradition though I was not formally received into the Church until four years later. At Westminster Art School were I was from 1919 to 1921, I had student friends who were Catholic and who – apart from obvious influences – unwittingly and in ways which they themselves least imagined turned my thoughts to the whole complex matter of poiesis, of 'making', of signa and of the signum-making proclivity of man. It was clear that the Catholic religion took it for granted that this sign-making was not peripheral but central to man,

So central indeed that the Church's central act was not only an act of poiesis, [*erasure*]

(2) XXX

This recalling of my own reactions of four decades back may seem too autobiographical, for which I apologize.

In 1918 when Bridges published the first edition of <u>Poems of Gerard Manley Hopkins</u> I was in the army and heard nothing of this extremely important literary event; but when at the end of 1918 I was demobilised I resumed my art-school studies which had been broken by three years or more previously. But as my concern was with the visual arts as it has been for [illegible] the name 'Hopkins' did not register though I occasionally heard [illegible]

[*page 30*]

[*this page in pencil*]
[XXX *in grey pencil in top right-hand corner*]
(2)

23

This recalling of my own reactions of four decades back may seems too autobiographic, for which I apologize.

In 1918 when Bridges published the first edition of <u>Poems of Gerard Manley Hopkins</u> I was in the army and heard nothing of this extremely important literary event and when at the end of 1918 I was demobilized I resumed my art-school studies which had been broken off three years or more previously. But as my concern was with the visual arts as it had been from childhood, the name 'Hopkins' did not register though I occasionally heard

Greetings telegram

Mrs [illegible]

40 Gaythorne Rd

S.E. 23

Happy Day

much love

David.

[*page 31*]

[*this page in pencil*]

Greetings telegram[153]

Mrs George Hyne
40 Garthorne Rd
S.E 23

Happy Day
much love
David.

[153] 'Mrs George Hyne' is Alice Mary Jones, Jones's older sister, born 29 April 1891. In his biography of Jones, Thomas Dilworth reports that on 14 April 1967 Jones attended a party for Alice's fiftieth wedding anniversary. She married George Hyne on 14 April 1917 at St James's Hatcham. See Dilworth, *David Jones: Engraver, Soldier, Painter, Poet*, 337.

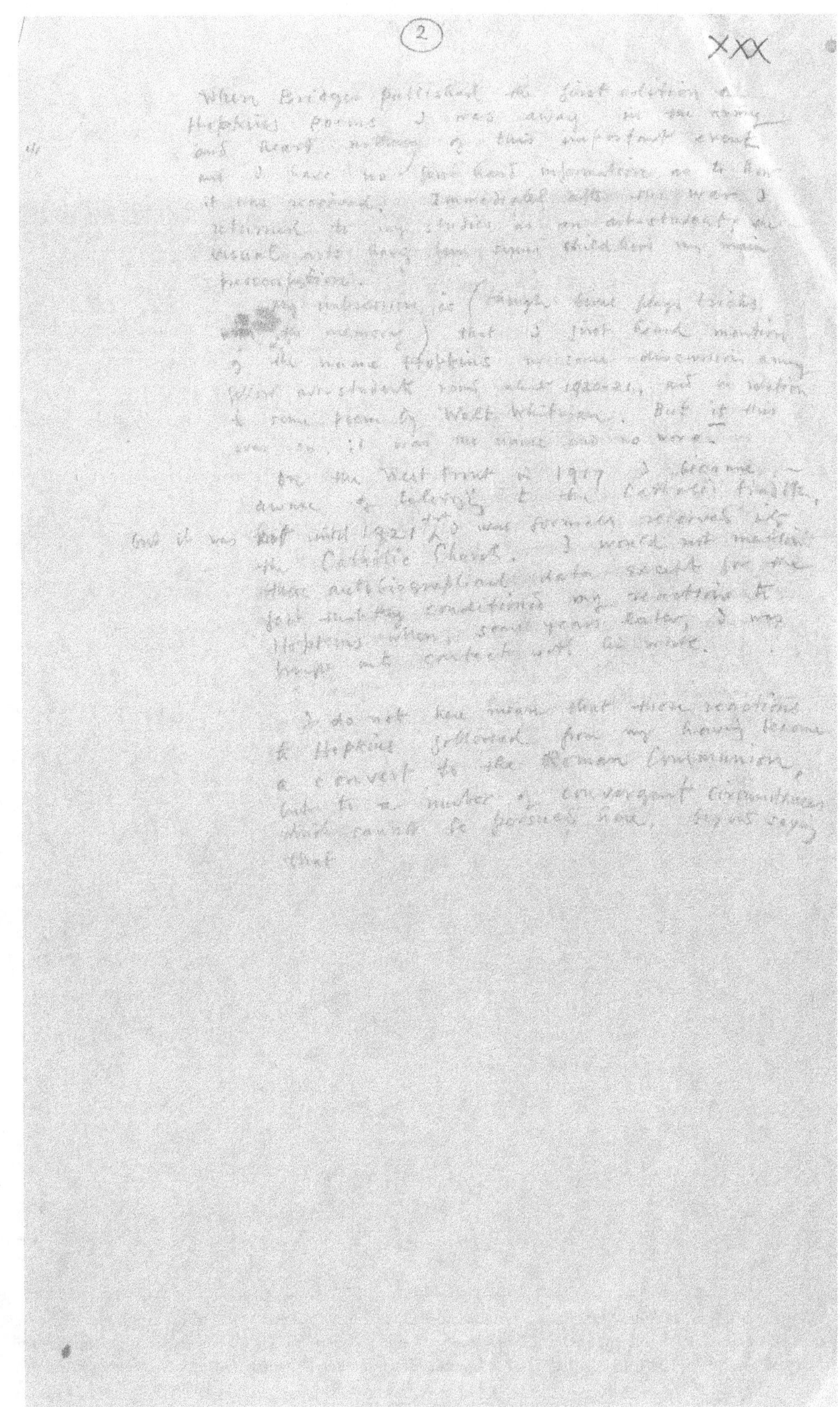

(2) XXX

When Bridges published the first edition of Hopkins poems I was away in the army and heard nothing of this important event and I have no first hand information as to how it was received. Immediately after the war I returned to my studies as an art student, the visual arts having from early childhood my main preoccupation.

My impression is (though time plays tricks with the memory) that I first heard mention of the name Hopkins in some discussion among fellow art-students round about 1920–21, and in relation to some poem by Walt Whitman. But if this was so, it was the name and no more.

In the West Front in 1917 I became aware of belonging to the Catholic tradition, but it was not until 1921 that I was formally received into the Catholic Church. I would not mention these autobiographical data except for the fact that they conditioned my reactions to Hopkins when, some years later, I was brought into contact with his work.

I do not here mean that these reactions to Hopkins followed from my having become a convert to the Roman Communion, but to a number of convergent circumstances which cannot be pursued here, except saying that

[*page 32*]

[*this page in pencil except for circled numeral 2 at top center and* XXX *in top right-hand corner, both in black ink*]

(2)

41

When Bridges published the first edition of Hopkins poems I was away in the army and heard nothing of this important event and I have no first hand information as to how it was received. Immediately after the war I returned to my studies as an art-student; the visual arts having been since childhood my main preoccupation.

My impression is (though time plays tricks with the memory) that I first heard mention of the name Hopkins in some discussion among fellow art-students round about 1920–21, and in relation to some poem by Walt Whitman. But if this was so, it was the name and no more.

On the West Front in 1917 I became aware of belonging to the Catholic tradition, [*the next three words added in left-hand margin*] but it was not until 1921 <^that> I was formally received into the Catholic Church. I would not mention these autobiographical data except for the fact that they conditioned my reactions to Hopkins when, some years later, I was brought into contact with his work.

I do not mean that those reactions to Hopkins followed from my having become a convert to the Roman Communion, but to a number of convergent circumstances which cannot be persued here, beyond saying that

The invitation to write something as a tribute to, or memento of, Gerard Manley Hopkins, in this centenary year of his entering the Novitiate of the Society of Jesus, might appear a not only congenial but fairly simple task in that there is so much which, over the years, the name 'Hopkins' has evoked.

But it becomes, at least in my case, a far from simple task, once one begins to actually make that tribute. For one thing, so much has been written in appraisement of this man and his works: Studies ranging from the intensive two volume work by Dr W. H. Gardner, published in 1944 & 1949 to the various articles & books of the nineteen-twenties & thirties and those written since 1949 making available additional material or concentrating on a one particular aspect of the works or life or character of Hopkins.

It occurred to me that perhaps my contribution to this collection in this issue of The Month might take the form of an attempt to recall the circumstances of my first hearing about or my reading or hearing read the works of Fr Hopkins, and my reactions to what I read or heard.

To-day, exactly half a century since the first publication of a collection of his poems, and seventy-nine years since the poet's death, Hopkins' work is part of the canon of English poetry; he is 'accepted'. Once his poetry was known it was, I think, certain that sooner or later, such acceptance would follow. But what is 'accepted' is always in danger of being taken for granted, and while a taking for granted, whether of works or of persons is never a good thing, it would be particularly unfortunate in the case of Hopkins and his works.

[*page 33*]

[XX *in pencil in top right-hand corner*]
Hopkins (1) <u>The Month</u>

7

[*the above in pencil, the below in pen*]

The invitation to write something as a tribute to, or memento of, Gerard Manley Hopkins, in the centenary year of his entering the Novitiate of the Scociet of Jesus, might appear a not only congenial but fairly simple task in that there is so much which, over the years, the name 'Hopkins' has evoked.

But it becomes, at least in my case, a far from simple task, [*four cancelled words illegible*] once one begins to actually make that tribute.

For one thing, so much has been written in appraisement of this man and his works: Studies ranging from the intensive two volume work by D[r] W. H. Gardner, published in 1944 & 1949 to the various articles and books of the nineteen-twenties & thirties and those written since 1949 making available additional material for concentrating on some particular aspect of the works or life or character of Hopkins.

It occurred to me that perhaps my contribution to this collection in this issue of <u>The Month</u> might take the form of an attempt to recall the circumstances of my first hearing about or my reading or hearing read the works of F[r] Hopkins, and my reactions to what I read or heard.

To-day, exactly half a century ~~since~~ since the first publication of a collection of his poems, and seventy-nine years since ~~since~~ the poet's death, Hopkin~~'~~s' work is part of the canon of English poetry; he is 'accepted'. Once his poetry was known it was, I think, certain that sooner or later, such acceptance would follow.

But what is 'accepted' is always in danger of being taken for granted, and while a taking for granted, whether of works ~~of~~ or of persons is [*the rest of the page in pencil*] never a good thing, it would be particularly unfortunate in the case of Hopkins and his works

(2) XXXX

In 1918 when Bridges' first edition of Poems
of Gerard Manley Hopkins was published I
was away in the army and heard nothing
of this event and so have no first hand
knowledge of its immediate reception.

In January 1919 I resumed my studies
as an art-student. My main concern was
with the visual arts as it had been since
childhood, so that, speaking in very general
terms, the people I most mixt with were more
aware, or more concentrated upon, the contemporary
problems to do with the visual arts than with
the written or aural arts. I do not at
all mean that we were not interested
in or did not discuss those other arts
but only that as students we were involved
in a contactual, immediate, day-by-day,
manual fashion with the intractable
problems of form and content in the
making of a drawing or a painting,
whereas we were not immediately involved
in those same problems as they occur
in the making of a written work, a
poem or a musical score.

But it so happened that this period
of my return to my studies as an
art-student was also the period of my
becoming a Catholic — and here I can
use the word 'becoming' in the sense of
a process toward, for that process had
begun ~~in 1917 in the trenches of the West Front in the neighborhood of the Ypres Salient~~ and it was now 1920–21.
1916-17,

Among my fellow-students were some who
were Catholic and it was natural that not
only did the ~~[illegible]~~ central dogma
of the Church and its implications become
part of our conversation but also all
sorts of matters involving Catholics.
Yet, as far as I can now recall, the

[*page 34*]

[*four* Xs *in black ink in top right-hand corner enclosed in a rectangle; the final* X *appears to have been added after the first three*]

(2)

74

In 1918 when Bridges' first edition of Poems of Gerard Manley Hopkins was published I was away in the army and heard nothing of this event and so have no first hand knowledge of its immediate reception.

In January 1919 I resumed my studies as an art-student. My main concern was with the visual arts as it had been since childhood, so that, speaking in very general terms, the people I most mixt with <^were> more aware, or more concentrated upon, the contemporary problems to do with the visual arts than with the written or aural arts. I do not at all mean that we were not interested in or did not discuss those other arts but only that as students we were involved in a contactual, immediate, day-by-day, manual fashion with the intractable problems of form and content in the making of a drawing or a painting, whereas we were not immediately involved in those same problems as they occur in the making of a written work, a poem or a muscieal score.

But it so happened that this period of my return to my studies as an art-student was also the period of my becoming a Catholic – and here I can use the word 'becoming' in the sense of a process toward, for that process had begun ~~in 1917 in the neighborhood the Ypres Salient,~~ <in the trenches of the West Front in 1916–17,> and it was now 1920–21.[154]

Among my fellow-students were some who were Catholic and it was natural that not only <^did> the ~~<^was>~~ [*cancellation illegible*] central dogma of the Church and its implications become part of our conversation but also all sorts of matters involving Catholics.

Yet, as far as I can now recall, the

[154] On this period of the war, during which Jones, in search of firewood, stumbled on a byre in which a military chaplain was celebrating a Catholic Mass, see his letter to René Hague of 9–15 July 1973 in *Dai Greatcoat*, 248–50, and Dilworth's account in *David Jones in the Great War*, 152–3.

(3) XXXX

name Hopkins did not crop up, except, I fancy, once, in relation to some poem by Walt Whitman. But, in any case, the significance of the name did not, as far as I was concerned, register.

It was not until round about 1927 that I can recall with absolute certainty a feeling of the impact of Hopkins.

[*page 35*]

[*four* Xs *in black ink in top right-hand corner enclosed in a rectangle*]

(3)

28

name Hopkins did not crop up, except, I fancy, once, in relation to some poem by Walt Whitman. But, in any case, the significance of the name did not, as far as I was concerned, register.

It was not until round about 1927 that I can recall with absolute certainty a feeling of the impact of Hopkins. ~~works~~.

(3) XXX

But it happened that the period of my return to my studies as an art-student was also the period of my becoming a Catholic — and here I can use the word 'becoming' in the sense of a process toward, for this process had begun in 1917 in the neighborhood of the Ypres Salient, and it was now 1919 or '20. Among my fellow art-students there were Catholics and it was natural that not only the Church's central dogma and its implications cropped up a good deal in our conversation, but also all sorts of matters involving Catholics.

As far as I can now recall, the name, Hopkins, did not occur, except, I think, once in relation to some poem of Walt Whitman's. But in any case, at that date, 1920–21, the significance of the name, as far as I was concerned, did not register.

I mention this because by that time the literary critics & reviewers had expressed their varied opinions — the first appears to have been in January 1919.

To the best of my recollection, it was not until about 1927 that I felt the impact of Hopkins.

I can recall with vividness a happening of about that time, but cannot recall the circumstances or the persons concerned.

Conversation had turned to the poetry of Hopkins and someone of the half dozen or more people present, read aloud one or two of Hopkins shorter works, which they were I cannot recall. At the conclusion I expressed the conviction that whether or no Hopkins was a Welshman he certainly was conversant with Welsh medieval metrical forms and the complex also used compound words in a very Welsh fashion.

(over)

[*page 36*]

[*three* Xs *in black ink in top right-hand corner*]

30 (3)

But it happened that this period of my return to my studies as an art-student was also the period of my becoming a Catholic – and here I can use the word 'becoming' in the sense of a process toward, for this process had begun in 1917 in the neighborhood of <^the> Ypres Salient, and it was now 1919 or '20. Among my fellow art-students there were Catholics and it was natural that ~~in conversation~~ not only ~~the~~ the Church's <^central> dogma and its implications cropped up a good deal in our conversation, but also all sorts of matters involving Catholics.

As far as I can now recall, the name, Hopkins, did not occur, except, I think, once in relation to some poem of Walt Whitman's

But in any case, at ~~at~~ that date, 1920–'21, the significance of the name, ~~did not register~~ as ~~far~~ far as I was concerned, did not register.

I mention this because by that [*one cancelled word illegible*] time the literary critics & reviewers had expressed their varied opinions – the first appears to have been in January 1919.[155]

To the best of my recollection, it was not until <^about> 1927 [*one or two cancelled words illegible*] that I felt the impact of Hopkins.

I can recall with vividness a happening of about that time, but cannot recall the circumstance [*a period absorbed into the* o *of the following word*] or the persons concerned.

~~Someone~~

~~The poetry of Hopkins was~~

Conversation had turned to the poetry of Hopkins and someone of the half dozen or more people present, ~~had~~ read aloud one or ~~more~~ <two> of Hopkins shorter works, which they were I cannot recall. At the conclusion I ~~ventured to~~ [*one cancelled word illegible*] expressed the conviction that whether [*the next four words inserted in the left-hand margin*] ~~or no~~ or no Hopkins was ~~eithe~~ a Welshman <^he certainly was> ~~or a man extremely influenced by and~~ conversant with [*the next two words inserted in the left-hand margin*] the complex Welsh medieval metrical forms and · – also used compound words in a very Welsh fashion.

(over)

[155] The first traced review appeared on 2 January 1919. See Dunne, *Gerard Manley Hopkins: A Comprehensive Bibliography*, 14.

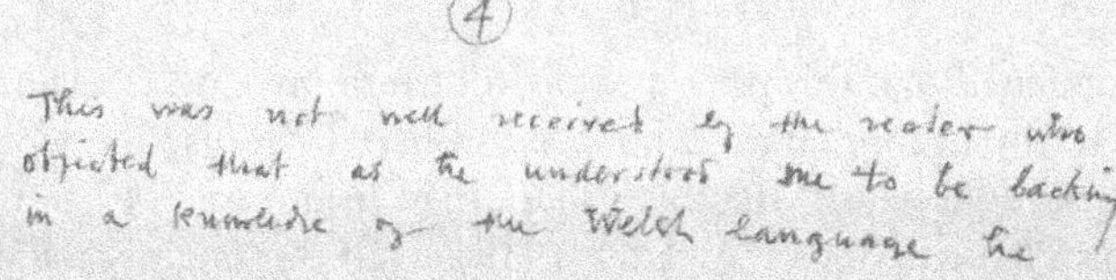

(4)

This was not well received by the reader who objected that as he understood me to be lacking in a knowledge of the Welsh language he

[*page 37*]

(4)

This was not well received by the reader who objected that as he understood me to be lacking in a knowledge of the Welsh language he

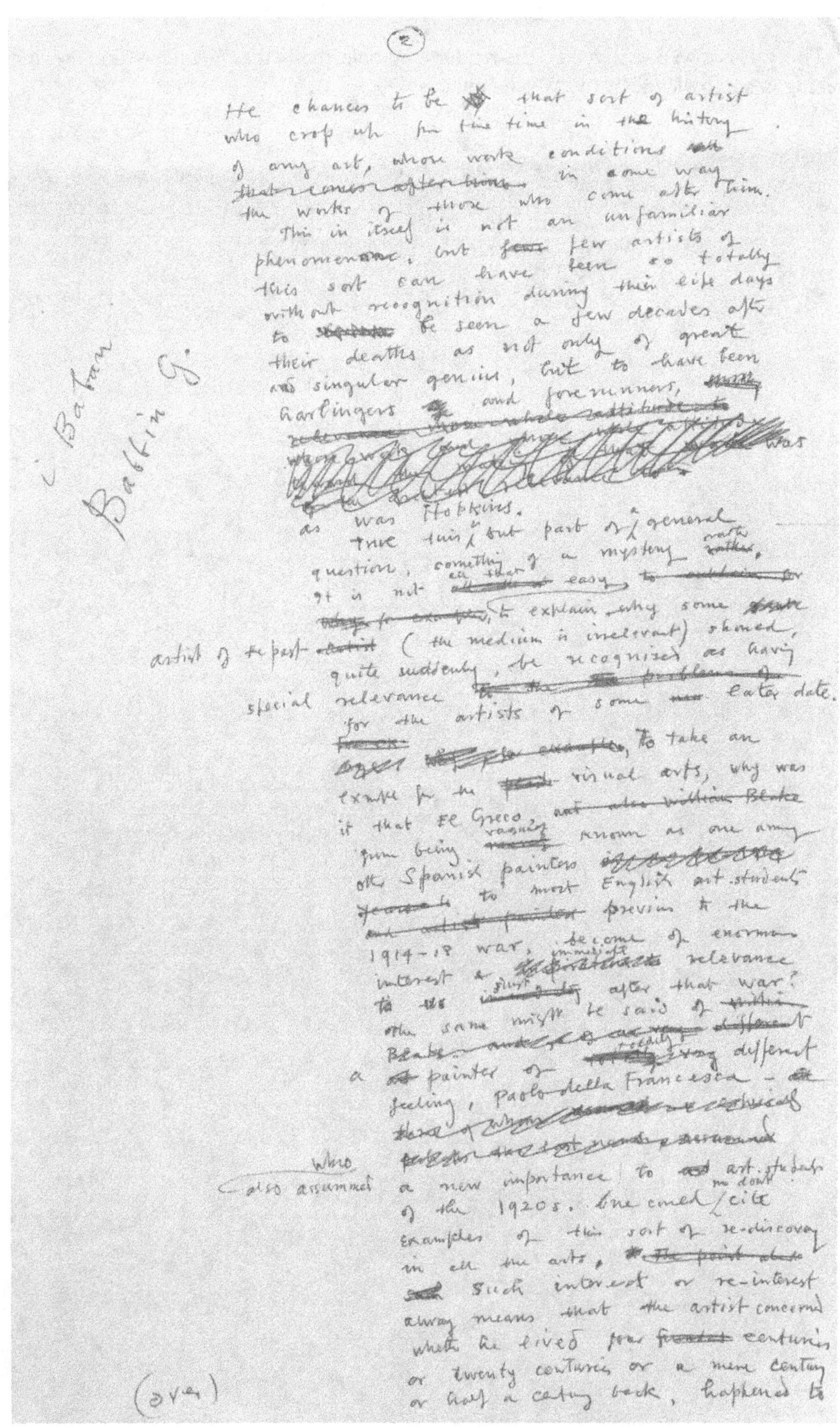

(2)

He chances to be that sort of artist who crop up from time to time in the history of any art, whose work conditions in some way the works of those who come after him.
This in itself is not an unfamiliar phenomenon, but few artists of this sort can have been so totally without recognition during their life days to be seen a few decades after their deaths as not only of great singular genius, but to have been harbingers and forerunners, as was Hopkins.

True this is but part of a general question, something of a mystery, it is not all that easy to explain why some artist of the past (the medium is irrelevant) should, quite suddenly, be recognized as having special relevance for the artists of some later date. To take an example from the visual arts, why was it that El Greco, from being vaguely known as one among Spanish painters to most English art students previous to the 1914–18 war, become of enormous interest & immediate relevance after that war? The same might be said of a painter of a very different feeling, Paolo della Francesca – who also assumed a new importance to art students in London of the 1920s. One could cite examples of this sort of re-discovery in all the arts. Such interest or re-interest always means that the artist concerned whether he lived four centuries or twenty centuries or a mere century or half a century back, happened to

(over)

Baten
Babbin G.

[*page 38*]

(2)

He chances to be [*illegible cancellation*] that sort of artist who crop up from time time in the history of any art, whose work conditions ~~all that comes after him.~~ in some way the works of those who come after him.

This in itself is not an unfamiliar phenomenon, but ~~fews~~ few artists of this sort can have been so totally without recognition during their life days to ~~become~~ be seen a few decades after

[*in left-hand margin:* i Baban [/] Babbin g.[156]]

their deaths as not only of great and singular genius, but to have been harbingers ~~of~~ and forerunners, ~~having relevance whose whole attitude to whose work and whose whole attitude toward the making of that work was of the greatest relevance to.~~ as was Hopkins.

True this <^is> but part of <^a> general question, something of a mystery ~~rather~~ <rather>. It is not <all that> easy ~~to explain for why, for example,~~ to explain [*comma cancelled*] why some ~~great~~ artist of the past ~~artist~~ (the medium is irrelevant) should, quite suddenly, be recognized as having [*the next word added in left-hand margin*] special relevance ~~to the the problems of~~ for the artists of some [*illegible cancellation*] later date.

~~For ex-~~

~~age why, for example,~~ [*in the next word a capital* T *overwrites a lowercase* t] To take an example from the ~~plastic~~ visual arts, why was it that El Greco, ~~and also William Blake~~ from being ~~merel~~ <vaguely> known as one among other Spanish painters ~~in the pre-1914 years to~~ to most English art-students ~~and artists painters~~ previous to the 1914–18 war, become of enormous interest & ~~inspiration to~~ <immediate> relevance to us ~~immediately~~ <right> after that war? The same might be said of ~~William Blake and of~~ [*the next word added in the left-hand margin*] a ~~an very different art~~ painter of ~~totally~~ <totally> ~~very~~ different feeling, Paolo della Francesca – ~~all three of whom assumed—especially perhaps the last named – assumed~~ [*the next three words added in the left-hand margin*] <^who> also assumed a new importance to ~~art~~ art-students of the 1920s. One could <^no doubt> cite examples of this sort of re-discovery in all the arts. ~~The point about such~~ Such interest or re-interest alway means that the artist concerned whether he lived four ~~hundred~~ centuries [*in left-hand margin:* (over)] or twenty centuries or a mere century or half a century back, happened to[157]

[156] If Welsh, the phrase 'i Baban' means 'to/for Baban'. The Welsh noun *baban* means 'baby'. Jones uses it in a letter to Aneirin Talfan Davies of 17 August 1970; see David Jones, *David Jones: Letters to a Friend*, ed. Aneirin Talfan Davies (Swansea: Triskele, 1980), 105. 'Babbin' is a habitation surname.

[157] In his biography of Jones, Thomas Dilworth reports that Jones attended the Blake (1757–1827) centenary exhibition at the Tate Gallery in 1927. See Dilworth, *David Jones: Engraver, Soldier, Painter, Poet*, 100. Before the war, in a major exhibition of October–December 1913, the Tate (then the National Gallery of British Art) had shown 102 of Blake's works. See Colin Trodd, *Visions of Blake: William Blake in the Art World 1830–1930* (Liverpool: Liverpool University Press, 2012), 443–4. Robin Ironside, in his *David Jones* (Harmondsworth: Penguin, 1949), reports, 'His actual enthusiasms at this period [between 1919 and 1921] were reserved for the English water-colourists, and for Blake. Feelings graver than enthusiasm had been deeply stirred in him by the first appearance at the National Gallery, in 1919, of El Greco's *Agony in the Garden*.' (7) In his biography, Dilworth reports that Jones visited this painting (now attributed to the Studio of El Greco) repeatedly and in a letter of 17 June 1923 to Petra Gill called it 'the best painting in the world' (59). Folder CF2/16 of the David Jones Papers at the National Library of Wales, Aberystwyth, contains drafts of a letter by Jones to the editor of *The Tablet* in response to an article by Anthony Bertram, 'The Altering Eye', pp. 457–8 in the issue of 23 November 1957, marking Blake's bicentenary. Against Bertram's recommendation to *The Tablet*'s Catholic readership of Blake 'as a teacher' in spite of the, for Bertram, misguided attempt of Roger Fry and 'Bloomsbury' to enter Blake's art in the lists of 'significant form' (458), Jones writes, 'It was precisely those who were to some degree susceptible to the notion of "significant form" that were foremost in appreciating Blake's watercolours and engravings. That this was so in 1919–1920 I can myself vouch. Those art-students who felt the compulsion of El Greco (until then unknown to most of us) felt also the compulsion of Blake. Moreover, with regard to the written works of Blake, my impression is that, at that time, "Bloomsbury" led the way.' In another version of this passage, Jones replaces the word 'compulsion' with the word 'relevance', using it in the special sense that it accrues in the drafts of the Hopkins essay. In this same alternate version Jones replaces the parenthetical remark about El Greco with one reminiscent of the language he uses of Hopkins in these drafts: '(previously a name only)'.

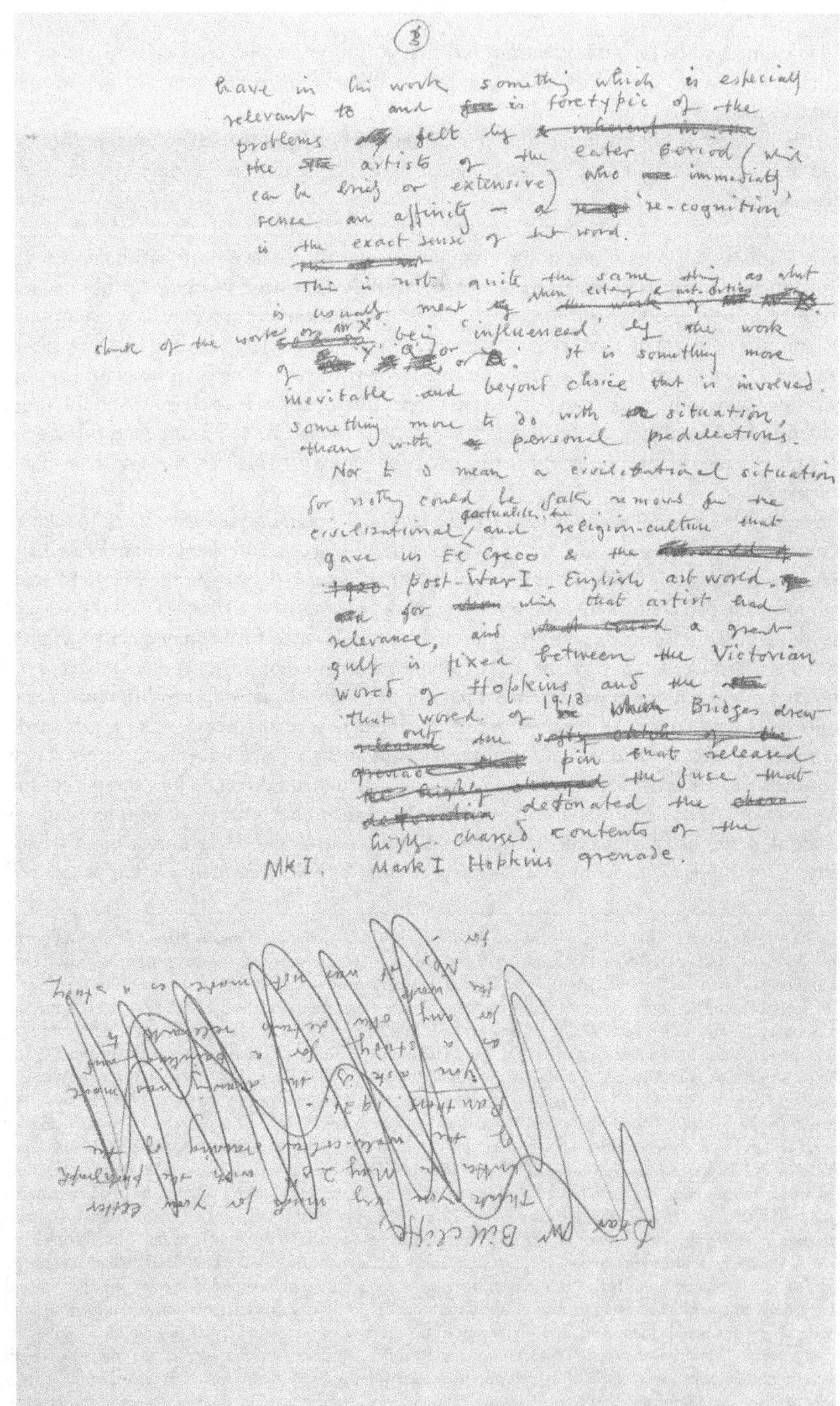

(3)

have in his work something which is especially relevant to and is foretypic of the problems felt by the artists of the Later Period (which can be brief or extensive) who immediately sense an affinity — a 're-cognition' is the exact sense of the word.

This is not quite the same thing as what is usually meant when artists think of the works of X being 'influenced' by the work of Y, Z or B. It is something more inevitable and beyond choice that is involved. Something more to do with situation, than with personal predilections.

Nor do I mean a civilizational situation for nothing could be further removed from the civilizational factualities, the and religion-culture that gave us El Greco & the post-War I English art world. for which that artist had relevance, and a great gulf is fixed between the Victorian world of Hopkins and the that world of 1918 Bridges drew out the pin that released the fuse that detonated the highly charged contents of the

MkI. Mark I Hopkins grenade.

[*page 39*]

(3)

26
have in his work something which is especially relevant to and ~~fore~~ is foretypic of the problems [*one cancelled word illegible*] felt by ~~& inherent in the~~ the ~~the~~ artists of the later period (which can be brief or extensive) who ~~are~~ immediately, sense an affinity – a ~~re-go~~ 're-cognition' is the exact sense of that word.

~~This~~ [*one cancelled word illegible*] ~~not~~

This is not quite the same thing as what is usually meant ~~by~~ <when literary and art-critics [*the next seven words added in left-hand margin*] speak of the work of Mr X> ~~the work of Mr Mr X. so & so~~ being 'influenced' by the work of ~~Mr A,~~ <'y'> ~~B~~ [*overwritten by* Q], <'Q'> or <or> 'C.' It is something more inevitable and beyond choice that is involved. Something more to do with the situation, than with ~~a~~ personal predilections.[158]

Nor do I mean a civilizational situation for nothing could be farther removed from the civilizational <^factualities> and <the> religion-culture that gave us El Greco & the ~~art-world of 1920~~ post-War I. English art world ~~of~~ ~~and~~. for ~~whom~~ which that artist had relevance, and ~~what could~~ a great gulf is fixed between the Victorian world of Hopkins and the ~~the~~ that world of ~~on~~ <1918> when [*overwrites* which] Bridges drew ~~released~~ <out> the ~~safety catch of the grenade that~~ pin that released ~~the highly charged~~ the fuse that ~~detonation~~ detonated the ~~charg~~ highly. charged contents of the [*added in the left-hand margin:* Mk I.] Mark I Hopkins grenade.[159]

[*The following script appears upside-down at the bottom of this page*]

"~~Dear Mr Billcliffe,~~[160]
~~Thank you very much for your letter written on May 20th with the photograph of the water-colour drawing of the Panthers, 1931. –~~
~~You ask if the drawing was made as a study for a painting and for any other details relevant to the work.~~
~~No, it was not made as a study for~~

[158] Compare Jones's letter to William Blissett of 21 November 1954 in William Blissett, *The Long Conversation: A Memoir of David Jones* (Oxford: Oxford University Press, 1981), 4: 'But then it's all very tricky, isn't it, this business of what complex of causes makes one generation or series of generations have an instinctual interest in some one poet of the past & not in another? Sometimes one can see clearly that the interest, or lack of it, is to do more with the techniques of the past poet – how much he does or does not, in some way appear to have some of the same, or similar *formal* problems as those that occupy the attention of this or that later generation of poets. Of course "content" no less than "form" is involved in these fluctuations of interest. It's just the same in the visual arts. The *enormous interest* in, e.g., Piero della Francesca & then in El Greco that has occurred in my time among art-students & artists is suggestive of what I mean re the poets.' In his biography, Dilworth reports that Jones admired Piero's *The Baptism of Christ* and *The Nativity*, both Victorian-era acquisitions of the National Gallery. See Dilworth, *David Jones: Engraver, Soldier, Painter, Poet*, 59. For a discussion of Roger Fry's 'Post-Impressionist' Piero, see Caroline Elam, *Roger Fry and the Re-Evaluation of Piero Della Francesca* (New York: Frick Collection, 2004).

[159] For Jones's handling of hand grenades during the war, see Dilworth, *David Jones: Engraver, Soldier, Painter, Poet*, 42, and *In Parenthesis*, 169. On the British grenades of the war, see Anthony Saunders, *Weapons of the Trench War, 1914–1918* (Stroud: Sutton, 1999), especially chapters one and four, pp. 1–27 and 67–94. The Mills No. 5 Mk I hand grenade was first issued in late spring 1915. See Saunders, 79. On its considerable liabilities, see Saunders, 82–5. See also Jones, *In Parenthesis*, 13.

[160] The addressee is Roger Billcliffe, at the time of writing Assistant Keeper of British Art at the Walker Art Gallery, Liverpool, which owns Jones's *Panthers in Regent's Park Zoo*, pencil and watercolour on paper, signed 1931 (Walker inventory number 1253). The Walker's object file for this artwork holds the letter drafted here as Jones sent it, dated 22 May 1968.

(3)

The significance and relevance may be after the passing of centuries, or, as in the case of Hopkins, a matter of a few decades.

It might be objected that in this particular case there is no mystery in that had the work of Hopkins been made available soon after his death in 1889 instead of thirty years later there would have been the same realisation of his qualities by the more perceptive critics and the same recognition of his immediate relevance for those engaged in writing poetry as there was when the work became known after its publication in 1918. I ought to say that by 'immediate relevance' I mean 'immediate' in the sense of being tied up inescapably with the work in hand.

It is impossible to know for certain but my own guess is that had the work of Hopkins been published at some earlier date, it would have received much more adverse comment from the literary critics than it did & many fewer artists would have seen its significance and relevance to them.

Obviously it is impossible to know, but it may well be that the decade 1918–1928 was an auspicious period for the reception of Hopkins.

If I am wrong in this supposition and had the Hopkins MSS been published in the 1890s or in the first decade of the 20th Century, and had they been well received by the critics and seen to be of great relevance to the writers of

(over)

[*page 40*]

(3)

28

The significance and relevance may be after the passing of centuries, or, as in the case of Hopkins, a matter of a few decades.

It might be objected that in the particular case there is <^no> mystery in that had the work of Hopkins been made available soon after his death in 1889 instead of thirty years later there would have been the same [*three or four cancelled words illegible*] realization of his qualities by the more perceptive critics and the same recognition of his immediate relevance for those ~~makers~~ engaged in ~~poiesis~~ writing poetry as there was ~~in 1918~~ when ~~the work became available late in 1918.~~ the work became known [*one cancelled word illegible*] after its publication in 1918. I ought to say that by 'immediate relevance' I mean ~~by~~ 'immediate' in the sense of <^being> tied up inescapably with the work in hand.

It is impossible to know for certain but my <^own> guess is that had the work of Hopkins been published at some earlier date~~—1909 of ?instance it would not have. its fewer critics critics & artists. would have perceived its worth & its most adverse~~ it would have received much more adverse ~~criticism~~ comment from the literary critics <than it did,> & many ~~fewer~~ fewer artists would have seen its significance and relevance ~~to~~ to them.

Obviously <^it is> impossible to ~~know, but it is rather like one of those fruitless questions such as how different would the history of such & such a country have <^been> had not~~ [*the next three words cancelled*] ~~so & so such & such an a battle gone other than it did.~~ [*the next word added in the left-hand margin*] know, but it may well be that the decade 1918–1928 was an auspicious period for the reception of Hopkins. If I am wrong in this supposition and <^had> the ~~ma~~ Hopkins ~~mater~~ MSS been published in the 1890s or in the first decade of the 20th Century, and had ~~their implications been –~~ they been well received ~~with~~ by the critics and seen to <^be> of great relevance to the writers of

(over)

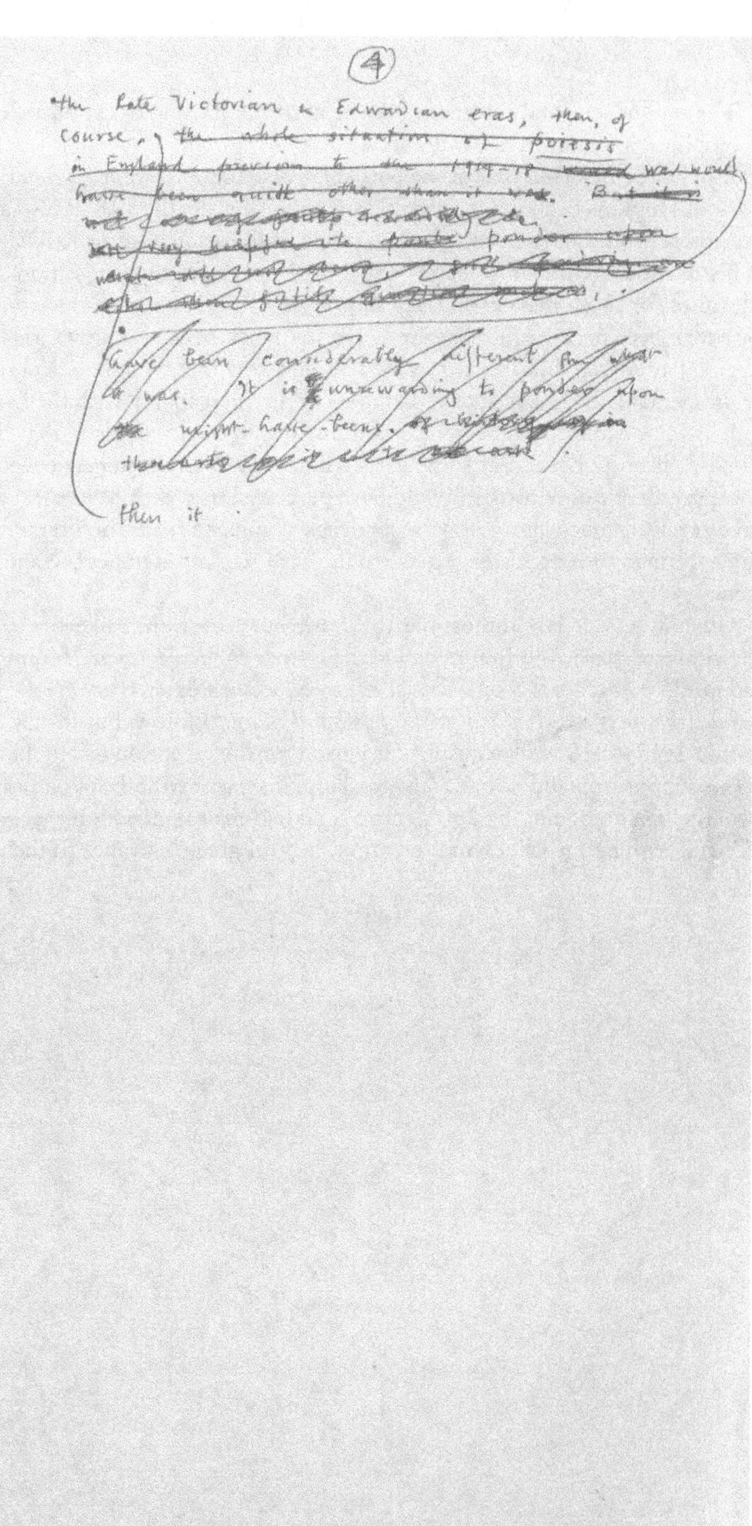

(4)

the late Victorian & Edwardian eras, then, of course, ~~the whole situation of poiesis in England previous to the 1914–18~~ war would ~~have been quite other than it was.~~

have been considerably different from what it was. It is unrewarding to ponder upon the might-have-beens.

then it

[*page 41*]

(4) [*overwrites* 3]

the late Victorian & Edwardian eras, then, of course, ~~the whole situation of poiesis in England previous to the 1914–18~~ [*the next word cancelled*] ~~would war would have been quite other than it was. But it is not a very ?fruitful rewarding~~ [*the next cancelled word illegible*] ~~not very helpful to ponde ponder upon what did not occur, such ponderings are like those futile questions such as,~~
~~have been considerably different from what it was. It is unrewarding to ponder upon the might-have-beens. of history of in these arts as it is to ask ask.~~
then it ·

(3)

Though this matter of the recognition of some past artist by artists of a later date is a general phenomenon, there is something of mystery about it.

It is not all that easy to explain why some particular artist (the medium is irrelevant) should quite suddenly, or relatively so, be recognized as having a significance for the practitioners of some later date.

The relevance may be after the passing of centuries, or, as in the case of Hopkins a matter of a few decades.

It might be objected that in this particular case there is no mystery in that had the poetry & other material of Hopkins been made available soon after his death in 1889 instead of thirty years later, there would have been the same recognition by the more perceptive critics and the same awareness by poets of the relevance of Hopkins to them in the decade following the belated publication in 1918.

It is impossible to know – but my guess is that, one way and another,

[*page 42*]

(3)

31

Though this matter of the recognition of some past artist by artists of a later date is a general phenomenon, there is something of mystery about it.

It is not all that easy to explain why some ~~particla~~ particular artist (the medium is irrelevant) should quite suddenly, or relatively, so, be recognized as having a significance for the practitioners of some later date.

The relevance may be after the passing of centuries, or, as in the case of Hopkins, a matter of ~~a~~ a few decades.

It mi[*the* i *overwrites* a]ght be objected that in this particular case there is no mystery in that had the ~~Hopkins m·~~ poetry & other material of Hopkins been made available soon after his death in 1889

~~or in 1909 (when for some reason Bridges refused Fr Keating S.J. the suggestion that the turned down the wish of Fr Keating S. J. to publish an edition of the poems.~~

~~or at some other date much earlier than late in 1918 there would have been the same recognition by critics of perception and the same sense by poets of the relevance to them as was in fact the case.~~

instead of thirty years later, there would have been the same recognition by the more perceptive critics and the same ~~aware of~~ awareness ~~of~~ by poets of the relevance of ~~this mate· Hopkins to the practitioners of :~~

Hopkins ~~to~~ <to them> ~~when in 1918 the work was at last available.~~

~~wh~~ in the decade following ~~1918~~ the belated publication in 1918.

It is impossible to know – but my guess is that, one way and another,

(3)

~~This matter of~~

Though this matter of the relevance of ~~[illegible]~~ the work of a past figure for the artists of a future generation is general enough, yet something of a mystery.

[*page 43*]

(3)

29

~~This matter of~~ ·

Though this matter of the relevance of ~~a past of work~~ the work of a past figure for the artists of a future generation is general enough, yet ~~a~~ something of a mystery ·

[*page 44*]

(3)

~~Thic~~ ·
~~This~~ :
~~A~~

(2)

Hopkins chanced to be that sort of artist who crops up from time to time whose work is destined to condition in a special way the works of those who come after him.

This, in itself, is no unfamiliar thing, we all know, for example, that the painting of that essentially English artist, John Constable who died in the year of Victoria's accession, was to have a delayed-action effect on the French impressionist movement of the late 19th Century.

1919
1929
1939
1949
1959
1969

(2)

15

Hopkins chanced to be that sort of artist who crops up from time to time whose work is destined to condition in a special way the works of those who come after him.

This, in itself, is no unfamiliar thing, We all know, for ~~expo~~ example, that the ~~landscape~~ <painting> of that essentially English [*the next word and the comma that follows it added in the right-hand margin*] artist, ~~painter~~, John Constable who died in the year of Victoria's accession, was to ~~have its a~~ [*the next two words added in the left-hand margin*] have a ~~its~~ delayed-action effect on the French impressionist[s *overwritten by* t] [*the next word added in the left-hand margin*] movement of the late 19th Century.[161]

1919
1929
1939
1949
1959
1969

[161] Of the French on Constable (1776–1837), Jones writes to William Blissett in a letter of 16 May 1967 (on or about the date of these drafts), 'Constable they praised highly as influencing their Impressionists, but the genius of Turner seemed to escape them.' See Blissett, *The Long Conversation*, 41.

(2)

Hopkins chanced to be that rare sort of artist who crops up from time to time whose work is destined to condition in various ways the works of those who come after them.

This in itself is no unfamiliar thing, we all know, for example, that the ~~painting of~~ landscapes of that exceeding ~~Constable~~ ~~English painter, John Crotch~~ [illegible] ~~who died in the year of~~ [illegible] [illegible] ~~English late 18th century~~ [illegible]

English artist (1776 – 1837)

[*page 46*]

(2)

16

Hopkins chanced to be that rare sort of artist who crops up from time to time whose work is destined to condition in various ways the works of those who come after them.

This in itself is no unfamiliar thing. We all know, for example, that the ~~paintings of Constable~~ landscapes of that exceeding ~~English painter, John Constable (1776–1837) who died in the year of Queen Victoria's accession~~
~~English late 18th Century painter (1776–1837)~~
English artist (1776–1837)

(2)

He chanced to be that sort of artist who crops up from time to time in the history of any art whose work conditions, in some special way, the works of those who come after them.

This in itself is not an unfamiliar thing, but few artists of this sort can have been so totally without recognition during their life days as Hopkins, to be seen a few decades after their deaths as not only of great and singular genius but have been, as with Hopkins, harbingers and forerunners.

True, this is but part of a general question, something of a mystery, rather. For it is not all that easy to explain why some artist of the past – the near past or the far past (the medium is irrelevant) should be quite suddenly, or relatively so, recognized as having a special relevance for the artists of some later date.

To take an example from the visual arts, why was it that El Greco, from being but vaguely known as a painter of 16th Century Spain to most English art-students of the pre-1914–18 War, became to us just after that war a painter of great interest and immediate relevance? There were a number of contributary causes which themselves do little more than pose further questions. All I wish to note here is that in 1919–20 that particular painter among others was seen by us to have been concerned with problems of a formal nature which had a much kinship with our own problems at that date.

[*page 47*]

[*Entire page cancelled with a slash*]

(2)

18

He chanced to be that sort of artist who crops up from time to time in the history of any art whose work[*the arm and leg of the* k *extended to overwrite a final* s] conditions, ~~in some way in~~ i[*the* i *overwrites an* s]n some special way, the works of those who come after them [*overwrites* him].

This in itself is not an unfamiliar thing, but few artists of this sort can have been so totally without recognition during their life days as Hopkins, to be seen a few decades after <^their> deaths as not only of great and singular genius but to have been, as with Hopkins, harbingers and forerunners.

True, this is but part of a ~~geen~~ general question, something of a mystery, rather. For it is not all that easy to explain why some artist of the past – the near past or the far past (the medium is irrelevant) should quite suddenly, or relatively so, be recognized as having a special relevance for the artists of some later date.

To take an example from the visual arts, why was it that E[*overwrites a lowercase* e]l Greco, from being but vaguely known as a [*one cancelled word illegible*] painter of [*overwrites* in] 16th Century Spain to most English art-students of the pre-1914–18 War, became to us just after that war <^a painter> of great interest and immediate relevance? There were a number of contributary causes which themselves do little more than pose further questions. All I wish to note here is that in 1919–20 that particular painter among others, was seen by us to have been ~~formally~~ concerned with problems of a formal nature which had a much kinship with our own problems at that date.

(2)

Hopkins chanced to be that sort of artist who crops up from time to time, whose work is destined to condition in some special way the works of those who come after them.

This, in itself, is no unfamiliar thing; but few artists of this sort can have been more totally without recognition during their life days, to be seen a few decades after their deaths as not only of great and singular genius but as harbingers and fore-showers and hence of immediate relevance to the 'makaris' of a later epoch.

True, this is part of a general question, something of mystery rather. For it is not all that easy to explain why some particular artist (the medium is irrelevant) showed quite suddenly, or relatively so, be recognized as having a special relevance for men of some later date.

The relevance may be after the passing of centuries, or, as in the case of Hopkins a matter of a few decades.

It might be objected that there is no mystery here in that had Hopkins' work been made available some decades before 1918 it would have been recognized at once as having that relevance which it was seen to have by certain perceptive poets and critics early in 1919, — a perception which has been amply shown to be valid.

So much so that today, nearly five decades later, it requires quite an effort to understand the state of mind of the more unrestrained of the adverse critics..

Hence I very much wonder whether

[*page 48*]

(2)

14

Hopkins chanced to be that sort of artist who crops up from time to time, whose work is destined to condition in some special way the works of those who come after them.

This, in itself, is no unfamiliar thing; but few artists of this sort can have been more totally without recognition during their life days, to be seen a few decades after <^their> deaths as not only of great and singular genius but as harbingers and fore-showers and hence of immediate relevance to the ~~'makars'~~ 'makaris' of a later epoch.

~~This~~ ·

True, this is part of a general question, something of a mystery rather,

~~Fort~~ For it is not all that easy to explain why some particular artist (the medium is irrelevant) should quite suddenly, or relatively so, be recognized as having a special relavance for men of some later date. ~~that date may be~~ ·

The relevance may be after the passing of centuries, or, as in the case of Hopkins a matter of a few decades.

It might be objected that there is no mystery here in that had Hopkins' work been made available some decades before 1918 it would have been ~~seen at~~ recognized at once as having that relevance

[*In the left-hand margin in red ink or pencil:* 113 in Vat. [/] Opus anglicana][162]

which it was seen to have by certain perceptive ~~critics~~ poets and critics early in 1919, ~~when the~~ – a perception which ~~gathered momentum~~ has been amply shown to be valid. ~~and which has gathered momentum~~ ·

So much so that to-day, five decades nearly five decades later, it ~~is requires~~ requires quite an effort to understand the state of mind <^of> the more unrestrained of the adverse critics.

Hence I very much wonder whether

[162] The Vatican's 1295 inventory lists 113 pieces of Opus Anglicanum, 'English work', medieval English embroidery. For a recent survey of this art, see the Victoria and Albert Museum's 2016–17 exhibition catalogue, *English Medieval Embroidery: Opus Anglicanum*, ed. Clare Browne, Glyn Davies, and M. A. Michael (New Haven, CT, and London: Yale University Press, 2016). For Jones's 'enduring interest in historical costume and embroidery', see Dilworth, *David Jones: Engraver, Soldier, Painter, Poet*, 28. In an undated manuscript essay, 'An Aspect of the Art of England', in *The Dying Gaul and Other Writings*, ed. Harman Grisewood (London: Faber & Faber, 1978), Jones speaks of Opus Anglicanum and Gerard Manley Hopkins in the same breath: 'When one tries to conjure up an image signifying this distinguishing quality [of English art], a fretted, meandering, countered image emerges. And when further it is remembered that *the* one art which has taken its name from us, is that kind of needlework called "Opus Anglicanum", we get a further hint, and another in the unique character of the early English miniatures, as those of Nicholas Hillyarde (1547–1619). We see very plainly how that deeply native poet, G. M. Hopkins, when he wrote his "Pied Beauty" was expressing an intensely native feeling'. (59) In *The Anathemata*, 196 n. 2, Jones cites a book in his personal library, Ffransis George Payne, *Guide to the Collection of Samplers and Embroideries* (Cardiff: National Museum of Wales and the Press Board of the University of Wales, 1939). See Huw Ceiriog Jones, *The Library of David Jones*, 223. Thanks to Thomas Goldpaugh for the reference. Goldpaugh is preparing an edition of Jones's complete *Grail Mass*, the second line of which mentions 'opus anglicanum case-stitch'.

(4)

While I can make no claim to a study of the reasons for Bridges' delay, I feel that *if* the true reason was that he judged the 1890s, or the year 1909 (the year in which Fr Keating S.J. desired him to publish a complete edition of Hopkins' poems) to be too soon for anything but adverse reception, but that he sensed that 1918 was 'the acceptable year', then I think Bridges' prescience remarkable. I don't know what augurs he consulted, but the determining formula Aves admittunt would seem to me to have been reclaimed just about on time.

That a Victorian Englishman of Liddon's Oxford, a priest of the Society of Jesus, who wrote poetry and in notes, diaries, letters discoursed on his theory of metrics should have turned out to be of the greatest possible interest to the men who either served in, or had come to manhood during, the 1914–18 war is hardly what one would suppose likely. Yet, such was in fact the case, so much so that any conversation in the 1920s or '30s that chanced to turn to discussing some living writer – St Jean Perse or Joyce or Eliot would sooner or later involve Hopkins. In fact it was hard to remember that his work was made in Victoria's England for we discussed it as though the author was a contemporary figure.

[*page 49*]

[*crossed check-mark in black ink in top right-hand corner*]
(4) [*overwrites* 3]

44

While I can make no claim to <^a> study of the reasons for Bridges' · delay, I feel that <u>if</u> the true reason was that he judged the 1890s, or the year 1909 (the ~~when~~ year in which Fr Keating S.J. desired him to publish a complete edition of Hopkins' poems) to be too soon for anything but adverse reception, but that he sensed that 1918 was 'the acceptable year', then I think Bridges' prescience remarkable. [*The next sentence in pencil*] I don't know what augers he consulted, but the determining formula <u>Aves admittunt</u> would seem to me to have been declaimed just about on time. [*The rest of the page resumes in pen*]

That a Victorian Englishman of ~~the Oxford~~ [*one cancelled word or part-word illegible*] Liddon's Oxford, a priest of the Society of Jesus. who wrote poetry and in notes diaries, letters ~~continuously~~ discoursed on his theory of metrics should have turned out to be ~~of the greatest <vital> of interest and~~ [*one cancelled word or part-word illegible*] ~~to the men who~~ of the greatest possible interest to the men who either served in, or had come to manhood during, the 1914–18 war is hardly what one would suppose likely.

Yet, such was in fact the case. So much so that any conversation in the 1920s or '30s that chanced to turn to discussing some living writer – St Jean Perse or Joyce or Eliot would sooner or later involve ~~the~~ Hopkins.

In fact ~~it~~ it was hard to remember that his work was made in Victoria's England for we discussed it as though [*the next word added in the right-hand margin*] the [*the next word added in the left-hand margin*] author ~~he~~ was a contemporary figure.

Hopkins (The Month)

10 The invitation to write something as a memento,
tribute to or recalling of Gerard Manley
Hopkins in this centenary year of his entry into the Society
of Jesus might appear at first
sight a not only welcome and congenial
but fairly simple task, in that there is so
much which, over the years, the
name 'Hopkins' has evoked.

But it becomes, at least in my own case, a far
less simple matter, once one tries to write
down a tribute. For one thing, so much
has been written in appraisement of Hopkins
and his works ranging from
Dr W. H. Gardner's intensive two volume study
published in 1944 & 1949, to the various
books and articles of the nineteen twenties
& thirties and more written since 1949, including
available additional material as well
as concentrating on some particular aspect of
the man or his work.

Anyway, to-day, exactly half a century
since his poems were first published and seventy-
nine years since his death, Hopkins is
firmly established in the canon of English
poetry. He is 'accepted'. Once his works
became known it was inevitable that,
sooner or later, acceptance would follow.
What is 'accepted' is always in danger
of being 'taken for granted' and while, in
any context, a taking for granted is never
a good thing it would be for a number of reasons, be especially undesirable
in the case of Hopkins.

As indicated above, so much has been written
since Bridges first released a collection of
Hopkins poems in 1918, I do not feel
in any position to add to what has
been expressed by competent & perceptive
writers who have made Hopkins & his
works their special study — in any case
I have not the qualifications. But it
occurred to me I might try &
record the impact of Hopkins upon
myself when first I came into
contact with his work.
This is, necessarily a, so to say, personal
testimony, and may appear to dwell

Hopkins The Month [*enclosed in rectangle*]

10

The invitation to write something as a memento, tribute to or recalling of Gerard Manley Hopkins in this <^centenary> year of his entry into the Society of Jesus might ~~at first sight~~ appear at first sight a not only welcome ~~by but~~ and congenial but fairly simple task, in that there is so much ~~over the years~~ which, over the years, the name 'Hopkins' has evoked.

But it becomes, at least in my own case, <^a> far less simple matter, once one tries to write down a tribute. For one thing, so much has been written <^in> appraisement of Hopkins and his ~~poetry~~ works ranging from W. H. Gardner's intensive two volume study published in 1944 & 1949, to the various books and articles of the nineteen twenties & thirties and more written since 1949 making available additional material ~~and~~ as well as concentrating on some particular aspect of the ~~poets~~ man or his work.

Anyway, to-day, ~~three~~ exactly half a century since his poems were first published and seventy-nine years since his death, Hopkins is firmly established in the canon of English poetry. He is 'accepted'. Once his works became known it was inevitable that, sooner or later, acceptance would follow. What is 'accepted' is always in danger of being 'taken for granted' and while, in any context, a taking for granted is never a good thing it would, <^for a number of reasons, be> especially undesirable in the case of Hopkins.

As indicated above, so much has been written since Bridges first released a collection of Hopkins ~~poetry~~ poems in 1918, I do not feel in any position to add to what has been expressed by competent & perceptive writers who have made Hopkins & his works their special study – in any case ~~I am not~~ [*the next three cancelled words illegible*] I have not <^the> qualifications. But it occurred to me that I might try & record the impact of Hopkins upon myself when first I came into contact with his work. ~~This may~~ [*the next word added in the left-hand margin*] This is, necessarily a, so to say, personal testimony, and may appear to dwell ~~too~~

(2)

too much on matters of an autobiographical nature. If so, I apologize, but this attempt to recall a few memories of hearing about Hopkins and of reading or hearing read some of his work and the reaction of various friends and my own reactions seems about all I can do in this brief salute to this unique 'makar'— and here the Lallan word for poeta seems especially evocative & appropriate for when we think of Dunbar's Lament for the Makaris, we make memento of Fr Hopkins, for whatever our personal response to his poetry, whether we place it very high indeed or admire some of it but not all of it or even if we don't care, must say, for it — we must admit that in him there was the single minded determination to make a work in which, at whatever cost, the words from the Vulgate psalm 121, verse 3, '...cujus participatio ejus in idipsum' were imperative. The unity of the parts without which there can be no whole, the most exacting conjoinery, the making one of a diversity of parts & the juxtapositioning of diverse elements whereby a 'whole' is achieved and 'form' and 'content' become inseparable, all this is indeed the crucial problem for all artists whether they know it or not. But with Hopkins the nature of the struggle is evident and, regardless of our reactions to this 'making', he was quintessentially a 'makar'.

When Bridges published the first edition

* Hopkins c 1918 I heard nothing of it

(and on demobilisation I re-continued my studies as an art-student after three years service in the army. My interests since childhood had been concentrated on the visual arts, and

over

[*page 51*]

(2)

too much on matters of an autobiographical nature. If so, I apologise, but ~~it seems about the only way~~ this attempt to recall a few ~~personal~~ memories of hearing about Hopkins and of reading or hearing read some of his work and the reaction of various friends and my own reactions seems about all I can do in this brief salute to this unique 'makar' – and ~~Dunbar's Lallan word~~[163] here the Lallan word for poeta seems especially evocative~~, for~~ & apropriate for when we think of Dunbar's Lament for the Makaris we make ~~mem~~ memento of Fr Hopkins, for ~~whether we~~ whatever our personal response to his poetry, whether we place it very high indeed or admire some of it but not all of it or even if we don't care <^much> for <^any of> it – we must admit that ~~the~~ in [*the next three words added in the left-hand margin*] him there was ~~making of it~~ the single minded determination to make a work in which, at whatever cost, the words from the Vulgate psalm 121, verse 3, '. . . cujus participatio ejus in idipsum' were imperative.[164] The unity of the parts ~~with~~ without which there can be no whole, the most exacting conjoinery, the making one of a diversity of parts ~~and <^the> juxtaposing of (in the case of poetry, words)~~ [*two cancelled words illegible*] & the juxtapositioning of ~~the~~ diverse elements whereby a whole is achieved, and 'form' and 'content' become insepable. All this is indeed the crucial problem for all ~~make~~ artists whether they know it or not. But with Hopkins the nature of the struggle is evident, and regardless of our reactions to this ~~work~~ <'making'> he was ~~first & quit~~ quintessentially a 'makar'.

~~But to return to~~

When Bridges published the first edition

[*Added in left-hand margin:* + Hopkins in 1918 [/] ~~I was abroad~~ [/] I heard nothing of it] ~~of Hopkins poems in 1918 I was in the serving in the army and have no direct knowledge at all of~~ and ~~when~~ on demobilization I re-continued my studies as an art-student ~~which I had had been interrupted for years~~ after three years service in the army My interests since childhood had been concentrated on the visual arts, and

.

over

[163] See Jones's letter of 20 April 1962 to Vernon Watkins in Staudt, 'David Jones: Eight Previously Unpublished Letters to Vernon Watkins', 83: 'The Scots are lucky, because of this continuous & great tradition of having the Low-land tongue [*the next ten words inserted in the margin*] "lallan" I believe it's called, but I can't spell it. – which is only a dialect of English, but which has made possible the impact of the Scottic thing within the English tradition. We have nothing like that.'

[164] This phrase describes Jerusalem as a city 'whose parts are united in one', as Jones translates it in a 1940 essay in appreciation of the recently deceased Eric Gill, who, Jones writes there, as he would of Hopkins later, took it to heart as a paradigm of aesthetic integrity. See Jones, 'Eric Gill, *an Appreciation*' [italics in table of contents, p. 10], *Epoch and Artist*, 301. This essay was first published in *The Tablet* on 10 November 1940, 'that is to say almost immediately upon Mr. Gill's death', Jones writes in a footnote on p. 296. Gill died on 17 November, having entered hospital on 4 November. See the biography by Fiona MacCarthy, *Eric Gill* (London: Faber & Faber, 1989 [paperback 1990]), 292. For another use of this verse of Ps. 121, a Jonesian motto, see Jones, *Letters to a Friend*, 18 and 81.

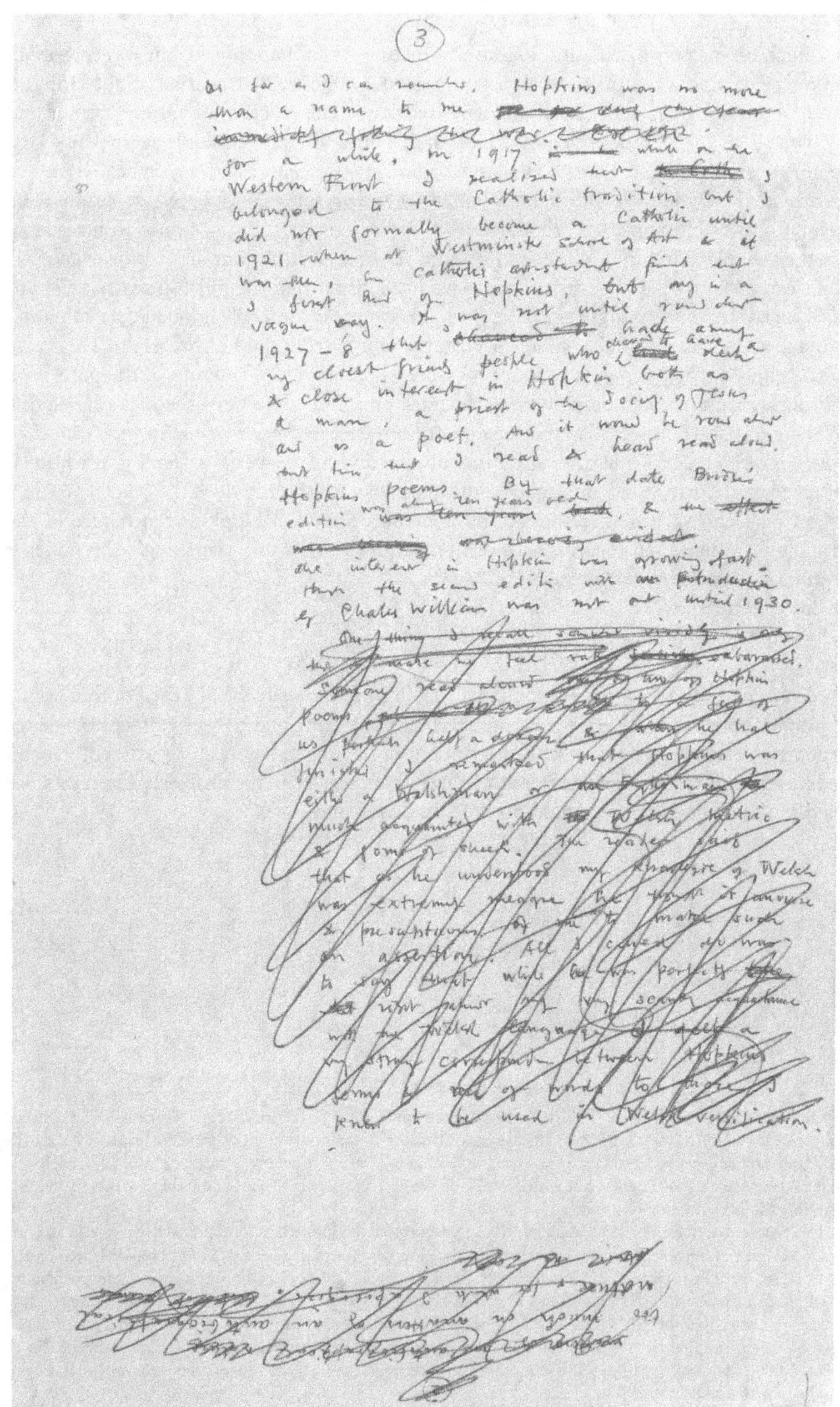

(3)

as far as I can remember, Hopkins was no more than a name to me for a while. In 1917 while on the Western Front I realised that I belonged to the Catholic tradition but I did not formally become a Catholic until 1921 when at Westminster School of Art a Catholic art-student friend [illegible] was then, [illegible] I first heard of Hopkins, but only in a vague way. It was not until round about 1927–8 that I had among my closest friends people who chanced to have a close interest in Hopkins both as a man, a priest of the Society of Jesus and as a poet. And it would be round about that time that I read & heard read aloud Hopkins poems. By that date Bridges' edition was already ten years old, & the interest in Hopkins was growing fast. though the second edition with an Introduction by Charles Williams was not out until 1930.

[*page 52*]

(3)

37

as far as I can ?remember, Hopkins was no more than a name to me ~~for~~ [*two cancelled words illegible*] ~~the years immediately following the war. By 192~~ · for a while, in 1917, ~~in~~ [*one cancelled word illegible*] while on the Western Front I realized that ~~the Cath~~ I belonged to the Catholic tradition but I did not formally become a Catholic until 1921 when at Westminster School of Art & it was then, from Catholic art-student friends that I first heard of Hopkins, but only in a vague way. It was not until round about 1927–'8 that <I> ~~chanced to~~ had among my closest friends people who <^chanced to have a> ~~had~~ [*one word illegible*] & close interest in Hopkins both as man, a priest of the Society of Jesus and as a poet. And it would be round about that time that I read & heard read aloud, Hopkins poems. By that date Bridges' edition ~~was ten years back~~ <was already ten years old>, & the ~~effect was becoming~~ ~~was becoming evident~~. the interest in Hopkins was growing fast, though the second edition with an introduction by Charles Williams was not out until 1930.[165]

~~One thing I recall somewhat vividly is that it made me feel rather foolish embarassed. Someone read aloud one or two of Hopkins poems at a~~ [*one cancelled word illegible*] ~~to a few of us perhaps half a dozen & when he had finished I remarked that Hopkins was either a Welshman or an Englishman~~ [*one cancelled word illegible*] ~~much acquainted with~~ [*the next word cancelled*] ~~the Welsh metric & forms of speech. The reader said that as he understood my knowledge of Welsh was extremely meagre he thought it unwise & presumptuous of me to make such an assertion. All I could do was to say that while~~ [*the next word overwrites* it] ~~he was perfectly~~ [*the next two words cancelled*] ~~true that right about my very scanty acquaintance with the Welsh language I feel a very strong correspondence between Hopkins forms and use of words to those I knew to be used in Welsh versification.~~

[*The following script at the bottom of the page upside-down*]

~~matters of an autobiographical nature.~~
~~too much on matters of an autobiographical nature, for which I apologise. but it seems about the only~~ ·

[165] This second edition was the first to gain for Hopkins a wide audience. For details of Jones's personal copies, one of which was a gift from his father, Christmas 1930, see Huw Ceiriog Jones, *The Library of David Jones*, 140.

The invitation to write something as a memento or recalling of Gerard Manley Hopkins in this Centenary year of his entry into the Society of Jesus might appear at first sight not only a welcome but a fairly simple task, in that there is so much which over the years, the name 'Hopkins' has evoked.

But what seems a simple task, becomes, at least in my case, by no means so simple once one tries to write down ones tribute.
For one thing so much has been written in appraisal of Hopkins and his poetry ranging from Dr W. H. Gardner's exhaustive two volume work subtitled <u>A Study of Poetic Idiosyncracy in Relation to Poetic Tradition</u>, published in the nineteen-forties, to books and articles of varying apperception, ten to twenty years before Dr Gardners volumes and still more in the two decades since 1947. While I cannot claim to have read anything more than a very small fraction of these various studies, it is clear that, one way and another, the man and his work have been carefully discussed & appraised by people well qualified to do so, and I don't think I can add anything to what is already known regarding the

All I can do is to try to recall something of my personal reactions on first coming into contact with the works of Fr Hopkins.

It is now exactly half a century since Bridges collection of Hopkins poems appeared, and the poet had then been dead for three decades.

In 1918, when this first publication appeared I was in the army and knew nothing whatever of this important event. When I returned my three years service it was to resume my studies at an art-school, the visual arts being my main preoccupation since childhood. It was, I suppose, round about 1926 that I first heard of the name Hopkins and not until 1927 or '28 that I can recall

[*page 53*]

2

The invitation to write something as a memento or recalling of Gerard Manley Hopkins in this centenary year of his entry into the Society of Jesus might appear at first sight not only a welcome but a fairly simple task, in that there is so much which over the years, the name 'Hopkins' has evoked ·

But what seems a simple task, becomes, at least in my case, by no means so simple once one tries to write down one's tribute. ·

[*pencilled in left-hand margin:* BBC Publications [/] Box 1 AR][166]

For one thing so much has been written in appraisal of Hopkins and his ~~work~~ poetry ranging from Dr W. H. Gardner's exhaustive two volume work subtitled A Study of Poetic Idiosyncracy in Relation to Poetic Tradition, published in the nineteen-forties, to books and articles of varying apperception ten to twenty years before ~~that~~ or Gardner's volumes and still more ~~since~~ in the two decades since 1947. While I cannot claim to have read anything more than a <^very small> fraction of these various studies, it is clear that, one way and another, the man and his work have been carefully discussed & appraised [*one cancelled word illegible*] ~~many differing~~ by people well qualified to do so, and I don't think I can add anything to what is already known regarding the

All I can do is to try ~~and~~ to recall ~~some something~~ something of my personal reactions on first coming into contact with the works of Fr Hopkins.

It is now exactly half a century since Bridges collection of Hopkins' poems appeared, and the poet had then been dead for three decades.

In 1918, when this first publication appeared I was in the army and knew nothing whatever of this important event. When I returned from my three years service it was to resume my studies at an art-school, the visual arts being my main preoccupation since childhood. ~~I supp~~ It was, I suppose, round about 1926 that I first heard of the name Hopkins and not until 1927 or '28 that I can recall

[166] The address of the BBC Publications office in the late 1960s was Box 1 AR, 35 Marylebone High Street, London W1.

Byr. ~~[illegible]~~ 1018

18 eggs
2 NZ butter
3 [illegible]
4 Ross Lime Juice
1 Bath Oliver biscuits
1 Cheese biscuits
2 Pears Soap
1 [illegible]/flat
1 [illegible] tea.

[*page 54*]

[*in red-brown ink or pencil*]

Byr. ~~1307~~ 1018[167]

18 eggs
2 NZ butter
3 Dairylea cheeselets
1 Rose's Lime Juice
1 Bath Oliver's biscuits
1 Ginger biscuits
2 Pears Soap
1 [*one word illegible*] toil/flat
1 Lapsang tea

[167] 'Byr.' (Byron) was one of the telephone exchange names for South Harrow, where Jones had lived from December 1947 until April 1964, at the boarding house Northwick Lodge in Harrow on the Hill. His new address, 2 Northwick Park Road, Harrow, the Monksdene Residential Hotel, was covered by the telephone exchange 'Har.' (Harrow). He moved to Calvary Nursing Home, Sudbury Hill, Harrow on the Hill, on 6 June 1970, after his stroke and subsequent fall in March 1970. See Dilworth, *David Jones: Engraver, Soldier, Painter, Poet*, 343–4.

(2)

reading or hearing read any of his poems.
It chanced that about that time various of
my closest friends were
particularly interested in Hopkins, both as a
poet and as a priest of the Society of Jesus.
I recall very vividly an occasion when someone
a visitor who happened to call while the
conversation had turned upon Hopkins,
and after a while he read aloud some of
Hopkins verses. At the conclusion of
his reading I remarked that Hopkins must
either have been a Welshman or an
Englishman who had been greatly influenced
by Welsh forms. The reader said
that he understood that I knew next to
nothing of the Welsh language, in which
case, how could I make such an
assertion. To which I could only reply that
while it was true that my acquaintance
with Welsh was minimal, none the less
I was convinced that, in various ways,
Hopkins metrical form & use of words
indicated a strong Welsh influence of
some sort.

(2)

[*a squiggle in the left-hand margin in the same red-brown ink or pencil used to write the shopping list on page 54*]

40

reading or hearing read any of his poems.

It chanced that about that time various of my closes friends were [*one cancelled word illegible*] ~~differing~~ [*one cancelled word illegible*] particularly interested in Hopkins, both as a poet and as a priest of the Society of Jesus.

I recall very vividly an occasion when someone a visitor who happened to call while the ~~subje~~ conversation had turned upon Hopkins,

~~and he too was~~

and after a while he read aloud some of Hopkins verses. At the conclusion of his reading I remarked that Hopkins must either have been a Welshman or an Englishman who had been greatly influenced by Welsh forms. The reader ~~said that~~ said that he understood that I knew next to nothing of the Welsh ~~languag~~ language, in which case, ~~it was but~~ how could I make such an assertion. To which I could only reply that while it was true that ~~I~~ my acquaintance with Welsh was minimal, none the less I was convinced that, in various ways, Hopkins metrical form & use of words ~~bore a strong resemblance to~~ indicated a strong Welsh influence of some sort.

(1)

The invitation to contribute something to a 'Homage to Hopkins' issue of The Month on the centenary of ~~his~~ his entry into the Novitiate of the Society of Jesus might appear a not only congenial but fairly simple task in that there is so much which the name 'Hopkins' has evoked over the last half century.

But when it comes to actually making a contribution of some sort the task, at least for the present writer, becomes far from simple.

For one thing, so much has been written ~~written of this man and his works.~~ ~~The appraisa~~ in appraisement of this remarkable man and his works. The studies range from that comprehensive ~~[illegible]~~ study and intensive two volume ~~work~~ by Dr W. H. Gardner published in 1944 and 1949 back to the many articles and some books of the nineteen ~~twenties~~ thirties and twenties and forward to other studies during the nineteen fifties & sixties. Some making available additional material, others concentrating on some particular facet or aspect of the work or the man.

So that to-day, exactly half a century since the initial publication of ~~of a body of his poems~~ a collection of his poems and seventy-nine years since the poet's death, Hopkins ~~[illegible]~~ ~~[illegible]~~ stands indisputably and fixedly within the canon of English poets: his work is 'accepted', so much so that any anthology of English verse in which no poem of Hopkins was included is hardly possible.

But with 'acceptance' there not infrequently comes a 'taking for granted' — never a good ~~thing~~ either with regard to things or persons and to take Hopkins for granted would be to cancell & make void his ever having a place in the canon.

~~His poiesis chances to be of that sort that occurs from time to time in the history of any given art [illegible] can be quite like [illegible] [illegible] for those practicing that same~~ ~~[illegible]~~ particular art.

[*page 56*]

(1)

3

The invitation to contribute something to a 'Homage to Hopkins' issue of <u>The Month</u> on the centenary of ~~his~~ his entry into the Noviciate of the Society of Jesus might appear a not only congenial but fairly simple task in that there is so much which the name 'Hopkins' has evoked over the last half century.

But when it comes to actually making a contribution of some sort the task, at least for the present writer, becomes far from simple.

For one thing, so much has been [*the next word added in the right-hand margin*] written ~~written of this man and his works.~~ ~~in appais~~ in appraisement of this remarkable man and his works. The studies range from that ~~great work~~ <comprehensive> and intensive two volume ~~work~~ <study> by Dr W. H. Gardner publised in 1944 and 1949 back to the many articles and some books of the nineteen ~~twenties~~ thirties and 'twenties and forward to other studies during the nineteen fifties & sixties. Some making available additional material, · others concentrating on some particular facet or aspect of the work or the man.

So that to-day, exactly half a century since the initial publication [*the next word added in the right-hand margin*] of ~~by Bridges of his friend's~~ a collection of his poems and seventy-nine years since the poet's death, Hopkins ~~has become~~

[*The rest of the script (in pen) on this page overwrites erased script in pencil*]

stands indisputably and fixedly within the canon of English poets: his work is 'accepted', so much so that any anthology of English verse in which no poem of Hopkins was included is hardly possible.

But with 'acceptance' there not infrequently comes a 'taking for granted' – never a good, ~~thing~~ either with regard to ~~works~~ <things> or persons and to take Hopkins for granted would be to cancell & make void his ever having a place in the canon.

~~His <u>poiesis</u> chances to be of that sort that occurs from time <sort> to time in the history of any given art, whereby nothing can be quite the same again for those practicing that particular art.~~ ~~(over)~~

(2)

What I am thinking of is not the same as what is meant by that 'influence'. over-worked word 'influence'.

But few such artists can have lived their lives with so total an exclusion of their particular genius, as to become some few decades after their deaths, such discussed and written-about figures and what is far more to the point, figures whose work has had a vivifying effect.

It is

[*page 57*]

(2)

~~it is not a question of 'influence' in the sense so much by art critics~~

~~What I am thinking of is not the same as~~ [*the next word cancelled*] ~~that what is meant by that 'influence'.~~
~~word 'influence' as~~ [*one cancelled word illegible*] ~~used so~~ ·
~~over-worked word 'influence'~~

~~But few~~ [*the next word cancelled*] ~~artists such artists can have lived their lives with so total an occlusion of their particular genius, to become, some few decades after their deaths, such discussed and written-about figures and what is far more to the point, figures whose work has had a~~ [*the next word cancelled*] ~~vitalizing vivifying effect.~~
It is ·

(2)

When Bridges made available to the public the first collection of Hopkins poems I was away in the army and wholly unaware of this important event. And when I was demobilised in December 1918 I at once resumed my studies as an art-student which I had laid aside three to four years previously. It must have been a year or more later that I first heard the name of Hopkins, but it was no more than a name mentioned by a fellow art-student, I think in relation to a poem of Walt Whitman's. Anyway, at that date, my concentration was so much upon the problems of the visual arts, as indeed it had been since childhood, that Hopkins was to remain for me not much more than a name for some little while yet.

In 1917 in the trenches of the West Front I became, so to say, interiorly aware of belonging to the Catholic tradition, though it took until 1921 to be formally received into the Church.

Inevitably this strand and that strand drew together and varying personal influences from among art-student friends which helped me to become a Catholic conditioned me also toward that habit of thought which would respond to the poetry of Hopkins. Nevertheless it was not until after 1927 that I recall reading and hearing read some of Hopkins poetry. Or, at all events that was about the time, when I realised that here was something,

[*page 58*]

(2)

21

When Bridges ~~fi~~ made available to the public the first collection of Hopkins poems I was away in the army and wholly unaware of this important event. And when I was demobilized in December 1918 I [*one cancelled word illegible*] at once resumed my studies as an art-student which <^had been> laid aside three to four years previously. It must have been a year or more later that I first heard the name of Hopkins, but it was no more than a name ~~ng inter.~~ mentioned by a fellow art-student, I think in relation to a poem of Walt Whitman's. Anyway, at that date, my concentration was [*one cancelled word illegible*] so much upon the problems of the visual arts as indeed it had been since childhood, that Hopkins was to remain for me not much more than a name for some little while yet.

In 1917 ~~while serving on~~ <in the trenches of> the West Front I became, so to say, interiorly aware ~~?that~~ of belonging to the Catholic tradition, though it took until 1921 to be formally received into the ~~Church Catholic~~ Church. ~~Inevit~~

Inevitably this ~~stan~~ strand and that strand draw together and varying personal influences from among art-student friends ~~who were Catholic~~ which helped me to become a Catholic conditioned me also toward that habit of thought which would respond to the poetry of Hopkins.

Nevertheless it was not until about 1927~~–28 that I~~ that I recall ~~first realising the nature of this~~ reading and hearing read some of Hopkins poetry. Or, at all events ~~?of~~ that was about the time, when [*the next word overwrites* a] I ~~realisation~~ realised that here was something.

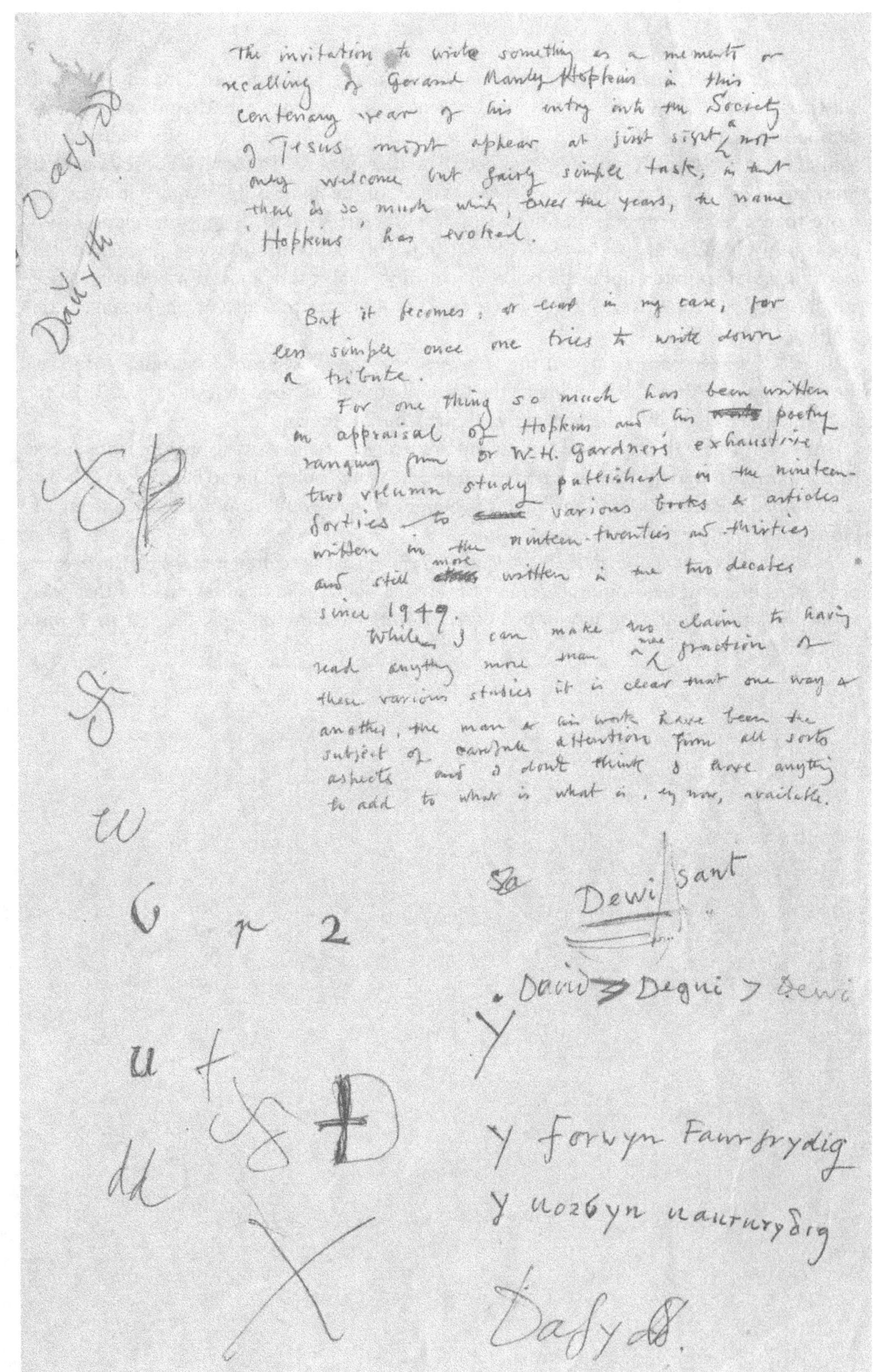

The invitation to write something as a memento or recalling of Gerard Manley Hopkins in this centenary year of his entry into the Society of Jesus might appear at first sight a not only welcome but fairly simple task, in that there is so much which, over the years, the name 'Hopkins' has evoked.

But it becomes: or least in my case, far less simple once one tries to write down a tribute.

For one thing so much has been written in appraisal of Hopkins and his ~~works~~ poetry ranging from Dr W. H. Gardner's exhaustive two volumn study published in the nineteen-forties to ~~some~~ various books & articles written in the ninteen-twenties and thirties and still ~~others~~ more written in the two decates since 1949.

While I can make no claim to having read anything more than a mere fraction of these various studies it is clear that one way or another, the man & his work have been the subject of carefule attention from all sorts aspects and I don't think I have anything to add to what is what is, by now, available.

[*page 59*]

9
[*a variety of interrelated marginalia down the left-hand margin and at the bottom of the page*][168]

The invitation to write something as a memento or recalling of Gerard Manly Hopkins in this centenary year of his entry into the Society of Jesus might appear at first sight <^a> not only welcome but fairly simple task, in that there is so much which, over the years, the name 'Hopkins' has evoked.

But it becomes, at least in my case, far less simple once one tries to write down a tribute.

For one thing so much has been written in appraisal of Hopkins and his ~~works~~ poetry ranging from Dr W. H. Gardner's exhaustive two volume study published in the nineteen-forties. [*the full-stop subsumed into the following* t] to ~~some~~ various books & articles written in the nineteen-twenties and thirties and still ~~others~~ <more> written in the two decades since 1949.

While I can make no claim to have read anything more than a <^mere> fraction of these various studies it is clear that one way & another, the man & his work have been the subject of carefull attention from all sorts aspects and I don't think I have anything to add to what is what is, by now, available.

[168] In the margins of this page Jones doodles the Old English letters eth and thorn and explores the etymology and orthography of his first name. 'Dewi sant' is Saint David, patron saint of Wales. The Welsh phrase 'y forwyn fawrfrydig' (which Jones transcribes in older orthography in the line below), 'the magananimous virgin', could refer to the Virgin Mary. See *Dai Greatcoat*, 74, for Jones's letter of 3 July 1935 to René Hague: 'Don't you think the sound of the words for Blessed V. Mary good—they are Fendigedig Fair Forwyn, pronounced roughly Vendigedig Vire (like i in fire) Vorwein.' This phrase, translated as 'the majestic maiden', appears in *Kilhwch and Olwen*, a tale included in the Charlotte Guest *Mabinogion*, as an epithet of Gwenllian Deg. See *The Mabinogion*, trans. Lady Charlotte Guest (London: Dent, 1913), 106. A copy of this edition is in Jones's personal library. See Huw Ceiriog Jones, *The Library of David Jones*, 183. Thanks to Francesca Brooks and Paul Robichaud for this information.

The invitation to contribute something to a 'Homage to Hopkins' issue of The Month.

[*page 60*]

32

The invitation to contribute something to a 'Homage to Hopkins' issue of The Month ·

[*page 61*]

(3)

the publication of Hopkins ·

Having been asked to write something as a
recalling of the hundredth anniversary of
Gerald Manley Hopkins' entry
into the Society of Jesus, I think the
only possible to me to try to
make a few perhaps disconnected and
oblique remarks of an entirely personal
nature, concerning, in the main, my
first contacts with with the 'poiesis'
that is the written poiesis of this
sacerdos.
I use the word poiesis rather than the
English word 'poetry', because what
he wrote was but one of the forms
of 'making' with which his life was
occupied — and as a priest of the Order
of Melchisedech he was inevitably committed
to that manual act and spoken words
at the Mensa Domini which constitute
the supreme 'making' where signa and what
is signified are one and the same. In
all 'poetry' the artist strives to make
in this or that medium an effectual
re-calling of something other, he tries to
'make present' under the forms of his
art some
reality — no matter what.

[*page 62*]

1

Having been asked to write something as a recalling of the hundredth anniversary of ~~the~~ Gerald Manly Hopkins' ~~becoming~~ entry into the Society of Jesus, I think the only possible to me to try [*one cancelled word illegible*] to ~~m~~ make a few perhaps disconnected and oblique remarks of an entirely personal nature, concerning, in the main, my first contacts with with the '~~poetry'~~ [*the next word added in the right-hand margin:*] poiesis ~~of~~ that is the written poetry <~~poiesis~~> of this ~~astonishing man~~ sacerdos. ~~I wrote~~

[*pencilled in the left-hand margin with an arrow pointing to the following line:* Begin]

I use the word poiesis rather than the English word 'poetry', because what he wrote was but one of the forms of 'making' [*the following word overwrites* wh] to <with his> which ~~he was~~ life was ~~dedicated~~ <occupied> – and as a Priest of the Order of Melchisdech,[169] he was inevitably committed to that manual act and spoken words at the Mensa Domini[170] which [*one cancelled word or part-word illegible*] constitute the supreme 'making' where signa and what is signified are one and the same. In all 'poetry' the artist strives to make in this or that medium an effectual re-calling of something other, he tries to 'make present' under the forms of his art some ~~actuality—it may be reality~~ – no matter what.

[*the rest of the script on this page cancelled*]

The question that has so harrassed our epoch [*one cancelled word illegible*] touching <the> ~~non~~ 'abstract' and 'non-abstract' is unaffected by the this precondition for all art is [*one cancelled word illegible*] abstract and all art re-presents.

But only the poiesis at the altar ·

[169] In endnote 38 to 'Part Four' of *In Parenthesis*, 210, where, at the end of his boast, Dai Greatcoat mentions 'Melchizzydix!' (84), Jones refers the reader to Heb. 7.3. See also 'from *The Book of Balaam's Ass*', in David Jones, *The Sleeping Lord and Other Fragments* (London: Faber & Faber, 1974), 108, n. 4, and 'The Preface to *The Anathemata*', in *Epoch and Artist*, 129. In the Epistle to the Hebrews, where he quotes Ps. 110.4, Paul establishes Christ as a priest in the order of Melchisedec: without genealogy, and so eternal.

[170] The 'Table of the Lord', i.e. the altar.

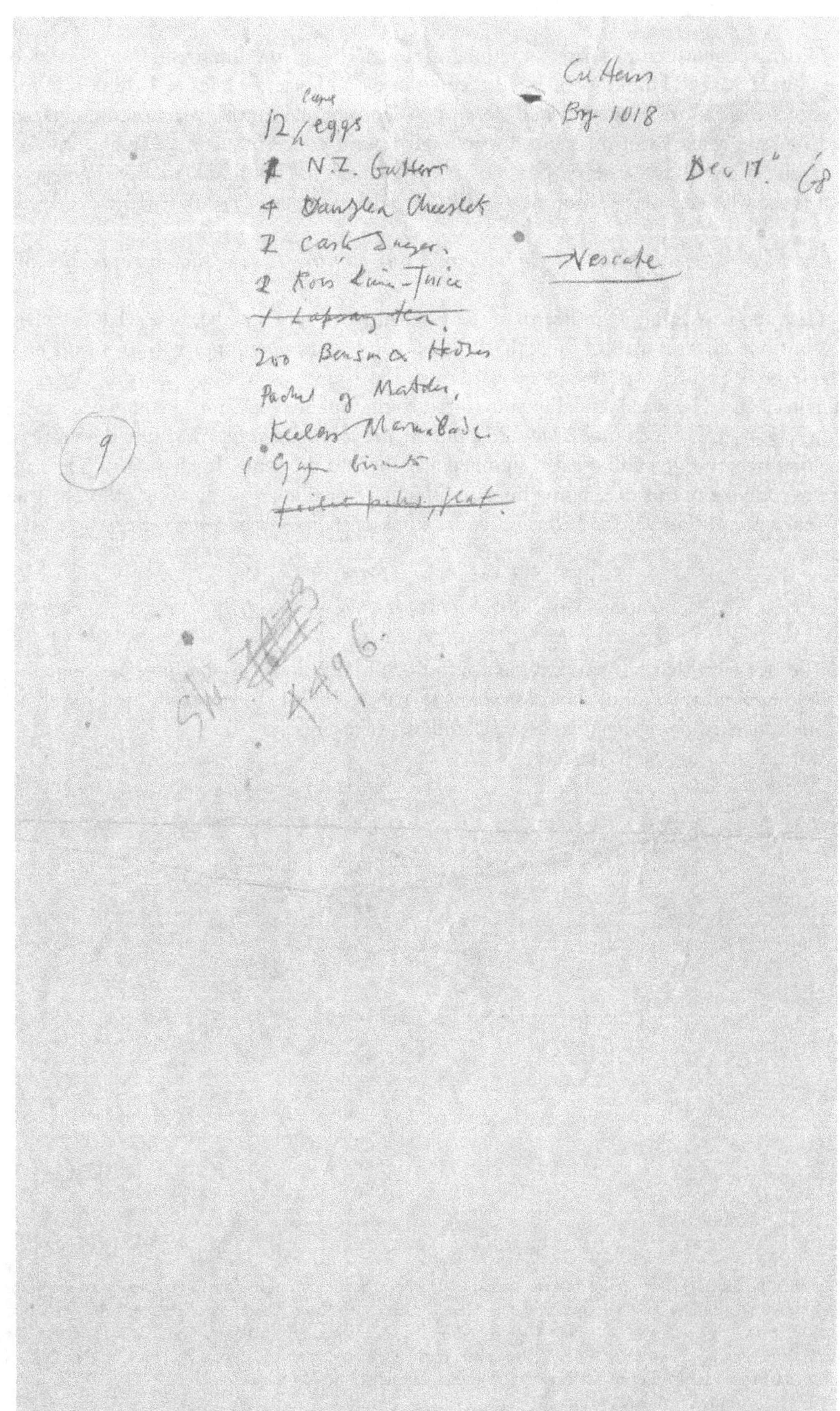
Cutters
Bry 1018
Dec 17th 68
12 large eggs
N.Z. Butter
4 Danish Cheeselets
2 cash Sugar.
2 Ross Lime-Juice
~~1 Lapsang tea.~~
200 Benson & Hedges
Packet of Matches,
Keiller Marmalade
1 Ginger biscuits
~~toilet rolls, flat.~~
Nescafe
9

[*page 63*]

Cullens[171] [/] Byr 1018 [/] Dec 17th. '68

12 <^large> eggs
1 [*overwrites* 2] N.Z. {*New Zealand*} butters
4 Dairylea Cheeslets
1 caster sugar
2 Rose's Lime-Juice Nescafe
~~1 Lapsang tea.~~
200 Benson & Hedges
Packet of Matches.

[*a circled numeral 9 in left-hand margin at the following line*]

Keiller's Marmalade
1 Ginger biscuits
~~toilet packs, flat.~~
[*in pencil:*] She ·[172] ~~7473~~ [/] 4496.

[171] The grocers Cullen's, receipts from which dating 1961–9 are preserved among Jones's personalia in folder P2/2/6 of the David Jones Papers at the National Library of Wales, Aberystwyth.
[172] 'She' is short for the 'Shepherd's' (Shepherd's Bush) telephone exchange.

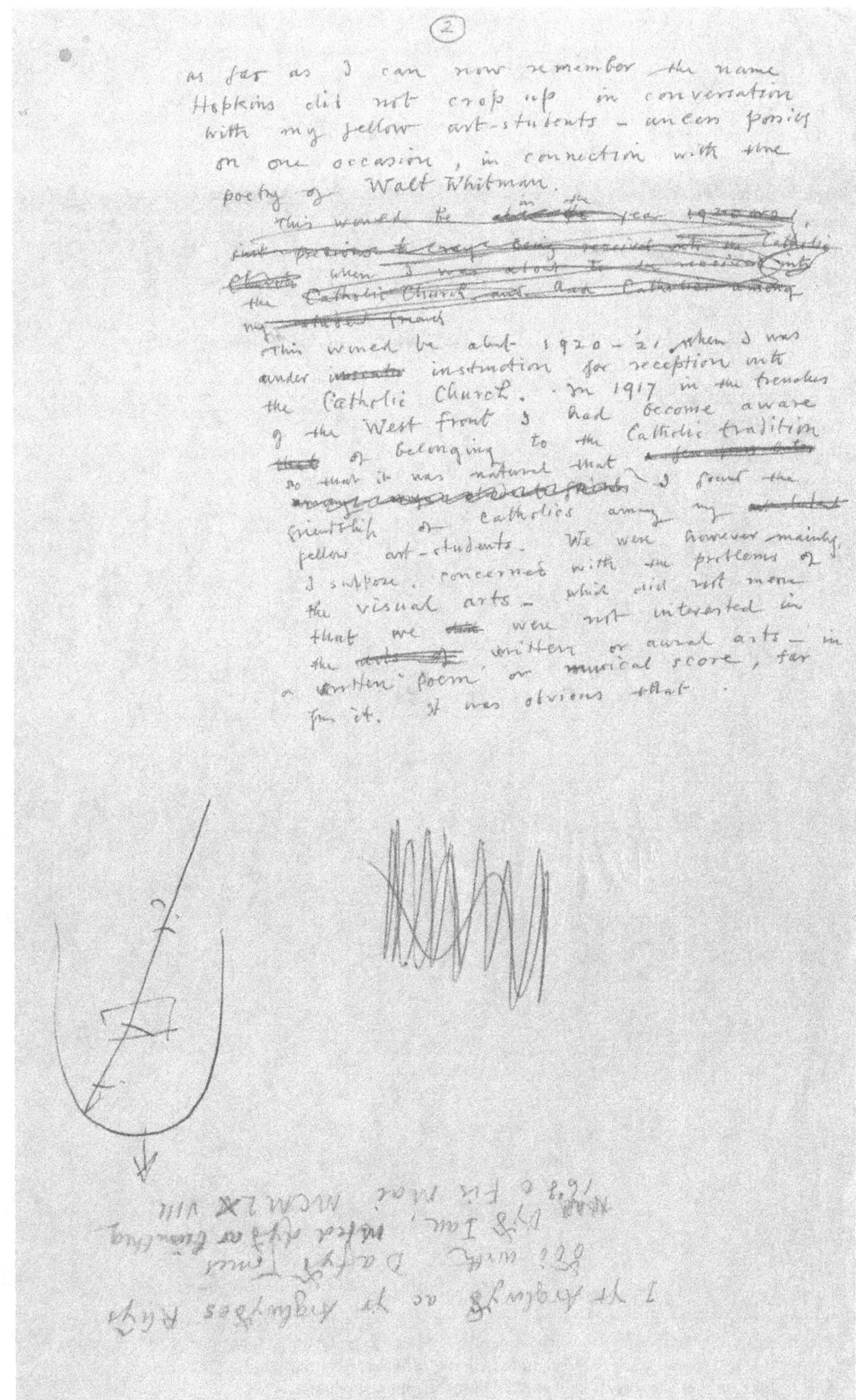

(2)

as far as I can now remember the name Hopkins did not crop up in conversation with my fellow art-students – unless possibly on one occasion, in connection with the poetry of Walt Whitman.

~~This would be in the year~~ ...

This would be about 1920–21, when I was under instruction for reception into the Catholic Church. In 1917 in the trenches of the West Front I had become aware of belonging to the Catholic tradition so that it was natural that I found the friendship of catholics among my fellow art-students. We were however mainly, I suppose, concerned with the problems of the visual arts – which did not mean that we were not interested in the written or aural arts – in a written poem or musical score, far from it. It was obvious that .

[*page 64*]

(2)

25

As far as I can now remember the name Hopkins did not crop up in conversation with my fellow art-students – unless possibly on one occasion, in connection with the poetry of Walt Whitman.

[*The following sentence cancelled*] This would be ~~about the~~ <in the> year 1920 or 21, just ~~previous to my being received into the Catholic Church~~ when I was about to be received into the Catholic Church and had Catholics among my student friends

This would be about 1920–'21 when I was under ~~inseuti~~ instruction for reception into the Catholic Church. In 1917 in the trenches of the West Front I had become aware ~~that~~ of belonging to the Catholic tradition ~~among my student friends~~ so that it was natural that ~~a few years later~~ I found the friendship of Catholics among my ~~art-student~~ fellow art-students. We were however mainly, I suppose, concerned with the problems of the visual arts – which did not mean that we ~~did~~ were not interested in the ~~arts of~~ written or aural arts – in a written 'poem' or musical score, far from it. It was obvious that ·

[*The following script appears upside-down in pencil at the bottom of this page*]

I Yr Arglwyð ac yr Arglwyðes Rhŷs
oði wrth Dafyð Jones
~~Mai~~ Dyð Iau unfed dyð ar bumtheg
16^{eg} o Fis Mai MCMLX VIII[173]

[173] Translation from the Welsh by Paul Robichaud: 'To the Lord and Lady Rhŷs / from David Jones / Thursday the sixteenth day of May / 16th of May 1968.' 'Lord and Lady Rhŷs' could designate the Welsh prince Rhys ap Gruffydd (1132–97), traditionally referred to as 'the Lord Rhys', and his wife Gwenllian ferch Madog. Rhys ap Gruffydd was ruler of the southern Welsh kingdom of Deheubarth and, from 1163, ally of Henry II of England until the latter's death in 1189. See John Davies, *A History of Wales*, rev. edn (London: Penguin, 2007), 122–5. Davies, 125, notes that 'Rhys ap Gruffydd was referred to on occasion as *proprietarius princeps Sudwalliae* (the proprietory [sic] prince of south Wales).' 'Lord and Lady Rhŷs' could also refer to Richard Charles Uryan Rhys, 9th Baron Dynevor (19 June 1935–12 November 2008) and his wife, Lucy Catherine King Rothenstein (16 October 1934–). They wed on 7 January 1959, and she was styled Lady Dynevor of Dynevor from 1962 until the marriage was dissolved in 1978. The couple's only son, Hugo Griffith Uryan Rhys, 10th Baron Dynevor, was born on 19 November 1966. Richard Rhys's Black Raven Press published Peter Levi's poetry collection *Fresh Water, Sea Water* in 1966 with Jones's painted inscription *Extensis manibus* (made for Levi's ordination in 1964) reproduced on its cover. Thanks to Sarah Rhys and Ceridwen Lloyd-Morgan for this information.

(3)

It might be objected that in this particular case of Hopkins there is no mystery in that had his works been made ~~availa~~ available soon after his death in 1889 instead of thirty years ~~latter~~ later there would have been the same realization of his qualities by the more perceptive critics and reviewers and the same recognition of his immediate relevance for those engaged in the writing of poetry. ~~[illegible]~~ Or to put it in another way his effect on the men of the late Victorian and Edwardian eras would have been much the same as it was on the men of the post-World War I era.

~~It is impossible to know for certain, but our guess is that~~ –

[*page 65*]

(3)

34

It might be objected that in this particular case of Hopkins there is no mystery in that had his works been made ~~avaible~~ available soon after his death in 1889 instead of thirty years ~~lather~~ later there would have been the same realisation of his qualities by the more perceptive critics and reviewers and the same recognition of his immediate relevance for those engaged <^in> the writing of poetry. ~~As~~ Or to put it another way his effect on the men of the late Victorian and Edwardian eras would have been much the same as <^it> was on the men of <the> post-World War I era.

~~It is impossible to know for certain, but our guess is that~~ –

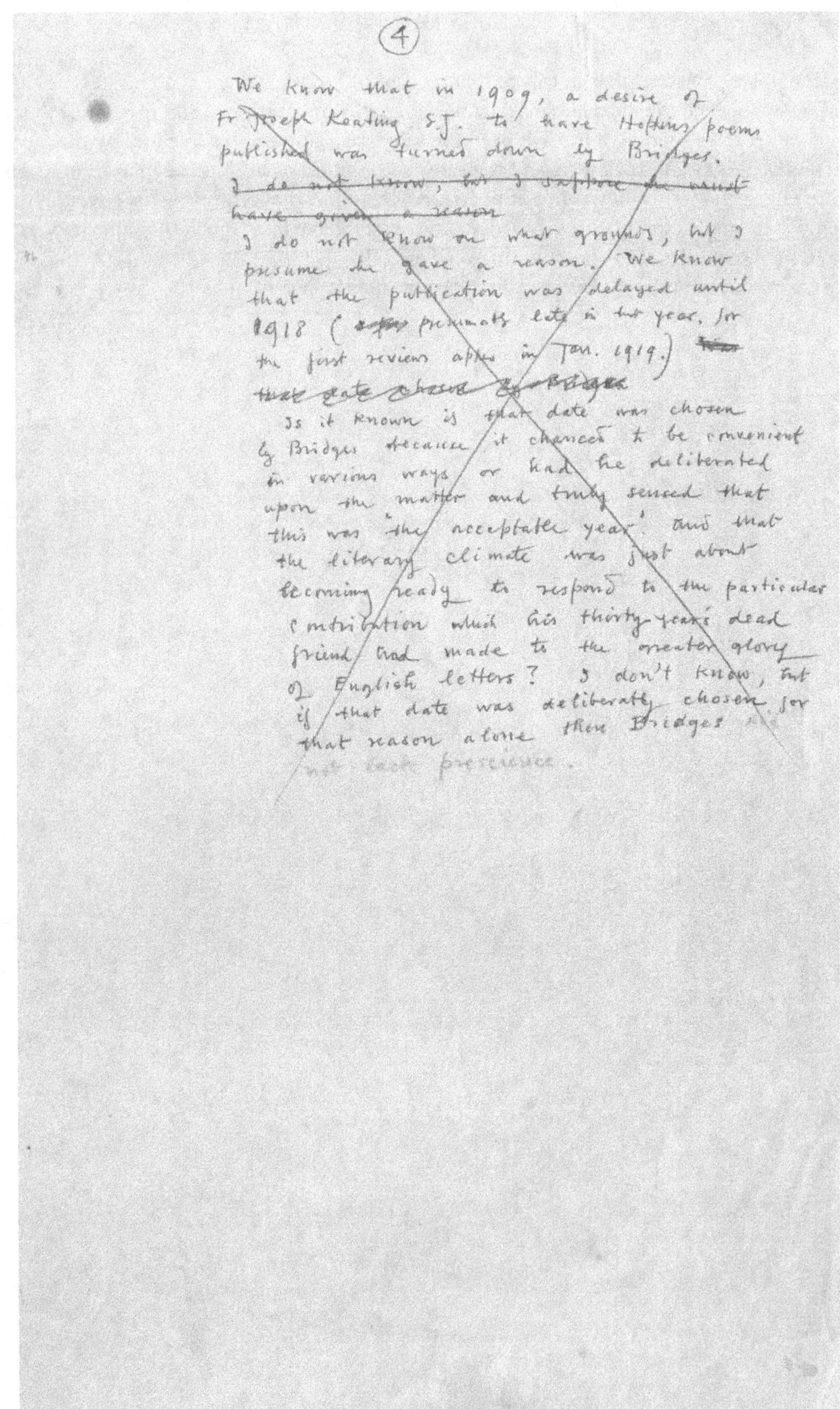

(4)

We know that in 1909, a desire of Fr Joseph Keating S.J. to have Hopkins' poems published was turned down by Bridges. ~~I do not know, but I suppose he would have given a reason~~ I do not know on what grounds, but I presume he gave a reason. We know that the publication was delayed until 1918 (~~after~~ presumably late in the year, for the first reviews appear in Jan. 1919.) ~~that date chosen by Bridges~~

Is it known if that date was chosen by Bridges because it chanced to be convenient in various ways or had he deliberated upon the matter and truly sensed that this was 'the acceptable year' and that the literary climate was just about becoming ready to respond to the particular contribution which his thirty-years' dead friend had made to the greater glory of English letters? I don't know, but if that date was deliberately chosen for that reason alone then Bridges did not lack prescience.

[*page* 66]

(3)

46

[*this entire page cancelled with an* X]

We know that in 1909, a desire of Fr Joseph Keating S. J. to have Hopkins poems published was turned down by Bridges.

~~I do not know, but I suppose he must have given a reason~~

I do not know on what grounds, but I presume he gave a reason. We know that the publication was delayed until 1918 (presumably late in that year, for the first reviews appeared in Jan. 1919.) ~~Was that date chosen by Bridges~~

Is it known if that date was chosen by Bridges because it chanced to be convenient in various ways or had he deliberated upon the matter and truly sensed that this was 'the acceptable year' and that the literary climate was just about becoming ready to respond to the particular contribution which his thirty-years' dead friend had made to the greater glory of English letters? I don't know, but if that date was deliberately chosen for that reason alone then Bridges [*the next four words and final full-stop in pencil*] did not lack prescience.

(3)

Then there's the other sort of chap, of which, I (personally) think G. M. Hopkins is a shining example. Not a large output, but practically <u>all</u> bloody good. Perhaps had he lived longer or had been ~~by profession~~ 'by profession' a poet in that Victorian Age and not by vocation, a priest, he too might have written a lot of stuff that was not '<u>o'r gorau</u>'! who should say? But I feel sure it was the tension & stress of his make-up & his vocation that went a long way to making his <u>poiesis</u> so terrifically good.

Then there are the other blokes, such as Turner, totally professional and of <u>vast</u> output &, by & large, great all the while.

So you are concentrating on Dürer. Well, there again, like yourself, I in the past, never got on much with Dürer – perhaps as with Rembrandt you may help me to appreciate Dürer better. I've always loved the one of Our Lady with the butterfly on her himation – ~~[illegible]~~ 'The Virgin with the Irises', but the engravings not much. Not up my street, that's all. I think it's mainly to do with the whole 'late-Gothic' world – & the German thing.

[*page 67*]

(3)

52

Then there's the other sort of chap, of which, I (personally) think G. M. Hopkins is a shining example. Not a large output, but practically all bloody good. Perhaps had he lived longer or had been ~~by profession~~ 'by profession' a poet in that Victorian age. and not by vocation, a priest, · he too might have written a lot of stuff that was not O'r gorau![174] Who should say? But I feel sure it was the tension & stress of his make-up & his vocation that went a long way to making his poiesis so terrifically good.

Then there are other blokes such as Turner, totally professional and of vast output &, by & large, great all the while.[175]

So you are concentrating on Dürer. Well, there again, like yourself, I in the past, never got on much with Dürer – perhaps as with Rembrandt you may help me to appreciate Dürer . better. I've always loved the one of Our Lady with the butterfly on her himation – ~~Our Lad~~ 'The Virgin with the Irises', but the engravings not much. Not up my street, that's all. I think it's mainly t do with the whole 'late-Gothic' ~~thing~~ world – and the German thing.[176]

---

[174] In a letter of 3 April 1967 to the art historian Kenneth Clark (1903–83), now among the Clark papers at the Tate Gallery Archive, London, Jones employs this Welsh expression and gives his translation: '"indisputably O.K"' [sic]. For an annotated transcription of this letter, see Thomas Dilworth, 'Letters from David Jones to Kenneth Clark', *Burlington Magazine* 142, no. 1165 (April 2000): 215–25, where this letter appears on pp. 224–5, its '*O'r gorau*' on p. 225. At the end of his transcription of the letter Dilworth notes, 'Here the letter breaks off, presumably before a last page on which Jones would have signed off, as usual, "Yours ever David"' (225). The three pages of the unaddressed, unsigned, undated, and incomplete draft letter preserved with the Hopkins essay drafts are almost certainly Jones's studies for the missing 'last page' that Dilworth surmises here. At the end of the presumed draft, transcribed in this edition of the Hopkins essay drafts, Jones signs off with, 'Well, good-bye for now, love David.' See p. 266 below.

[175] Jones esteemed Turner highest among British painters. See Jones, *Letters to a Friend*, 15. In a letter of 16 May 1967 to William Blissett, Jones calls Turner 'easily in my view the greatest of all British painters by world standards (quite apart from how one may react to him)'. See Blissett, *The Long Conversation*, 41. Blissett reports a conversation of 9 September 1972 in which Jones discerns a family resemblance between Turner and Hopkins in their 'very Victorian . . . love of shipwrecks'. See Blissett, *The Long Conversation*, 111.

[176] Jones refers to *The Virgin and Child (The Madonna with the Iris)*, an oil of c. 1500–10, now attributed to the workshop of Albrecht Dürer by the National Gallery of Art, London, for which Clark, as director, acquired it in 1945. See James Stourton, *Kenneth Clark: Life, Art, Civilisation* (London: Collins, 2016), 96. See Jones's note to his use of 'himation' (an outer garment) in *The Anathemata*, 194, n. 5: 'See Dürer's painting the "Virgin with the Irises". The madonna is in a red dress with a purple cloak upon the paler purple lining of which a butterfly has alighted. From the Doughty House Collection, now in the National Gallery.' Writing of Rembrandt here, Jones probably refers to Kenneth Clark, *Rembrandt and the Italian Renaissance* (London: John Murray, 1966), based on lectures that Clark delivered at the Metropolitan Museum of Art, New York, in April 1964. Jones likely has Spengler in mind when he mentions 'the German thing' and the Gothic 'springtime'.

(3)

Then there's the other sort of chap, of which I personally think G.M. Hopkins is a shining example. Not a large output — but practically all bloody good. Perhaps had he lived longer, or, had he been a 'professional poet' in that Victorian age & had not been, by vocation, a priest, he too would have written a lot of stuff that was not O'r goreu! Who can say? But I feel sure it was the tension & stress of his make-up & vocation that went a long way to making his poiesis so good. Then there are the other blokes such as Turner, totally professional & of vast output who, by & large, remain good artists all the while.

So you are concentrating on Dürer. Well, again I, like you, have not, in the past, ever found much to my liking, excepting in occasional works. Perhaps, as with Rembrandt, you may help me to appreciate him, Dürer, better. I've always liked the thing of Our Lady with the butterfly — it's marvellous. But, on the whole, the Engravings, not much — marvels of technique but the 'feel' not up my street. It's something to do with that whole 'Late-Gothic' world & the German thing. I've often noticed in German writers that they think of 'Gothic' in terms of 'Late-Gothic', whereas the real, fresh, 'springtime' 'Gothic' is surely French, or Chartres. I should have [illegible] — summer etc. I look forward to [illegible]. Anyway, what you have to say on Dürer — & needless to say — should greatly enjoy a visit from you as you suggest in yr letter, sometime.

To return to that forthcoming issue of Agenda — it may, I think, turn out to be interesting — too early to say before one actually sees the thing, but—

I may be biassed a bit in Hopkins case, owing to his getting so much from the complex medieval Welsh metric & for his being a Catholic as well, but even taking my prejudices in his favour on those two counts, he does surely remain a most remarkable poet.

I have a rather amusing anecdote touching Hopkins which forgive me if I've told you before: Round about 1927 I was in Chelsea in the [illegible] of a friend (Hopkins was at that time little more than a name to me) and a very pro-Hopkins, able, well-read rather donnish man read aloud a poem of Hopkins (I've forgotten which poem) and I said 'Well, I don't know if that poet was a Welshman, but he certainly knew, by some means or other, much that is characteristic of Welsh poetry.' And the reader said 'What right have you to say that when you don't know the Welsh language' and he went on to say that there were various sources from which Hopkins might have developed his particular feeling & technique. I could do no more than say that it was true that I had very little knowledge of Welsh but none the less was convinced that I was right in supposing a Welsh influence in Hopkins. I was then told not to presume upon matters about which I knew nothing. And being young I left it at that, for the chap in question really was a learned & intelligent informed man. This was years & years before Dr Gardner (among others) had demonstrated in detail Hopkins' indebtedness to his study of Welsh metric. A few years later I had a temptation to send a p.c. to this man on this matter, but of course I did not.]

[*page 68*]

(3)

Then there's the other sort of chap, of which, I personally, think G. M. Hopkins is a [*overwrites* an] <^shining> example. Not a large output – but practically all bloody good. Perhaps had he lived longer, or, had he been a 'professional poet' in that Victorian age & had not been, by vocation, a priest, he too would have written a lot of stuff that was not O'r gorau! Who can say? But I feel sure it was the tension & stress of his make-up & vocation that went a long way to making his poiesis so good.

~~So you~~ Then there are the other blokes such as Turner, totally professional & of vast output who, by & large, remain great artists all the while.

So you are concentrating on Dürer. Well, again I, like you, have not, in the past, ever found much to my liking, except in occasional works. Perhaps, as with Rembrandt, you may help me to appreciate him, Dürer, better. I've always liked the thing of Our Lady with the butterfly – its marvellous. But, on the whole, the engravings, not much – marvels of technique but the 'feel' not up my street. It's something to do with that ~~late~~ whole 'late-Gothic' world & the German thing. I've often noticed in German writers that they think of 'Gothic' ~~as~~ in terms of late-Gothic whereas the real, fresh, 'springtime' of 'Gothic' is surely French. – summed up in Chartres, I should have thought. Anyway, I look forward to what you have to say on Dürer – & needless to say – should greatly enjoy, sometime, a visit from you as you suggest in y'r letter.

To return to that forthcoming issue of Agenda[177] – it may, I think, turn out to be interesting – too early to say – before one actually sees the thing, but

[177] See Kenneth Clark, 'Some Recent Paintings of David Jones', *Agenda* 5, nos 1–3 (Spring–Summer 1967): 97–100. This was *Agenda*'s first 'David Jones Special Issue'. A second appeared during Jones's lifetime: *Agenda* 11, no. 4–12, no. 1 (Autumn–Winter 1973–4). For the history of Jones's association with *Agenda*, see Tom Dilworth, 'William Cookson, David Jones, and *Agenda*', *Agenda* 48, nos 3–4 (11 November 2014): 9–12.

(3)

Then there's the other sort of chap, of which I personally think G.M. Hopkins is a shining example. Not a large output – but practically all bloody good. Perhaps had he lived longer, or, had he been a 'professional poet' in that Victorian age & had not been, by vocation, a priest, he too would have written a lot of stuff that was not Ór goran! Who can say? But I feel sure it was the tension & stress of his make up & vocation that was a long way to making his poiesis so good. Then there are the other blokes such as Turner, totally professional & of vast output who, by & large, remain great artists all the while.

So you are concentrating on Dürer. Well, again I, like you, have not, in the past, ever found much to my liking, perhaps excepting in occasional works. Perhaps, as with Rembrandt, you may help me to appreciate him, Dürer, better. I've always liked the thing of Our Lady with the butterfly, it's marvellous. But, on the whole, the engravings, not much – marvels of technique but the 'feel' not up my street. It's something to do with that whole 'late-Gothic' world & the German thing. I've often noticed in German writers that they think of 'Gothic' in terms of 'late-Gothic', whereas the real, fresh, 'Gothic' is surely French, 'springtime' of Chartres, I should have thought – summer etc. Anyway, I look forward to what you have to say on Dürer & needless to say – should greatly enjoy a visit from you as you suggest in yr letter sometime.

To return to that forthcoming issue of Agenda – it may, I think, turn out to be interesting – too early to say before one actually sees the thing, but

I may be biassed a bit in Hopkins case, owing to his getting so much from the complex metrical Welsh metric & for his being a Catholic as well. But even taking my prejudices in his favour on those two counts, he does surely remain a most remarkable poet.

I have a rather amusing anecdote touching Hopkins, will forgive me if I've told you before: Round about 1927 I was in Chelsea in the (Hopkins was at that time little more than a name to me) and a very pro-Hopkins, able, well-read, rather donnish man read aloud a poem of Hopkins (I've forgotten which poem) and I said 'Well, I don't know if that poet was a Welshman, but he certainly knows, by some means or other, much that is characteristic of Welsh poetry.' And the reader said 'What right have you to say that? You don't know the Welsh language' and he went on to say that there were various sources from which Hopkins might have developed his particular feeling & technique. I could do no more than say that it was true that I had very very little knowledge of Welsh but none the less was convinced that I was right in supposing a Welsh influence in Hopkins. I was then told not to presume upon matters about which I knew nothing. And being young I kept it at that, for the chap really was a learned (& intelligent) informed man. This was years & years before Dr Gardner (among others) demonstrated in detail Hopkins' indebtedness to his study of Welsh metric. A few years later I had a temptation to send a p.c. to this man on this matter, but of course did not.

[*page 68*] (continued)

[*the following marginal note in green ink starting at the top of the left-hand margin and working down the page until it moves into the footer*]

I may be biassed a bit in Hopkins case, owing to his [*one cancelled word illegible*] getting so much from ~~Welsh~~ the complex medieval Welsh metric & for his being a Catholic as well. but even taking [*one cancelled word illegible*] my prejudices in his favour on those two counts, he does surely remain a most remarkable poet.

I have a rather amusing anecdote touching Hopkins, which forgive me if I've told you before: Round about 1927 [*one cancelled word illegible*] I was in Chelsea[178] in the house of a friend [*one cancelled word illegible*] (Hopkins was at that time little more than a name to me) and a very pro-Hopkins, able, well-read, rather donnish man read aloud a poem of Hopkins (I've long forgotten which poem) and I said "Well, I don't know if that poet was a Welshman, but he certainly knew, by some means or other, much that is characteristic of old Welsh poetry." And the reader said "What right have you to say that <^when> you don't <^even> know <the> Welsh, [*the previous comma subsumed into the following* l] language" and he went on to say that there were various sources for which Hopkins might have developed his particular feeling & technique. I could do no more than say that it was true that I had very, very little knowledge of Welsh but none the less was convinced that I was right in supposing a Welsh influence in Hopkins. I was then told not to presume upon matters about which I knew nothing. And being young I left it at that, for the chap in question really was a learned <^intelligent> & informed man. This was years & years before Dr Gardner (among others) had demonstrated in detail Hopkins indebtedness to his study of Welsh metric. A few years later I had a temptation to send a p.c. {*postcard*} to this man on this matter but of course did not. D

[178] This is a tale that Jones had also told to Aneirin Talfan Davies in a letter of November 1962. See Jones, *Letters to a Friend*, 79. William Blissett records the outlines of a conversation of 25 September 1970, in which Jones retells it, and Thomas Dilworth, writing in 1985, reports hearing it as well, although he does not say when. See Blissett, *The Long Conversation*, 59, and Thomas Dilworth, 'David Jones and Gerard Manley Hopkins', in Richard F. Giles (ed.), *Hopkins Among the Poets: Studies in Modern Responses to Gerard Manley Hopkins* (Hamilton, Ontario: International Hopkins Association, 1985), 54.

(4)

William Cookson has certainly laboured hard to get it into some sort of shape — I think it will be about 160-170 pages. As for the reproductions of the drawings, inscriptions etc, well we shall see. He's managed to get the printers to have a large one of the detail of the right hand corner of the Annunciation drawing, by having it folded & also one, again folded, of the whole drawing, and if the final printed version is as good as the proof it should convey at least something of the original. It's an awful problem, as you no doubt know, to get illustrations put 'even' remotely in some sort of relationship to the text — for the current fashion of putting all illustration in a bunch in one section of the book is so prevailing that it requires a somewhat decided insistence to get them put otherwise — this William C. has managed to do. I hope some papers may review the little book — for Agenda is not widely known & being a virtually entirely one-man production has hardly ever been noted by the press, we shall see — I hope, for William Cookson's sake alone, that after all his care to get this issue out, it may receive some notice.

Yes, very odd that thing you mention, about 'bad' reproductions in cheap newspaper being frequently better than grand de luxe ones. I imagine it's largely a fluke — but the chief point of interest is, I think, just as you say, what is got is 'an analogy' & not an 'imitation'. All one can ever have is an 'analogy' — there is no alternative to that, other than a most expensively produced 'facsimile' — as in some, at all events, of those Ganymed prints. Yes, I think the softness of the paper has something to do with it too — but it's pretty chancy. I'm interested that you have noticed the same thing on various occasions. But I also think that it depends enormously on the kind of work, as in my own case the works are the very devil to reproduce

and it's an absolute toss-up as to whether even the finest 'analogy' comes through. There is one in this Agenda [illegible] photograph [illegible] analogy [illegible] reproduction [illegible] lost [illegible] original [illegible] Dai's [illegible]

[*page* 69]

(4)

51

William Cookson[179] has certainly laboured hard to get it into some sort of shape – I think it will be about 160–170 pages. As for the reproductions of the drawings, inscriptions, etc., well we shall see.

He's managed to get the printers to have a large one of the detail of the right hand corner of The Annunciation drawing, by having it folded & also one, again folded, of the whole drawing. and if the final printed version is as good as the proof it ~~does will~~ should convey at least something of the original.[180]

It's an awful problem, as you no doubt know, to get illustrations <^put> even remotely in some sort of relationship to the text – for the current fashion of putting all illustrations in a bunch in one section of the book is so prevailing that it requires a somewhat decided insistence [*one cancelled word illegible*] to get them put otherwise – this William C. has managed t do. I hope some papers may review the little book – for ~~it's~~ Agenda is not widely known & being ~~an~~ a virtually entirely one-man production has hardly ever been noted by the press, We shall see – I hope, for William Cookson's sake alone, that after all his care to get this issue out, it may receive some notice.

Yes, very odd that thing you mention, about 'bad' reproductions on cheap newspaper being frequently better ~~no~~ than grandly done ones. I imagine its largely a fluke. – but the ~~chief~~ point of interest is, I think, <^just> as you say, what is got is 'an analogy & less of an imitation,'

All one can expect is an 'analogy' – there is no alternative to that, other than a most expensively produced 'facsimile' – as in some, at all events, of those Ganymed prints.[181] Yes, I think the softness of the paper has something to do with it too – but it's pretty chancy

[179] Cookson (1939–2003) was the founding editor of *Agenda*. See Dilworth, 'William Cookson, David Jones, and *Agenda*'.

[180] See the fold-out plates in *Agenda* 5, nos 1–3 (Spring–Summer 1967), facing pages 97 and 98. This is *Y Cyfarchiad i Fair* ('The Greeting to Mary'), a drawing in pencil, crayon, and watercolour made c. 1963 and owned by the National Museum Cardiff.

[181] For an account of Jones's 1951 correspondence with John Roberts of the Ganymed Press, London, concerning the colour facsimile reproduction of his watercolour *The Chapel in the Park* (1932), see Dilworth, *David Jones: Engraver, Soldier, Painter, Poet*, 263–4.

(4)

William Cookson has certainly laboured hard to get it into some sort of shape – I think it will be about 160–170 pages. As for the reproductions of the drawings, inscriptions etc. well we shall see. He's managed to get the printers to have a large one of the detail of the right hand corner of The Annunciation drawing, by having it folded & also one, again folded, of the whole drawing. and if the final printed version is as good as the proof it should convey at least something of the original. It's an awful problem, as you no doubt know, to get illustrations put 'even' remotely in some sort of relationship to the text – for the current fashion of putting all illustrations in a bunch in one section of the book is so prevailing that it requires a somewhat decided insistence to get them put otherwise – this William C. has managed to do. I have some papers may review the little book – for Agenda is not widely known & being a virtually entirely one-man production has hardly ever been noted by the press, we shall see – I know, for William Cookson's sake alone, but after all his care to get this issue out, it may receive some notice.

Yes, very odd that thing you mention, about 'bad' reproductions on cheap newspaper being frequently better than grandly done ones. I imagine it's largely a fluke. – but the chief point of interest is, I think, just as you say, what is got is "an analogy & less of an imitation". All one can expect is an 'analogy' – there is no alternative to that, other than a most expensively produced 'facsimile' – as in some, at all events, of those Ganymed prints. Yes, I think the softness of the paper has something to do with it too – but it's pretty chancy. It's interesting that you have noticed the same thing on various occasions. But I also think that it depends enormously on the kind of work, as in my own case the works are the very devil to reproduce

[*page 69*] (continued)

I'm interested that you have noticed the same thing on various occasions. But I also think that it depends enormously on the kind of work, and my own case the works are the very devil to reproduce

[*continues up left-hand margin*]

and it's an absolute toss-up as to whether even the barest 'analogy' comes through. There is one in this Agenda of Yaks at Regents' Park, <^1930>, a photograph of which I happened to have & the photograph gets an 'analogy' very well indeed.[182] ~~but I~~ I thought it would work perfectly in the ~~prop~~ reproduction, but it does not. Whatever it was that gave the analogous feeling of the original is largely lost – it's not so bad, but nothing like as good as I had hoped ?for the photograph. I chance, now, to have the original, & one can see why, is that it depends greatly on pale bits of cool & bits of warm colour – but why the photograph seemed to work without these colours – but not the reproduction remains a mystery. Well, good-bye for now, love David.

---

[182] See the plate facing page 81 in *Agenda* 5, nos 1–3 (Spring–Summer 1967). This is the watercolour drawing whose title as given on p. 4 of this issue of *Agenda* is *The Old Animal from Tibet in Regents Park Zoo* (1930). It is owned by the National Museum Cardiff.

FIGURE 2: David Jones responding to a question from the interviewers Margaret Aeron-Thomas and Leo Aylen. Film still from the Mabon Studios interview at Calvary Nursing Home, Harrow, 1973 (David Jones Society).

CHAPTER FOUR

David Jones, Mabon Studios Interview, 31 August–3 September 1973

JASMINE HUNTER EVANS AND ANNE PRICE-OWEN

INTRODUCTION

'The first experiences are the things that stay'

—The Lost 1973 Mabon Studios Interview with David Jones

David Jones died on Monday, 28 October 1974, just four days before his seventy-ninth birthday. Between 31 August and 3 September 1973 he agreed to be interviewed by Margaret Aeron-Thomas, the founder of the Mabon Studios production company based in The Attic Gallery in Swansea.[1] She and her team travelled to Calvary Nursing Home in Harrow, London, to converse with Jones in his room.[2] During the filming Jones read passages from *The Anathemata* and *The Sleeping Lord* and was interviewed by both Margaret, whom he had known since 1962, and the director Leo Aylen.[3] This interview survives only in fragments. Indeed, the recordings were preserved on a varied assortment of sound tapes and 16mm film reels that Margaret kept for over forty years. On deciphering the name 'David Jones' on the labels, Margaret's son Mark Aeron-Thomas presented

[1] The Attic Gallery, first known as the Dillwyn Gallery, was established by Margaret Aeron-Thomas at 61–2 Wind Street, Swansea, in 1962. It was Wales's first commercial art gallery and aimed to promote Welsh and Wales-based artists. For a history of the Attic Gallery, see Ceri Thomas, David Roe, and Alexandra Roe, *Attic Gallery at Fifty: 1962–2012* (Swansea: Attic Gallery, 2012). It was from the same address that Margaret also ran the production company Mabon Studios. The archive that contains this interview with Jones is Mabon Studios' only known surviving material. It was presented to the David Jones Society by her son, Mark Aeron-Thomas, after Margaret's death in 2013.

[2] Margaret Aeron-Thomas was not a filmmaker. It appears that her decision to film Jones led her to enlist the help of Andrew Quicke, who worked for the London world-news agency Visnews. After the filming, Margaret and Andrew viewed the raw footage from the filming, or rushes (entitled 'This Thing Other'), but decided not to progress further with production of the film at that time.

[3] Margaret Aeron-Thomas appears to have come into contact with Jones at least as early as 1962 through her interest in displaying his artwork. In 1963 she curated the 'Painting and Sculpture from Wales' exhibition, which toured Welsh artists' work to Clare College, Cambridge, Kingsley Amis's house in Cambridge, and St Hilda's College, Oxford. For letters from Margaret Aeron-Thomas to David Jones, see CT4/1, Redfern, Tate, Arts Council, and CT3/4, Letters, 1961–1965, David Jones Papers, National Library of Wales, Aberystwyth. Leo Aylen is a poet, director, and screenwriter, born in KwaZulu, South Africa, who first met Jones at this interview, having been brought in by Andrew Quicke to direct the piece.

them to the David Jones Society in 2014 with no knowledge about the material that he was delivering, except that his mother had carried these tapes and reels with her during her extensive travels since the 1970s.[4] While much of the film is missing – in part due to the use of certain sequences in Aylen's 1976 HTV Wales production *Steel Be My Sister*[5] – the majority of the interview survives on ten sound tapes. The sound quality is variable, some sections of the recording appear to have disappeared forever, and the continuity of the discussion is broken by the gaps caused by the changing of the tapes. Nonetheless, there remain more than three hours of material that has until now not been digitized or transcribed, and for this reason alone the interview is a valuable resource. As the last filmed interview to capture Jones's thoughts before he died, it reveals a retrospective inclination to look back over his life and experiences and through wider historical and mythical themes to explore his own origins and those of the culture he spent his life trying to preserve.[6]

Jones often admitted to an antipathy to interviews. In a letter to René Hague in 1966, he explained that for him it was an 'awful business' due to the 'impromptu questions'. He continued:

> When you consider how bloody difficult it is to say anything remotely accurate in writing a considered article or something, it becomes ludicrously crude & sometimes positively the opposite of what one intends when asked point blank some direct question – a 'question' which is impatient of an 'answer' without going into endless stuff & making presuppositions of all sorts.[7]

This difficulty was acknowledged by Douglas Cleverdon, the BBC producer and friend of Jones, in his 1972 essay 'David Jones and Broadcasting'. While he had tried to record Jones on a number of occasions, Cleverdon claimed that 'the sight of a microphone inhibits him, I think, from the unaffected spontaneity that characterizes his conversation'.[8] One of the few interviews Cleverdon deemed a success was the BBC programme broadcast in 1965 for the *Writers' World* series in which Jones was filmed in conversation with the Welsh poet, playwright, and political activist Saunders Lewis.[9] Jones claimed that it was the 'rather special common view and . . . "shared background"' between Lewis and himself that made this interview one of the 'only occasions when "impromptu"

---

[4] Information received from Mark Aeron-Thomas when he delivered the Mabon material to Anne Price-Owen in September 2014.

[5] Leo Aylen made the 1975 film *Steel Be My Sister* about David Jones's life and work for Harlech Television (HTV). In an interview with the authors on 8 February 2015, Aylen stated that Margaret gave him permission to use the material from 'This Thing Other' in his new film and it was then that the majority of the poetry readings and interview footage were cut out of the rolls of rushes, leaving, in most cases, just the beginnings and ends of the shots. The whereabouts of the original film negative remains a mystery.

[6] Peter Orr made audio recordings of Jones in 1973, but these were not filmed. They went on to be used in the creation of Jones's essay '*In illo tempore*', in David Jones, *The Dying Gaul and Other Writings* (London: Faber & Faber, 1978), 19–29. For further information on this essay, see n. 20 below.

[7] David Jones, letter to René Hague, 8–16 June 1966, in CD1/15, René Hague Letters, David Jones Papers, National Library of Wales, Aberystwyth. Excerpts from this letter also appear in David Jones, *Dai Greatcoat: A Self-portrait of David Jones in his Letters*, ed. René Hague (London: Faber & Faber, 1980), 221–5, but this particular passage is not included there.

[8] Douglas Cleverdon, 'David Jones and Broadcasting', *Poetry Wales* 8, no. 3 (Winter 1972): 79.

[9] For a transcript of this interview, see David Jones and Saunders Lewis, 'David Jones: Writer and Painter Interview', *BBC Writers' World* (15 March 1965), in Jasmine Hunter Evans, 'You're Awfully Unorthodox, David', *New Welsh Review* 104 (25 May 2014): 24–31.

recordings seem to be any good'; 'I completely forgot the presence of about six or more chaps in the room with lights, cameras, microphones, etc. I suppose because of the complete understanding between Saunders and myself'.[10]

As this BBC interview represents the only other extant filmed conversation with Jones, it is pertinent to compare it to the Mabon Studios footage. Jones's health had declined considerably in the eight years since 1965. While Jones's concern to articulate his ideas and beliefs remains unchanged, the Mabon interview reveals both the frailty of his voice and the impairment of his hearing. In the 1965 interview, Lewis and Jones finish each other's sentences, share sentiments, and laugh together as if in private. This was not simply the result of clever editing but a testament to their 'common view' through which Lewis appears to comprehend the depth of meaning in Jones's words. In the raw footage captured in 1973, we see more clearly the difficulty Jones encountered both in articulating his beliefs and in making himself understood. To some extent this accounts for Jones's meandering answers and the hiatuses that accompany them until he grasps the concept he truly wants to discuss, sometimes regardless of the initial question. Yet, like Jones's poetic footnotes or complex annotations and additions to his letters, these pauses, lacunae, asides, allusions, and anecdotes are often subtly pertinent to the surrounding discussion; they appear tangential only due to the labyrinthine character of Jones's line of thought, which represents myriad associations that have slowly been assimilated and consolidated in the artist's mind. In this sense, overarching themes emerge from the extensive array of topics covered by the questions, including war, history, literature, politics, Catholicism, and art, which can provide some form of coherence and unity to the whole. One such strand of thought underlying the interview is Jones's delicate exploration of the relationship between Wales and the nature of origins. Jones draws together two central conceits that he had developed throughout his life but which took on a more profound significance in his final years – his desire both to preserve cultural continuity and to reposition his own formative experiences within this wider cultural tradition.

As Jeremy Hooker observes, the 'awareness of the present as a time of "ends" is very strong in David Jones's writings'.[11] Indeed, Jones viewed his contemporary world as a time of severance, in his terms represented by the 'Break' in the continuity of past and present. Due to his fear that the 'Break' would soon become 'an unbridgeable chasm',[12] Jones ensured that his works consistently alluded to the beginnings of culture and tradition – whether of geological formation, man's fundamental role as artist, the emergence of cultural identities or the origins of language, signs, and religious observance.[13] Embedded in his vision of history was the conviction that all artists serve as the 'custodians' or 'rememberers' for their societies and that their works preserve continuity (or in Jones's terms build a 'bridge') between the ancient past and the modern commercial, industrial, and culturally destructive present. So when he looked to the past Jones searched

---

[10] David Jones, letter to René Hague, 8–16 June 1966, in CD1/15, René Hague Letters, David Jones Papers, National Library of Wales, Aberystwyth.

[11] Jeremy Hooker, 'Ends and New Beginnings', *Poetry Wales* 8, no. 3 (Winter 1972): 22.

[12] David Jones, letter to Harman Grisewood, 12 March 1960, in CD2/7, Letters to Harman Grisewood and Jim Ede 1925–1973, David Jones Papers, National Library of Wales, Aberystwyth.

[13] For examples of Jones's explanation of 'the Break', see David Jones, letter to Harman Grisewood, 1967, in CF1/16: Letters to friends 1944–1982, David Jones Papers, National Library of Wales, Aberystwyth, number 38; David Jones, preface to *The Anathemata* (London: Faber & Faber, 1952), 15–16.

instinctively for origins.[14] When asked by Aylen in the interview, 'how physically do you imagine . . . [Arthur]? How do you feel him in your mind?', Jones responds by focusing on Arthur's historical origin and the way in which he represents the inauguration of a cultural inheritance for an entire people:

> I think of him as a Romano-Briton, therefore more or less *Roman*. Because Wales *alone* of the composite peoples of this island, come [sic] directly, I mean were formed, *before* the Roman imperium had broken down. While all the other people were attackers of the province of Britain.[15]

Like Arthur, Wales itself emerged from a mixed Celtic and Roman heritage, so when Jones 'imagines' Arthur he also envisages the origin of the Welsh nation and the Welsh people. This is simply one example of the way Jones consistently strives to return to the earliest form of any myth, text, historical occurrence, or cultural development, in order to gain access, as far as possible, to the origin of any aspect of culture that he wished to be preserved in the present. As he stated in a similar discussion of Arthur, Rome, and Wales twenty years earlier, 'it is axiomatic that the origin of things conditions their ends in however obscure, roundabout, mutated or even quite contradictory a manner.'[16] Yet it is also significant that this example, alongside many others present in the interview, focuses explicitly on the Welsh cultural tradition and its intrinsic, and unique, position within British culture.

The interview reveals Jones looking back to the origins and development both of his particular love of Wales and of the Welsh culture itself; it intertwines his personal history with the whole cultural tradition which he was determined to protect. To 'remember', for Jones, was an act of remaking and revivifying the past in the present, and so, by drawing together strands of his own memories and situating them within a reconsideration of the wider culture, he is following a vision of positive cultural protection previously explored by his friend the cultural historian Christopher Dawson. In a 1949 article 'Tradition and Inheritance: I. Wales and Wessex', which he sent to Jones in the year it was published, Dawson reaffirmed his long-standing belief in the importance of family tradition in the preservation of culture. In language reminiscent of that with which Jones presents his vision of the 'Break', Dawson states:

> [W]e cannot dismiss the past as dead or unimportant. If it is dead, it deserves to be recorded, no less than any other vanished civilization. If it is not dead, but only in a state of revolutionary change, we must study the past in order to discover what elements in its tradition can be recovered, what is lost beyond recall and what is indispensable to the continuity, and the identity of Western culture.[17]

---

[14] For Jones's discussion of the poet as 'custodian', see Jones, preface to *The Anathemata*, 21; as 'rememberer', see David Jones, 'Past and Present' (1953), in *Epoch and Artist* (London: Faber & Faber, 1959), 141. For Jones's use of the term 'bridge', see David Jones, 'In a Statement to the Bollingen Foundation, 1959', in *The Dying Gaul,* 17. For further discussion of Jones's concept of *poiesis* as building a 'bridge', see Jasmine Hunter Evans, 'Bridging the Breaks: David Jones and the Continuity of Culture', *Flashpoint* 18 (Summer 2016), available online at http://www.flashpointmag.com/hunterevans.pdf.

[15] David Jones, Mabon Studios Interview with David Jones, 31 August–3 September 1973, in this volume, p. 289 below.

[16] David Jones, 'Wales and the Crown' (1953), in *Epoch and Artist*, 45.

[17] Christopher Dawson, 'Tradition and Inheritance: I. Wales and Wessex', *The Wind and the Rain* 5, no. 4 (Spring 1949): 210. David Jones's copy is enclosed in 'Letter from Dawson to Jones, 28 April 1949', in CT5/2, Letters C-D 1943–1970, David Jones Papers, National Library of Wales, Aberystwyth.

His answer to this crisis was to 'record' and 'recover' family traditions, because in past societies each individual was a synthesis of all the cultural and social history that they inherited, and make use of these to bolster and maintain the wider cultural tradition.[18] For this reason Dawson ensured that his article considered his own family, heritage, and early memories alongside his broader vision of Western culture and his belief in the need for its protection and regeneration in the face of the destructive power of 'the new urbanized and mechanized type of civilization'.[19] Jones, in the Mabon interview, covers the same material from his own perspective, and due both to the similarity of their outlooks and his reliance on Dawson's theories and works throughout their long friendship, it is probable that he understood the way in which Dawson interlaced family tradition and cultural preservation. Whether Jones intentionally assimilated Dawson's theory or not, the close connection in Jones's discussion of Wales – between his personal memories and conversations about history and culture – reveals an acceptance that recording his own inheritance was part of the preservation of the expansive nature of Welsh culture. Bringing the autobiographical material to bear on the discussion of culture permeating the interview is a productive way to explore such a complex source, as it engenders a more nuanced understanding of the relationship that binds Jones's own heritage and experiences to his outlook on culture.

In this interview, as in other pieces recorded and written during his final years, Jones re-examines his life and subtly investigates the powerfully formative nature of beginnings. Indeed, Jones's last essay, '*In illo tempore*', was assembled from interviews with Peter Orr in 1973 precisely because he was interested in 'setting down some recollections of his life'.[20] Jones would always dismiss the idea of intentionally 'writing something autobiographical . . . [because] it all takes away from' the creative work itself.[21] However, he had long accepted the centrality of his own heritage and experience in the formation of his works.[22] In the preface to *The Anathemata* (1952) he explained that all his works were 'conditioned and limited by and dependent upon his being indigenous to this island . . . within which insularity there are the further conditionings contingent upon his being a Londoner, of Welsh and English parentage, of Protestant upbringing, of Catholic subscription'.[23] Jones understood that his works were created within a specific national, cultural, and religious

[18] Dawson, 'Tradition and Inheritance: I. Wales and Wessex', 210–11.

[19] Dawson, 'Tradition and Inheritance: I. Wales and Wessex', 211.

[20] Peter Orr, 'An introductory note by Peter Orr', in 'Fragments of an Attempted Autobiographical Writing', *Agenda* 13, no. 1 (Winter–Spring 1975): 96. This piece in *Agenda* represents Orr's cohesive assembly of Jones's thoughts from multiple interviews in 1973 together with other autobiographical sources. It was reprinted, with further small additions of autobiographical material and formatting changes, as '*In illo tempore*' (1966–73), in *The Dying Gaul*, 19–29. Peter Orr was head of the British Council's Department of Recorded Sound (1955–75) and a close friend of Jones since 1964, having interviewed him previously on 24 November 1964 for Orr's series *The Poet Speaks*. For a transcript of this interview, see David Jones, 'Interview with Peter Orr, 24 November 1964', in *The Poet Speaks, Interviews with Contemporary Poets Conducted by Hilary Morrish, Peter Orr, John Press and Ian Scott-Kilvert* (London: Routledge & Kegan Paul, 1966), 97–104. For a memoir of their friendship, see Peter Orr, 'Mr. Jones, your legs are crossed: A Memoir', *Agenda* 15, nos 2–3 (Summer–Autumn 1977): 110–25.

[21] Jones, Mabon Studios Interview, p. 295 below. While Jones was reluctant to create poetry or art directly from autobiographical material, he was comfortable discussing his life and experiences in his essays. See, for example, Jones, 'Autobiographical Talk' (1954), in *Epoch and Artist*, 25–31.

[22] Jones's growing interest in writing and publishing autobiographical material in his later years could simply be put down to the natural tendency of older generations to turn to memoir. Yet, as Jones explicitly connects this material with his artistic and critical development, it would be hasty to assume it had no relevance to our understanding of his broader corpus, or of the ways in which his ideas and beliefs changed throughout his life.

[23] Jones, preface to *The Anathemata*, 11.

milieu; that his entire output 'draws all the time upon things of a quasi-experiential nature'.[24] This 'quasi-experiential' material therefore brings together both his own lived experiences and choices – in his words, the 'things I saw, felt, & was part of'[25] – and the culture he inherited through the identity, traditions, and localities of his family that he situated within the wider British cultural tradition. Jones may have questioned the efficacy of deliberately creating art from 'something autobiographical', but he was clearly committed to exploring the personal experiences and perceived cultural inheritance that shaped his life and works.

Jones proceeds through the interview in a mood of retrospection as he covers a vast array of his own formative experiences. He speaks at length about the Great War, covering his attempts to enlist in the 'Welsh Horse' (Jones's term for the Royal Welsh Yeomanry) and at a recruiting station in the vicinity of St Paul's Cathedral, as well as his memories of German soldiers, such as the time when his battalion captured an officer.[26] Influential friendships are discussed – including those with Saunders Lewis, Eric Gill, and Christopher Dawson – along with the impact of his time at Westminster Art School, during which he formulated his earliest comprehension of the 'analogy' between the Mass and Art. Jones also examines his particular vision of Catholicism and looks back to the time before his conversion: 'I was already Catholic in my heart, but I didn't formally become one until 1921.'[27] While versions of many of these anecdotes and thoughts have been published elsewhere, this late interview reveals the way in which hindsight allows Jones delicately to redefine some of his theories. When discussing his long-established belief that the loss of chivalry occurred in 1916 during the Battle of the Somme, which to him represented a fundamental 'change' in the nature of the war symptomatic of the wider 'Break',[28] Jones muses:

> I've since wondered, more recently, whether it [his perception of the loss of chivalry] was because I happened to arrive in the actual line just before Christmas 1915. And it's rather like things in one's childhood – the first experiences are the things that stay. Supposing I'd been, for whatever reason, not in line and in action until the next year, I might have felt the same about that.[29]

Similarly, Jones allows that his strict differentiation between man-the-artist and animals, which he examines comprehensively in 'Art and Democracy' (1942–3), needed more nuance: 'I believe they have found that a certain kind of ape in India, that they carry away dead ones and *howl*. It is getting sort of near . . . it isn't a chant, or Michelangelo, but at least it isn't purely *utile*.'[30] These small reconsiderations demonstrate a degree of tolerance towards updating long-held beliefs while the interview as a whole testifies to the

[24] David Jones, letter to W. F. Jackson Knight, 11 October 1952, in EUL MS75, Jackson Knight Family Papers, Special Collections GB 0029, University of Exeter Library, 2–3.

[25] David Jones, preface to *In Parenthesis* (London: Faber & Faber, 1937), ix.

[26] Jones, Mabon Studios Interview, pp. 284–7 below. For further details of Jones's attempts to enlist, see Thomas Dilworth, *David Jones in the Great War* (London: Enitharmon, 2012), 35–7.

[27] Jones, Mabon Studios Interview, p. 295 below.

[28] For Jones's discussion of this 'change', see Jones, preface to *In Parenthesis*, ix.

[29] Jones, Mabon Studios Interview, p. 285 below.

[30] Jones, Mabon Studios Interview, p. 296 below. For the original essay and its particular discussion of man-the-artist with respect to non-human animals, see David Jones, 'Art and Democracy' (1942–3), in *Epoch and Artist*, 85–8. In this essay, Jones argues that while animals make things they cannot be artists in the same way as man because an animal's creativity is never gratuitous: 'If we could catch the beaver placing never so small a twig *gratuitously* we could make his dam into a font, he would be patient of baptism – the whole "sign-world" would be open to him, he would know "sacrament" and would have true culture. For culture is nothing but a sign, and the *anathemata* of a culture, "the things set up", can be set up only to the gods' (88).

importance of retrospective reflection in both amending and reinforcing areas of Jones's sentiments. Throughout the autobiographical material Jones covers during the interview the clearest theme that emerges is his undiminished and very personal passion for Wales and Welsh culture. Jones might question his own self-ascribed Welshness – self-ascribed because he positions himself as one of 'those who, by blood or inclination, feel a kinship with the more venerable culture in that hotch-potch which is ourselves'[31] – but the interview reveals a poet and artist who understands the deep and formative influence of Wales, as a physical landscape, a cultural tradition, and a family inheritance, upon his imagination and his convictions.

This interview further testifies to the way in which Jones became, in Thomas Dilworth's words, 'obsessed' with Wales.[32] Although close friends such as René Hague dismissed his fixation as 'no more than a sentimental love',[33] Jones's works and letters reveal that his personal association with the Welsh culture as his own tradition and inheritance only grew more pronounced in later life. Peter Orr's series of interviews with Jones in 1973 incorporates much material that illuminates the sources of Jones's strong affinity for Wales as do many letters written in his final years.[34] For example, Jones's letter to the editor of *Poetry Wales* magazine, Meic Stephens, delves into his earliest memories – such as his feeling that 'the Rubicon had been passed' when he first saw Wales.[35] The Mabon interview similarly elicits Jones's reflections upon his family life, his Welsh heritage, and his sense of Welshness:

> By the time I was nine or ten, well actually before then, I'd decided I was Welsh because my father was, and I used to go up to North Wales to see his sisters, my aunts, cousins and people – but they thought I was absolutely *crackers* because they were all terrific Anglophiles, they couldn't understand it! Well, perhaps that's being a bit unfair, but they thought it was very odd.[36]

Jones scrutinized at some length what might have been the origins of these intense yet youthful feelings of belonging to the Welsh people and culture. He admits that 'I haven't the foggiest idea – it started when I was six or seven' but goes on to explain, 'It certainly wasn't because I had any less love for my mother, because I hadn't. I was lucky, damned lucky, in having two parents who were not only jolly nice to each other but also to me.'[37] Jones's father, James Jones, 'realized' his son's interest in Wales and gave him English-language books about Wales 'for birthday presents and things' – such as those by 'Owen

---

[31] Jones, preface to *In Parenthesis*, xiii.

[32] Thomas Dilworth, 'Antithesis of Place in the Poetry and Life of David Jones', in Alex Davis and Lee M. Jenkins (eds), *Locations of Literary Modernism: Region and Nation in British and American Modernist Poetry* (Cambridge: Cambridge University Press, 2000), 81.

[33] René Hague, 'Notes by the Editor', in *Dai Greatcoat*, 23.

[34] This is evident, for example, in Jones's last letter to his nephew Tony Hyne on 18 May 1972, in which he describes his aunt Gladys's house in the lee of the mountain Bryn Euryn in Llandrillo-yn-Rhos, North Wales: 'Aunt Gladys's house was on the sea front and not far from the little Capel Trillo . . . The altar stone was . . . there . . . and beneath the altar the *ffynnon* [spring] of very cool fresh water. It seemed a marvelous [sic] thing that this fount of living water, utterly devoid of saline flavour should be here at the very rim of salt surf breakers.' See Anthony Hyne, 'David Jones: A Man of Letters', *David Jones Journal* (1999): 10.

[35] David Jones, 'A Letter from David Jones', *Poetry Wales* 8, no. 3 (Winter 1972): 7.

[36] Jones, Mabon Studios Interview, p. 290 below. For another text in which Jones discusses his early feeling of 'Welshness', see Jones, '*In illo tempore*', in *The Dying Gaul*, 23. See also Thomas Dilworth, *David Jones: Engraver, Soldier, Painter, Poet* (London: Jonathan Cape, 2017), 17–20.

[37] Jones, Mabon Studios Interview, p. 291 below.

M. Edwards – published in *The Story of the Nations* series – and then John Rhys's book called *The Welsh People* . . . Well I lapped that up! Then Giraldus Cambrensis, *The Mabinogion*, Lady Guest.'[38] Yet Jones admitted that 'my father was himself not interested in Welsh history, he was only interested in religion'.[39] Far from being coerced into developing his sense of Welsh identity, Jones presents himself as actively rejecting the anglicization promoted by his family. Like his friend and fellow painter Arthur Giardelli, who prized his Italian heritage through his father (in direct contrast to his only brother who was 'not remotely interested in Italian'),[40] Jones's appropriation of Welshness was disproportionate in degree to that of his siblings or indeed to his English locality, language, or family ethos.[41]

Despite never mastering the Welsh language, Jones was deeply dismayed by the decline of Welsh as a spoken language both within his own family and in wider Welsh society.[42] He describes in the interview how his father 'used to sing to us in Welsh, and tell us stories about the local area of Flintshire where he was brought up',[43] yet his grandparents had dissuaded their son from speaking the language despite it being their mother tongue:

> My father was born in 1860. Well, *his* father prevented him as far as he could from speaking Welsh at home. Of course, he was beaten if he spoke it at school. Again, you see, that would give more reason for the old man to think that you must be able to thoroughly speak English grammatically and understandably, otherwise you'll never get a job. But he and his wife (my grandfather and his wife) spoke to themselves in nothing *but* Welsh. Nor did they bother about the younger children. (My father was the oldest son.)[44]

Jones saw the decline of spoken Welsh within his own family as both aiding and symbolizing the broader campaign since the Tudor period to promote the English language over the Welsh. During a conversation concerning the Welsh gentry at the Tudor court who prevented their sons from speaking Welsh, Jones exclaims, 'Oh yes – that's interesting to me – because my own grandfather was exactly the same, on a much lower level, strata, of society', as, from the Tudors onwards, there was a belief that 'unless you speak the Queen's English you can't have any sort of success'.[45] Jones referred to his lack of proficiency in the Welsh language as 'my misery', alleging that it gave him 'no right to speak about' Welsh literature despite his autodidactic passion for learning about 'the nature of the Welsh language and its history'.[46] Along with the language, Jones also expressed in the interview his early love of the Arthurian tales, as he would ask his sister

---

[38] Jones, Mabon Studios Interview, p. 291 below.

[39] Jones, Mabon Studios Interview, p. 291 below.

[40] Jones, Mabon Studios Interview, p. 292 below.

[41] Jones had an older brother, Harold, who died in 1910 at the age of twenty-one, and an older sister, Alice (1891–1974). See Dilworth, *David Jones: Engraver, Painter, Soldier, Poet*, 24.

[42] Thomas Dilworth, *The Shape of Meaning in the Poetry of David Jones* (Toronto: University of Toronto Press, 1988), 270, n. 4.

[43] Jones, Mabon Studios Interview, p. 291 below. Jones's father sang Welsh songs and hymns, including 'Mae hen wlad fy nhadau' ('Land of my Fathers') and 'Ar hyd y nos' ('All Through the Night') at home. See David Blamires, *David Jones: Artist and Writer*, 2nd edn (Manchester: Manchester University Press, 1978), 2, and Dilworth, *David Jones: Engraver, Painter, Soldier, Poet*, 17.

[44] Jones, Mabon Studios Interview, p. 292 below.

[45] Jones, Mabon Studios Interview, p. 292 below.

[46] Jones, Mabon Studios Interview, p. 294 below.

to read him works like 'The Knight of the Sparrow Hawk'.[47] While he admitted that 'he couldn't be without Malory', Jones quickly comprehended Malory's debt to the medieval Welsh romances and tales of the *Mabinogion* and became convinced that the Arthurian myth first developed in ancient Wales.[48] Arthur was the hero of *Kilhwch and Olwen*, the earliest of *Mabinogion* tales, a scene from which Jones poetically reimagined in his poem 'The Hunt,' collected in *The Sleeping Lord* in 1974. This early understanding of his own entwined Welsh and English heritage – through the languages of his family and the connections between the literature of both countries – provided Jones not only with the materials that would shape his later works but also with an acute understanding of his shared inheritance. His belief in the essential unity of the deposits and culture of Britain encouraged Jones to accept, and celebrate, the way in which his works were 'conditioned and limited by and dependent upon being indigenous to this island'.[49]

Other formative experiences covered in the interview include Jones's memories of living at Capel-y-ffin in the Black Mountains of Wales, the art he produced there, and the effect the Welsh landscape had on the development of his artistic style:

> The bards of an earlier Wales referred to themselves as 'carpenters of song'. Carpentry suggests a fitting together and the English word 'artist' means someone concerned with a fitting together of some sort. Well, it would seem to me, that round about 1924 I was at last understanding [the] particular 'carpentry' which most sorted with my inclinations and limitations.
>
> Because at this propitious time the circumstances occasioned my living in Nant Honddu [Honddu valley], there to feel the impact of the strong hill-rhythms, the bright counter-rhythms of the *afonydd dyfroedd* [rivers of water], which makes so much of Wales such a 'plurabelle'.[50]

The impact of living in Wales on his artistic approach, or his 'particular carpentry', is visible in his artwork from 1924 onwards; his works became invigorated with a new intellectual energy which drew together the rhythms of the hills, rivers, and trees to reveal how they 'fit together' in harmony.[51] For Jones, this sojourn in Wales 'marked a new beginning', as all his later works could 'truthfully be said to hinge on that period'.[52] This interview stands as further testament to the formative nature of Jones's relationship with Wales, which influenced his works, outlook, and life, from his earliest memories to his final recollections. By reconsidering his own origins in this way, Jones positions himself firmly within the Welsh cultural tradition and endeavours to preserve and promote an inheritance at once his own and, according to his own sensibilities, essential to all the diverse inhabitants of the island of Britain.

---

[47] Jones, Mabon Studios Interview, p. 290 below. This tale is often called 'Sir Geraint and the Knight of the Sparrow Hawk' or 'Prince Geraint and Fair Enid'. For further discussion of Jones's reading of this tale, see Dilworth, *David Jones in the Great War*, 20.

[48] Jones, Mabon Studios Interview, p. 290 below. For further discussion of Malory and his sister reading to him, see Jones, '*In illo tempore*', in *The Dying Gaul*, 25.

[49] Jones, preface to *The Anathemata*, 11.

[50] Jones, Mabon Studios Interview, p. 302 below. This passage from the interview also appears in discrete, practically verbatim, sections in 'Autobiographical Talk', in *Epoch and Artist*, 29–30.

[51] See, for example, the pencil, watercolour, and chalk drawing *Hill-Pastures at Capel-y-ffin* (1926), and *Y Twmpa, Nant Honddu* (1926), both reproduced in Ariane Bankes and Paul Hills, *The Art of David Jones: Vision and Memory* (Farnham: Lund Humphries, 2015), 46, 50.

[52] Jones, 'Autobiographical Talk', *Epoch and Artist*, 28.

In the Mabon interview, Jones's persistent return to the history, culture, heritage, and contemporary plight of Wales brings together his own feeling of Welshness, which he viewed as his personal cultural inheritance, and his desire, shaped by the experiences of his life, to uphold the continuity of the Welsh cultural tradition. Jones reveals his grief at the loss of elements of the Welsh culture – whether these were misunderstood, forgotten, or actively destroyed – at various points in history. He laments the way in which early translations of Geoffrey of Monmouth's *Historia Regum Britanniae* 'changed the actual names', and thus lost relevant connections with earlier mythic traditions, and that such distortions in history resulted in inaccuracies so that 'they put the court of Arthur as Caerleon on Usk, but there is nothing in the native tradition about that'.[53] While Jones can celebrate the wider European Arthurian tradition and marvel at the process of metamorphosis that had almost disguised the Welsh origin of the tales, he nonetheless compares these apparently small changes of 'names' to the notion that 'Longfellow made the . . . Sioux Indians or something, believe that's their *real* history. Nearest parallel that I can think of.'[54] This sense of cultural loss is similarly present in Jones's association of the demise of classical education, the destruction of the Welsh language, and the changes to the Catholic liturgy by the reformers of the Second Vatican Council (1962–5), which, Jones declares, 'wrecked a whole cultural heritage':[55]

> [S]upposing a chap wrote a poem which referred to Aphrodite, let's say, and chaps had never heard of Aphrodite – you see it wouldn't ring the bell, would it? It's rather like that.
>
> As a matter of fact (and this is subjective, I mean) my thing about the destruction of the Latin liturgy, and the chant which goes with it, is giving me just the same kind of the misery as the disappearance of Welsh, and I know a little more Latin than Welsh, but not very much more, really. Do you know what I mean? To me, it's a sort of deprivation.[56]

These sentiments, and indeed these very examples, recur in many of Jones's essays and letters and represent his profound fear concerning the decline of Western culture.[57] He was particularly anxious about the survival of Welsh culture because it 'belongs to the mores of Britain, and affords a direct, living, unbroken series of links with Antiquity and so with the formative period and the foundational things of this Island'.[58] In his poetic and visual explorations of Welsh culture Jones was thus intent on recovering the ancient

---

[53] Jones, Mabon Studios Interview, p. 289 below.

[54] Jones, Mabon Studios Interview, p. 289 below.

[55] Jones, Mabon Studios Interview, p. 294 below.

[56] Jones, Mabon Studios Interview, p. 295 below. For an example of a similar passage in which Jones connected the loss of the Latin Mass to the decline of the Welsh language and knowledge of the classics, see David Jones, letter to Harman Grisewood, 6 July 1964, in *Dai Greatcoat*, 207–9.

[57] For further examples of Jones using 'Aphrodite' to explore the impact of the loss of classical learning, see David Jones, letter to Vernon Watkins, 11 April, 1962, in *David Jones: Letters to Vernon Watkins*, ed. Ruth Pryor (Cardiff: University of Wales Press, 1976), 57, 61. For Jones's lament at the loss of the Welsh language, see David Jones, untitled writing on 'the Welsh language struggling for survival' (n.d.), in CF1/15, Draft Letters and Articles 1932–1964, David Jones Papers, National Library of Wales, Aberystwyth; Jones, 'Preface by the Author' (1958), in *Epoch and Artist*, 11–18, 16; David Jones, draft letter to *The Times* (n.d.), in CF2/27, Letters to the Press 1932–1961, David Jones Papers, National Library of Wales. For Jones's criticism of the loss of the Latin Mass, see David Jones, draft letter to *The Tablet* (n.d.), in CF2/27, Letters to the Press 1932–1961, David Jones Papers, National Library of Wales; David Jones, letter to René Hague, 6 January 1965, in CD1/15, René Hague Letters, David Jones Papers, National Library of Wales; David Jones, 'Letter on "The Latin Mass"', *The Tablet*, 2 December 1967, 25.

[58] David Jones, 'Message from Mr. David Jones' (1960), quoted in Neil Corcoran, *The Song of Deeds: A Study of* The Anathemata *of David Jones* (Cardiff: University of Wales Press, 1982), 14.

origins of myths and symbols. In the interview, Margaret Aeron-Thomas questions why the figure of the Virgin Mary in Jones's painting *Y Cyfarchiad i Fair* (*The Greeting to Mary*) (1963), who simultaneously represents pre-Christian classical and Welsh goddesses, holds a foxglove.[59] Jones explains that he used this flower both because it is native to the Welsh landscape at Capel-y-ffin (which he redrew from memory as the setting for his visual interpretation of the Annunciation) and because he wished to rectify the mistranslation in the *Mabinogion* regarding the heroine Olwen, as 'When they talk about Olwen and her cheeks are "redder than the reddest roses", and the word isn't *roses* at all its *foxgloves*.'[60] In Jones's opinion, it was essential to understand the origin and development of cultural traditions because, as he explains in his 1953 essay 'Past and Present', 'The entire past is at the poet's disposal' and so art should 'show forth, recall, discover and re-present those things that have belonged to man from the beginning'.[61]

A fundamental impetus for Jones's creative production was the protection and reinvigoration of the Welsh culture which he celebrated as one of the diverse heritages essential for the unity and continuance of the wider cultural tradition of the British Isles. In Jones's quest to revivify the symbolic and historical significance of cultural objects (whether sign, myth, language, or landscape) that represented unbroken connections between the ancient and modern world, Wales became his exemplar. Jones stressed the ways in which the modern Welsh rituals, traditions, and language were traceable back to the Celts and Romans. He was determined to reveal these long-standing cultural aspects of Wales as a means of encouraging the Welsh to nurture their indigenous and unique heritage, which had been threatened in the past but was now facing the onslaught of forces including machine technologies, materialism, consumerism, and globalization with the power to destroy cultural diversity. Jones was profoundly aware of the dangers facing the survival of Welsh culture – both historical and modern. He reveals in the interview that it was 'a miracle' that the "'Welshness" of Wales' had 'remained alive', 'because that Tudor Act of Union debarred the Welsh language from all the courts of justice, lesser or bigger'.[62] His frustration with the Welsh in the Tudor period for not being 'resistant' to these laws is equalled by his anger at the hypocritical attitude of the English government towards the destruction of the Welsh landscape in the twentieth century.[63] Jones protests against both the impositions of the English on Wales – such as the way in which 'officially, Wales in the English law, just doesn't exist' – and the impact of modernity: 'That is the *awful* danger now – of mass media which is far more destructive than the Lords Marcher.'[64]

[59] The 1963 painting *Y Cyfarchiad i Fair* (also known as *Annunciation in a Welsh Hill Setting*), pencil, crayon, and watercolour, in National Museum Cardiff. The figure in this painting has been associated with Minerva, Rhiannon, and Olwen. For further discussion, see Arthur Giardelli, 'Three Related Works by David Jones', *Poetry Wales* 8, no. 3 (Winter 1972): 60–71. 'The Greeting to Mary' is a literal translation as the title represents the standard Welsh term for the Annunciation.

[60] Jones, Mabon Studios Interview, p. 301 below. Here, Jones appears to interpret Lady Charlotte Guest's decision to use 'roses' in her 1838–45 translation of the *Mabinogion* as an accident rather than as a deliberate mistranslation to encourage engagement from her Anglophone readership.

[61] Jones, 'Past and Present' (1953), in *Epoch and Artist*, 138, 140.

[62] Jones, Mabon Studios Interview, p. 292 below.

[63] Jones, Mabon Studios Interview, p. 295 below. For Jones's accusations of hypocrisy over the aerodrome built on the Llyn Peninsula in 1936, see Jones, Mabon Studios Interview, p. 292 below.

[64] Jones, Mabon Studios Interview, p. 291 below. For further examples of Jones discussing Wales's lack of nation status, see David Jones, draft letter to Gwynfor Evans, 1966, in CF1/12, in letters to Welsh correspondents 1940–1972, David Jones Papers, National Library of Wales, Aberystwyth; for the Lords Marcher, see Jones's letter to Jonah Jones (n.d), in CF1/12, in letters to Welsh correspondents 1940–1972, David Jones Papers, National Library of Wales, Aberystwyth.

In response to these issues, Jones traced and retraced Welsh history, literature, and myth in a variety of his essays, letters, and interviews in an attempt to reinvigorate a sense of continuity within Welsh culture.[65] In this interview alone he covers, among other topics, Wales's Celtic and Roman origins, early Welsh Arthurian myth, Geoffrey of Monmouth, Llywelyn the last prince of Wales, the Edwardian conquest, Owain Glyndŵr, the Welsh presence in the War of the Roses, the impact of the Tudors, the suppression of the monasteries and of Roman Catholicism, the penalization of the Welsh language in the nineteenth century, the Welsh in the Great War, and the subsequent decline of the knowledge of Welsh culture in the twentieth century.[66] While Welsh history might reveal a pattern of disunity, internal and external conflict, defeat by the English, and the decay of precious elements of the Welsh heritage, Jones finds hope in the precarious survival of the Welsh language, literature, landscape, and national identity that has its origins in the distant past. This was at once his own inheritance and the rich legacy of all of Britain. Ultimately, in his position between the Welsh and the English, Jones took upon himself the role of the artist who '"shows forth", "recalls", [and] "re-presents"' the culture of both peoples to reveal their diversity and their interconnectedness.

By combining his own early memories and family history with a defence of the whole cultural history of Wales, Jones revealed a vision of the past in which the inheritance of each individual, each family, each community, and each nation was essential to the culture of the whole of the British Isles, or indeed Western civilization. Like Dawson before him, Jones promoted this productive vision of diversity in unity by examining the origin and development both of Welsh culture and of his own sense of Welshness and situating these within the wider British tradition. Working with raw interview footage will always raise more questions than can be definitively answered. For example, we can only speculate on why Jones, in a discussion of the origins of his literary career, offhandedly says 'it might have been better if I had not ever started on that damn book'.[67] Yet footage of this kind also provides a point of direct access into Jones's mindset unmediated by his own revision. Jones believed that an artist 'must necessarily show forth what is his by this or that inheritance',[68] and the Mabon interview stands as yet another testament to the necessity Jones felt to 'show forth' his Welsh heritage. Indeed, Jones's endeavour to pursue and develop his childhood affinity for Wales intimately shaped not only the corpus that survives him but also the artistic principles on which he created all his works. As Peter Levi proclaimed in his funeral eulogy for David Jones in Westminster Cathedral on 13 December 1974, just over a year after this interview was filmed:

> David Jones's tradition was Welsh. He is a last innocent witness to the cultural massacre of the Welsh people by the English and by the modern world. But in David's life the whole Welsh thing became something different, more intense, more suffering and more noble than we had known it to be. That is the work of Christ, it is the spirit of God crying out to the Father.[69]

---

[65] For examples, see David Jones, 'Welshness in Wales' (1957), in *Epoch and Artist*, 51–3; 'The Myth of Arthur' (1942), in *Epoch and Artist*, 212–59; 'The Welsh Dragon' (1966), in *The Dying Gaul*, 108–16.

[66] Jones, Mabon Studios Interview, pp. 285–301 below.

[67] Jones, Mabon Studios Interview, p. 294 below. The context suggests Jones is referring to *In Parenthesis*, but the tape cuts out at this point. Leo Aylen has no recollection of this part of the conversation.

[68] Jones, preface to *The Anathemata*, 10.

[69] Peter Levi, SJ, 'In Memory of a Maker: The text of a sermon delivered in Westminster Cathedral at the Solemn Requiem for the poet and painter, David Jones, on 13 December 1974', *The Tablet*, 4 January 1975, 7.

FIGURE 3: David Jones. Film still from the Mabon Studios interview at Calvary Nursing Home, Harrow, 1973 (David Jones Society).

FIGURE 4: David Jones listening to the interviewers Margaret Aeron-Thomas and Leo Aylen. Film still from the Mabon Studios interview at Calvary Nursing Home, Harrow, 1973 (David Jones Society).

ANNOTATED TRANSCRIPT

Provenance

Ten ¼-inch sound tapes labelled 'David Jones', given to the David Jones Society, Swansea, Wales, in September 2014 by Mark Aeron-Thomas, son of Margaret Aeron-Thomas, founder of Mabon Studios, The Attic Gallery, 61–2 Wind Street, Swansea, Wales. These tapes will be deposited in The National Screen and Sound Archive of Wales in the National Library of Wales.

This interview was conducted by Margaret Aeron-Thomas (**MAT**) and the director Leo Aylen (**LA**). The cameraman was John Pike and the sound recordist Ian Hills. Shooting took place at the Calvary Nursing Home, Harrow, north London, where Jones had been resident since the summer of 1970. His previous lodgings, which he entered in 1964, consisted of a large room in the Monksdene Hotel, Harrow. There, in March 1970, he suffered a slight stroke so that his 'mouth was a bit out of the straight'.[70] This was followed two days later by a nasty fall, which resulted in his hospitalization where he underwent a hip operation from which he never really recovered, being unable to walk without support. Following convalescence in the Bethany Nursing Home, Highgate, Jones finally moved to Calvary Nursing Home in Harrow on 6 June 1970. He died there four years later on 28 October 1974.

Alongside the film, which is extant only in fragments, the interview and associated poetry readings were recorded on ten ¼-inch sound tapes. This transcript represents all the audible material from these tapes.[71] The frailty of Jones's voice, the difficulty he encountered articulating his thoughts, and particularly the subsequent deterioration of the sound recording on tapes which had not been stored in conditions conducive to their preservation,[72] have inevitably affected both the sound and the quality of the tapes from which this transcript has been made. Rather than a cohesive or progressing conversation, the transcript more closely resembles a series of vignettes exploring Jones's thoughts, stories, and beliefs – not least because passages of the interview were not recorded when the ¼-inch tapes were changed. To highlight these gaps in the recording, the changes of tape have been noted. The poetry readings have not been included in the transcript; they are of passages from *The Anathemata* (1952), 'The Tutelar of the Place' (1961), 'The Hunt' (1965), and 'A, a, a, Domine Deus' (1967).[73] A supplement (pp. 302-3 below) contains three fragmentary passages that Leo Aylen confirms were part of the original recording, but which were cut from the film reels and now survive only in his 1975 documentary *Steel Be My Sister*.[74]

---

[70] David Jones, letter to Colin Hughes, 5 December 1970, in *Dai Greatcoat: A Self-portrait of David Jones in his Letters*, ed. René Hague (London: Faber & Faber, 1980), 230.

[71] In this transcript inaudible passages are marked with an ellipsis enclosed in brackets ('[. . .]'), pauses with an ellipsis without brackets ('. . .').

[72] The ten sound tapes, along with seven rolls of 16mm film of varying lengths and five rolls of magnetic sound track were wrapped in polythene bags and kept in a series of large cardboard boxes that Margaret Aeron-Thomas took with her on her travels, according to her son, Mark, who delivered the material to Anne Price-Owen in September 2014.

[73] As tapes seven, nine, and ten contain only poetry, we indicate only six tape-changes in the transcript.

[74] This film is available from Leo Aylen. Write to him at leo@leoaylen.com. The surviving 16mm film and magnetic soundtrack from the original Mabon Studios interview were consulted during the transcription process, but they include no new areas of the interview not covered by the ¼-inch sound tapes.

Interview, 31 August–3 September 1973[75]

[START OF TAPE RECORDING]

MAT: And they still had the altar and the seats are all still in use and they play live theatre there, because we could see the numbers on the seats. And I did a dreadful thing, I stole three tiny little bits of stone, of the marble, which had fallen onto the floor. I didn't take them out of the wall. It was such a marvellous place, it really was numinous. You could feel that it's been around since Mycenaean times. And I've got three little bits of marble: one for you – it's in the car, Johnny's got it packed away –and one for Ian McKellan and one for Leo.[76] And I thought Apollo wouldn't mind, you sort of keep it in the trade – I wouldn't take one for myself. I'll bring it to you next time I come.[77]

LA: I'm intrigued by the way we have been brought up to think of Greece as very much as the rational arts, and the rational gods and so on, and really, I suspect that the actuality of Apollo for the Greeks was much more like the Welsh pre-Christian thing.

DJ: Yes, a much more the Dionysiac thing. I have a friend – who's not officially a classical scholar – who says that the English tradition that we teach in university of Greece and Athens leaves out altogether, the other much more *wild* and – well Macedonian [tradition], really.[78]

LA: Yes certainly, it brings it in line a little bit more with our own heritage.

DJ: Yes – it's extraordinary how Plato in British academic circles, or for that matter, anywhere – is taken as a moral for good behaviour and so on.[79] Whereas for the Nazis, to them, he was absolutely crucial. But it's so odd – that so totally opposite perceptions should arise.

LA: I always see him as rather a villain – with all his ideas of the elitist society, I must say I see his ideas as rather nearer the Nazi thought than the idea of British democracy.

---

[75] This date-range is the most precise information available about the schedule of interview sessions.

[76] According to a close friend of Mark Aeron-Thomas, the filmmaker Nigel Wattis, Wattis in conversation with Anne Price-Owen, 21 January 2015, Johnny was Margaret Aeron-Thomas's travelling companion when she went to Greece in 1973. We have been unable to identify Ian McKellan.

[77] The tapes begin *in media res* with Margaret Aeron-Thomas discussing a recent trip to an ancient Greek theatre, which we have been unable to identify.

[78] At Aylen's proposition that the 'Welsh pre-Christian thing' is comparable to the Greek Apollonian culture, Jones instead prefers to associate the lifestyle of the ancient Celts with his perception of Dionysian and Macedonian values, implying that these represent a wilder tradition of ritual ecstasy, madness, wine, and violence. The friend Jones alludes to is most likely the prolific Catholic historian of religion and culture Christopher Dawson (1889–1970), who lectured at a number of universities, including Exeter, Liverpool, and Edinburgh, and held the Charles Chauncey Stillman Chair of Roman Catholic Studies at Harvard University 1958–62. According to Thomas Dilworth, 'Jones found the scope, depth and clarity of Dawson's conversation breathtaking . . . and learned more from him than anyone else.' See Thomas Dilworth, *David Jones: Engraver, Soldier, Painter, Poet* (London: Jonathan Cape, 2017), 122, 136. Jones owned no fewer than a dozen of the twenty-two books by Dawson, including *The Age of the Gods: A Study in the Origins of Culture in Prehistoric Europe and the Ancient East* (London: John Murray, 1928), *Progress and Religion: An Historical Enquiry* (London: Sheed & Ward, 1929), and *Beyond Politics* (London: Sheed & Ward, 1939). Jones places Dawson first in the list of over fifty people to whom he acknowledges a debt of gratitude in the preface to *The Anathemata: Fragments of an Attempted Writing* (London: Faber & Faber, 1952), 36.

[79] Jones was not beyond criticizing philosophers and writers he found contentious. In an unpublished letter dated 'Midsummer Eve', 1955, to his friend the collector H. S. (Jim) Ede, Jones writes, 'I agree with you that Augustine was WRONG, i.e. "joy" & "singing", but then he was "wrong" about all kinds of things as it seems to me, to which of course we don't really know the background with sufficient intimacy but the late Roman world was a pretty tough place no doubt. But then Plato & in our day, Tolstoi were both "wrong" about the arts . . .' See correspondence from David Jones, Kettle's Yard Museum and Art Gallery, University of Cambridge, folder labelled KY/EDE/1/8.

DJ: You thought who was . . .?

LA: Plato.

DJ: Well yes, he had a – not that I ought to talk about him at all really: I've only read his stuff in English – but he was perfectly awful about poetry as the enemy of the state, wasn't he?

LA: I'm sure that in 1914 the Germans were much more doctrinaire about what they were doing than the British were.

DJ: Were they?

LA: Did you have moral indoctrination sessions of any kind in the first war?

DJ: In the first war? Oh no! Only the one thing which everybody detested – they had it at base camps, one was at Rouen, and also in England – where you were instructed in bayonet fighting, you see. And then it was absolutely *appalling*, apart from being extremely badly stated by a boring drill sergeant. Funnier still, if you'd already been fighting for some time – it wasn't taken very well. But I can't recall anything else of that nature. And it was very much disliked by everybody that I knew, in the ranks I mean. Of course we know it was disapproved of by people who wrote [. . .] like Siegfried Sassoon, about the very artificiality and absurdity of it.[80] But not only that, there was no political thing, no attempt, as far as I can remember, to explain *why* we were at war with Germany. It only came out in this way.

Oh! I'll tell you something, we had lectures, but [. . .] they were just fudges, generalized. As a matter of fact when we came home on leave, it was one of the most acute embarrassments to try to explain, as people asked us endless questions, as to what the thing was like. Because you see with the second war, everybody was so involved. [. . .]

LA: How close did you come to any Germans personally? Did you ever get caught up in a kind of personal situation with some of them on the front line?

DJ: Well, in a sort of way, yes – I remember on the Somme, when we half-captured a thick wood. But of course, another very odd aspect which is difficult to get across is the sort of chaos that was there. You could be fifty yards from the next British soldier, it was very odd that feeling, that is to say, once you were in a thing like a wood which was all fallen trees, fallen line and shellfire, it was a most peculiar feeling. I remember the Germans led by a very immaculate lieutenant. You know those in German field gray – especially their greatcoats, they fitted them absolutely superbly and they had some sort of red piping.[81] This chap came to surrender two people under his command, because, well, we'd surrounded them you see. But, he saluted the Welsh officer with *such* astonishing smartness and all the rest of it.[82] We got tired of hearing this chap [the Welsh Officer] talk to – I'm

[80] For Jones's discussion of his meeting with Sassoon, see David Jones, letter to Harman Grisewood, 17 July 1964, in David Jones, *Dai Greatcoat: A Self-portrait of David Jones in his Letters*, ed. René Hague (London: Faber & Faber, 1980), 210–11. Jones notes that he and Sassoon 'talked about [Edmund] Blunden and [Robert] Graves and the Welch Fusiliers – Mametz, Limerick etc. [H]e said that however much he tried he could never get that 1st War business out of his system, which is exactly the case with me.' See Jones, *Dai Greatcoat*, 210.

[81] It is typical of Jones to notice and remember detail in others' attire, particularly military uniforms. Thomas Dilworth calls Jones 'a bit of a dandy'. See Thomas Dilworth, *David Jones in the Great War* (London: Enitharmon, 2012), 31. Jones's own uniform, that of the Royal Welch Fusiliers, was 'of brethyn-llwyd (a hard-wearing brown Welsh cloth) . . . fairly smart and therefore popular'. See Colin Hughes, *Mametz: Lloyd George's 'Welsh Army' at the Battle of the Somme* (Gerrards Cross: Orion Press, 1982), 28.

[82] The capture of Germans is not documented in any of Jones's published letters or essays.

sure he went on until the end of the war talking to – recruits about it, because we had parade drill and had to salute all of them. [. . .] I can't remember much about it, but I know I remembered at the time. In fact, it was only the same sort of highly graded discipline the Germans go in for now.

LA: That's part of what you were talking about when you wrote about the difference before the Somme and after the Somme, that before there was a kind of chivalry.

DJ: Oh yes – enormous chivalry.[83] I've since wondered, more recently, whether it was because I happened to arrive in the actual line just before Christmas 1915. And it's rather like things in one's childhood – the first experiences are the things that stay. Supposing I'd been, for whatever reason, not in line and in action until the next year, I might have felt the same about that. But I think the special thing about the Somme was that it was the first time the new armies were used in a concerted fashion for big-scale attacks. And mechanization hadn't yet . . . it didn't really mean that much. I mean the ordinary troops had enforced marches on foot because there was nothing else available. We marched from the area around La Bassée, we'd been there from Christmas [1915] until the end of May [1916], or the beginning of June actually, when we marched down to the Somme – I don't know how many miles it was, but it was a good distance.[84]

[TAPE CHANGE]

MAT: You had a choice? You said you wanted to go into a Welsh regiment?

DJ: Yes, I did, but they were so long in forming the London Welsh battalion.[85] I think they wanted to be like the London Scottish division.[86] I think most of the people who would

---

[83] For Jones's discussion of 'chivalry' in the trenches and the change in the nature of war during the march to the River Somme, see David Jones, preface to *In Parenthesis* (London: Faber & Faber, 1937), ix.

[84] Jones's battalion was stationed at La Bassée, in the north-east of France just south of Neuve Chapelle and Givenchy, for six months preceding the march south to the Somme. They spent five days on the march before stopping for ten days to practise on training grounds for the anticipated battle on the Somme. They marched for a further four days and then moved towards Mametz Wood, in readiness for the order to attack on 10 July. The distance between La Bassée and the Somme is approximately eighty miles. See Colin Hughes, *David Jones: The Man Who Was on the Field:* In Parenthesis *as Straight Reporting* (Manchester: David Jones Society, 1979), 14–18.

[85] Jones was keen to sign up for a Welsh regiment, and on the advice of his father he agreed to wait until a London-Welsh battalion was constituted. He enlisted on 2 January 1915 and was appointed to the 15th Battalion (London-Welsh) of the 113th Brigade of the Royal Welsh Fusiliers (23rd Foot) of the 38th (Welsh) Division. The majority of his army training took place at Llandudno on Wales's north coast, about forty-three miles west of Holywell, where Jones had first met his father's family 'in 1904 or thereabouts'. See David Jones, '*In illo tempore*', in David Jones, *The Dying Gaul and Other Writings*, ed. Harman Grisewood (London: Faber & Faber, 1978), 23. Dilworth observes that 'when off duty, he [Jones] was able to visit Llandrillo-yn-Rhos, which was only five miles away. As a child he had gone there for several holidays to visit his cousins.' See Dilworth, *David Jones in the Great War*, 47. Jones described the place in a broadcast for the BBC Welsh Home Service on 29 October 1954, published as David Jones, 'Autobiographical Talk', in David Jones, *Epoch and Artist*, ed. Harman Grisewood (London: Faber & Faber, 1959), 27. On this initial training expedition, among Jones's companions many of the London-Welsh infantry were actually London Cockneys who, like himself, were Welsh 'by blood or inclination'. See Jones, preface to *In Parenthesis*, xiii. Jones believed he qualified on both counts: his father was Welsh, and Jones himself declared that '[f]rom about the age of six, I felt I belonged to my father's people and their land'. See David Jones, '*In illo tempore*', in *The Dying Gaul*, 23. In August 1915, Jones and his unit moved from Wales to Winchester in the south of England, the site of the Army practice grounds of Winnall Down and Salisbury Plain. More advanced training with the entire 38th (Welsh) Division followed before the march on 1 December of seventeen miles to the Southampton docks and departure for France on 2 December.

[86] For information on David Lloyd George's efforts to raise 'a Welsh army', see Dilworth, *David Jones in the Great War*, 36, and Colin Hughes, *David Jones: The Man Who Was on the Field*, 7.

have been in that battalion just joined other infantry battalions available, you know. I tried various things. One was the Artists Rifles, but the thing about this was that my chest expansion wasn't fit for the . . . because they kept up the regular army standard, you see.[87] It was a question of 'breathe in, breathe out,' and that had to be dead on! I mean I don't know what the measurements were, but it looked awfully strange written solemnly down.[88] So that then they relaxed this standard, and that's why there were so many real Cockneys and chaps of all kinds, I mean anybody, because they had to make the tally up of something.

Most of the officers were Welsh or Anglicized Welsh, but not all – on the whole more Welsh than me. The colonel, who was in the Indian army and had charge of Gurkhas – when they arrived at Winchester for training, he informed the civvies in this menacing fashion – actually he was such a nice man – he said, [. . .] they're the best soldiers here. He was awfully proud of the Gurkhas.[89]

Oh yes, also [. . .] they did raise a unit of Welsh Horse or Welsh Yeomanry.[90] Since I was child I'd always wished that I could ride – an ambition I had, I don't mean in a very big sort of way but I very much wanted to ride, and I couldn't – so I thought, well, now's my chance. Some recruiting officer I think weighed in. [He was] perfectly round, terribly smart, regular, amazingly young, including an eye glass without any attachment. I thought it was perfectly nice of him actually – he had some paper in his hand; I don't know how I got in there; I must've been taken into his room, by an NCO or something – and I can't remember any more, but I was facing him over the table, and he said, 'Look, I understand that you wish to become enlisted in this Welsh Horse?' (If it was called the Welsh Horse, I can't remember.) He said, 'Do you know anything about horses?' I said, 'Nothing at all.' 'Well, do your family have anything to do with horses?' 'No Sir, 'fraid not.' He said, 'Well, I would love to enlist you in this mob, but I strongly advise you for your own sake not to enlist with us, because in any kind of cavalry division, it's horse first, man second, and in a very big way. If you know nothing whatever about horses you would have a very, very tough time of it.' He said I should wait a bit and join the Welsh Infantry, which they were forming. I thought that was rather nice. The Welshman was almost a caricature of what majors are supposed to look like in immaculate pale khaki drill riding on a horse.[91]

LA: Have you ever been on a horse since?

DJ: No.

LA: Never at all? So it remains a dream.

---

[87] For information about the Artists Rifles, a regiment of the British Army Reserve raised in 1859, see Barry Gregory, *A History of The Artists Rifles 1859–1947* (Barnsley: Pen & Sword, 2006).

[88] The 'regular army standard' in 1914 was thirty-four inches.

[89] See Dilworth, *David Jones in the Great War*, 41, and Colin Hughes, *David Jones: The Man Who Was on the Field*, 6.

[90] The Welsh Horse Yeomanry was a mounted regiment raised on 18 August 1914, in South Wales. See Colin Hughes, *Mametz: Lloyd George's 'Welsh Army'*, 39.

[91] For an earlier version of this story, see David Jones and Saunders Lewis, 'David Jones: Writer and Painter', *BBC Writers' World*, an interview of 15 March 1965, in Jasmine Hunter Evans, 'You're Awfully Unorthodox, David', *New Welsh Review* 104 (25 May 2014): 26. Jones's interest in joining a cavalry regiment may have been shaped by his early memory of seeing the cavalry ride past his home in Brockley. See Jones, '*In illo tempore*', in *The Dying Gaul*, 19–21.

DJ: Yes.

LA: You've done a lot of drawings of horses . . .[92]

DJ: Well I may have been on a farm – I assume down in Sussex – I may have ridden a horse in that sense, but I've not any idea, and of course he was quite right, you know, in the war itself watering the horses was the first thing you did before breakfast.

[. . .] And another thing, rather revealing, terribly typical of this country, there was a recruiting station, the east end of St Paul's Cathedral, I mean opposite, I suppose it was designed in sight of the cathedral. There was a fierce looking chap that wagged his moustaches you know, just standing at the doorway, and I went up the steps 'Oi! What do you want?' I said 'Well, I want to join the Territorial Army.' (I don't know why I said that, because I wasn't thinking particularly of that.) And he said, 'Then you can 'oppit – this is the bloody Army.' I mean this struck me as very odd because they were *screaming* for chaps, you see.[93]

LA: I always imagine that the Welsh, the whole Welsh tradition wasn't very military, and that the Welsh regiments weren't very much the fighters – what did it seem? Not so much like the Scots?

DJ: Well you see, whereas there was in the British army an enormous Scottish division, there was no such thing in the corresponding place in Wales. It was a historical accident, wasn't it? Heavens above, they did nothing else but fight in the Middle Ages, and even after the Edwardian conquests, which they viewed very sensitively.

LA: Yes of course, they were bowmen.

DJ: Oh yes, bowmen.

LA: But it somehow seems that the Welsh tradition is less dependent on that militarist thing than the Highland Scottish, certainly. The Welsh haven't needed to be winning battles. It's been more a matter of small raids over the border?

MAT But, David, they are very proud of this society they have, of people who can prove their descent from a Welshman who was at Crécy, and quite a number of them meet regularly, and pride themselves on this station.[94]

DJ: Well you see, officially, Wales in the English law, just doesn't exist.[95] But certainly, they fought and lost terrible numbers in the War of the Roses, because you see, the distant

---

[92] Among Jones's artworks featuring horses, see *The Lancers* (1926), *Wounded Knight* (1929–30), *The Four Queens find Launcelot Sleeping* (1941), all reproduced in Ariane Bankes and Paul Hills, *The Art of David Jones: Vision and Memory* (Farnham: Lund Humphries, 2015), 38, 45, 132.

[93] The recruiting station that Jones visited was in sight of Christopher Wren's seventeenth-century St Paul's Cathedral. Jones must have mistaken this station for that of the Territorial Army's recruiting station, which during the First World War was at the Inns of Court in central London.

[94] The Battle of Crécy, 26 August 1346, was fought against the French king, Philip VI, in northern France. Edward III's English-Welsh victory over the French was the battle in which his son, Edward of Woodstock, the Black Prince of Wales (mentioned in Dai's Boast in *In Parenthesis*, 79), won his spurs and acquired the emblem of the Three White Feathers.

[95] Here Jones refers to the Act of Union of 1536 whereby Wales was declared 'incorporated, united and annexed' to the English realm. Effectively and in practice, English laws and justice were similarly applied to Wales. See John Davies et al. (eds), *The Welsh Academy Encyclopaedia of Wales* (Cardiff: Welsh Academy, 2008), 12.

Lord Marchers were such a tangled patchwork of Lancasters and Yorkists that the men had to follow whichever their lords chose, this sign or that.[96]

LA: But in general I wonder whether is it fair to say that Wales as a nation is more defined by its poetry tradition, than anything else, all the art and the language is what has kept it alive?

DJ: Yes, I agree about that. But it's very complicated, the *history* of the relationship, particularly after the Tudors. Because lots of quite eminent Welshmen under Elizabeth [. . .] . . . but even before that when under Thomas Cromwell, Henry the VIII, rather later in his reign, they had this Act of Union and in the same year the suppression of the lesser monasteries, which in the case of Wales meant virtually all. They [the Welsh] were so ludicrously obsessed with this idea of the Tudors on the throne of Britain that they paid special attention to that.[97]

LA: In a sense, I suppose, the great Welsh poetic tradition is when Wales was Catholic. It was after the Reformation that the tradition was to a certain extent broken?

DJ: Yes, it became . . . You see, as to the religious business, they had no real leaders.

[TAPE CHANGE]

DJ: As everybody was in constant lawsuits over land, they never were able to add to what they'd got. And I don't think in Edward III's time,[98] though it may have been so later on, it was not necessarily conscious that they feared – in the British government in London – they feared that if there was a descendant of the real authentic princes, especially of Gwynedd,[99] the very name would cause people to rally to him whether he likes it or not. And of course that's one of the reasons why the Owain Glyndŵr thing arose.[100]

LA: I suppose that the whole Arthurian thing, of *Hic iacet Arthurus, rex quondam, rexque futurus*, it was always strong in the actual Welsh consciousness – that the king would come back?[101]

---

[96] The Wars of the Roses, between the House of York (white rose) and the House of Lancaster (red rose), began in 1455. The Lords Marcher were powerful noblemen who lived on the borders of Wales and England, and recruited their troops from Wales. The Welsh were involved in the continual battles between the two countries, and often their loyalties lay with their respective Lord Marcher. In 1485 Henry Tudor, who claimed Welsh blood, took up the banner of the Red Dragon of Cadwaladr (a former king of Gwynedd), and this appealed to the people of Wales, who allegedly made up a third of his army. They defeated Richard III of York at the Battle of Bosworth, 22 August 1485.

[97] Jones refers here to the First Suppression Act of 1536.

[98] Edward III, born in 1312, reigned from 1327 until his death in 1377. In 1905 Jones painted a watercolour entitled *Edward III Entering Calais, 1347*. See Dilworth, *David Jones in the Great War*, 20.

[99] Gwynedd was an ancient principality in north-west Wales that Jones believed had been ruled since the fifth century AD by a royal line beginning with Cunedda and ending with the death of Llywelyn ap Gruffudd in 1282. For an example of Jones's discussion of this line of princes, see David Jones, 'Wales and the Crown' (1953), in *Epoch and Artist*, 41–2.

[100] In 1400, when Owain Glyndŵr was proclaimed Prince of Wales, he led a Welsh uprising which lasted more than a decade. It began with a dispute with Reginald de Grey, lord of Rhuthun, but ended in a full-scale war against Henry IV. The revolt was suppressed by Henry IV, but Owain was never captured.

[101] 'Here lies Arthur the once and future king'. This alludes to the prophecy that despite being laid to rest upon his death, Arthur would return to the land as a redeemer. The quotation is from Sir Thomas Malory's *Morte d'Arthur*, which was completed in 1469 and published by William Caxton in 1485.

DJ: Well, yes. But *after* Geoffrey of Monmouth, in his *Historia.* But even Llywelyn, our last prince, argued that case with Archbishop Peckham.[102] But Edward I himself, in correspondence with the papacy, claimed Scotland on precisely the same grounds. An incredible influence.

LA: Of Arthur?

DJ: No, of Geoffrey of Monmouth really. Because it's very difficult to find out what bits have historical foundations and what haven't. Because he obviously *has* sources, native sources, whereas the French think [otherwise]. It's a strange thing, his *History of the Kings of Britain* I think was published first in 1130-something, but, you see, by 1200, Chrétien de Troyes and all that line of French Romance had continued to Germany, Wolfram von Eschenbach.[103] And you see, I mean, Geoffrey is concerned more with history and politics. It's amazing that this great cycle of romance literature should have come from him. Because he altered and changed the names, you see, and it's a great headache to scholars who specialize in that sort of thing. I think there has been a slight swing back – I hear that you can't dismiss the whole Geoffreyan thing as people did. I think he was damn useless in that sense because he wrote this stuff in Latin and it was very quickly translated into Welsh and [. . .] they changed the actual names – oh, for one thing, they put the court of Arthur at Caerleon on Usk, but there is nothing in the native tradition about that. It's astonishing, it's as though Longfellow made the – I dunno what – Sioux Indians or something, believe that's their *real* history. Nearest parallel I can think of.[104]

LA: When actually you are thinking or working over anything to do with Arthur, how physically do you imagine him? How do you feel him in your mind?

DJ: Well, it's very difficult to answer. I think (though I've no right to say so, as [. . .] it couldn't be more complex, for historians and stuff) I think of him as a Romano-Briton, therefore more or less *Roman.* Because Wales *alone* of the composite peoples of this island, come [sic] directly, I mean were formed, *before* the Roman Imperium had broken down. While all the other people were attackers of the province of Britain. The fact that they were unable to unite, and constantly at war with each other, is a characteristic

---

[102] Geoffrey of Monmouth published his *Historia Regum Britanniae* (*History of the Kings of Britain*) in 1138. Written in Latin and translated into Welsh by the middle of the thirteenth century, it skillfully blends truth and falsehood. Notoriously, Geoffrey gives the British a Trojan lineage through the Roman statesman Brutus. John Peckham, Archbishop of Canterbury 1279–92, a critic of Llywelyn and the Welsh Laws, was involved in negotiations between Edward, the first son of Henry III, and Llywelyn ap Gruffudd, whom Henry III had recognized as Prince of Wales in 1267. Edward (Edward I after his father's death in 1272) continually diminished Llywelyn's powers and had him beheaded on 11 December 1282. Edward appealed to Pope Martin IV to endorse his claim on Wales, as he had also done with regard to Scotland. See Davies et al., *The Welsh Academy Encyclopaedia of Wales*, 263–4, 309, 656.

[103] Chrétien de Troyes was a twelfth-century French *romancier* who wrote poetry based on the Arthurian legends. These works were part of the developing tradition of *courtoisie* in French literature, often associated with later notions of 'courtly love', a phenomenon that spread throughout Europe, influencing the twelfth- and thirteenth-century German poet Wolfram von Eschenbach's romance *Parzival*, a variant of the legendary tale concerning Peredur in the *Mabinogion.*

[104] Jones compares the pseudohistorical location of the Court of Arthur at Caerleon, Newport, Wales, on the River Usk, to the representation of the history of the indigenous peoples of North America by Henry Wadsworth Longfellow in his epic poem *The Song of Hiawatha* (1855).

(perhaps more characteristic) of Celtic peoples – I don't even know that, I mean, it could be accidental.[105]

But on other hand, as I was brought up, as a child, I read about Arthur – well I couldn't read when I was a child, I was disgraceful, and I asked my sister to read to me. There were in those days, in 1902 or so, a series of paperbacks called *Books for the Bairns*, one of these was about the Knight of the Sparrow Hawk. I remember she said, 'Well, first of all you ought to be *ashamed* of yourself for not being able to read it', and I said, 'Please read to me about the Knight of the Sparrow Hawk.'[106]

Then soon after, just when Caxton's edition of Malory . . . I've never quite understood why Malory doesn't figure more eminently in English literature, because he has a superb grasp of a certain kind of English, and his curious double negatives! I suppose it was just on the turn when he wrote it, he was in prison, wasn't he? In the War of the Roses – supposedly cattle-stealing, or rape or whatever, I mean, God knows. I suppose when the Lancastrians and the Yorkists got their hands on you they'd put you in jail for anything. [. . .] At that time I was almost wholly interested in the visual arts, I just read what I wanted, you know. But Malory . . . I couldn't be without Malory.

LA: It's a marvellous book. But everyone really is going to come to Arthur through the legendary aspects via Malory now, and perhaps in a way that's right, because somehow Arthur has become different from the Celtic material.

DJ: But what people *won't* believe . . . well it's perfectly obvious if they know anything at all of Welsh literature. I don't know why some people get very angry, because all this stuff certainly came to its splendour in the French and then the following – about a hundred years, 1200 to 1300, this thing went on and Tristan was translated into Czech[107] – it's very remarkable. Now that's taken me away from what I wanted to say . . .

By the time I was nine or ten, well, actually before then, I'd decided I was Welsh because my father was, and I used to go up to North Wales to see his sisters, my aunts, cousins and people – but they thought I was absolutely *crackers* because they were all terrific Anglophiles, they couldn't understand it![108] Well, perhaps that's being a bit unfair, but they thought it was very odd.

LA: What made up your mind that you were Welsh?

---

[105] Jones links the figure of Arthur to Welsh history more broadly in his essay 'Wales and the Crown' (1953), in *Epoch and Artist*, 45–6: 'the beginnings of specifically Welsh history were tied up with the end of a Romanic Brittania . . . This is clearly exemplified in the case of Arthur, the sixth-century Roman cavalry leader who, by various metamorphoses takes on the attributes of a Celtic cult-figure of pre-history, and then by further metamorphoses, from elsewhere, returns to our traditions in the guise of a medieval king. Because the fifth and sixth centuries were the formative age in Wales the man who was in fact defending what was left of Roman Britain became assumed into a Celtic mythology of immemorial antiquity'.

[106] On Jones's youthful enthusiasm for 'Arthurian things', see Dilworth, *David Jones in the Great War*, 19–20. These works gave him a notion of gallant soldiers fighting for noble causes. As his art teacher at Camberwell Art School noted, he was 'an incurable romantic'. See A. S. Hartrick, *A Painter's Pilgrimage through Fifty Years* (Cambridge: Cambridge University Press, 1939), 234.

[107] By the end of the fourteenth century.

[108] David Jones's grandfather, John Jones, born 1834 in Ysceifiog, Flintshire, north-east Wales, was a plasterer by trade. He married Sarah (née Jones), in 1852. Their son James was born in 1860 in Treffynnon (Holywell), Flintshire, Wales. In 1885 James moved to London, where in 1888 he married Alice Ann Bradshaw, born in London in 1855, with whom he raised a family in Brockley, Kent. In 1889 their son Harold Thomas Peart was born, and in 1891 their daughter Alice Mary. Walter David Jones was born in 1895.

DJ: I haven't the foggiest idea – it started when I was six or seven. My father, when he realized this, used to give me [books] for birthday presents and things – there weren't many books in English about Welsh things at that date. One of the first things was Owen M. Edwards – published in *The Story of the Nations* series – and then John Rhys's book called *The Welsh People*. [. . .] Well I lapped that up! Then Giraldus Cambrensis, *The Mabinogion*, Lady Guest.[109]

It certainly wasn't because I had any less love for my mother, because I hadn't.[110] I was lucky, damned lucky, in having two parents who were not only jolly nice to each other but also to me. But my father was himself not interested in Welsh history. He was only interested in religion.[111]

MAT: He used to sing to you in Welsh, your father?

DJ: Yes, he used to sing to us in Welsh, and tell us stories about the local area of Flintshire where he was brought up.

[TAPE CHANGE]

DJ: [The Welsh] would suffer defeat and yet turn up next day. Their weakness was that they wouldn't stand their ground and fight it out in a fixed engagement. Well of course that's true, but they would not have had modern information about the state of society, they couldn't very well do otherwise. I suppose it was really why the attempt of later princes to make [a united Wales] . . . well, as Llywelyn the Great[112] pretty well *did* – but it broke again as soon as he died. Because of this awful gavelkind, of dividing the property up, it's just quasi-tribal you see?[113] Those later princes saw that and tried to make them feudal. Well! Neither the Welsh, and certainly not the English king, wanted to have a strong feudal state so near at hand.

LA: Wales is a difficult country for communications, it always has been and always will remain. It seems a landscape and a people which fit terribly well together.

DJ: That is the *awful* danger now – of mass media which is far more destructive than the Lords Marcher.

---

[109] Owen M. Edwards, *Wales*, number 56 in *The Story of the Nations* series (London: T. Fisher Unwin, 1901); John Rhys and David Brynmor-Jones, *The Welsh People: Chapters on Their Origin, History, Laws, Language, Literature, and Characteristics* (London: T. Fisher Unwin, 1900); Gerald of Wales, *The Historical Works of Giraldus Cambrensis*, ed. Thomas Wright (London: George Bell & Sons, 1905); *The Mabinogion*, trans. Lady Charlotte Guest (London: Dent, 1902). See Dilworth, *David Jones in the Great War*, 25–6, and Dilworth, *David Jones: Engraver, Soldier, Painter, Poet*, 29–30.

[110] Jones's mother's ancestral line were Londoners from Rotherhithe on the River Thames. Her mother, Jones's grandmother, Ann Elizabeth Mockford, was born in Rotherhithe in 1829, the child of Joseph and Mary Ann Mockford. She married Ebenezer Bradshaw (son of Thomas and Hannah Bradshaw of London's Southwark on the Thames) in 1853. Ebenezer died in Rotherhithe in 1891; his wife died in 1907.

[111] Jones's father, James Jones, a printer's overseer for the *Christian Herald* newspaper, was a devout Anglican.

[112] Llywelyn ap Iorwerth (Llywelyn Fawr), Prince of Gwynedd (c. 1172–1240).

[113] Wales's gentry were bound by law to leave equal parts of their estates to their male heirs, which exponentially divided the country into small plots which was hardly conducive to instigating unity in times of crises. This system is similar to gavelkind, which is when the inheritance is divided into equal parts and distributed to family members. This applies to property where there is no will stating an heir. In contrast, the feudal system, where primogeniture was law, gave precedence to the eldest son, thus forming an essential part of the family infrastructure in preserving the unity of the estates.

LA: Most of the Welsh media seem very conscious of the necessity of preserving the 'Welshness' of Wales.

DJ: Yes, I know. It's a miracle really how the thing has remained alive, because that Tudor Act of Union debarred the Welsh language from all the courts of justice, lesser or bigger.[114] And you'd have thought, they would have been *so* resistant, but of course again you had to have leaders – and the leaders weren't going to chance offending the Tudor King. [. . .]

MAT: They discouraged speaking Welsh from those times onwards, didn't they? Don't you remember those letters from some minor Welsh gentry telling their son at the Tudor Court not to speak Welsh so he could 'get on'.

DJ: Oh yes – that's interesting to me – because my own grandfather was exactly the same, on a much lower level, strata, of society. I think it was the Chirburys – well, there are one or two accounts – but there's one specific thing I remember: when he was sending his son to Oxford, on *no* account was he to speak Welsh, not even to his closest friends in lodgings, because unless you speak the Queen's English you can't have any sort of success. And the Vaughans and Herberts, some of them, I know, sent their boys to a Welsh homestead to become acquainted with Welsh, but of course that indicated that at home and elsewhere it was not to be.[115] My father was born in 1860. Well, *his* father prevented him as far as he could from speaking Welsh at home. Of course, he was beaten if he spoke it at school. Again, you see, that would give more reason for the old man to think that you must be able to thoroughly speak English grammatically and understandably, otherwise you'll never get a job. But he and his wife (my grandfather and his wife) spoke to themselves in nothing *but* Welsh. Nor did they bother about the younger children. (My father was the oldest son.)

As to why I had this thing about Wales so early, I suppose it could be analysed by some analyst. I mentioned it to Art Giardelli, who said 'Well, you know, it's not really very odd, because my brother is not remotely interested in Italian, can't speak it or anything.' Whereas Arthur, you see, *is* . . . with Dante and all that . . .[116]

MAT: When did you start reading and get to know about things like *Y Gododdin* and 'Men Went to Catraeth'.[117] Was that after you met Saunders [Lewis]?

DJ: No, I heard of Saunders when he was sent to prison, because I sent him a copy of my war book [*In Parenthesis* (1937)]. His wife took it to him, but apparently if you have books in prison, you're not allowed to bring them out again. [. . .] They made him librarian.

LA: What was he in prison for?

DJ: Oh, there was an aerodrome of some sort that was going to be built. Well, I presume it *was* built, on the Llyn Pennisula, opposite Ynys Enlli where the pilgrims used to go.

---

[114] See n. 95 above.

[115] The Metaphysical poets Henry Vaughan (1621–95) and George Herbert (1593–1633). See Jones's marginal note in his copy, in the National Library of Wales, of Wyn Griffith, *The Welsh* (Harmondsworth: Penguin, 1950), 103: 'Vaughan, Traherne, Donne, Herbert, all of Welsh affinities'.

[116] The Welsh artist of paternal Italian descent Arthur Giardelli (1911–2009) was a close friend of Jones. As Arthur was also known to Margaret Aeron-Thomas, and a film of Giardelli at an exhibition of Jones's artwork was discovered with the Mabon materials, it may be that Giardelli was involved in the making of this film. Although Giardelli's university degree was in Modern Languages, he devoted himself to the visual arts, and to championing other artists.

[117] Each section of *In Parenthesis* is preceded by quotations taken from *Y Gododdin*, the early Welsh epic poem attributed to the sixth-century poet Aneirin. The poem commemorates the raid by 300 Welshmen, at Catraeth, northern England, which was disastrous for Wales as only three men escaped with their lives, including the poet.

They'd written letters to *everybody* in the government with a whole vast quantity of signatures – [. . .] eminent men, all the associate people in fact – and they tried to get an interview with the Prime Minister, but they wouldn't have anything to do with it, you see, wouldn't even see them. Saunders and a chap called Valentine, who was a minister at Llandudno, and a schoolmaster in Pembrokeshire, decided that the only thing to do was to do something against the law whereby they would be . . . well, they would give themselves up [. . .] and that would bring attention. Which is what they did. I think he mentioned it in his defence at Caernarvon Assizes, because the jury couldn't come to a verdict.[118]

You know the Holy Island, part of the Farne Islands, where St Cuthbert was, off the coast of Northumbria? Well, they wanted to do a thing like that there, and the Archbishop of York, and of Canterbury, and God knows who, soon got that squashed! I don't know who the Prime Minister would be, it was 1926, wasn't it?[119]

LA: Was Saunders born a Catholic?

DJ: No, I think, like myself, he became a Catholic inside, after the First World War.[120]

LA: You think it was because of that?

DJ: He read those French authors, Barrès . . . I don't know about French. Have you seen that book published, *Introducing Saunders Lewis*, it's called?[121]

LA: No I haven't seen that.

DJ: He's a most remarkable man. He can *see* things *dead* straight, and of course it's terribly unliked by the majority of Welshmen. [. . .] He is a very good French scholar and Italian especially, and, I mean, if I showed him a drawing or something, he'd *never* say he thought it was all right if it isn't.

MAT: Did you learn about the *cynghanedd* and the old Welsh poetic forms from him, David, or did you know them by that time?[122]

---

[118] In 1936 the writer and Welsh nationalist Saunders Lewis (1893–1985) was gaoled for arson at the RAF bombing school at Penyberth on the Llyn Peninsula, opposite Bardsey Island, North Wales. He was accompanied by two companions, D. J. Williams and the Reverend Lewis Valentine, a schoolteacher and a vicar respectively, who like him wished to promote the Welsh language to official status in Wales. The three were tried at Caernarfon Assizes, but the jury failed to reach a decision, so the trial was moved to London. All three were sentenced to nine months' imprisonment. For further information and for Lewis's speech in his own defence, see Saunders Lewis, 'The Caernarfon Court Speech', 13 October 1936, in Alun R. Jones and Gwyn Thomas (eds), *Presenting Saunders Lewis*, 2nd edn (Cardiff: University of Wales Press, 1983), 115–26.

[119] Jones was mistaken about the date, 1926, and it is likely that he meant 1936 as this relates back to his conversation about Saunders Lewis and links to the attempt to institute a programme of bombing near Holy Island in 1935–6. The proposal was mentioned in Parliament on 19 December 1935 but not taken forward. For this proposal, see 'Bombing Practice, North-East Coast', House of Commons debate, 19 December 1935, *Hansard Archive*, vol. 307, col. 1996 W. Lindisfarne, the island in question, lies off the north-east coast of England and is also known as Holy Island. In 1935 Archbishop Cosmo Gordon Lang was incumbent in Canterbury, Archbishop William Temple was incumbent in York, and Stanley Baldwin was Prime Minister of Great Britain.

[120] Lewis was received into the Roman Catholic Church in 1932. He was formerly a member of the Methodist Church.

[121] For Jones's letter, which acts as an introduction to *Presenting Saunders Lewis*, see 'Introduction', in Jones and Thomas, *Presenting Saunders Lewis*, xv–xvii. Maurice Barrès (1862–1923) was a French Catholic writer and ethnic nationalist.

[122] *Cynghanedd* ('harmony') is a technique of intricate alliteration, stress-management, and rhyme along a line in Welsh-language verse dating back to the sixth century.

DJ: Oh, well, *he* knows the whole thing inside out, you see! That is my misery, that I've got no right to speak about it. I know about the nature of the Welsh language and its history . . .

As you know, he [Lewis] prefers to write plays. Well, I can only read them in English. There's one he called *Brad* about the Nazis in Paris – I was thinking that had that been written in English, I think it would've become quite an important book.[123] You know [his plays] are very grim, but only because of his intense regard for reality, and he never presumes to be more than he is. I've forgotten when he first knew about my paintings. But after all, until 1928 I still was wholly concerned with painting.

LA: I wonder now if you would see yourself as more a writer or more a painter?

DJ: I can't make any distinction really. Except that I sometimes wonder if it might have been better if I had not ever started on that damn book, because for a long while . . .[124]

[TAPE CHANGE]

DJ: You can't do anything about it. You can only carry on. I know that the people in the Roman Church to which I adhere – they don't seem to understand that you can't help what they call modern man by just saying things in such a way that they are *acceptable*. Because as a matter of fact they're bloody well wrong!

Because, in a full way, these wild chaps with long hair are often much more, underneath . . . You know they have this supernatural thing.[125] They are rebelling quite naturally against this bloody materialism! But it's not my kind of game to talk about that. They [the Vatican Council] wrecked a whole cultural heritage, such as chant, and having exchanged the things, they imagine that it won't offend sensibilities of current fashions of thought. Which rather alarms me as a Catholic, of course, because whatever the horrors they may have committed in the past, they seem to have had a deep understanding of the *psychology* of man. I mean, let's leave out whether it's true or not, just on *that* ground, the tactics are all wrong.[126]

LA: I'm interested by the way in which so much of the important creative writing now, poetry and some prose, about the nature of the Mass, has been made by people who are converts. I wonder whether this has something to do with the fact that the establishment has lost its touch and that there is a strength in coming from outside, because you know exactly what it is that you are doing.

DJ: Well, I think ecclesiastics, as such you see, have always been *philistines* because their job is more like . . . They can be frightfully good, holy, and all that, but their actual job is

---

[123] The English title of the play is *Treason* (1958). There are seven cast members, one female and six men. They are high-ranking officials in the German army. The first two acts take place in the afternoon and evening of Thursday, 20 July 1944, and the last act in the morning three days later. For further information and for a translation of *Brad* into English by Elwyn Jones, see Saunders Lewis, '*Brad*', in Jones and Thomas, *Presenting Saunders Lewis*, 301–58.

[124] For a further discussion of Jones's belief in the lack of distinction between being a writer or painter, see David Jones, 'Interview with Peter Orr, 24 November 1964', in *The Poet Speaks: Interviews with Contemporary Poets Conducted by Hilary Morrish, Peter Orr, John Press and Ian Scott-Kilvert*, ed. Peter Orr (London: Routledge & Kegan Paul, 1966), 98, 100. The 'damn book' is probably *In Parenthesis* (1937).

[125] Jones probably refers to London's hippie scene and its early–1970s aftermath.

[126] Compare David Jones, 'Letter on "The Latin Mass"', *The Tablet*, 2 December 1967, 25.

more like the efficient director of a company. They've always been terrified of being thought ascetic.

LA: I think it makes the poets terribly important now. In a sense, almost, they are the people there to defend the tradition because it is their job to see the tradition.

DJ: Yes. But you see, it's awfully difficult. Well, I mean apart from my happening to be ill this way, people say 'I don't see that all this liturgical stuff need worry you, you can get on with your work', but of course it *does* because it's about the whole of 'man' [. . .][127] I'm thinking of a good example, supposing a chap wrote a poem which referred to Aphrodite, let's say, and chaps had never heard of Aphrodite – you see it wouldn't ring the bell, would it? It's rather like that.

As a matter of fact (and this is subjective, I mean), my thing about the destruction of the Latin liturgy, and the chant which goes with it, is giving me just the same kind of the misery as the disappearance of Welsh, and I know a little more Latin than Welsh but not very much more, really. Do you know what I mean? To me, it's a sort of deprivation [. . .]

LA: I was interested in reading your accounts of the relationship between man-the-maker of signs and the centrality of the Mass . . .

DJ: Well, no, what I really like writing is the stuff itself, which, I have the conceit to think, could be a great deal better, but is not all that bad. You know what I mean? When people say *why* couldn't you write something autobiographical, well I suppose I could, but it all takes away from . . .

[. . .] Yet one word, you see, you've got to get all the words dead right or the thing's useless, and that takes a frightful time.

LA: Coming back to the relationship of poetry and the Sacrament itself. I was wondering, would you say that the Sacrament is the kind of sign which gives the greatest possibility for poetry?

DJ: Oh yes – by analogy – it is the same thing, as to say 'artists'. I was saying this to chaps, causing a fearful stink, when I came back from the first war, in Westminster Art School. I was already Catholic in my heart, but I didn't formally become one until 1921, but I argued with students at Westminster Art School that this *thing* which the post-Impressionists brought out in their manifestos (quite regardless of whether the work was good or bad) was *awfully* like the seemingly preposterous sayings the Church made as regard the bread and wine on the altar becoming identical with whatever happened in the manger or at the Last Supper. The few Catholics – there were only a couple there – they thought this was positively blasphemous! But don't you think that that's so? I mean, you see in the arts – in any of them – you take something, you hold it up and you say 'this signifies something other'. And in the jargon of art students – I don't know what they would say now (I'm talking about 1919) – but I remember one [. . .] drawing – a pretty bad drawing actually – of a mountain, and he [the student] says but that *is* mountain under the sign of paint, or pencil or whatever it was. It's terribly difficult for people to

---

[127] Compare Jones and Lewis, 'David Jones: Writer and Painter', 30.

comprehend it.[128] What surprises me is that quite genuinely religious chaps are almost the *worst* – they think in moral terms. I think, well, that's okay, but you can't have morals based on nothing.

LA: In some ways, I think it's a great advantage. I mean if you are asked the justification of poetry, actually it is rather difficult to justify poetry. But it is very easy as a Catholic: you can say it is like a sacrament.

DJ: Well, I think, you see, at least I've said to people, it is just extraneous to technological man – a sheer waste of bloody time for chaps to have ceremonies in Church or for that matter for chaps to send roses Interflora to the one they love. I mean man is obviously *bound* to this thing of doing . . . you know, *utile* things – if you pull a lever, it works – but he also has this other thing of performing acts [. . .] not sacred necessarily at all, which are purely *signs*, aren't they?

But I know a psychologist would say, 'Well, don't talk nonsense – this is just how human beings are.' But precisely *why* are they? I suspect it goes beyond human beings too. It's becoming, I understand from certain biologists, that certain creatures, not human, also in a very elementary way as far as we can see . . . I believe they have found that a certain kind of ape in India, that they carry away dead ones and *howl*. It is getting sort of near . . . it isn't a chant, or Michelangelo, but at least it isn't purely *utile*.[129]

LA: Obviously some birds sing just for the sake of singing, don't they? It's not all courtship and mating?

DJ: No – I believe a lot of *that* is pretty aggressive, they do it to keep chaps off their patch . . .

LA: But it's in a sense a fundamental demand of human beings to do something, to make processions – if they can't process to Church they will process behind a political leader.

DJ: That's terribly true. My friend . . . did you ever hear of the cultural historian, meta-historian, Christopher Dawson?[130] He was the most astounding chap – disgracefully

---

[128] In his essay 'Art and Sacrament' (1955), Jones puts this point quite succinctly: 'the more rewarding notions implicit in the post-Impressionist idea was that a work is a 'thing' and not (necessarily) the impression of some other thing'. See Jones, *Epoch and Artist*, 172. Jones goes on to identify a parallel between post-Impressionist theory and his understanding of *anamnesis*, as he claims that a work of art 'is a "thing" an object contrived of various materials and so ordered . . . as to show forth, recall and re-present, strictly within the conditions of a given art and under another mode, such and such a reality. It is a *signum* of that reality and it makes a kind of anamnesis of that reality' (174). In a letter to Harman Grisewood of 4 September 1971 Jones declares that the post-Impressionist doctrine 'that a painting must be a thing and not the impression of something has an affinity with what the Church said of the Mass, that what was oblated under the species of Bread and Wine at the Supper was the same *thing* as what was bloodily immolated on Calvary'. See Jones, *Dai Greatcoat*, 232. Jones's understanding of the interrelationship of the Last Supper, the Crucifixion, and the Mass was shaped by his engagement, since 1922, with the Eucharistic theology of the French Jesuit Maurice de la Taille (1872–1933). See Maurice de la Taille, *The Mystery of Faith & Human Opinion, Contrasted & Defined*, trans. J. B. Schimpf (London: Sheed & Ward, 1934), a book that survives (dated 1 November 1934) in Jones's personal library preserved in the National Library of Wales, Aberystwyth. See Huw Ceiriog Jones, *The Library of David Jones (1895–1974): A Catalogue* (Aberystwyth: National Library of Wales, 1995), 85.

[129] Compare David Jones, 'Use and Sign' (a talk broadcast on the BBC Third Programme on 26 April 1962), in *The Dying Gaul*, 183: 'She were better affianced to a baboon, for even those primates have, according to certain observers, an elementary apperception of some otherness in that they are said ceremonially to mourn their dead. Which report, if true, betrays an extra-utile tendency.'

[130] See n. 78 above.

unknown in this country. He had an almost disgusting ability . . . what he hadn't read, God alone knows, nothing! Mostly chaps like that make one feel rather foolish, but somehow he made one feel as though one knew stuff as well. Now, how did that come in – what were we talking about just before then?

LA: The innate necessity for ritual of man.

DJ: Oh bother, no, it wasn't that – such a nuisance when one forgets . . . Oh, hell!

[TAPE CHANGE]

DJ: Oh, another thing about him [Dawson] was, his first essay was about early Welsh literature! I went to stay with him – he was pretty well-to-do, but had always complained he wasn't, but he had houses all over the place, and his father's house was in Burnsall, Yorkshire, or Wharfedale,[131] and I was staying up there, and you could hardly move for books, I mean, as you go into the room where his desk was, it was like a lane. I noticed on the landing – you know it was one of those houses that had a – hideous houses actually, Victorian – it had a double staircase, and on the first landing I noticed copies of Lady Guest's *The Mabinogion*, the first one with big, big illustrations – you can't get it now. And then there was Skene's *Four Ancient Books of Wales*.[132] I asked him, 'Why? Aren't you proud of it?' But he said, 'Oh, well, you see, it was my first love.' I said, why the *hell* didn't you go on with it? He said 'Well . . .', and I quite see what he meant. He didn't *know*, nothing the matter with him, but just that he was more and more spreading into other things. So I didn't know until then that on his mother's side he *was* Welsh. I always thought it was Yorkshire because of his father, and his mother was a Bevan I think. Odd tracing the genealogical tree. That's very typical, isn't it? I knew her because she was near Capel-y-ffin. It's an odd place, and he said that it was neither Welsh nor English, but quite a separate enclave – like, do you know Berwick-on-Tweed? I just happened, I had to go to Northumberland, and went to Berwick-on-Tweed and there was a positive hostility to being called Scots or English.[133]

MAT: I went to Capel-y-ffin the other day, David, just before I went to Greece. I don't think it has changed much since you were there? Was it in 1921 that you went? It was after you met Eric Gill, wasn't it?

---

[131] Jones refers to Dawson's inherited family house, Hartlington Hall, near Skipton in Wharfedale, North Yorkshire. Jones visited in the summer of 1935. See Dilworth, *David Jones: Engraver, Soldier, Painter, Poet*, 177.

[132] Jones may be referring to the second edition of Lady Charlotte Guest's translation of *The Mabinogion*, three volumes in seven parts, with forty-nine woodcuts (London and Llandovery: Longmans, 1849). The Scottish antiquary William Forbes Skene transcribed and translated a selection of texts from *The Black Book of Carmarthen*, *The Book of Taliesin*, *The Book of Aneirin*, and *The Red Book of Hergest*, collected in a two-volume edition entitled *The Four Ancient Books of Wales* (Edinburgh: Edmonston and Douglas, 1868).

[133] Jones first went to Northumberland to visit Helen Sutherland (1881–1965), the art patron, to whom he was introduced by his friend Jim Ede, in August 1929. Sutherland, the wealthy daughter of a shipping magnate, leased Rock Hall, four miles north of Alnwick. A generous art collector, she often invited writers, artists, and musicians to stay. David Jones accepted her patronage and hospitality. Rock is in the parliamentary constituency of Berwick-on-Tweed, a border town straddling the English–Scottish border. Jones spent a fortnight with Dawson at Hartlington Hall in the summer of 1935 before going on to Rock. See Dilworth, *David Jones: Engraver, Soldier, Painter, Poet*, 121, 177. Jones lived from 1924 to 1926 with Gill and Gill's family and community (some transferred from Ditchling) at the former Benedictine monastery Capel-y-ffin in the Ewyas Valley in the Black Mountains. Dawson's mother, Mary Louisa Dawson (née Bevan), was the eldest daughter of the Archdeacon of Brecon William Latham Bevan, of Hay Castle, Hay-on-Wye, Powys, Wales, where Dawson was born. Hay Castle lies eight miles north of Capel.

DJ: Yes, that's another mistake people make (although it doesn't really matter), but they say that I came and knew Eric and became a Catholic, but it wasn't at all like that. I knew a man, Father John O'Connor,[134] who was Chesterton's Father Brown, although I could *never* see any resemblance, and I was friendly with him from art school. It was under Father O'Connor's instructions, and he said, 'Do you by any chance know Eric Gill?' and I said, 'No, I don't' – though most people did, I mean the thing at Westminster Cathedral.[135] And he said, 'I think you'd be interested to go down and look at that community at Ditchling, it might interest you.' So that's how I came to know him. I didn't go there until a year later [1921] because I'd got a government grant to Westminster Art School, and that's when I had all the haranguing under old Sickert![136]

MAT: And you met Petra at Ditchling when you went there?[137] Petra was living there with Eric Gill, she was Eric Gill's daughter, wasn't she?

DJ: Oh, wait a minute. Let me get this straight. I *liked* what I saw of it, the people working at Ditchling because I always laughed about art schools, because they were *wholly* . . . all you did was to try to imitate the style of the masters you had. I mean, chaps want to paint, the first thing they teach you to do is to paint a door. How technical is that? And Sickert was just about going. He'd been there all through the war. Only he used to come and lecture to us, and I used to go out to tea with him sometimes. Terribly funny bloke! He was so terrified of being thought an aesthete – he used to wear sort of stable-boy's clothes, leggings and sometimes sucking a straw. I think he's a *superb* artist, but why he had to teach drawing at Westminster, I can't imagine.

MAT: But then when you saw what they were doing at Ditchling, they were all real artists, craftsmen, weren't they? Johnston and all those people?[138]

DJ: Oh Johnston – I didn't see Johnston – I saw him much later once, after Eric was dead actually. I don't think he was much admired really. He was a fairly straightforward 'Hilary Pepler printer', you see. Then there was some kind of ruckus between Hilary Pepler and Eric, and when Bobby wrote his biography of Eric, he was just a little bit annoyed with me, because he said, 'Now, you were there, can you tell me what caused what happened,

---

[134] Fr John O'Connor (1870–1952) arranged Jones's first meeting, on 29 January 1921, with the Catholic sculptor and letter-carver Eric Gill in Gill's community of Catholic craftsmen in Ditchling, Sussex. O'Connor received David Jones into the Church on 7 September 1921. See Dilworth, *David Jones: Engraver, Soldier, Painter, Poet*, 63–4, 68.

[135] Jones's first encounter with Eric Gill was in January 1921, at Ditchling in Sussex, where Gill had co-founded, together with Desmond Chute (who had studied at the Slade School of Art), and also Hilary Pepler (see n. 139 below), the Guild of Saints Joseph and Dominic, a religious fraternity for those who wanted to work with their hands. Gill was a mentor to Jones and looked upon him as a son. Jones refers here to Gill's carvings of the Stations of the Cross installed in Westminster Cathedral 1914–18, when Jones was studying at Westminster Art School.

[136] Walter Sickert (1860–1942) was a leading painter and printmaker who taught Jones at Westminster Art School in 1919–21.

[137] Petra (1906–99) was Eric Gill's second daughter. Jones first met her at Ditchling, where they were betrothed in a formal ceremony on 24 April 1924. Jones was distraught by her decision to end the engagement in 1927. They remained friends until Jones's death. See Dilworth, *David Jones: Engraver, Soldier, Painter, Poet*, 79–82, 102–4.

[138] Edward Johnston (1872–1944) was a typographer who designed the sans-serif Johnston typeface for the London Transport Authority in 1913. Eric Gill was one of his students, and Johnston joined the Ditchling community in 1912, and lived there until his death.

because I can't get anybody to tell me!'[139] I said, 'Well, because they don't *bloody well know*, I certainly don't.' I think it was just a clash of temperaments, you know. Hilary was rather romantic – he'd get some old lady wanting to build a house and he'd get her down to Ditchling. Eric, of course . . . he wasn't intolerant, nothing like that, but he kept a day book, every *penny* he spent, and he did all his own income tax forms. [. . .] When I went to stay with them at Capel, we were on quite another footing, I think I went there as a guest – I used to go to Caldey half the time from there.[140]

MAT: But you were engaged to Petra by that time weren't you, David?

DJ: I was engaged to Petra for I suppose three years, but it doesn't . . . I mean, it didn't cause any rumpus, mercifully, and she married Denis Tegetmeier.[141] Now they've got grandchildren and I wouldn't be surprised if there are great-grandchildren!

MAT: She must have been very beautiful.[142]

DJ: I haven't seen her . . . I saw her on my seventieth birthday, which is seven years ago, because she happened to be staying in London near Douglas Cleverdon.[143]

MAT: Does she remember the day that you took the trap to meet her at Capel station?

DJ: Oh! I drove the trap – yes.[144]

MAT: I don't think you had much gift for horses, did you, David?

DJ: Oh no, obviously. That was what Major Billy Davies observed when I tried to become a [mounted soldier].[145] No, this was when Petra was coming to the nearest station to Capel. I think the line is probably closed by now, isn't it? And there was no one, either they were ill, or something, there was no one else but myself to drive the trap. I put on the harness, did that all right, trouble with the horse was that it was *far* too slow, so I had a whip and whipped it, and it started to go like a racehorse and didn't stop, I could hardly stop it until I got to the station! On this road, one of the lanterns and all these other attachments all fell off. I was just on time, the train was just coming into the station. Petra said, 'Well, Ma will be terribly angry about these things,' which I took for criticism, so I said, 'What do you mean?' 'Oh,' she said 'let's just go very slow.' We did, every now and again, I think, we did find some of the things.

MAT: You must have looked very dishevelled, David. Judging by what she said to you?

---

139 Hilary Douglas Clark Pepler (1878–1951) was Eric Gill's working partner. Together they established St Dominic's Press at Ditchling in 1916. Pepler married Gill's youngest daughter, Joanna. Robert (Bobby) Speaight (1904–76) was an actor and author who wrote, among other biographies, *The Life of Eric Gill* (London: Methuen, 1966).

140 Jones visited Caldey Island, off the coast of Tenby, south-west Wales, on a number of occasions in 1926–7, when he was living at Capel-y-ffin.

141 Denis Tegetmeier (1909–87) was a painter and printmaker and member of Gill's Ditchling community. Petra broke off her engagement to Jones on 4 February 1927, and in 1930 married Tegetmeier.

142 Jones sketched, made wood-engravings, and also painted three watercolour portraits of Petra: *Petra with Cherries* (1929), in the Glynn Vivian Art Gallery, Swansea; *Petra im Rosenhag* (1930–1), in the National Museum Cardiff; and *Petra, Seated Mother, Autumn* (1932), in a private collection. See Bankes and Hills, *The Art of David Jones*, 78–80.

143 Douglas Cleverdon (1903–87) was a Bristol bookseller who commissioned several works from Jones, including his copperplate engravings to *The Rime of the Ancient Mariner* (1929). Cleverdon later joined the BBC and put Jones on the air.

144 See Dilworth, *David Jones: Engraver, Soldier, Painter, Poet*, 85.

145 Jones alludes to the story he told earlier in the interview about his attempt to join the Welsh Horse. See nn. 90–91 above.

DJ: Oh, that thing about walking?

MAT: No – I mean that you were standing by this contraption with your hair on end.

DJ: Did you mean the thing about . . . I'd been for a walk with Petra and when we came back, I couldn't help it but I heard her sister say to her 'Have you had a nice walk, Petra?' She said, 'Well, David had a nice walk. I had a nice run!' Well it made me realize in future that I should slow down a bit. That's why I hate this particular thing that makes it impossible for me to run, as I like to move quickly.[146]

MAT: There is still something that you made at Capel, isn't there, that Arthur [Giardelli] was telling me he was concerned that it was getting rather rusty. Is it a bit of sculpture or something?

DJ: Well, the thing on the wall – a large crucifix with two columns of lettering down each side – which is bound to go because it was painted with ordinary artists' coloured paint straight onto a lime-washed, plastered wall. And a chap sent to Cardiff Museum, asking if something could be done about it, and they got some experts and they said, 'Well, it could be [preserved], but it would cost the earth.' But they can do almost anything. And I said then that I shouldn't bother. While I *knew* they couldn't help it, the very damp climate, and I said, 'Well it's not like a Giotto or something or other, so forget about it.' What I *was* worried about was the tabernacle on the altar, and that was on metal, and I hoped that that wouldn't rust. I'm afraid there is only one very bad photograph of it. It doesn't give any idea of what the thing looks like.[147]

[TAPE CHANGE]

LA: I was intrigued, and I wanted to ask you, about these figures of Flora and indeed Guinevere, too, mingling with the figure of Our Lady in your pictures and your poetry and wondered whether – if – you regarded that as orthodox Catholicism?[148]

DJ: Well, I regard it as Catholicism. But . . . you see, theologians are like a lot of other trades, you can't, if you start nailing things down, you find they *won't* have it, and quite rightly, I mean. I always liked the thing about Tennyson. There were three figures in some poem by Tennyson, and someone said, 'Oh, Tennyson, I take it that these figures stand in some way for Faith, Hope and Charity?' And Tennyson said 'Well, you can think what you *bloody well like* as far as I'm concerned. They can stand for what you say, I don't object to that. You know, I mean I won't be *bound down*.'[149]

---

[146] For an account of Jones's fall on 21 March 1970, at least two days after his stroke, see Dilworth, *David Jones: Engraver, Soldier, Painter, Poet*, 343. The 'particular thing' Jones mentions may be his walker, visible in the film.

[147] Jones refers to the refectory wall on which he painted a mural of the crucified Christ with lettering on either side of the figure. Owing to the damp climate of the valley, the paint started to flake off the wall even before autumn 1928 when Gill and his supporters vacated Capel-y-ffin and moved to Pigotts, a farmstead five miles north of High Wycombe in Buckinghamshire. Jones constructed a metal tabernacle for the chapel at Capel-y-ffin. See images of the mural and the tabernacle's door in Nicolete Gray, *The Painted Inscriptions of David Jones* (London: Gordon Fraser, 1981), 23. The tabernacle can also be seen in Aylen's film *Steel Be My Sister* (1975).

[148] In Jones's work, which often dwells on the eternal feminine archetype, the Virgin Mary could appear as the epitome, and culmination, of womanhood by displaying some of the characteristics of other figures, such as Flora, goddess of Spring, and also Guinevere, queen of Arthur, beloved of Lancelot. Compare Jones's painting *Aphrodite in Aulis* (1940–1), now in Tate Britain, and *The Anathemata*, 128

[149] For an earlier version of this anecdote, see Jones's letter to Helen Ede (wife of Jim Ede), 28 August 1949, in Jones, *Dai Greatcoat*, 150–1.

MAT: But why did you paint her in a South Wales landscape, David?[150] She's got the hills of Breconshire around and a little Welsh mountain ponies [sic] on one side and she's got a foxglove in her hand, not a lily?[151] I wondered why you did that?

DJ: A foxglove?

MAT: She's holding a foxglove.

DJ: It's only because – it's the only thing on places like Capel, the only flower after the spring flowers were foxgloves. That's why. And as she's in this setting and Ffion is the collective name for the flower in Welsh. And you know in *The Mabinogion*, when they talk about . . . well for one thing, when they talk about Olwen and her cheeks are 'redder than the reddest roses', the word isn't *roses* at all, its *foxgloves*.[152] See, I mean, it was natural to an English person translating that, of a girl's cheeks, to say roses, I don't think I've got any complaint with that, but in fact it is a foxglove. It couldn't mean roses . . . but it could mean some another sort of red, reddish, flower.

MAT: Well, she is very, very beautiful. Quite lovely.

DJ: I don't know why – they are very hardy, I suppose, foxgloves.

[END OF TAPE RECORDING]

FIGURE 5: David Jones. Film still from the Mabon Studios interview at Calvary Nursing Home, Harrow, 1973 (David Jones Society).

[150] The painting under consideration here is *Y Cyfarchiad i Fair* (*The Greeting to Mary*), also known as *The Annunciation in a Welsh Hill Setting* (1963), now in the National Museum Cardiff. Many of the tropes that are associated with Jones's *oeuvre* appear in this work, including the young Madonna receiving Gabriel's announcement of her Divine impregnation. For a discussion of this work, see Bankes and Hills, *The Art of David Jones*, 164.

[151] Traditionally, lilies are the flowers associated with paintings of the Annunciation, but as Jones observes, cultivated lilies do not thrive in the mountainous regions of Wales.

Fragments of the Mabon interview extant only in Steel Be My Sister

According to Leo Aylen, these three fragments were recorded during the Mabon Studios interview with Jones but do not appear on the ten ¼-inch sound tapes. They survive only as sound bites in Aylen's 1975 HTV documentary *Steel Be My Sister*. These fragments are very similar to written passages by Jones which appear in his letters and essays; we have noted these associations in the footnotes. From the clarity, pace, and deliberation with which Jones speaks during these sections, they appear to have been prepared in advance of the interview sessions for recitation during them. They represent interesting variations on passages by Jones previously published elsewhere.

Fragment 1

DJ: From about the age of five my main obsession was with drawing and painting. To attempt to convey on paper this or that object seemed to me as natural a desire as, say, stroking a cat, and I couldn't understand why my brother and sisters [sic] had not the same compulsion.

Animals were what I usually drew . . . Hence, when I should have been having Latin declensions and the elements of Greek knocked into me . . . I was . . . making drawings of plaster casts of such works of classical antiquity as the Aphrodite of Melos (that most serene and gracious of the works in the academic tradition) . . . or the 'Dying Gaul' from Pergamon. I naturally like him, for he epitomized for me so much of Celtdom, or what little I knew of it in 1909–10. At least I sensed the continuity of struggle, the continuity of loss. I could not recall hearing of works celebrative of victory, but only of relentless resistance culminating in defeat. But from each defeat, the living embers to feed the fires of the resistance yet to be.[153]

Fragment 2

DJ: The bards of an earlier Wales referred to themselves as 'carpenters of song'. Carpentry suggests a fitting together and the English word 'artist' means someone concerned with a fitting together of some sort. Well, it would seem to me, that round about 1924 I was at last understanding [the] particular 'carpentry' which most sorted with my inclinations and limitations.

Because at this propitious time the circumstances occasioned my living in Nant Honddu [Honddu Valley], there to feel the impact of the strong hill-rhythms and the bright counter-rhythms of the *afonydd dyfroedd* [river brooks], which makes so much of Wales such a plurabelle.[154]

---

[152] *Kilhwch and Olwen* is a story in *The Mabinogion* in which Kilhwch, a cousin of Arthur, is challenged to capture and kill a wild boar. See Jones's poem 'The Hunt', in David Jones, *The Sleeping Lord and Other Fragments* (London: Faber & Faber, 1974), 65–9.

[153] This passage appears in discrete, almost verbatim, sections in '*In illo tempore*', in *The Dying Gaul*, 23–4, 26. It occurs in *Steel Be My Sister* at 5:12–6:45.

[154] This passage appears in discrete, almost verbatim, sections in David Jones, 'Autobiographical Talk', in *Epoch and Artist*, 29–30. It occurs in *Steel Be My Sister* at 10:35–11:43.

Fragment 3

DJ: I stayed in Jerusalem for two months, and almost everything that I have written since 1934 has arisen out of that. At that period Palestine was a British mandated territory, and British Tommies looked very familiar to me from the First World War – seeing them in the very different conditions, very bronzed, extremely short khaki shorts, shirts, tin hats at the usual sideways angle, and sometimes we saw groups of them with riot shields. It gave me the instant impression of Roman soldiers in the first century, and that impression has reminded me ever since.[155]

[155] This passage is similar to the text of a letter Jones wrote to Saunders Lewis in April 1971, reprinted in *Dai Greatcoat*, 56–7. It occurs in *Steel Be My Sister* at 16:10–17:06. This visit to Jerusalem was organized by Jones's friends, including Tom Burns, to help Jones recover from his first nervous breakdown in 1933.

Conclusion

Pursuing the Question

KATHLEEN HENDERSON STAUDT

When I began reading and writing about David Jones in the late 1970s, the poet had just recently died and Jones criticism was entering what I now think of as an early 'second generation' of critical studies. Many of those writing on Jones initially had known or met the man, and the first wave of posthumous biographical material was surfacing. In 1980 René Hague published *Dai Greatcoat: A Self-portrait of David Jones in his Letters*, alerting readers to the voice and creativity in Jones's trove of letters.[1] William F. Blissett's *The Long Conversation: A Memoir of David Jones* appeared in 1981 and drew on both the author's years of friendship with Jones and unpublished letters.[2] This basic biographical work, as well as early introductions by David Blamires and Samuel Rees,[3] laid the groundwork for critics to turn their attention to the formal and thematic study of Jones's major poetic works.

During the late 1970s and 1980s, Thomas Dilworth and I were both working on monographs that sought to break fresh ground by offering readings of the form and theme of all of Jones's major published works. In 1984, as part of the research for my book, I came upon a largely uncatalogued collection of Jones manuscripts, letters, and drawings in the Burns Library at Boston College. This collection included the essays on Gerard Manley Hopkins and Adolf Hitler freshly edited for the present volume. The abridged edition of the Hopkins essay I produced at the time provided a 'reader's version' that gave access to the main ideas of the essay without claiming to be the complete transcription that Thomas Berenato provides here.[4] Similarly, the excerpts from the Hitler essay provided important material for the essay on David Jones and fascism that

[1] David Jones, *Dai Greatcoat: A Self-portrait of David Jones in his Letters*, ed. René Hague (London: Faber & Faber, 1980). Major deposits of David Jones's letters and manuscripts can be found at the National Library of Wales in Aberystwyth, Yale University's Beinecke Library, the Booth Family Center for Special Collections at Georgetown University Library, the John J. Burns Library at Boston College, and Kettle's Yard, University of Cambridge. Jones's letters to René Hague are deposited at the Thomas Fisher Rare Book Library at the University of Toronto.

[2] William F. Blissett, *The Long Conversation: A Memoir of David Jones* (Oxford: Oxford University Press, 1981).

[3] David Blamires, *David Jones: Artist and Writer*, 2nd edn (Manchester: Manchester University Press, 1978); Samuel Rees, *David Jones* (Boston: Twayne, 1978).

[4] See Kathleen Henderson Staudt, 'David Jones: An Unpublished Appreciation of Gerard Manley Hopkins', *Agenda* 31, no. 3 (Autumn 1993): 72–80. Reprinted, with permission, pp. 321–5 below in this volume.

Thomas Dilworth produced at this time.[5] Meanwhile, Dilworth had found the manuscripts of *The Anathemata* and *In Parenthesis*, along with many other Jones manuscript materials housed in the David Jones Collection at the National Library of Wales, Aberystwyth.[6] These manuscripts give important insights into David Jones's working methods and formal imagination, and they continue to offer deeper insights into the poet's process and formal strategies. Dilworth's *The Shape of Meaning in the Poetry of David Jones*[7] brings together biography, explication, annotation, and critical readings based on his study of the manuscripts; it remains a foundational interpretive study. My own book, *At the Turn of a Civilization*, also drawing on Jones manuscripts and annotations, sought to integrate literary readings of the poetry with insights into modern and postmodern poetics and cultural, religious, and mythological contexts, including the role of the feminine in Jones's work.[8] Dilworth, the most prolific of contemporary Jones scholars, has recently published the first full-dress biography of David Jones. Its appearance should help to inspire more of the kind of textual, historical, and contextual study of the poet and his era that the present volume represents.[9]

The canon of poetry published during Jones's lifetime and with his approval closed with *The Sleeping Lord and Other Fragments*, which appeared in 1974.[10] Its title gives a clue to the poet's own sense that the published work is only a fragment of a much larger body of work, and indeed the collections of manuscript materials have proven to be vast. Two posthumous publications, *The Roman Quarry and Other Sequences*[11] and *The Dying Gaul*,[12] both edited by close friends of David Jones, appeared as early outcroppings of the deposits of David Jones's manuscript material that still remain to be explored, edited, and annotated by scholars. Thomas Goldpaugh, writing over the past two decades and more, has given us samplings of the cultural and theological insights contained in the unpublished manuscripts of poetry including that from which *The Anathemata* and the Roman poems were drawn. These manuscripts encompass material published in *The Sleeping Lord* and *The Roman Quarry* but include much more still awaiting thorough editing and commentary.[13]

This present volume reflects a fresh scholarly effort to learn about the poet's context, particularly his religious, political, and cultural views, by attending closely to unpublished

[5] Thomas Dilworth, 'David Jones and Fascism', *Journal of Modern Literature* 13, no. 1 (March 1986): 149–62.

[6] A description of this collection can be found at https://www.llgc.org.uk/collections/learn-more/archives/david-jones-papers (accessed 17 November 2017).

[7] Thomas Dilworth, *The Shape of Meaning in the Poetry of David Jones* (Toronto: University of Toronto Press, 1988).

[8] Kathleen Henderson Staudt, *At the Turn of a Civilization: David Jones and Modern Poetics* (Ann Arbor: University of Michigan Press, 1994).

[9] Thomas Dilworth, *David Jones: Engraver, Soldier, Painter, Poet* (London: Jonathan Cape, 2017).

[10] David Jones, *The Sleeping Lord and Other Fragments* (London: Faber & Faber, 1974). To this canon one could add 'The Narrows', published in both *The Anglo-Welsh Review* 22, no. 50 (Autumn 1973) and the second David Jones special issue of *Agenda* 11, no. 4–12, no. 1 (Autumn–Winter 1973–4). This poem was edited with an introduction by Roland Mathias as David Jones, *The Narrows* (Budleigh Salterton, Devon: Interim Press, 1981). See Keith Alldritt, *David Jones: Writer and Artist* (London: Constable, 2003), 181–4.

[11] David Jones, *The Roman Quarry and Other Sequences*, ed. Harman Grisewood and René Hague (New York: Sheep Meadow Press), 1981.

[12] David Jones, *The Dying Gaul and Other Writings*, ed. Harman Grisewood (London: Faber & Faber, 1978).

[13] See Tom Goldpaugh, 'On the Traverse of the Wall: The Lost Long Poem of David Jones', *Journal of Modern Literature* 19, no. 1 (Summer 1994): 31–53; Tom Goldpaugh, 'To Make a Shape in Words: The Labyrinthine Text of David Jones', in Belinda Humfrey and Anne Price-Owen (eds), *David Jones: Diversity in Unity* (Cardiff: University of Wales Press, 2000), 132–152; Thomas Goldpaugh, 'David Jones and the Cost of Empire', *Flashpoint* 10 (Summer 2010). Goldpaugh's complete edition of Jones's poetic manuscripts is in preparation.

manuscript drafts. Both the Hitler essay and the Hopkins essay included in this volume sound the theme of 'asking the question', reflecting a quality of David Jones's sensibility and his work that is fundamentally interrogative and exploratory rather than dogmatic or ideological.[14] So it seems worthwhile to sketch out some of the dimensions of the cultural and political 'question' that David Jones seeks to ask and to consider the variety of ways that Jones scholars are currently framing and pursuing this question.

We know that much of Jones's most original thinking about politics, culture, and religion emerges from his attraction and struggles with the work of Oswald Spengler, manifest in his annotations to *The Decline of the West.*[15] One of these annotations is particularly telling for Jones's view of himself in relation to the civilizational 'turn' that he discerns in his own time. Spengler writes about the importance of accepting 'our destiny'. Those who are living in a declining civilizational phase must accept it, he insists, without looking for alternatives or lying to themselves. 'He who does not acknowledge this in his heart,' Spengler writes, 'ceases to be counted among the men of his generation, and remains either a simpleton, a charlatan or a pedant.'[16] Jones responds in an annotation: 'He might be simply an intelligent person who knows he is living in a kind of hell.' This is the ground on which Jones stands in his writings and attempted writings on culture and politics: he observes, describes, and acknowledges the Waste Land around him, but he refuses to 'abandon the Muses for technics'[17] (as, he says, Spengler implicitly demands) or accept the contemporary technocracy as determinative of his identity as man, artist, and lover of the 'things of which one is oneself made'.[18]

We hear this refusal to accept a civilizational destiny in Dai Greatcoat's exhortation at the centre of *In Parenthesis*. At the climax of his bardic boast about his presence with soldiers throughout myth and history, Dai turns to his listeners in the trenches and says:

> You ought to ask: Why,
> what is this,
> what's the meaning of this.
> Because you don't ask,
> although the spear-shaft
> drips,
> there's neither steading – not a roof-tree.[19]

The passage alludes to *Peredur,* the Welsh iteration of the Parsifal story, in which the violence of battles and the destruction of the kingdom is attributed to the hero's failure

---

[14] Jones uses this same allusion to describe the poet's task in his posthumously published essay 'Art in Relation to War', where he writes of his essay, 'Because the land is Waste (or seems so to the writer) it seeks to do what the hero in the myth was rebuked for not doing, i.e. it seeks to "ask the Question". Although, alas, unlike the myth, this essay does not suppose that in asking the question the land can be "restored". Although if all the world asked the question perhaps there might be some fructification – or some "sea-change"'. See Jones, *The Dying Gaul*, 123.

[15] Kathleen Henderson Staudt, 'The Decline of the West and the Optimism of the Saints: David Jones' Reading of Oswald Spengler', in John Matthias (ed.), *David Jones: Man and Poet* (Orono, ME: National Poetry Foundation, University of Maine: 1989), 443–63.

[16] Oswald Spengler, *The Decline of the West*, trans. Charles Francis Atkinson (London: George Allen & Unwin, 1926), 44, quoted from David Jones's copy in the National Library of Wales, Aberystwyth. See Huw Ceiriog Jones, *The Library of David Jones (1895–1974): A Catalogue* (Aberystwyth: National Library of Wales, 1995), 274.

[17] Jones, *The Dying Gaul*, 129.

[18] David Jones, preface to *The Anathemata: Fragments of an Attempted Writing* (London: Faber & Faber, 1952), 10.

[19] David Jones, *In Parenthesis* (London: Faber & Faber, 1937), 84. All published editions give 'not a roof-tree', when one expects 'nor'.

to ask the questions 'Why, / what is this, / what's the meaning of this'?[20] or, to evoke the Grail myth more directly, 'Why is the land waste?'[21]

Much of Jones's poetry is fundamentally interrogative: in *The Anathemata* all but the first and last books begin with a question, and the whole poem ends with the rhetorical question 'What did he do other / Riding the Axile Tree?'[22] Jones's 1967 poem 'The Sleeping Lord' proceeds similarly as a series of questions. For Jones, questions call for exploration, not answers. So it is not surprising that in the Mabon Studios interview published in the present volume, Jones speaks of his reluctance to be interviewed on camera because of the expectation that he will immediately answer the questions posed. His preferred procedure is to bring questions into conversation with other questions, texts, and contexts, letting the question be illuminated by possible answers that raise new questions.[23] This is the method of Jones's writings that readers and students of his work must grasp.

'Why . . . what's the meaning of this'? and 'Why is the land waste?' These are the questions that Spengler's steely determinism forbids. They are political questions for Jones because of his love of place, landscape, and the Welsh tradition and his conviction that what is valuable in Welsh culture has been threatened by the forces of technology and empire. He regularly depicts lovers of the Celtic landscape and those who treasure an indigenous heritage as victims of the 'levelling' influence of imperial and technological power. Opposed to empire is the reality of our human identity as 'man the artist', an identity basic to Jones's theology and aesthetic and always, in his view, subversive to rulers and empires. In his essay on Hitler, Jones raises versions of the hero's question: how did we get to this place in the life of Europe? What does this new leader have to offer that might somehow restore the Waste Land? The essay on Hopkins casts the poet in the prophetic role of 'asking the question' that could heal the Waste Land.

Four interrelated dimensions of Jones's questioning have occupied Jones scholars over the years, each dimension suggesting its own way to pursue the deeper 'question' about the modern Waste Land and its meaning that is at the core of Jones's thinking about culture and politics. The first dimension encompasses what I will call 'Man-and-Artist' questions: wondering who David Jones was, how his life experience, relationships, and cultural context helped to shape his work and his aesthetics. Related to this is a second question: in what contexts can we best make sense of David Jones's work, including his identity as a veteran and survivor of the Great War, as a Catholic convert working in the period between the wars, and as an artist shaped by other aspects of what Jones calls 'one's own "thing", which *res* is unavoidably part and parcel of the Western Christian *res*, as inherited by a person . . . indigenous to this island . . . is necessarily insular . . . contingent upon his being a Londoner, of Welsh and English parentage, of Protestant upbringing, of Catholic subscription'?[24] These contexts give rise to what I would call the dialogic dimension of the question, inhabiting which scholars have placed Jones's works in dialogue with other works, traditions, and disciplines. Thomas Berenato's edition of Jones's essay on Hopkins in this book exemplifies how Jones's work can be considered in

[20] Jones, *In Parenthesis*, 210.
[21] See Rowan Williams's foreword to the present volume, p.xvii above.
[22] Jones, *The Anathemata*, 243.
[23] See the Mabon Studios interview with Jones in this volume, p. 271 above.
[24] Jones, *The Anathemata*, 11.

dialogue with particular poets and artists, some of them known to him and others not.[25] Perhaps the most important of these dialogues are those between the poetry and the artwork, the poetic theory and the aesthetic theory. Finally, from poets, critics and long-time readers alike, there is the question of how we might invite others into the experience of reading a text by Jones, an experience certain to be enhanced by forthcoming manuscript work on both the poems and the letters.

Man and poet/man and artist

Jones has described his poetic project as an effort 'to make a shape out of the very things of which one is oneself made'.[26] As the material included in the present volume testifies, these 'things' that have shaped his work and thought include his experience and identity as a veteran of the Great War, and his identity and vocation as an artist, a poet, a Catholic. Emerging from these connections we see also his affinity with Welsh culture and accompanying sympathy for the diversities of people, cultures, and landscapes that fall victim to the levelling imperialism that he sees in modernity.

The question of Jones's voice among the war poets has been explored in great depth, beginning with John H. Johnston's 1962 essay, which Jones pronounced 'the only decent analysis of *I.P.* that's ever appeared'.[27] William Blissett published '*In Parenthesis* among the War Books'[28] during the poet's lifetime and has continued to explore *In Parenthesis* and the war experience in his many writings around what he is coming to call the 'Great Misadventure' that was the war in Jones's eyes.[29] Particularly valuable for understanding the formative effect of Jones's war experience is Colin Hughes's early work on *In Parenthesis* in relation to Jones's experience in the Great War, and his accounts of his conversations and friendship with the poet. His long essay *David Jones: The Man Who Was on the Field*, first published in 1979, provided strong historical context for Jones's experience in the Great War.[30] Most recently, Thomas Dilworth's detailed study *David Jones in the Great War* provides a compelling view of the relationship between David Jones the art student and Jones the war veteran, offering an account of childhood influences, the formative effect of his art school training, and the details of the war experiences in which Jones's unit was engaged.[31] It is clear that Jones's perspective on twentieth-century politics and culture is rooted in his first-hand experience of the war, offering a foot soldier's perspective rather than the officer's view that we find in Owen, Sassoon, and other well-known Great War poets. Jones as war poet received renewed attention in 2016 amidst commemorations of the centenary of the Somme, including an

[25] See Thomas Berenato's introduction to the Hopkins essay in this volume, pp. 101–17 above.

[26] Jones, *The Anathemata*, 10.

[27] In a letter to Harman Grisewood of 22 May 1962, in Jones, *Dai Greatcoat*, 188.

[28] William Blissett, '*In Parenthesis* among the War Books', *University of Toronto Quarterly* 42, no. 3 (Spring 1973): 258–88.

[29] See, among others, William Blissett 'The Efficacious Word', in Roland Mathias (ed.), *David Jones: Eight Essays on His Work as Writer and Artist* (Llandysul: Gomer Press, 1976), 22–49; William Blissett, 'The Syntax of Violence', in Matthias, *David Jones: Man and Poet*, 193–208; William Blissett, 'To Make a Shape in Words', *Renascence* 38, no. 2 (Winter 1986): 67–81.

[30] Colin Hughes, *David Jones: The Man Who Was on the Field:* In Parenthesis *as Straight Reporting* (Manchester: David Jones Society, 1979), a pamphlet revised as 'David Jones: The Man Who Was on the Field: *In Parenthesis* as Straight Reporting', in Matthias, *David Jones: Man and Poet*, 163–92.

[31] Thomas Dilworth, *David Jones in the Great War* (London: Enitharmon, 2012).

operatic version of *In Parenthesis* by the English composer Iain Bell. The trauma of the war, both civilizational and personal, colours Jones's efforts to make sense of the political and cultural trends of the mid-twentieth century and continues to attract critical attention. The essays collected in the present book demonstrate, for example, how deeply Jones's disillusionment with the romanticized war propaganda of the First World War affected his reaction to the war propaganda and liberal political arguments in the late 1930s and made him an admirer of Neville Chamberlain's proclamation of 'peace for our time'.

While Jones has received wide attention as a poet of the Great War, the conversation about his thinking between the wars, as he was reading Spengler and engaging in theological and philosophical conversations with fellow Catholics, continues to attract further exploration. In the late 1980s and 1990s, when there seemed to be widespread suspicion or dismissal of Christian poetry in the literary academy, some of us writing on Jones were eager to present him as a figure less parochial than the tag 'Catholic writer' had come to signify. But Jones himself claims this identity in the preface to *The Anathemata*: he is an artist 'of Welsh and English parentage, of Protestant upbringing, of Catholic subscription'.[32] Recent scholarship has engaged with Jones in relation to some of his Catholic contemporaries in ways that reflect the importance of his particular expression of a Catholic Christian historical sense, national identity, and theological orientation. This discussion is laid out in Adam Schwartz's important study of Jones's work in relation to that of G. K. Chesterton, Graham Greene, and Christopher Dawson.[33] Jones stayed in London during the Blitz; he appears to have thrived, perhaps reverting to some of his instincts as an old soldier.[34] The drafts of *The Anathemata* date from this period. The collections of letters to Tom Burns and Harman Grisewood, as well as the *Wedding Poems* that Thomas Dilworth has edited, invite further scholarly exploration.[35] It is perhaps the most fruitful period of Jones's poetic career, and it merits further study.

Jones's experiences with Eric Gill in the 1920s – first in the community of craftsmen at Ditchling Common in Sussex, then at Capel-y-ffin in Wales beginning in 1926, and eventually in the community of letter-cutters that gathered around Gill at Pigotts farmstead in Buckinghamshire between 1929 and 1933 – make up another collection of those 'things' of which the poet is made. Jones's relationship to these Catholic communities, their artistic and religious practices, and the thought of writers such as Jacques Maritain and Maurice de la Taille, to whom he was exposed at this time, is multifaceted and shows him exploring his core question, 'What is the meaning of this?' Some of the research on Ditchling and Capel-y-ffin, especially by scholars who focus on Jones's visual art, has opened questions about the man and his intimate relationships that continue to invite further critical evaluation. Paul Hills pursues this question in his now-classic essay on Jones's representations of the Crucifixion, provocatively entitled 'The Pierced Hermaphrodite'.[36] Jonathan Miles interrogates Jones and Gill's relationship at Capel-y-ffin in his biographical study, raising

[32] Jones, *The Anathemata*, 11.

[33] Adam Schwartz, *The Third Spring: G. K. Chesterton, Graham Greene, Christopher Dawson, and David Jones* (Washington, DC: Catholic University of America Press, 2005). See also Martin Potter, *British and Catholic? National and Religious Identity in the Work of David Jones, Evelyn Waugh and Muriel Spark* (Oxford: Peter Lang, 2013).

[34] See Jones, *Dai Greatcoat*, 90–131, and Alldritt, *David Jones: Writer and Artist*, 121–34.

[35] David Jones, *Wedding Poems*, ed. Thomas Dilworth (London: Enitharmon, 2002). The largest collection of the Grisewood letters is in the Beinecke Library at Yale University, while the letters to Tom Burns are at the National Library of Wales, Aberystwyth.

[36] Paul Hills, '"The Pierced Hermaphrodite": David Jones' Imagery of the Crucifixion', in Matthias, *David Jones: Man and Poet*, 425–40.

probing questions about Jones's personal relationships, psychological and emotional state, and sexuality.[37] Miles continues this approach with Derek Shiel in their major study of Jones's art, aptly titled *David Jones: The Maker Unmade*.[38] Miles and Shiel focus on connections between the artwork and events in David Jones's historical and emotional life, relying largely on a psychoanalytic framework which does not always do justice to the complex relationships among personal history, theology, and historical-cultural exploration that shape Jones's work.[39] The work of Anne Price-Owen,[40] Paul Hills, and Ariane Banks[41] exemplifies the variety and depth of questions that can be brought to the complex role of the feminine principle in Jones's artworks. Thomas Dilworth attends to the importance of sex and 'coupling' as motifs in Jones's work, and my own work on Jones has focused on the role of the feminine in his writings.[42]

Jones's treatment of feminine figures raises important interpretive and contextual questions. How does his mythic notion of the feminine shape his understandings of culture and art? What is the importance to his life and work of his intense friendships with several women over his lifetime, including Lady Prudence Pelham, Valerie Wynne-Williams, and others? This remains important territory to be explored through scholarly editing and commentary on Jones's unpublished letters as well as further biographical work.[43]

Wider critical contexts: Jones, the War, Catholicism, and Wales

The study of Jones's work has been moving gradually out of the realm of specialists and into wider cultural conversations in several important contexts, notably the distinctiveness of his voice among the war poets, as challenged and critiqued by Paul Fussell, and his connection with Catholic conservative politics in the period between the wars, first described in Elizabeth Ward's controversial account and examined in depth in the present volume. We are also beginning to see broader appreciations of Jones's importance as a voice for Welsh culture and indeed for indigenous cultures anywhere that are challenged by imperialism and by modernity's break with the past.

Paul Fussell's *The Great War and Modern Memory* placed Jones's work into dialogue with the work of other important poets of the Great War. Critics are in wide agreement now in refuting Fussell's contention that Jones's work expresses a nostalgic, romanticized view of war, but it could be argued that his critique occasioned readings of *In Parenthesis*

---

[37] Jonathan Miles, *Eric Gill and David Jones at Capel-y-ffin* (Bridgend: Seren, 1992).

[38] Jonathan Miles and Derek Shiel, *David Jones: The Maker Unmade* (Bridgend: Seren, 1995 (repr. 2003)).

[39] See Muriel Whitaker's review of *David Jones: The Maker Unmade*, in *The Chesterton Review* 23, nos 1–2 (February and May 1997): 223–6.

[40] Anne Price-Owen, 'Feminist Principles in David Jones's Art', in Belinda Humfrey and Anne Price-Owen (eds), *David Jones: Diversity in Unity* (Cardiff: University of Wales Press, 2000), 91–106.

[41] See Ariane Banks and Paul Hills, *David Jones: Vision and Memory* (Farnham: Lund Humphries, 2015), 123–33.

[42] See Dilworth, *The Shape of Meaning*, 206–56; Staudt, *At the Turn of a Civilization*, 85–182.

[43] On Jones and women, see also the films directed by Derek Shiel, especially *David Jones Between the Wars: The Years of Achievement*, 2013, available online: http://www.dailymotion.com/video/x13fk5l_david-jones-between-the-wars-the-years-of-achievement_creation (accessed 17 November 2017), and *David Jones: Innovation and Consolidation* (2014). See the website of the David Jones Society, http://www.david-jones-society.org/research-resources.html (accessed 17 November 2017), for further information. See also Dilworth, *David Jones: Engraver, Soldier, Painter, Poet*, 100–4, 175–7.

that reflect the complexity of Jones's view of the threat to our humanity caused by the 'break' between the wars of the past and the mechanized and impersonal civilization in which we now live.[44] Notable among recent appreciations of Jones's war experience for contemporary readers is poet Tom Sleigh's essay 'To Be Incarnational', which reassesses *In Parenthesis* as distinct from other war poets including Wilfred Owen, and in relationship to other civilizational traumas of the last century.[45]

In the early generations of Jones scholarship there was some reluctance to engage in analysis of Jones's relationship to his fellow Catholics and particularly to right-leaning and proto-fascist ideas among Catholics between the wars. Elizabeth Ward's early study of Jones fleshed out this relationship and provided some useful historical and cultural context for the development of Jones's political and cultural ideas.[46] But her analysis is marred by an insistence on finding fascist political ideas in the poetry and questioning the value of Jones's work as a whole as a result.[47] Especially at the time that Ward's book appeared (1983), when Blissett's and Hague's admiring memoirs and letter collections were just being assimilated, and Jones scholarship was invested in making Jones more accessible and available to a wider public, Ward's work found a mostly hostile audience among Jones scholars, and was roundly refuted by Thomas Dilworth and in my own study of David Jones.[48] More recent work has offered a more consequential and reasoned exploration of Jones's political views between the wars, and the publication of Jones's 1939 essay on Hitler in this volume with Tom Villis's commentary, together with Oliver Bevington's edition of and commentary on Jones's 1938 letter to Chamberlain, testify to this. The groundwork for this discussion has been laid by Villis himself in his study of British Catholics and fascism, as well as by Adam Schwartz's historical study of what he calls 'The Third Spring'. Schwartz studies the lively exchange of ideas and the attractiveness of a deeply conservative ideology to Catholics who were converted between the wars, notably Chesterton, Dawson, and Jones. He stresses the appeal of Catholicism as a way to stand in opposition to modern culture, and for him Jones's insistence, drawn from Maritain, on the 'gratuitous' practice of the arts, in opposition to the 'utile' values dominating liberal industrial culture, typifies the dualism that makes Catholicism attractive to this group. For them, Catholicism represented a connection to European culture, an assertion of value against the growing agnosticism of English democratic culture, and a preserver of those aspects of traditional culture that they experienced as humanizing and moral.[49] Jones participated in what Ward labels the 'Chelsea group' of Catholic intellectuals that gathered frequently at the home of Tom Burns for conversation about literature and culture. For them, Mussolini's and Hitler's appeals to folk tradition, religion, and land in

---

[44] William Blissett, review of Fussell, *The Great War and Modern Memory*, *University of Toronto Quarterly* 45, no. 3 (Spring 1976): 268–74. See also Staudt, *At the Turn of a Civilization*, 18–20.

[45] Tom Sleigh, 'To Be Incarnational', *Poetry Magazine* 203, no. 2 (November 2013): 187–206; available online: http://www.poetryfoundation.org/poetrymagazine/articles/detail/70066 (accessed 17 November 2017). For another thoughtful exploration of Jones's poetics in relationship to *In Parenthesis*, modernism, and modernity, see Jack Dudley, 'Transcendence and the End of Modernist Aesthetics: David Jones's *In Parenthesis*', *Renascence* 65, no. 2 (Winter 2013): 103–24.

[46] Elizabeth Ward, *David Jones, Mythmaker* (Manchester: University of Manchester Press, 1983). See also Tom Villis, *British Catholics and Fascism: Religious Identity and Political Extremism Between the Wars* (Basingstoke: Palgrave Macmillan, 2013), 175–9.

[47] See Schwartz, *The Third Spring*, 289, n. 18.

[48] Dilworth, 'David Jones and Fascism'. See also Staudt, *At the Turn of a Civilization*, 20–6.

[49] Villis, *British Catholics and Fascism*, 105, and Schwartz, *The Third Spring*, 1–29.

opposition to atheistic communism had the appeal of what Roger Griffin has termed 'the sense of a beginning' that fascism in its early stages seemed to offer to a continent weary and broken by war and economic stagnation.[50] This area of discussion is thoroughly pursued in the introductions to the Hitler essay and the Chamberlain letter in this book.

Less fully explored is the effect of one of Jones's journeys abroad after his war service, namely his trip to British-occupied Palestine in the 1930s, prescribed as a remedy for his 'neurasthenia'. He writes in some of the published letters of his sense of affinity with the British soldiers stationed there, and further exploration and editing of the manuscripts of *The Fatigue* and other Roman poems centring on the Crucifixion, promise fuller insights into the connections between Jones's ambivalence toward empire and his recurring focus on the Passion of Jesus as a key to the question 'What is the meaning of this'?[51]

Dai Greatcoat's question, coming as it does at the centre of *In Parenthesis* and in the voice of the bard who has experienced generations of European warfare, also engages a key context for Jones: the embeddedness of his work in history. Paul Robichaud's 2007 study, *Making the Past Present: David Jones, the Middle Ages, and Modernism*, charts a fruitful direction that scholars have taken with the questions central to Jones's work, recognizing his core understanding of the poet as bridge-builder in a time when traditional understandings of the relationship between poetry and history are unravelling and modernism's sense of a 'Break' with the past calls for exploration and problematization.[52]

Conversations and dialogues

Jones compares his writing to 'a longish conversation between two friends, where one thing leads to another; but should a third party hear fragments of it, he might not know how the talk had passed from the cultivation of cabbage to Melchizedek, king of Salem'.[53] A number of critics have noted the labyrinthine and rambling form of his work which nonetheless draws the reader into explorations that reach toward meaning, engaging the Grail hero's neglected question 'Why, What is the meaning of this?'[54] What Thomas Dilworth has called the 'shape of meaning' in Jones's work often takes the form of associations, cross-references, and intersecting conversations. This is illustrated quite strikingly in Jones's 1943 drawing 'Map of Themes in the Artist's Mind', which visually traces the complex mythic and cultural associations that are the foundation of Jones's work both as artist and poet.[55] Given this dimension of the poet's mind and process,

---

[50] Roger Griffin, *Modernism and Fascism: The Sense of a Beginning Under Mussolini and Hitler* (Basingstoke and New York: Palgrave Macmillan, 2007).

[51] See Jones, *Dai Greatcoat*, 55–8, and Alldritt, *David Jones: Writer and Artist*, 87–90. See also Thomas Goldpaugh, 'David Jones and the Cost of Empire', *Flashpoint* 13 (Summer 2010).

[52] Paul Robichaud, *Making the Past Present: David Jones, the Middle Ages, and Modernism* (Washington, DC: Catholic University of America Press, 2007). For a more recent development of this historical exploration, see Jasmine Hunter Evans, 'Bridging the Breaks: David Jones and the Continuity of Culture', *Flashpoint* 18 (Summer 2016).

[53] Jones, *The Anathemata*, 33.

[54] See especially Dilworth, *The Shape of Meaning*, 152–8; Goldpaugh, 'To Make a Shape in Words', 232–52; Kathleen Henderson Staudt, 'Opening Out and Gathering In: The Three-Dimensional Form of *The Anathemata*', *David Jones Journal* 1 (1997): 41–9.

[55] See Merlin James, *David Jones 1895–1974: A Map of the Artist's Mind* (London: Lund Humphries, 1995). The drawing is included as frontispiece to *The Roman Quarry*. It can also be viewed online at http://www.david-jones-society.org/research-resources.html (accessed 17 November 2017).

I believe it is significant that some of the most stimulating observations concerning David Jones's work have appeared in volumes of essays centred on a broadly defined topic of conversation. The earliest of these, John Matthias's contribution to the National Poetry Foundation's 'Man and Poet' series, is still a classic point of reference for contexts and conversations.[56] Two volumes coming out of the celebration of Jones's 100th birthday anniversary in 1995 reflect the state of conversation on Jones at that time. Paul Hills brought together literary critics and art historians from a 1995 conference at the University of Warwick for a volume focused on form, materiality, and theme in Jones's work.[57] Anne Price-Owen and Belinda Humfrey gathered the papers from a 1995 conference in Lampeter on the theme of 'Diversity in Unity' to shape a conversation that deepens the reader's understanding of Welsh and Celtic themes and processes in Jones's work.[58] The David Jones Society, founded by David Blamires after the poet's death and waning by the mid-1990s, was revived following a conversation between Anne Price-Owen, Derek Shiel, and Tom Durham at the Lampeter conference. Price-Owen formally inaugurated the David Jones Society in London in 1996, with the poet-priest R. S. Thomas as its honorary president (succeeded in 1998 by William Blissett).[59] The David Jones Society sponsors biannual international conferences on Jones and publishes the *David Jones Journal* on an occasional basis and the *David Jones Society Newsletter* at seasonal intervals. The Society also sponsors one- and two-day events in the United Kingdom that bring together scholars and readers who are interested in Jones's work, and it has been responsible for carrying forward a lively conversation around Jones's poetry, art, and thought over the years.[60]

William Blissett has suggested that especially with a poet like Jones, the academic conference becomes a kind of pilgrimage, where the face-to face engagement and conversation between scholars becomes transformative.[61] Two editions of the online journal *Flashpoint* published in recent years take as their focus the conversations proposed by North American David Jones conferences. The 2010 edition, *Flashpoint* 13, includes essays that consider Jones as a Christian artist consciously in dialogue with a post-Christian culture. The pieces included in that issue are drawn from a 2009 conference on Jones on the theme 'A Christian Artist in a Post-Christian World', held at the Cathedral College of Washington National Cathedral, as well as other essays solicited on the occasion. A North American branch of the David Jones Society was quietly inaugurated at this conference, with myself as convener. The North American branch sponsored a second conference in 2012, which forms the basis of *Flashpoint* 18. This issue centres on an exhibition of Jones's prints and book illustrations organized by Bradford Haas, as well as papers that explore the relation between culture and artifice in Jones's work, placing

[56] See Matthias, *David Jones: Man and Poet*.

[57] Paul Hills (ed.), *David Jones: Artist and Poet* (Aldershot: Scolar Press, 1997).

[58] Belinda Humfrey and Anne Price-Owen (eds), *David Jones: Diversity in Unity* (Cardiff: University of Wales Press, 2000).

[59] Blissett might be seen as a founder of David Jones studies in the literary academy. His body of work has helped to define the thematic and biographical contexts for study of Jones's work for two generations. In an excerpt from a longer keynote address of 2012 he offers his own list of important questions remaining for David Jones scholars to pursue. See William Blissett, 'With David Jones after Seventy Years', *Flashpoint* 18 (Summer 2016), http://www.flashpointmag.com/Blissett70.pdf (accessed 17 November 2017).

[60] See the website of the David Jones Society: www.david-jones-society.org (accessed 17 November 2017).

[61] Blissett, 'With David Jones after Seventy Years'.

him in the context of modernist and postmodernist artistic and literary practice.[62] More recently, a 2014 conference took place at the University of Oxford to address the question 'David Jones: Christian Modernist?' Embedded within these conversations is what I call the 'Jones-and . . .' theme, the search for conversation partners for David Jones's work, within and beyond the modernist canon.[63]

David Jones's aesthetic theory brings together in his own particular way his early exposure to post-Impressionist theory at Camberwell Art School, his work as a poet who seeks to make 'a shape in words',[64] and his understanding of sacramental theology, which blossomed well before he was received into the Roman Catholic Church.[65] Post-Impressionist art theory undergirds what we might call Jones's 'both-and' approach to art and to history, where apparent opposites are often in dialogue with one another and dialectics are rarely resolved.[66] He tells us in 'Art and Sacrament' that the post-Impressionists taught that a work of art is at once a 'thing' and 'a representation of a thing', and he draws from that the axiom that 'all art is "abstract" and that all art "re-presents"'.[67] A fruitful conversation has been emerging, especially among Jones scholars who begin from his visual artwork, about the complex relationship between the material of Jones's artworks and its strongly referential 'literary' tendencies, especially in the later work. Paul Hills and Anne Price-Owen have been among the most eloquent students of the relationship between word and image in Jones's work, notably his painted inscriptions, which are quintessentially art made out of words, speaking through both their materiality and their referentiality, and often through the embeddedness of a text in a tradition. This awareness of the importance of inscriptions opens the way for readings of his poetic works that acknowledge at once the materiality of a Jones text, its tendency to foreground itself as 'thing', and its immersion in the 'sign-world' including myth and history, which a Jones text is always consciously exploring.[68] If students of Jones the artist help to demonstrate the radical character of his devotion to the materiality of the work, literary interpreters

---

[62] Bradford Haas, 'Culture and Artifice: The Major Book Illustrations of David Jones: A PDF catalogue', *Flashpoint* 18 (Summer 2016), available at www.flashpointmag.com/fp18_Culture_and_Artifice_Major_Book_Illustrations_of_David_Jones.htm (accessed 17 November 2017).

[63] See, for example, Jacques Darras, 'Sleep of the Tongue: Pound, Eliot, Jones and Europe', in Hills, *David Jones: Artist and Poet*, 122–31; Ivan Phillips, 'Penmen and Brushmen: The Remediation of Word and Image in the Work of Wyndham Lewis and David Jones', *Word & Image* 24, no. 1 (2008): 103–14; Steven Matthews, 'Provincialism and the Modern Diaspora: T. S. Eliot and David Jones', *English* 58, no. 220 (2009): 57–72; Calum Macfarlane, '"There is No Escape from Incarnation": Sacramental Particularity as an Antidote to Technocracy in David Jones and Gerard Manley Hopkins', *Flashpoint* 13 (2010), available at http://www.flashpointmag.com/joneshopkins.htm (accessed 17 November 2017); Kathleen Henderson Staudt, '"Acts of Ars" in David Jones's *The Anathemata* and W. H. Auden's *Horae Canonicae*', *Flashpoint* 18 (2016), available at http://www.flashpointmag.com/staudtars.pdf (accessed 17 November 2017).

[64] See the preface to *In Parenthesis*, x.

[65] See the Mabon Studios interview in this volume, p. 295 above: 'I was already Catholic in my heart, but I didn't formally become one until 1921, but I argued with students at Westminster Art School that this *thing* which the Post-Impressionists brought out in their manifestos (quite regardless of whether the work was good or bad) was *awfully* like the seemingly preposterous sayings the Church made as regard the bread and wine on the altar becoming identical with whatever happened in the manger or at the Last Supper.'

[66] See Peter Larkin, 'Tutelary Visitations', in Hills, *David Jones: Artist and Poet*, 141–7.

[67] David Jones, *Epoch and Artist* (London: Faber & Faber, 1959), 173.

[68] See Anne Price-Owen's important essay 'From Medieval Manuscripts to Postmodern Hypertexts in the Art of David Jones', in Rui Carvalho Homem and Maria de Fátima Lambert (eds), *Writing and Seeing* (New York and Amsterdam: Rodopi, 2006), 355–68; see also Ariane Bankes and Paul Hills, *David Jones: Vision and Memory* (Farnham: Lund Humphries, 2015), 151–65.

have sometimes offered illuminating readings of the visual art. Notable here are Thomas Dilworth's editions of Jones's engraved illustrations to *The Rime of the Ancient Mariner* and his insightful reading of Jones's woodcuts for *The Chester Play of the Deluge* in relation to the development of *The Anathemata*.[69]

When Jones writes in 'Art and Sacrament' that 'all art is "abstract" and that all art "re-presents"', he is invoking the theological concept of *anamnesis*, the belief that in the celebration of the Eucharist, there is a 're-calling' of the events of the Passion of Christ. His sacramental theology draws on the work of Jacques Maritain and Dom Gregory Dix and perhaps even more significantly on that of the Jesuit theologian Maurice de la Taille, whose view of the continuity of the Last Supper and the Passion as a single action provides a core formal principle in the structure of *The Anathemata*. Jones was also drawn to de la Taille's understanding of the Mystery of the Incarnation, in which, he writes, the incarnate God in becoming human 'placed himself in the order of signs'.[70]

It has become commonplace for Jones scholars to write of the 'sacramental' or 'incarnational' quality of Jones's writing, prompted by Jones's essay 'Art and Sacrament'.[71] Scholars writing in Catholic journals have probed the analogy between what Jones writes about sacrament and the orthodox teachings of the Church about the Mass, sometimes suggesting that a lack of understanding of Catholic doctrine is part of the reason for widespread neglect of Jones's work.[72] Jones scholars have noted the connections between Jones, Maritain, and de la Taille in ways that illuminate the themes and symbols of Jones's work, and they have studied how the sacramental analogy informs themes of unity and diversity in Jones's work and poetics. Jones's sacramental aesthetic has qualities that mark him as a theological autodidact, for whom the ideas of incarnation and sacrament were part of his effort to 'ask the question' about the place of 'man the artist' in his particular historical era. Theologian Paul Fiddes has shown how Jones's use of sacramental theology engages contextual issues important to both modernism and a postmodern or late-modern approach to art making.[73] Erik Tonning has proposed the term 'Christian Modernism' as a category that could help us make sense of Jones's affinities with and distinctiveness from modernism,[74] while Thomas Goldpaugh and I have both begun to

---

[69] David Jones, *The Rime of the Ancient Mariner*, ed. Thomas Dilworth (London: Enitharmon, 1997); Thomas Dilworth, 'From *The Deluge* to *The Anathemata*: Engraving towards Poetry,' in Hills, *David Jones: Artist and Poet*, 43–53.

[70] Dom Gregory Dix, *The Shape of the Liturgy* (London: A & C Black, 1945), 161–2; Maurice de la Taille, *The Mystery of Faith & Human Opinion, Contrasted & Defined*, trans. J. B. Schimpf (London: Sheed & Ward, 1934), 212.

[71] The beginnings of this conversation are well summarized in Tony Stoneburner's review essay 'So Primitive, So Civilized: The Eucharistic Vision of David Jones', *Anglican Theological Review* 55, no. 4 (October 1973): 484–91. Staudt, *At the Turn of a Civilization*, 39–50; Robert Ombres, OP, 'The Cult-Man Stands Precariously: David Jones and the Liturgy', *Chesterton Review* 23, nos 1–2 (February and May, 1997): 113–26; Sleigh, 'To Be Incarnational'; Stephen McInerny, 'David Jones's Blessed Rage for Order: The "Will Toward Shape"', *Logos* 14, no. 2 (Spring 2011): 59–81; Thomas Goldpaugh, 'The *Signum* of Some Otherness: David Jones and a Eucharistic Theory of Art,' *Flashpoint* 18 (2016), available at http://www.flashpointmag.com/goldpaughost.pdf (accessed 17 November 2017); Malcolm Guite, 'Imagination, Bodies and Locality: The Incarnational Thrust of David Jones' Art', *Flashpoint* 18 (Summer 2016), available at http://www.flashpointmag.com/guiteimag.pdf (accessed 17 November 2017).

[72] See, for example, Anthony Domestico, 'Words in Action: The Sacramental Poetry of David Jones', *Commonweal*, 11 January 2013, 12–16.

[73] Paul Fiddes, 'The Sacramental Modernism of David Jones and the World as Text', in Rebecca White (ed.), *David Jones: The Furrowed Line, Catalogue of an Exhibition* (Oxford: Fellowship of St Alban and St Sergius, 2014), 51–74.

[74] Erik Tonning, *Modernism and Christianity* (Basingstoke: Palgrave Macmillan, 2014).

suggest ways that Jones's debt to de la Taille reflects a poetics of resistance and openness that has more in common with what might be called a postmodern aesthetic, attending to what Jones seems to have experienced as the countercultural character of his poetics in a post-Christian culture.[75] Wider interdisciplinary engagement with theologians interested in theology and aesthetics begins to illuminate the originality of Jones's theological aesthetics. Rowan Williams's inclusion of Jones in his exploration of 'Grace and Necessity' in Maritain and Flannery O'Connor gives us a start on this, especially in his argument for 'Art and Sacrament' as 'one of the most important essays of the twentieth century on art and the sacred'.[76] Catholic theologians William F. Lynch, David Tracy, and Catherine Pickstock have been proposed in various contexts as conversation partners for Jones's work, illuminating the ways that his sacramental aesthetic refuses to embrace a totalizing ideology, despite its roots in dogmatic theology, but rather reflects a labyrinthine or 'analogical' approach to the relationship between the material of an artwork and its signification.[77] These readings suggest that further engagement with theology may illuminate the originality of the way that Jones chooses to pursue questions of meaning and artistic practice in an era that he already recognizes (though without using these terms) as postmodern and post-Christian.

Reading David Jones: The Experience

It may be significant that many who have written on Jones over the years are also poets, including Thomas Dilworth, Jeremy Hooker, John Matthias, Paul Robichaud, and myself. Certainly some of Jones's earliest admirers and promoters were prominent poets: T. S. Eliot and W. H. Auden, Saunders Lewis, Kathleen Raine, R. S. Thomas, Elizabeth Jennings, and Rowan Williams, to name a few.[78] Many of these poet-critics revel in 'readings' of David Jones, essays that walk us through the poetry and show what it is doing, thereby gradually deepening our understanding. Jeremy Hooker's early study of the writings remains one of my favourite examples of a poet's appreciative reading.[79] W. H. Auden's review of *The Anathemata* offers this kind of reading,[80] as does R. S. Thomas's 'Meditations on Some Lines in *The Anathemata*', published in the *Diversity in Unity* collection.[81] *The Anathemata*, in particular, seems to inspire this kind of reading and suggests ways in which Jones, especially in this work, is a 'poet's poet', drawing fascinated attention from people who know first-hand the challenges of making art out of words. The

[75] Goldpaugh, 'The *Signum* of Some Otherness'; Kathleen Henderson Staudt, '"The Sagging End and Chapter's Close": Revisiting a Long Conversation with Jones's Poetry', *Flashpoint* 13 (2010), available at http://www.flashpointmag.com/jonestaudt.htm (accessed 17 November 2017).

[76] Rowan Williams, *Grace and Necessity: Reflections on Art and Love* (London: Continuum, 2005), 88.

[77] See Stephen McInerny, 'David Jones's Blessed Rage for Order'.

[78] The first section of Matthias's *David Jones: Man and Poet* (41–85) includes appreciations by a number of poets, including T. S. Eliot, W. H. Auden, Stephen Spender, Kathleen Raine, Michael Alexander, Guy Davenport, R. S. Thomas, John Montague, and Anne Beresford. See also Kathleen Henderson Staudt, '"To Find the Song": John Matthias and the Legacy of David Jones', in Robert Archambeau (ed.), *Word Play Place: Essays on the Poetry of John Matthias*, 154–67 (Athens, OH: Swallow Press, 1998).

[79] Jeremy Hooker, *David Jones: An Exploratory Study of the Writings* (London: Enitharmon, 1975).

[80] W. H. Auden, 'A Contemporary Epic', *Encounter* 2, no. 2 (February 1954), 67–71. Reprinted in Matthias, *David Jones: Man and Poet*, 45–9.

[81] R. S. Thomas, 'Time's Disc Jockey: Meditations on Some Lines in *The Anathemata*', in Humfrey and Price-Owen, *David Jones: Diversity in Unity*, 153–9.

allusiveness of all of Jones's works is often cited as an obstacle to wider appreciation of his poetry.[82] This is addressed comprehensively in Dilworth's recent commentary on all the works, aptly entitled *Reading David Jones*.[83] Further annotation and commentary of this sort will only be enhanced by continuing scholarly work on editions of unpublished letters and manuscripts, to which the present book makes a contribution.

I have framed these various areas of study and scholarship as ways of 'pursuing the question' that Jones describes in two of the essays presented in this volume. The Grail hero of the *Peredur* story stands in the same relationship to his time and place as Jones's anti-Spenglerian 'intelligent person who knows he is living in a kind of hell'.[84] Dai Greatcoat, at the centre of *In Parenthesis*, frames the questions 'Why, / what is this, / what's the meaning of this'? in a context that points to the Waste Land that results from the failure to ask. In writings both published and unpublished, Jones insists on seeking meaning, 'making sense', combing through the beloved fragments of an elusive tradition for clues to his own place, culture, and vocation as poet and artist. He is aware of being embedded in a particular 'culture-phase', shaped by and loving the 'things' belonging to other culture-phases. Unlike others among his contemporaries, he seems always in the process of constructing, de-constructing and shaping his understanding of the world; he cannot be identified with any single ideology or political programme, but there is much to be learned by the questions he frames about the land, about authority, about gender and myth, and about what is lost and what might one day return. This insistence on 'asking the question', even when there is no clear answer, marks the distinctiveness of Jones's voice in his late-modern context and in our own time as well.

As he reveals in his essay on Hopkins, Jones was fascinated by the reception of that Victorian's poetry, written in an era that would not have understood it, not discovered by a wider public until after the Great War, and influential on the major modernists of that later time. Jones may be considered a late modern or an early postmodernist, or perhaps as an outlier with ties to various categories we could construct for him. The interrogative mode of his body of work amounts to a resistance to the toxic fusion of technology, wealth, and political and imperial power that he discerns in his time, over against the long heritage and claim of his indigenous Celtic heritage, his adopted religion, and the land itself, especially the land of Wales. For him this act of questioning is a prophetic act. Asking 'What shall I write?', he echoes the prophet Jeremiah in a poem he revised multiple times over the course of his lifetime.[85]

The questions raised by his work must be the questions raised by 'artists, lovers and all kinds of unifying makers'.[86] In 'The Sleeping Lord', one of the last poems he published in his lifetime, Jones appropriates the Celtic myths of Arthur sleeping under the land, who will return again. The poem is shaped by questions, as the poet contemplates the landscape and asks where that saving presence may be resting and waiting under the mountains of Wales, untouched by the scars of the industrial landscape.[87] It is perhaps apposite, then,

[82] See Elizabeth F. Judge, 'Notes on the Outside: David Jones, "Unshared Backgrounds", and (the Absence of) Canonicity', *ELH* 68, no. 1 (Spring 2001): 179–213.

[83] Thomas Dilworth, *Reading David Jones* (Cardiff: University of Wales Press, 2008).

[84] See n. 15 above.

[85] Published as 'A, a, a, Domine Deus', in Jones, *The Sleeping Lord and Other Fragments*, 9. This poem also appears in different versions in Jones, *Epoch and Artist*, 179, and Jones, *The Roman Quarry*, 209–11.

[86] Jones, *Dai Greatcoat*, 92.

[87] See Kathleen Henderson Staudt, 'What's Under Works Up: The Prophetic Modernism of David Jones', in Hills, *David Jones: Artist and Poet*, 158–71.

that the title poem of the last volume whose publication he lived to oversee ends on a question that has to do with present, past, and future, and implies the persistence of some kind of culture, even in the Waste Land:

> Does the land wait the sleeping lord
> or is the wasted land
> that very lord who sleeps?[88]

[88] Jones, *The Sleeping Lord and Other Fragments*, 96.

Appendix

David Jones: An Unpublished Appreciation of Gerard Manley Hopkins

KATHLEEN HENDERSON STAUDT

Reprinted, with permission, from *Agenda* 31, no. 3 (Autumn 1993): 172–80[1]

INTRODUCTION

In 1968, *The Month* published a special issue in honour of Gerard Manley Hopkins, commemorating the centenary of Hopkins's entrance into the Novitiate of the Society of Jesus. David Jones was invited to contribute to this issue, which also included appreciations by Elizabeth Jennings, Paul Mariani, Philip Hobsbaum, and others. Although no essay by Jones is included, manuscripts recently discovered at the Boston College Library (Chestnut Hill, Massachusetts) reveal that Jones did indeed attempt to write an essay in appreciation of Hopkins for this special issue of *The Month*, but abandoned the project.[2] The manuscripts of this fragmentary essay illuminate some of David Jones's own views on the nature of literary tradition and influence, as well as his appreciation of Hopkins's contribution. In particular, they suggest that Jones perceived an analogy between the fate of Hopkins's poetry – ignored in his own time but of fundamental importance to a later literary generation – and the fate that he may have desired for his own work. The same hope is implicit in the epigraph from *King Lear* that he uses for *The Anathemata*: 'This prophecie Merlin shall make, for I liue before his time.'

In the process of composing this essay, Jones appears to have been concerned with two main directions of inquiry: 1) the question of historical context and 'influence' – probably the most original and provocative part of this essay – and 2) Hopkins's significance as a

[1] Grateful acknowledgement is made to the Trustees of the David Jones Estate for permission to publish previously unpublished material, and to the editors of *Agenda* for permission to reprint this article.

[2] There is, curiously enough, a *translation* by David Jones, of a French poem, 'Le Coeur du temps', by Jean Mambrino, SJ. The same poem is also dedicated to Jones. See *The Month*, New Series, 40, nos 1–2 (July–August 1968): 45. This translation is his only contribution to the 'Homage to Hopkins' number of *The Month*. Fr Mambrino has confirmed, to Thomas Dilworth, that Jones did in fact translate this poem, with the aid of some fellow residents at Harrow-on-the-Hill. (My thanks to Thomas Dilworth for providing this information.) This contribution seems worth noting, if only as an aside, in view of Jones's repeated laments about his lack of command of any foreign language.

poet – using for illustration the story of *Peredur*, in which the hero must 'ask the question' which will refresh the 'Waste Land' of contemporary culture.[3] The drafts show Jones roughing out two different approaches to this problem. One set of very rough drafts reflects on Jones's own earliest encounters with Hopkins's work and the impression he and his contemporaries had, in the years following the Great War, that Hopkins was a 'contemporary'. A larger set of drafts explores the questions of 'influence' and tradition in the arts. In putting together the edition of these manuscripts which follows, I have sought to include both lines of argument, although Jones himself seems to have pursued them as separate thoughts.

The manuscript drafts reflect Jones's typical method of prose composition – which parallels his poetic technique. He begins with one idea and rewrites repeatedly, revising one word or phrase at a time and leaving the rest as is, so that there are many draft pages which are almost identical, with only minor additions or changes. For example, there are sixteen drafts of a page containing the clause 'Hopkins chanced to be one of those "makaris"' (or 'makers'), many of them also pursuing the allusion to the theme of 'asking the question' in the story of Peredur.

My objective in editing these manuscripts has been to compile the most complete version of each of these lines of argument, and to put them into a logical order. It is impossible to know whether the progression of ideas I give here would have been that intended by the poet, since he evidently got discouraged and gave up the project. A shopping list on the back of these drafts, dated 17 December 1968, suggests that they were lying about Jones's workspace well after the Hopkins special issue appeared. The catalogue of David Jones's personal library at the National Library of Wales shows that Jones did indeed receive and keep a copy of this special issue of *The Month*.

AN EDITION OF THE MANUSCRIPT ESSAY DRAFTED FOR *THE MONTH*, NEW SERIES, 40, NOS 1–2 (JULY–AUGUST 1968)

To contribute something in homage to Hopkins in this centenary year of his entry into the Novitiate of the Society of Jesus might appear a not only congenial but fairly simple task in that there is so much which the name 'Hopkins' has evoked for many of us over the half-century. But when it comes to actually making some such contribution, the task, at least for the present writer, is far from simple.

For one thing, so much has been written in appraisal of this remarkable man and his works: studies of every sort seeking to assess every aspect of the writings of this great

[3] Jones uses this same allusion to describe the poet's task in his essay 'Art in Relation to War', where he writes, 'Because the Land is Waste (or seems so to the writer) it [this essay] seeks to do what the hero in the myth was rebuked for not doing, i.e. it seeks to 'ask the Question'. Although, alas, unlike the myth, it does not suppose that in asking the question the land can be "restored". Although if all the world asked the question perhaps there might be some fructification – or some "sea-change".' See David Jones, *The Dying Gaul and Other Essays*, ed. Harman Grisewood (London: Faber & Faber, 1978), 123. For other uses of this motif in Jones's work, see David Jones, *In Parenthesis* (London: Faber & Faber, 1937), 84, and David Jones, *The Anathemata* (London: Faber & Faber, 1952), 226. Reflections on the important role of the Grail hero's question in Jones's work can be found in John Terpstra, '"Bedad He Revives! See Where He Raises!": An Introduction to David Jones's *The Sleeping Lord*', *University of Toronto Quarterly* 52, no. 1 (Fall 1982): 98–9, and Thomas Dilworth, *The Shape of Meaning in the Poetry of David Jones* (Toronto: University of Toronto Press, 1988), 225.

metrist and of their author. The range and depth of what has been written varies from the comprehensive and intensive two volume study by Dr W. H. Gardner, published in 1944 and 1949, back to innumerable articles and a number of books written in the nineteen-thirties and 'twenties and forward to books and articles written in the 'fifties and 'sixties, some making available additional material, some concentrating on a particular facet or aspect of this *poeta-sacerdos*.

So that to-day, exactly fifty years since the first appearance of *Poems by Gerard Manley Hopkins*, edited with notes by Robert Bridges, and seventy-nine years since the poet's death, Hopkins stands indisputably within the received canon of English poetry. He was by some literary critics and the general public regarded for some time as, at the most, deuterocanonical but gradually a proto canonical status has been allowed him. His poetry has become 'accepted', so much so that it is difficult to imagine any anthology of English verse that did not include at least one poem by G. M. Hopkins.

But with 'acceptance', there not infrequently comes a 'taking-for-granted', never a good thing either with regard to works or persons and to take Hopkins for granted would be most unfortunate: it would indeed make void and cancel out his ever having become accepted and made available.

I say this because the particular nature of his contribution (the poems, diaries, letters, etc.) is of that sort which prompts, goads, alerts. To borrow from a motif in the romance-tale of Peredur (Perceval) in which everything hangs on the asking of a question, Hopkins requires us to 'ask the question' or rather a complex of questions. Should we fail in this, no amount of appreciation of the beauty of this or that of his poems will suffice against the danger of our taking him for granted.

Hopkins chanced to be that sort of artist who crops up from time to time whose work is destined to condition in a special way the works of those who come after him. This, in itself, is no unfamiliar thing, such artists crop up from time to time in any medium you like to name. We all know, for example, that the painting of that essentially English artist, John Constable, who died in the year of Victoria's accession, was to have a delayed action effect on the French Impressionist movement of the late nineteenth century. But few men of this sort can have experienced more isolation and less recognition during their life days than Hopkins, to be recognized a few decades after their deaths as not only of singular genius but as harbingers whose work would have a special relevance for the poets, artists, makers, call them what you will, of those few decades later.

True this is but part of a general question, something of a mystery, rather. It is not all that easy to explain why some artist of the past (the medium is irrelevant) should, quite suddenly, be recognized as having special relevance for the artists of a later date. To take an example from the visual arts, why was it that El Greco, from being vaguely known as one among other Spanish painters to most English art students previous to the 1914–18 war, became of enormous interest and immediate relevance to us just after that war? The same might be said of a painter of totally different feeling Piero della Francesca – who also assumed a new importance to art students of the nineteen-twenties. One could no doubt cite examples of this sort of re-discovery in all the arts. Such interest or re-interest always means that the artist concerned, whether he lived four centuries or twenty centuries or a mere century or half a century back, happened to have in his work something which is especially relevant to and is foretypic of the problems felt by the artists of the later period (which can be brief or extensive) who immediately sense an affinity – a re-cognition in the exact sense of that word.

I take it as axiomatic that it is always something in the civilizational situation that causes the men of such and such a period to respond to and see the relevance of the works of some man from the past, whether it be of the far past or, as in the case of Hopkins, of the near past.

It is, however, far harder to put one's finger on precisely what it is in the civilizational phase that impells the artists of that particular phase to recognise as immediately relevant to them and their problems this or that work made by a man of a very differing set-up from theirs. This relevance of which I speak is not to be confused with appreciation of the beauty or admiration of the skill of such and such a past work. It is something different in kind from such admiration. It is a relevance in the sense of having an immediate bearing on problems facing the men practising this or that art at a given time, something adjuvant to them in their own work, something confirmatory no matter how other in form, content and intention their work may be or how totally different their civilizational milieu. It is something which, whether it comes to them from across many centuries, or over a few decades to them, says, in the word of Eliot's Tiresias figure: I have foresuffered all.

This is not quite the same thing as what is usually meant when either literary or art-critics speak of the work of Mr. X as being 'influenced' by the work of 'Y' 'Q' or [*crossed out*]. It is something more inevitable and beyond choice that is involved. Something more to do with situation than with personal predictions.

Nor do I mean a civilizational situation for nothing could be farther removed from the civilizational actualities and the religion-culture that gave us El Greco and the post-War I-English art world for which that artist had relevance, and a great gulf is fixed between the Victorian world of Hopkins and that world of 1918 when Bridges drew out one pin that released the fuse that detonated the highly charged contents of the Mark I Hopkins grenade.

Away back in the nineteen-twenties when I first became aware of Hopkins it was not infrequently complained that Bridges was much to blame for not getting published the Hopkins MSS long before 1918. Whether the publication of Hopkins poems was delayed until late in 1918 by various accidents, or whether Bridges judged the moment now opportune (he appears to have turned down the notion in 1909 when Father Keating, S.J., wished for their publication) or indeed for what reasons Bridges found 1918 an appropriate date – I mean whether convenient in various ways, or whether he truly sensed that this was 'the acceptable year' and that the literary climate to appreciate the very particular contribution his thirty-years-dead friend had made to the greater glory of English letters, I do not know. But deliberate or not, there are reasons for thinking that the date of Hopkins' highly charged *materiel* was auspicious.

That a Victorian Englishman (and *how* Victorian!) of Liddon's Oxford, received into the Church by Newman, a priest of the Society of Jesus who wrote poetry and who in notes, diaries, letters discoursed in great detail upon his theory of metrics, who observed cloud formations, trees, flowers, the behaviour of streams, the stratification of rocks, and whose sensitive drawings of these natural phenomena remind one of Ruskin, should have turned out to be of the greatest possible interest to the men who had either served in, or had come to manhood during, the 1914–18 war is hardly what one would suppose most likely. Yet such was in fact the case; so much so that any conversation of the nineteen-twenties or 'thirties which chanced to turn on a discussion of some living writers, St.-J. Perse, Joyce, Eliot, would, sooner or later, almost certainly involve Hopkins.

Indeed it required a conscious effort of some sort to remember that the work of Hopkins was made in Victoria's England and that he was born ten years before the Crimean War and was dead a decade before the earliest motorcar would 'unselve the sweet especial scene' whether where Binsey's poplars once were felled or in Beuno's wilder land.

For we discussed him as though his contribution was contemporary. I can't think, off hand, of any other artist of the past of whom this could be said in quite the same way.[4]

---

[4] The nature of these early conversations about Hopkins's contemporaneity is further illumined by the following 'false start'. Jones writes:

> I think my contribution to this collection of tributes can only take the form of an attempt to recall something of the impact of Hopkins in the nineteen-twenties among my friends and acquaintances and on myself.
>
> When Bridges published the first edition of Hopkins poems I was away in the army and wholly unaware of this important event. In 1919 I resumed my studies as an art student and as far as I can now remember, the name Hopkins did not crop up in conversation with my fellow art students – unless possibly on one occasion, in connection with the poetry of Walt Whitman. This would be sometime in 1920 or '21, when I was under instruction to be received into the Catholic Church. Since 1917 in the trenches of the West Front I had realized that I belonged to the Catholic tradition, so it was natural that I should find close fellowship with certain Catholics among my fellow students when I returned from the war.
>
> We were mainly concerned with the visual arts – with the complex problems of form and content, in e.g. the making of a drawing or painting. This does not mean that we were uninterested in other forms of *poeisis*, written or aural as in a 'poem' or a musical score, or in that supreme example where all forms of *poeisis* converge and the lifted *signa* are what is signified. Our interest was also in the written poetry of the man whose vocation as a priest involved him in a special sense with that *poeisis* which is made at the altar. There was also the interesting fact that this English Victorian priest of the Society was attracted to that principle of individuation as understood in the *haecceitas* of Scotus and that this permeated his work as a 'makar' in much the same way as the work of a later literary artist of immeasurable importance was permeated by Thomistic discipline – who in 1904 wrote of himself as being 'steeled in the school of old Aquinas'.

The same draft breaks off with a fragmentary allusion to Jones's argument in 1927 with a Welsh don who very rudely challenged the poet's suggestion that Hopkins's work must have been influenced by Welsh metrics. A letter to Aneirin Talfan Davies gives a fuller account of this incident, which Jones seemed to enjoy relating because subsequent scholarship about Hopkins revealed he was indeed deeply indebted to the Welsh metric tradition. See David Jones, *David Jones: Letters to a Friend*, ed. Aneirin Talfan Davies (Swansea: Triskele, 1980), 79. See also William F. Blissett, *The Long Conversation: A Memoir of David Jones* (Oxford: Oxford University Press, 1981), 59.

BIBLIOGRAPHY

ARCHIVAL MATERIAL

Chapter one

David Jones, 'Correspondence: Jones to Chamberlain, Neville' (18 December 1938), 'Correspondence IV: Sent/Rec'd by David Jones', Harman Grisewood Papers 1, box 3, folder 1, in the Booth Family Center for Special Collections, Lauinger Library, Georgetown University Libraries, Georgetown University, Washington, DC. Component unique identifier: 42201. Finding aid available online: http://findingaids.library.georgetown.edu/repositories/15/archival_objects/1169824.

Chapter two

David Jones, '"Hitler Essay", 20-page typescript intended for *The Tablet*', John J. Burns Library, Boston College, David Jones Papers, MS 86–1, series II, subseries 1, box 2, folder 5.

David Jones, '"Hitler Essay", second typescript', John J. Burns Library, Boston College, David Jones Papers, MS 86–1, series II, subseries 1, box 2, folder 6.

David Jones, 'The Pursuit of Peace', David Jones Manuscripts, Harman Grisewood Papers 1, box 5, folder 22, in the Booth Family Center for Special Collections, Lauinger Library, Georgetown University Libraries. Component unique identifier 42307. Finding aid available online: http://findingaids.library.georgetown.edu/repositories/15/archival_objects/1169933.

David Jones, 'Paper re Peace' (11 May 1939), Michael Richey Papers 1, Booth Family Center for Special Collections, Lauinger Library, Georgetown University Libraries, box 1, folder 43. Unique component identifier: 65734. Finding aid available online: http://findingaids.library.georgetown.edu/repositories/15/archival_objects/1192657.

Chapter three

David Jones, 'Gerard Manley Hopkins, essay on, manuscript draft', John J. Burns Library, Boston College, Chestnut Hill, MA, David Jones Papers, MS 86–1, series II, subseries 1, box 2, folder 7.

Chapter four

Ten ¼-inch sound tapes labelled 'David Jones', given to the David Jones Society, Swansea, Wales, in September 2014 by Mark Aeron-Thomas, son of Margaret Aeron-Thomas, founder of Mabon Studios, The Attic Gallery, 61–2 Wind Street, Swansea, Wales. These tapes will be deposited in the National Screen and Sound Archive of Wales in the National Library of Wales.

Other archives consulted

David Jones (Artist and Writer) Papers, National Library of Wales, Aberystwyth. Description available online: https://archives.library.wales/index.php/david-jones-artist-and-writer-papers–2.

David Jones Papers (MS Coll 00196), Thomas Fisher Rare Book Library, University of Toronto. Finding aid available online: http://search.library.utoronto.ca/details?5432288.

David Jones, Letters to Harman Grisewood, General Collection, Beinecke Rare Book and Manuscript Library, Yale University, New Haven, CT. Description available online: http://hdl.handle.net/10079/bibid/11056697.

Correspondence from and relating to David Jones, Papers of Harold Stanley 'Jim' Ede, Kettle's Yard Museum and Art Gallery, University of Cambridge. Description available online: https://archiveshub.jisc.ac.uk/data/gb1759-ky/ede/ky/ede/1/8.

Correspondence with David Jones, Jackson Knight Family Papers, Special Collections Archives (GB 0029), University of Exeter. Reference number EUL MS 75/1.

PUBLISHED MATERIAL

Alldritt, Keith. *David Jones: Writer and Artist.* London: Constable, 2003.

Andrews, Charles. 'War Trauma and Religious Cityscape in David Jones's *In Parenthesis*', *Journal of the Midwest Modern Language Association* 40, no. 1 (Spring 2007): 87–96.

Aspden, Kester. *Fortress Church: The English Roman Catholic Bishops and Politics, 1903–63*. Leominster: Gracewing, 2003.

Auden, W. H. 'A Contemporary Epic', *Encounter* 2, no. 2 (February 1954): 67–71; repr. in John Matthias (ed.), *David Jones: Man and Poet*, 45–9.

Auden, W. H. and John Garrett. *The Poet's Tongue*. London: George Bell & Sons, 1935.

Aylen, Leo. *Steel Be My Sister*. Film. HTV, 1975.

Bankes, Ariane and Paul Hills. *David Jones: Vision and Memory*. Farnham: Lund Humphries, 2015.

Barnes, James J. and Patience P. Barnes. *Hitler's* Mein Kampf *in Britain and America: A Publishing History, 1930–39*. Cambridge: Cambridge University Press, 1980.

Barth, Karl. 'The Need and Promise of Christian Preaching'. In Karl Barth, *The Word of God and the Word of Man*, trans. with new foreword by Douglas Horton, 97–135. New York: Harper & Row, 1957.

Bell, Julian. 'Moon Behind Clouds: The Wounded Vision of David Jones', *Times Literary Supplement*, 5 April 1996, 9–10.

Belloc, Hilaire. *A History of England.* 4 vols. London: Methuen, 1925–31.

Belloc, Hilaire. 'Moscow or Berlin', *G. K.'s Weekly*, 14 January 1937, 367.

Benda, Julien. *La Trahison des Clercs*. Paris: Bernard Grasset, 1927.

Benda, Julien. *The Great Betrayal*, trans. Richard Aldington. London: Routledge, 1928.

Benda, Julien. *The Treason of the Intellectuals*, trans. Richard Aldington. New York: William Morrow, 1928.

Benjamin, Walter. 'The Storyteller', trans. Harry Zohn. In *Walter Benjamin: Selected Writings, Volume 3: 1935–1938*, ed. Howard Eiland and Michael W. Jennings, 143–66. Cambridge, MA, and London: The Belknap Press of Harvard University Press, 2002.

Bergonzi, Bernard. *The Roman Persuasion*. London: Weidenfeld & Nicolson, 1981.

Bertram, Anthony. 'The Altering Eye: The Bicentenary of William Blake', *The Tablet*, 23 November 1957, 457–8.

Binyon, Laurence. 'Gerard Manley Hopkins and His Influence', *University of Toronto Quarterly* 8, no. 3 (April 1939): 264–70.

Black, Kirsty. 'Representation and Re-Presentation in the Poetry of Wallace Stevens and David Jones'. In Gesche Ipsen, Timothy Matthews, and Dragon Obradović (eds), *Provocation and Negotiation: Essays in Comparative Criticism*, 105–20. Amsterdam and New York: Rodopi, 2013.

Blamires, David. *David Jones: Artist and Writer*. 2nd edition. Manchester: Manchester University Press, 1978.

Blissett, William. '*In Parenthesis* among the War Books', *University of Toronto Quarterly* 42, no. 3 (Spring 1973): 258–88.

Blissett, William. 'The Efficacious Word'. In Roland Mathias (ed.), *David Jones: Eight Essays on His Work as Writer and Artist*, 22–49. Llandysul: Gomer Press, 1976.

Blissett, William F. Review of Paul Fussell, *The Great War in Modern Memory*, *University of Toronto Quarterly* 45, no. 3 (Spring 1976): 268–74.

Blissett, William F. *The Long Conversation: A Memoir of David Jones*. London: Oxford University Press, 1981.

Blissett, William. 'To Make a Shape in Words', *Renascence* 38, no. 2 (Winter 1986): 67–81.

Blissett, William. 'The Syntax of Violence'. In John Matthias (ed.), *David Jones: Man and Poet*, 193–208. Orono, ME: National Poetry Foundation, University of Maine, 1989.

Blissett, William. 'With David Jones after Seventy Years', *Flashpoint* 18 (Summer 2016). Available online: http://www.flashpointmag.com/Blissett70.pdf (accessed 17 November 2017).

Borgmann, Albert. 'Technology'. In *A Companion to Heidegger*, ed. Hubert L. Dreyfus and Mark A. Wrathall, 420–32. Oxford: Blackwell, 2005.

Bridges, Robert. *The Selected Letters of Robert Bridges, Volume 1*, ed. Donald E. Stanford. Newark: DE University of Delaware Press, 1983.

Brogan, Denis [unsigned]. 'On the Teaching of Mr Belloc', *Order: An Occasional Catholic Review* 1, no. 4 (November 1929): 120.

Bronson, Bertrand H. 'Samuel Hall's Family Tree', *California Folklore Quarterly* 1, no. 1 (January 1942): 47–64.

Browne, Clare, Glyn Davies, and M. A. Michael, eds. *English Medieval Embroidery: Opus Anglicanum*. New Haven, CT, and London: Yale University Press, 2016.

Browning, Robert. *Robert Browning: Selected Poems*, ed. John Woolford, Daniel Karlin, and Joseph Phelan. London and New York: Routledge, 2013.

Burns, Jimmy. *Papa Spy: Love, Faith, and Betrayal in Wartime Spain*. London: Bloomsbury, 2009.

Burns, Tom. *The Use of Memory: Publishing and Further Pursuits*. London: Sheed & Ward, 1993.

Buxton, Charles Roden. Letter to *The Times* (London), *The Times*, 10 May 1939, 17.

Callison, Jamie. '"The Heart of Time" Revisited: A New Translation by David Jones', *PN Review* 42, no. 2 (November–December 2015): 11–14.

Carvalho Homem, Rui Manuel Gomes, and Maria de Fátima Lambert, eds. *Writing and Seeing: Essays on Word and Image*. Amsterdam and New York: Rodopi, 2006.

Catholic Herald. 'Germany and Europe', 5 February 1937, 8.

Catholic Herald. 'Catholics–BUF: Mosley Discusses their Relations', 21 July 1939, 1.

Catholic Herald. 'Hitler's Responsibility', 8 September 1939, 6.

Chamberlain, Neville. 'Speech by the Prime Minister at Birmingham on March 17, 1939', *The Avalon Project: The British War Bluebook*. Available online: http://avalon.law.yale.edu/wwii/blbk09.asp (accessed 6 June 2017).

Chesterton, G. K. *The Resurrection of Rome*. London: Hodder & Stoughton, 1930.

Churchill, Winston. *Great Contemporaries*. London: Butterworth, 1937.

Clark, Kenneth. *Rembrandt and the Italian Renaissance*. London: John Murray, 1966.

Clark, Kenneth. 'Some Recent Paintings of David Jones', *Agenda* 5, nos 1–3 (Spring–Summer 1967): 97–100.

Cleverdon, Douglas. 'David Jones and Broadcasting', *Poetry Wales* 8, no. 3 (Winter 1972): 72–81.

Cleverdon, Douglas, ed. *Word and Image IV: David Jones*. London: National Book League, 1972.

Collini, Stefan. *Absent Minds: Intellectuals in Britain*. Oxford: Oxford University Press, 2006.

Corcoran, Neil. *The Song of Deeds: A Study of* The Anathemata *of David Jones*. Cardiff: University of Wales Press, 1982.

Corcoran, Neil. 'Spilled Bitterness: *In Parenthesis* in History'. In John Matthias (ed.), *David Jones: Man and Poet*, 209–25. Orono, ME: National Poetry Foundation, University of Maine, 1989.

Darras, Jacques. 'Sleep of the Tongue: Pound, Eliot, Jones and Europe'. In Paul Hills, (ed.), *David Jones: Artist and Poet*, 122–31. Aldershot: Scolar Press, 1997.

Davie, Donald. 'A Grandeur of Insularity', *Times Literary Supplement*, 22 August 1980, 935.

Davies, John. *A History of Wales*. London: Penguin, 2007.

Davies, John, Menna Baines, Nigel Jenkins, and Peredur Lynch, eds. *The Welsh Academy Encyclopaedia of Wales*. Cardiff: Welsh Academy, 2008.

Davis, Alex and Lee M. Jenkins. *Locations of Literary Modernism: Region and Nation in British and American Modernist Poetry*. Cambridge: Cambridge University Press, 2000.

Dawson, Christopher. *The Age of the Gods: A Study in the Origins of Culture in Prehistoric Europe and the Ancient East*. London: John Murray, 1928.

Dawson, Christopher. *Progress and Religion: An Historical Enquiry*. London: Sheed & Ward, 1929.

Dawson, Christopher. 'If the Dictators Seek War, Then We Must Seek Peace', *Catholic Herald*, 7 October 1938, 9.

Dawson, Christopher. *Religion and the Modern State*. London: Sheed & Ward, 1938.

Dawson, Christopher. *Beyond Politics*. London: Sheed & Ward, 1939.

Dawson, Christopher. 'Tradition and Inheritance: I. Wales and Wessex', *The Wind and the Rain* 5, no. 4 (Spring 1949): 210–17.

Dawson, Christopher. *The Dynamics of World History*. London: Sheed & Ward, 1956.

Dilworth, Thomas. 'David Jones and Gerard Manley Hopkins'. In Richard F. Giles (ed.), *Hopkins Among the Poets: Studies in Modern Responses to Gerard Manley Hopkins*, 53–37. Hamilton, Ontario: International Hopkins Association, 1985.

Dilworth, Thomas. 'David Jones and Fascism', *Journal of Modern Literature* 13, no. 1 (March 1986): 149–62. Revised and expanded for publication in John Matthias (ed.), *David Jones: Man and Poet*, 143–59.

Dilworth, Thomas. *The Shape of Meaning in the Poetry of David Jones*. Toronto: University of Toronto Press, 1988.

Dilworth, Thomas. 'From *The Deluge* to *The Anathemata*: Engraving towards Poetry'. In Paul Hills (ed.), *David Jones: Artist and Poet*, 43–53. Aldershot: Scolar Press, 1997.

Dilworth, Thomas. 'Antithesis of Place in the Poetry and Life of David Jones'. In Alex Davis and Lee M. Jenkins (eds), *Locations of Literary Modernism: Region and Nation in British and American Modernist Poetry*, 66–88. Cambridge: Cambridge University Press, 2000.

Dilworth, Thomas. 'Letters from David Jones to Kenneth Clark', *Burlington Magazine* 142, no. 1165 (April 2000): 215–25.

Dilworth, Thomas. *Reading David Jones*. Cardiff: University of Wales Press, 2008.
Dilworth, Thomas. *David Jones in the Great* War. London: Enitharmon, 2012.
Dilworth, Thomas. *David Jones: Engraver, Soldier, Painter, Poet*. London: Jonathan Cape, 2017.
Dilworth, Tom. 'William Cookson, David Jones, and *Agenda*', *Agenda* 48, nos 3–4 (11 November 2014): 9–12.
Dix, Dom Gregory. *The Shape of the Liturgy*. London: A & C Black, 1945.
Domestico, Anthony. 'Words in Action: The Sacramental Poetry of David Jones', *Commonweal*, 11 January 2013, 12–16.
Dudley, Jack. 'Transcendence and the End of Modernist Aesthetics: David Jones's *In Parenthesis*', *Renascence* 65, no. 2 (Winter 2013): 103–24.
Dugdale, E. T. S. 'National Socialism in Germany', *English Review*, October 1931, 569.
Dunne, Tom. *Gerard Manley Hopkins: A Comprehensive Bibliography*. London: Oxford University Press at the Clarendon Press, 1976.
Ede, H. S. (Jim). *David Jones: A Memorial Exhibition*. Cambridge: Kettle's Yard, 1975.
Edwards, Alun. 'Interview with Colin Hughes', *Oxford University First World War Poetry Archive*, podcast, 18 February 2009. Available online: http://www.flashpointmag.com/jonesoxford.htm (accessed 17 November 2017).
Edwards, Owen M. *Wales*. London: T. Fisher Unwin, 1901.
Eiland, Howard and Michael W. Jennings, eds. *Walter Benjamin: Selected Writings, Volume 3: 1935–1938*. Cambridge, MA, and London: The Belknap Press of Harvard University Press: 2002.
Elam, Caroline. *Roger Fry and the Re-Evaluation of Piero Della Francesca*. New York: Frick Collection, 2004.
Eliot, T. S. 'Prose and Verse' (1921). In T. S. Eliot, *The Complete Prose of T. S. Eliot: The Critical Edition: The Perfect Critic, 1919–1926*, ed. Anthony Cuda and Ronald Schuchard, 324–32. Baltimore, MD, and London: Johns Hopkins University Press and Faber & Faber, 2014.
Eliot, T. S. *The Waste Land* (1922). In T. S. Eliot, *The Poems of T. S. Eliot: Volume 1: Collected and Uncollected Poems*, ed. Christopher Ricks and Jim McCue. Baltimore, MD, and London: Johns Hopkins University Press and Faber & Faber, 2015.
Ellmann, Richard. *James Joyce*. New and revised edition. London: Oxford University, 1982.
Erskine-Hill, Howard and Richard A. McCabe, eds. *Presenting Poetry: Composition, Publication, Reception*. Cambridge: Cambridge University Press, 1995.
Fiddes, Paul. 'The Sacramental Modernism of David Jones and the World as Text'. In Rebecca White (ed.), *David Jones: The Furrowed Line, Catalogue of an Exhibition*, 51–74. Oxford: Fellowship of St Alban and St Sergius, 2014).
Foster, OP, Kenelm. 'David Jones on Art and Religion', *Blackfriars* 4, no. 475 (October 1959): 421–5.
Frayn, Andrew. *Writing Disenchantment: British First World War Prose, 1914–30*. Manchester: Manchester University Press, 2014.
Fuchser, Larry William. *Neville Chamberlain and Appeasement*. New York: Norton, 1982.
Fussell, Paul. *The Great War and Modern Memory*. Oxford: Oxford University Press, 1975.
Gardner, W. H., *Gerard Manley Hopkins (1844–1889): A Study of Poetic Idiosyncrasy in Relation to Poetic Tradition*, Vol. 1 of 2. London: Martin Secker & Warburg, 1944.
Gerald of Wales. *The Historical Works of Giraldus Cambrensis*, ed. Thomas Wright. London: George Bell & Sons, 1905.
Giardelli, Arthur. 'Three Related Works by David Jones', *Poetry Wales* 8, no. 3 (Winter 1972): 60–71.

Giles, Richard F., ed. *Hopkins Among the Poets: Studies in Modern Responses to Gerard Manley Hopkins*. Hamilton, Ontario: International Hopkins Association, 1985.

Gittens, Anthony. 'Mussolini and Hitler', *The Tablet*, 29 September 1934, 409.

Gogarty, Oliver St. John. *As I Was Going Down Sackville Street*. London: Rich & Cowan, 1937.

Goldpaugh, Tom. 'On the Traverse of the Wall: The Lost Long Poem of David Jones', *Journal of Modern Literature* 19, no. 1 (Summer 1994): 31–53.

Goldpaugh, Tom. 'To Make a Shape in Words: The Labyrinthine Text of David Jones'. In Belinda Humfrey and Anne Price-Owen (eds), *David Jones: Diversity in Unity*, 132–52. Cardiff: University of Wales Press, 2000.

Goldpaugh, Thomas. 'David Jones and the Cost of Empire', *Flashpoint* 10 (Summer 2010). Available online: http://www.flashpointmag.com/goldjones.htm (accessed 17 November 2017).

Goldpaugh, Thomas. 'The *Signum* of Some Otherness: David Jones and a Eucharistic Theory of Art', *Flashpoint* 18 (Summer 2016). Available online: http://www.flashpointmag.com/goldpaughost.pdf (accessed 17 November 2017).

Goodman, Anthony. *The War of the Roses: Military Activity and English Society, 1452–97*. London: Routledge, 2002.

Graves, Robert. *But It Still Goes On*. New York: Jonathan Cape and H. Smith, 1931.

Gray, Nicolete. *The Painted Inscriptions of David Jones*. London: Gordon Fraser, 1981.

Gray, Nicolete, ed. *The Helen Sutherland Collection: A Pioneer Collection of the 1930s*. London: Lund Humphries, 1970.

Gregory, Barry. *A History of The Artists Rifles 1859–1947*. Barnsley: Pen & Sword, 2006.

Gregory, J. D. 'Germany', *English Review*, May 1934, 621–5.

Griffin, Roger. *Modernism and Fascism: The Sense of a Beginning Under Mussolini and Hitler*. Basingstoke and New York: Palgrave Macmillan, 2007.

Griffith, Llewelyn Wyn. *The Welsh*. Harmondsworth: Penguin, 1950.

Grisewood, Harman. *One Thing at a Time: An Autobiography*. London: Hutchinson, 1968.

Grossman, Allen. *The Sighted Singer: Two Works on Poetry for Readers and Writers*. Baltimore, MD: Johns Hopkins University Press, 1992.

Guite, Malcolm. 'Imagination, Bodies and Locality: The Incarnational Thrust of David Jones' Art', *Flashpoint* 18 (Summer 2016). Available online: http://www.flashpointmag.com/guiteimag.pdf (accessed 17 November 2017).

Haas, Bradford. 'Culture and Artifice: The Major Book Illustrations of David Jones: A PDF catalogue', *Flashpoint* 18 (Summer 2016). Available online: www.flashpointmag.com/fp18_Culture_and_Artifice_Major_Book_Illustrations_of_David_Jones.htm (accessed 17 November 2017).

Hartman, Charles O. *Free Verse: An Essay on Prosody*. Princeton, NJ: Princeton University Press, 1980.

Hartrick, A. S. *A Painter's Pilgrimage through Fifty Years*. Cambridge: Cambridge University Press, 1939.

Hayes, Kevin. Letter to *The Tablet*. *The Tablet*, 22 April 1939, 21–2.

Hebblethwaite, SJ, Peter. 'Letter from the Editor', *The Month*, New Series, 40, nos 1–2 (July–August 1968): 3–4.

Hegel, Georg Wilhelm Friedrich. *Aesthetics: Lectures on Fine Art: Volume 1*, trans. T. M. Knox. Oxford: Clarendon Press, 1975.

Heidegger, Martin. 'The Question Concerning Technology'. In Martin Heidegger, *The Question Concerning Technology and Other Essays*, trans. and intro. William Lovitt, 3–35. New York and London: Garland, 1977.

Hills, Paul. 'The Romantic Tradition in David Jones', *Malahat Review* 27 (July 1973): 39–80.

Hills, Paul. '"The Pierced Hermaphrodite": David Jones' Imagery of the Crucifixion'. In John Matthias (ed.), *David Jones: Man and Poet*, 425–40. Orono, ME: National Poetry Foundation, University of Maine, 1989.

Hills, Paul, ed. *David Jones: Artist and Poet*. Aldershot: Scolar Press, 1997.

Hitler, Adolf. 'Extract from Herr Hitler's speech to the Reichstag on April 28, 1939', *The Avalon Project: The British War Bluebook*. Available online: http://avalon.law.yale.edu/wwii/blbk13.asp (accessed 6 June 2017).

Hoare, Lottie. *Philip Hagreen: A Sceptic and a Craftsman*. Winchester: Ritchie Press, 2009. Available online: https://www3.nd.edu/~jsherman/hagreen/Hagreen–13Dec2012.pdf (accessed 17 November 2017).

Hollahan, Eugene, ed., *Gerard Manley Hopkins and Critical Discourse*. New York: AMS Press, 1993.

Hollis, Christopher. *The Two Nations: A Financial Study of English History*. London: Routledge, 1935.

Hollis, Christopher. *Foreigners Aren't Knaves*. London: Longmans, 1939.

Holmes, Colin. *Anti-Semitism in British Society, 1876–1939*. London: Edward Arnold, 1979.

Hooker, Jeremy. 'Ends and New Beginnings', *Poetry Wales* 8, no. 3 (Winter 1972): 22–31.

Hooker, Jeremy. *David Jones: An Exploratory Study of the Writings*. London: Enitharmon, 1975.

Hopkins, Gerard Manley. *Poems of Gerard Manley Hopkins, now first published, Edited with notes by Robert Bridges, Poet Laureate*. London: Humphrey Milford, printed at the Oxford University Press, 1918.

Hopkins, Gerard Manley. *Poems of Gerard Manley Hopkins, second edition, edited with notes by Robert Bridges, with an index of additional poems, and a critical introduction by Charles Williams*. London: Humphrey Milford, Oxford University Press, 1930.

Hopkins, Gerard Manley. *Notebooks and Papers of Gerard Manley Hopkins*, ed. Humphry House. London and New York: Oxford University Press, 1937.

Hopkins, Gerard Manley. *Poems and Prose of Gerard Manley Hopkins*, selected, intro. and notes W. H. Gardner. Harmondsworth: Penguin, 1967.

Hopkins, Gerard Manley. *The Collected Works of Gerard Manley Hopkins, Volume II: Correspondence 1882–1889*, ed. R. K. R. Thornton and Catherine Phillips. London: Oxford University Press, 2013.

Hughes, Colin. *David Jones: The Man Who Was on the Field:* In Parenthesis *as Straight Reporting*. Manchester: David Jones Society, 1979; a pamphlet revised as 'David Jones: The Man Who Was on the Field: *In Parenthesis* as Straight Reporting'. In John Matthias (ed.), *David Jones Man and Poet*, 163–92. Orono, ME: National Poetry Foundation, University of Maine, 1989.

Hughes, Colin. *Mametz: Lloyd George's 'Welsh Army' at the Battle of the Somme*. Gerrards Cross: Orion Press, 1982.

Humfrey, Belinda and Anne Price-Owen, eds. *David Jones: Diversity in Unity: Studies of His Literary and Visual Art*. Cardiff: University of Wales Press, 2000.

Hunter Evans, Jasmine. 'Bridging the Breaks: David Jones and the Continuity of Culture', *Flashpoint* 18 (Summer 2016). Available online: http://www.flashpointmag.com/hunterevans.pdf (accessed 17 November 2017).

Hunter Evans, Jasmine, ed. 'You're Awfully Unorthodox, David', *New Welsh Review* 104 (25 May 2014): 24–31.

Hyne, Anthony. 'David Jones: A Man of Letters', *David Jones Journal* (1999): 6–17.

Ironside, Robin. *David Jones*. Harmondsworth: Penguin, 1949.

James, Merlin. *David Jones 1895–1974: A Map of the Artist's Mind*. London: Lund Humphries, 1995.

Jerrold, Douglas. *England*. Bristol: Arrowsmith, 1935.

Jerrold, Douglas. 'Stop Those War Mongers!', *Catholic Herald*, 7 October 1938, 2.

John of the Cross. *The Complete Works of Saint John of the Cross, Doctor of the Church, Volume 1*. London: Burns, Oates & Washbourne, 1934–5.

Johnston, John H. *English Poetry of the First World War: A Study in the Evolution of Lyric and Narrative Form*. Princeton, NJ: Princeton University Press, 1964.

Jones, Alun R. and Gwyn Thomas, eds. *Presenting Saunders Lewis*. 2nd edition. Cardiff: University of Wales Press, 1983.

Jones, David. *In Parenthesis*. London: Faber & Faber, 1937.

Jones, David. 'Poetry and Anarchy'. Review of Herbert Read, *Poetry and Anarchism* (London: Faber & Faber, 1938), *The Tablet*, 16 July 1938, 77.

Jones, David. 'The Myth of Arthur'. In Douglas Woodruff (ed.), *For Hilaire Belloc: Essays in Honour of His 71st Birthday*, 174–218. London: Sheed & Ward, 1942.

Jones, David. *The Anathemata: Fragments of an Attempted Writing*. London: Faber & Faber, 1952.

Jones, David. 'Art and Sacrament: An Enquiry Concerning the Arts of Man and the Christian Commitment to Sacrament in Relation to Contemporary Technocracy'. In Elizabeth Pakenham (ed.), *Catholic Approaches*, 143–82. London: Weidenfeld & Nicolson, 1955.

Jones, David. *Epoch and Artist: Selected Writings by David Jones*, ed. Harman Grisewood. London: Faber & Faber, 1959.

Jones, David. 'Interview with Peter Orr, 24 November 1964'. In Peter Orr (ed.), *The Poet Speaks: Interviews with Contemporary Poets Conducted by Hilary Morrish, Peter Orr, John Press and Ian Scott-Kilvert*, 97–104. London: Routledge & Kegan Paul, 1966.

Jones, David. 'Letter on "The Latin Mass"', *The Tablet*, 2 December 1967, 25.

Jones, David. 'A Letter from David Jones', *Poetry Wales* 8, no. 3 (Winter 1972): 5–9.

Jones, David. *The Sleeping Lord and Other Fragments*. London: Faber & Faber, 1974.

Jones, David. *Letters to Vernon Watkins*, ed. Ruth Pryor. Cardiff: University of Wales Press, 1976.

Jones, David. *The Dying Gaul and Other Writings*, ed. Harman Grisewood. London: Faber & Faber, 1978.

Jones, David. *Letters to William Hayward*, ed. Colin Wilcockson. London: Agenda Editions, 1979.

Jones, David. *Dai Greatcoat: A Self-portrait of David Jones in his Letters*, ed. René Hague. London: Faber & Faber, 1980.

Jones, David. *David Jones: Letters to a Friend*, ed. Aneirin Talfan Davies. Swansea: Triskele, 1980.

David Jones. 'Letters to H. S. Ede', selected and ed. John Matthias. *PN Review* 22, volume 8, no. 2 (November–December 1981): 10–16.

Jones, David. *The Narrows*, ed. and intro. Roland Mathias. Budleigh Salterton, Devon: Interim Press, 1981.

Jones, David. *The Roman Quarry and Other Sequences*, ed. Harman Grisewood and René Hague. New York: Sheep Meadow Press, 1981.

Jones, David. *Inner Necessities: The Letters of David Jones to Desmond Chute*, ed. Thomas Dilworth. Toronto: Anson-Cartwright Editions, 1984.

Jones, David. *The Rime of the Ancient Mariner*, ed. Thomas Dilworth. London: Enitharmon, 1997.

Jones, David. *Wedding Poems*, ed. Thomas Dilworth. London: Enitharmon, 2002.
Jones, David and Saunders Lewis. 'Two Letters Introduced by Saunders Lewis', *Agenda* 11, no. 4–12, no. 1 (Autumn–Winter 1973–4): 17–29.
Jones, David and Saunders Lewis. 'David Jones: Writer and Painter', *BBC Writers' World*. Interview of 15 March 1965. In Jasmine Hunter Evans, 'You're Awfully Unorthodox, David', *New Welsh Review* 104 (25 May 2014): 24–31.
Jones, Huw Ceiriog, ed. *The Library of David Jones (1895–1974): A Catalogue*. Aberystwyth: National Library of Wales, 1995.
Joyce, James. *Anna Livia Plurabelle: Fragments of Work in Progress*. London: Faber & Faber, 1930.
Joyce, James. *Finnegans Wake*. London: Faber & Faber, 1939.
Joyce, James. *Poems and Shorter Writings*, ed. Richard Ellmann, A. Walton Litz, and John Whittier-Ferguson. London: Faber & Faber, 2001.
Judge, Elizabeth F. 'Notes on the Outside: David Jones, "Unshared Backgrounds", and (the Absence of) Canonicity', *ELH* 68, no. 1 (Spring 2001): 179–213.
Keating, SJ, Joseph. 'Impressions of Father Gerard Hopkins, S.J. I.', *The Month* 114, no. 541 (July 1909): 59–68.
Korostovetz, Vladimir. Letter to *The Tablet*, *The Tablet*, 29 April 1939, 21–2.
Larkin, Peter. 'Tutelary Visitations', in Paul Hills (ed.), *David Jones: Artist and Poet*, 141–7. Aldershot: Scolar Press, 1997.
Levi, SJ, Peter. 'In Memory of a Maker: The text of a sermon delivered in Westminster Cathedral at the Solemn Requiem for the poet and painter, David Jones, on 13 December 1974', *The Tablet*, 4 January 1975, 6–7.
Lochner, Louis P. 'Adolf Hitler Now Dictator of Germany', *The Gazette* (Montreal), 24 March 1933, 1 and 3.
Lothian, James R. *The Making and Unmaking of the English Catholic Intellectual Community, 1910–1950*. Notre Dame, IN: University of Notre Dame Press, 2009.
Lubac, Henri de. *The Eternal Feminine: A Study on the Text of Teilhard de Chardin, followed by Teilhard and the Problems of Today*, trans. René Hague. London: Collins, 1971.
Lunn, Arnold. *Spanish Rehearsal*. London: Hutchinson, 1937.
Lunn, Arnold. 'Bellicose Pacifism Is Not New', *Catholic Herald*, 7 October 1938, 5.
The Mabinogion, trans. Lady Charlotte Guest. London: Dent, 1902.
The Mabinogion, trans. Lady Charlotte Guest. London: Dent, 1913.
MacCarthy, Fiona. *Eric Gill*. London: Faber & Faber, 1989.
Macfarlane, Calum. '"There is No Escape from Incarnation": Sacramental Particularity as an Antidote to Technocracy in David Jones and Gerard Manley Hopkins', *Flashpoint* 13 (Spring 2010). Available online: http://www.flashpointmag.com/joneshopkins.htm (accessed 17 November 2017).
MacKay, Marina. *Modernism and World War II*. Cambridge: Cambridge University Press, 2007.
MacKenzie, Norman H. *A Reader's Guide to Gerard Manley Hopkins*. 2nd edition. Philadelphia: Saint Joseph's University Press, 2008.
Mackenzie, W. Mackay. *The Poems of William Dunbar*. Edinburgh: Porpoise Press, 1932.
Malory, Thomas, *Le Morte d'Arthur*, ed. Ernest Rhys. London: Dent, 1933.
Mambrino, SJ, Jean. 'Le Coeur du Temps', trans. David Jones. *The Month*, New Series, 40, nos 1–2 (July–August 1968): 45.
Mathias, Roland, ed. *David Jones: Eight Essays on His Work as Writer and Artist*. Llandysul: Gomer Press, 1976.
Matthews, Steven. 'Provincialism and the Modern Diaspora: T. S. Eliot and David Jones', *English* 58, no. 220 (2009): 57–72.

Matthias, John, ed. *David Jones: Man and Poet*. Orono, ME: National Poetry Foundation, University of Maine, 1989.
McDonough, Frank. *Neville Chamberlain, Appeasement, and the British Road to War*. Manchester: Manchester University Press, 1998.
McInerny, Stephen. 'David Jones's Blessed Rage for Order: The "Will Toward Shape"', *Logos* 14, no. 2 (Spring 2011): 59–81.
Miles, Jonathan. *Backgrounds to David Jones: A Study in Sources and Drafts*. Cardiff: University of Wales Press, 1990.
Miles, Jonathan. *Eric Gill and David Jones at Capel-y-ffin*. Bridgend: Seren, 1992.
Miles, Jonathan and Derek Shiel. *David Jones: The Maker Unmade*. Bridgend: Seren, 1995 (repr. 2003).
The Month, New Series, 40, nos 1–2 (July–August 1968).
Nichols, OP, Aidan. *Dominican Gallery: Portrait of a Culture*. Leominster: Gracewing, 1997.
Noon, SJ, William T. *Joyce and Aquinas*. New Haven, CT, and London: Yale University Press, 1963.
Noon, SJ, William T. *Poetry and Prayer*. New Brunswick, NJ: Rutgers University Press, 1967.
Ombres, OP, Robert. 'The Cult-Man Stands Precariously: David Jones and the Liturgy', *Chesterton Review* 23, nos 1–2 (February and May, 1997): 113–26.
Orr, Peter. 'An Introductory Note by Peter Orr'. In David Jones, 'Fragments of an Autobiographical Writing', *Agenda* 15, no. 1 (1975): 96–108.
Orr, Peter. 'Mr. Jones, your legs are crossed: A Memoir', *Agenda* 15, nos 2–3 (1977): 110–25.
Orr, Peter, ed. 'David Jones'. In Peter Orr (ed.), *The Poet Speaks, interviews with contemporary poets conducted by Hilary Morrish, Peter Orr, John Press and Ian Scott Kilvert*, 97–104. London: Routledge & Kegan Paul, 1966.
Pagnoulle, Christine. *David Jones: A Commentary on Some Poetic Fragments*. Cardiff: University of Wales Press, 1987.
Pakenham, Elizabeth, ed. *Catholic Approaches*. London: Weidenfeld & Nicolson, 1955.
Payne, Ffransis George. *Guide to the Collection of Samplers and Embroideries*. Cardiff: National Museum of Wales and the Press Board of the University of Wales, 1939.
Pearce, Joseph. *Literary Converts: Spiritual Inspiration in an Age of Unbelief*. London: HarperCollins, 1999.
Phillips, Catherine L. 'Robert Bridges and the First Edition of Gerard Manley Hopkins's Poems'. In Eugene Hollahan (ed.), *Gerard Manley Hopkins and Critical Discourse*, 293–307. New York: AMS Press, 1993.
Phillips, Ivan. 'Penmen and Brushmen: The Remediation of Word and Image in the Work of Wyndham Lewis and David Jones', *Word & Image* 24, no. 1 (2008): 103–14.
Pick, John, ed. *A Hopkins Reader*. London: Oxford University Press, 1953.
Pick, John, ed. *A Hopkins Reader*. Revised and enlarged edition. Garden City, NY: Doubleday Image Books, 1966.
Poetry Wales 8, no. 3 (Winter 1972).
Poole, Adrian. 'The Disciplines of War, Memory, and Writing: Shakespeare's *Henry V* and David Jones's *In Parenthesis*', *Critical Survey* 22, no. 2 (2010): 91–104.
Potter, Martin. *British and Catholic? National and Religious Identity in the Work of David Jones, Evelyn Waugh and Muriel Spark*. Oxford: Peter Lang, 2013.
Price-Owen, Anne. 'Feminist Principles in David Jones's Art'. In Belinda Humfrey and Anne Price-Owen (eds), *David Jones: Diversity in Unity*, 91–106. Cardiff: University of Wales Press, 2000.

Price-Owen, Anne. 'From Medieval Manuscripts to Postmodern Hypertexts in the Art of David Jones'. In Rui Carvalho Homem and Maria de Fátima Lambert (eds), *Writing and Seeing*, 355–68. New York and Amsterdam: Rodopi, 2006.

Price-Owen, Anne. 'Materializing the Immaterial: David Jones: Painter-Poet', *Flashpoint* 13 (Spring 2010). Available online: http://www.flashpointmag.com/priceowen.htm (accessed 17 November 2017).

Pugh, Martin. *'Hurrah for the Blackshirts!' Fascists and Fascism in Britain Between the Wars*. London: Jonathan Cape, 2005.

Quiller-Couch, Arthur, ed. *The Oxford Book of English Verse, 1250–1900*. Oxford: The Clarendon Press, 1915.

Quiller-Couch, Arthur, ed. *The Oxford Book of English Verse, 1250–1900*. Oxford: Clarendon Press, 1930.

Raine, Kathleen. *David Jones: Solitary Perfectionist*. Ipswich: Golgonooza, 1974.

Rees, Samuel. *David Jones*. Boston: Twayne, 1978.

Rhys, John and David Brynmor-Jones. *The Welsh People: Chapters on Their Origin, History, Laws, Language, Literature, and Characteristics*. London: T. Fisher Unwin, 1900.

Robichaud, Paul. 'David Jones, Christopher Dawson, and the Meaning of History', *Logos: A Journal of Catholic Thought and Culture* 6, no. 3 (Summer 2003): 68–85.

Robichaud, Paul. *Making the Past Present: David Jones, the Middle Ages, and Modernism*. Washington, DC: Catholic University of America Press, 2007.

Roosevelt, Franklin D. Telegram to Adolf Hitler, 14 April 1939. *Franklin D. Roosevelt Day by Day: A Project of the Pare Lorentz Center at the FDR Presidential Library*. Available online: http://www.fdrlibrary.marist.edu/daybyday/resource/april–1939–7/ (accessed 6 June 2017).

Saunders, Anthony. *Weapons of the Trench War, 1914–1918*. Stroud: Sutton, 1999.

Schloesser, Stephen. *Jazz Age Catholicism: Mystic Modernism in Postwar Paris, 1919–1933*. Toronto: University of Toronto Press, 2005.

Schramm, Percy Ernst. 'Adolf Hitler: Anatomie eines Diktators', *Der Spiegel* 5 (29 January 1964): 40–61. Available online: http://www.spiegel.de/spiegel/print/d–46162899.html (accessed 22 January 2016).

Schramm, Percy Ernst. *Hitler: The Man and the Military Leader*, trans. Donald S. Detwiler. London: Allen Lane, 1972.

Schwartz, Adam. *The Third Spring: G. K. Chesterton, Graham Greene, Christopher Dawson, and David Jones*. Washington, DC: Catholic University of America Press, 2005.

Self, Robert. *Neville Chamberlain: A Biography*. Aldershot: Ashgate, 2006.

Sencourt, Robert. 'These Are the Facts', *Catholic Herald*, 7 October 1938, 7.

Sencourt, Robert. Letter to *The Tablet*, *The Tablet*, 22 April 1939, 20–1.

Sherry, Vincent B. 'David Jones's *In Parenthesis*: New Measure', *Twentieth Century Literature* 28, no. 4 (Winter 1982): 375–80.

Shiel, Derek, dir. *David Jones: Innovation and Consolidation*. Film. David Jones Society, 2014.

Shiel, Derek and Adam Alive, dirs. *David Jones Between the Wars: The Years of Achievement*. Film. David Jones Society, 2013. Available online: http://www.dailymotion.com/video/x13fk5l_david-jones-between-the-wars-the-years-of-achievement_creation (accessed 17 November 2017).

Sitwell, Edith. *The Atlantic Books of British and American Poetry*. 2 vols. London: Victor Gollancz, 1959.

Sleigh, Tom. 'To Be Incarnational', *Poetry Magazine* 203, no. 2 (November 2013): 187–206. Available online: http://www.poetryfoundation.org/poetrymagazine/articles/detail/70066 (accessed 17 November 2017).

Soud, W. David. *Divine Cartographies: God, History, and* Poiesis *in W. B. Yeats, David Jones, and T. S. Eliot*. New York and Oxford: Oxford University Press, 2016.

Spender, Stephen. 'A Jesuit Poet', *Tribune*, 17 November 1944, 15–16.

Spengler, Oswald. *The Decline of the West*, trans. Charles Francis Atkinson. London: George Allen & Unwin, 1926.

Staudt, Kathleen Henderson. 'David Jones: Eight Previously Unpublished Letters to Vernon Watkins', *Anglo-Welsh Review* 87 (1987): 76–90.

Staudt, Kathleen Henderson. 'The Decline of the West and the Optimism of the Saints: David Jones' Reading of Oswald Spengler'. In John Matthias (ed.), *David Jones: Man and Poet*, 443–63. Orono, ME: National Poetry Foundation, University of Maine, 1989.

Staudt, Kathleen Henderson. 'David Jones: An Unpublished Appreciation of Gerard Manley Hopkins', *Agenda* 31, no. 3 (Autumn 1993): 172–80.

Staudt, Kathleen Henderson. *At the Turn of a Civilization: David Jones and Modern Poetics*. Ann Arbor: University of Michigan Press, 1994.

Staudt, Kathleen Henderson. 'Opening Out and Gathering In: The Three-Dimensional Form of *The Anathemata*', *David Jones Journal* 1 (1997): 41–9.

Staudt, Kathleen Henderson. 'What's Under Works Up: The Prophetic Modernism of David Jones'. In Paul Hills (ed.), *David Jones: Artist and Poet*, 158–71. Aldershot: Scolar Press, 1997.

Staudt, Kathleen Henderson. '"To Find the Song": John Matthias and the Legacy of David Jones'. In Robert Archambeau (ed.), *Word Play Place: Essays on the Poetry of John Matthias*, 154–67. Athens, OH: Swallow Press, 1998.

Staudt, Kathleen Henderson. '"The Sagging End and Chapter's Close": Revisiting a Long Conversation with Jones's Poetry', *Flashpoint* 13 (2010). Available online: http://www.flashpointmag.com/jonestaudt.htm (accessed 17 November 2017).

Staudt, Kathleen Henderson. '"Acts of *Ars*" in David Jones's *The Anathemata* and W. H. Auden's *Horae Canonicae*', *Flashpoint* 18 (Summer 2016). Available online: http://www.flashpointmag.com/staudtars.pdf (accessed 17 November 2017).

Stone, Dan. *Responses to Nazism in Britain, 1933–1939*. London: Palgrave Macmillan, 2003.

Stoneburner, Tony. 'So Primitive, So Civilized: The Eucharistic Vision of David Jones', *Anglican Theological Review* 55, no. 4 (October 1973): 484–91.

Stourton, James. *Kenneth Clark: Life, Art, Civilisation*. London: Collins, 2016.

Surette, Leon. *Dreams of a Totalitarian Utopia: Literary Modernism and Politics*. London: McGill-Queen's University Press, 2009.

The Tablet. 'Fascism as Cant Phrase', 3 October 1936, 438.

The Tablet. 'The Germans in Europe', 1 October 1938, 421.

Taille, Maurice de la. *The Mystery of Faith & Human Opinion, Contrasted & Defined*, trans. J. B. Schimpf. London: Sheed & Ward, 1934.

Teilhard de Chardin, Pierre. *Writings in a Time of War*. London: Collins, 1968.

Terpstra, John. '"Bedad He Revives! See Where He Raises!": An Introduction to David Jones's *The Sleeping Lord*', *University of Toronto Quarterly* 52, no. 1 (Fall 1982): 94–105.

Thomas, SJ, Alfred. 'Hopkins, Welsh and Wales', *Transactions of the Honourable Society of Cymmrodorion*, Session 1965, Part II (1966): 272–85.

Thomas, SJ, Alfred. *Hopkins the Jesuit: The Years of Training*. London: Oxford University Press, 1969.

Thomas, Ceri, David Roe, and Alexandra Roe. *Attic Gallery at Fifty: 1962–2012*. Swansea: Attic Gallery, 2012.

Thomas, R. S. 'Time's Disc Jockey: Meditations on Some Lines in *The Anathemata*'. In Belinda Humfrey and Anne Price-Owen (eds), *David Jones: Diversity in Unity*, 153–9. Cardiff: University of Wales Press, 2000.

Thurlow, Roger. *Fascism in Britain: From Oswald Mosley's Blackshirts to the National Front*. London: I.B. Tauris, 1998.

Thurston, Luke. 'David Jones' Disaster: *In Parenthesis*', *Almanac: Yearbook of Welsh Writing in English: Critical Essays* 16 (2012): 151–72.

The Times (London). 'Future of Bohemia', 17 March 1939, 18.

The Times (London). 'The Return to London: Mr. Chamberlain at No. 10', 17 September 1938, 10.

The Times (London). 'Mr. Chamberlain's Mission', 23 September 1938, 13.

Tonning, Erik. *Modernism and Christianity*. Basingstoke: Palgrave Macmillan, 2014.

Trodd, Colin. *Visions of Blake: William Blake in the Art World 1830–1930*. Liverpool: Liverpool University Press, 2012.

Vander Meulen, David L. and G. Thomas Tanselle. 'A System of Manuscript Transcription', *Studies in Bibliography* 52 (1999): 201–12.

Villis, Tom. *British Catholics and Fascism: Religious Identity and Political Extremism Between the Wars*. Basingstoke: Palgrave Macmillan, 2013.

Wall, Bernard [unsigned]. 'Commentary', *Colosseum* 1, no. 2 (June 1934): 7.

Wall, Bernard [unsigned]. 'Editorial', *Colosseum* 3, no. 12 (December 1936): 245.

Wall, Bernard. 'Germany and Racism', *Colosseum* 5, no. 20 (January 1939): 32–3.

Walsh, Michael J. *The Tablet, 1840–1990: A Commemorative History*. London: The Tablet Publishing Company, 1990.

Ward, Elizabeth. *David Jones, Mythmaker*. Manchester: University of Manchester Press, 1983.

Watkins, Vernon, ed. *Landmarks and Voyages*. London: Poetry Book Society, 1957.

Waugh, Evelyn [unsigned]. 'The Abyssinian Record', *The Tablet*, 2 May 1936, 546.

Waugh, Evelyn [unsigned]. 'Italy in Abyssinia', *The Tablet*, 13 June 1936, 750–1.

Weston, Jessie. *From Ritual to Romance*. Cambridge: Cambridge University Press, 1920.

Whitaker, Muriel. 'Review of Jonathan Miles and Derek Shiel, *David Jones: The Maker Unmade* (Bridgend, Seren, 1995) and David Jones, *David Jones: A Fusilier at the Front: His Record of the Great War in Word and Image*, ed. Anthony Hyne (Bridgend, Seren, 1995)', *Chesterton Review* 23, nos 1–2 (February and May 1997): 223–6.

White, Arnold. *The Hidden Hand*. London: Grant Richards, 1917.

White, Norman. *Hopkins: A Literary Biography*. Oxford: Oxford University Press at the Clarendon Press, 1992.

White, Rebecca, ed. *David Jones: The Furrowed Line, Catalogue of an Exhibition*. Oxford: Fellowship of St Alban and St Sergius, 2014.

Wilcockson, Colin. 'Presentation and self-presentation in *In Parenthesis*'. In Howard Erskine-Hill and Richard A. McCabe (eds), *Presenting Poetry: Composition, Publication, Reception*, 235–56. Cambridge: Cambridge University Press, 1995.

Williams, Charles. 'Gerard Hopkins', *Time and Tide* 26, no. 5 (3 February 1945): 102–3; repr. in Charles Williams, *The Image of the City*, ed. and intro. Anne Ridler, 48–51. London and New York: Oxford University Press, 1958.

Williams, Charles. *Arthurian Torso: Containing the Posthumous Fragment of* The Figure of Arthur. London: Oxford University Press, 1948.

Williams, Rowan. *Grace and Necessity: Reflections on Art and Love*. London: Continuum, 2005.

Wilson, Woodrow. 'Address to a Joint Session of Congress Requesting a Declaration of War Against Germany', 2 April 1917. Available online: https://www.ourdocuments.gov/doc.php?doc=61&page=transcript (accessed 21 May 2017).

Wood, Christopher S., ed. *The Vienna School Reader: Politics and Art Historical Method in the 1930s*. New York: Zone Books, 2000.

Woodruff, Douglas, ed. *For Hilaire Belloc: Essays in Honour of His 71st Birthday*. London: Sheed & Ward, 1942.

INDEX

www.ingramcontent.com/pod-product-compliance
Lightning Source LLC
Chambersburg PA
CBHW081355090726
47908CB00011B/2678

* 9 7 8 1 3 5 0 2 7 4 3 2 7 *